AF707002

PSYCHOLOGICAL ASSESSMENT OF **EMOTIONAL DYSREGULATION**

in Children and Adolescents

Important Notice

I have worked to ensure that all information in this book was accurate at the time of publication and is consistent with general mental health care standards. As research and practice continue to advance, however, therapeutic and assessment standards may change. Moreover, particular situations may require an assessment approach or therapeutic response not addressed or included in this book. For these reasons and because human and mechanical errors sometimes occur, it is recommended that readers follow the advice of psychologists or other clinicians directly involved in their care or the care of a member of their family.

Child specialists from diverse mental health backgrounds who share an interest in assessment will delight in this *tour de force*, which begins with a deep dive into conceptual issues and takes readers on a compelling journey through diversity-sensitive assessment procedures; the vexing nature of differential diagnosis (either/or vs. and/or conditions); and implications for treatment and education—areas in which Dr. Bram has already established his expertise. It concludes with five detailed case presentations, which provide a practical road map for navigating conceptual issues, differential diagnostic and treatment-related challenges, and translating assessment findings into a more accessible language for clinical reports.

—**James H. Kleiger, PsyD, ABAP, ABPP,** private practice, coeditor of *Psychological Assessment of Bipolar Spectrum Disorders* and coauthor of *Assessing Psychosis: A Clinician's Guide, Second Edition*

Bram's comprehensive and carefully reasoned approach to assessing emotional dysregulation in children and adolescents sets a standard of care for our profession. He provides an extensive review of relevant psychological tests and then models how to integrate them to make diagnostic decisions and useful treatment recommendations. I especially appreciated the sensitive, respectful case illustrations, which clearly reflect Bram's clinical wisdom, humility, and years of experience.

—**Stephen E. Finn, PhD,** President, Therapeutic Assessment Institute, Austin, TX

What is the young client's capacity for emotional regulation and how might this information be used to rule in or out a diagnosis of a bipolar spectrum disorder? In his text filled with compelling clinical examples, the very first on this topic, Bram provides the assessor with the tools to answer these questions with confidence and competence. Bram's use of a multimethod approach allows for the greatest precision in differential diagnosis. For all who assess younger clients, this text is a must-have.
—Virginia Brabender, PhD, ABPP (Cl), Emeritus Professor, Widener University, Chester, PA

This groundbreaking psychodiagnostician's handbook on dysregulation disorders in children and adolescents sets a new standard for evidence-based, multimethod, diversity-sensitive psychological assessment. Integrating transdiagnostic concepts, empirical data foundations, state-of-the-art evidence-based psychological assessment methods, differential diagnosis, treatment modalities, and rich case studies, *Psychological Assessment of Emotional Dysregulation in Children and Adolescents* extends, deepens, and reinvigorates the venerable Menninger tradition in personality assessment.
—Marvin W. Acklin, PhD, ABPP, ABAP, University of Hawaii School of Medicine, Honolulu

PSYCHOLOGICAL ASSESSMENT OF **EMOTIONAL DYSREGULATION** in Children and Adolescents

ANTHONY D. BRAM

The Bipolar Spectrum and Beyond

AMERICAN PSYCHOLOGICAL ASSOCIATION

Copyright © 2025 by the American Psychological Association. All rights, including for text and data mining, AI training, and similar technologies, are reserved. Except as permitted under the United States Copyright Act of 1976, no part of this publication may be reproduced or distributed in any form or by any means, including, but not limited to, the process of scanning and digitization, or stored in a database or retrieval system, without the prior written permission of the publisher.

The opinions and statements published are the responsibility of the author, and such opinions and statements do not necessarily represent the policies of the American Psychological Association.

Published by
American Psychological Association
750 First Street, NE
Washington, DC 20002
https://www.apa.org

Order Department
https://www.apa.org/pubs/books
order@apa.org

Typeset in Charter and Interstate by Circle Graphics, Inc., Reisterstown, MD

Printer: Gasch Printing, Odenton, MD
Cover Designer: Anthony Paular Design, Newbury Park, CA

Library of Congress Cataloging-in-Publication Data

Names: Bram, Anthony D., author. | American Psychological Association.
Title: Psychological assessment of emotional dysregulation in children and adolescents : the bipolar spectrum and beyond / Anthony D. Bram.
Description: Washington, DC : American Psychological Association, [2025] | Includes bibliographical references and index.
Identifiers: LCCN 2024020782 (print) | LCCN 2024020783 (ebook) | ISBN 9781433843259 (paperback) | ISBN 9781433843266 (ebook)
Subjects: LCSH: Emotions in adolescence. | Psychotherapy.
Classification: LCC BF724.3.E5 B73 2025 (print) | LCC BF724.3.E5 (ebook) | DDC 618.92/89075--dc23/eng/20240804
LC record available at https://lccn.loc.gov/2024020782
LC ebook record available at https://lccn.loc.gov/2024020783

https://doi.org/10.1037/0000430-000

Printed in the United States of America

10 9 8 7 6 5 4 3 2 1

With gratitude to the teachers, staff, and students at the New England Center for Children and the Landmark School.

Contents

Acknowledgments

This project evolved from a chapter on children and adolescents that Jim Kleiger and Irv Weiner asked me to write for their edited book *Psychological Assessment of Bipolar Spectrum Disorders* (2023). When my original submission was more expansive in content and exceeded the page limits that Jim and Irv had in mind, they buffered their feedback that I needed to make significant cuts with the observation that what I had written had the makings of another book, which they encouraged me to pursue. I am grateful to each of them. I am also appreciative of Kate Edwards, who coauthored the chapter "Assessment of Bipolar Spectrum, Disruptive Mood Dysregulation Disorder, and ADHD [Attention-Deficit/Hyperactivity Disorder] in Children and Adolescents" in *Psychological Assessment of Bipolar Spectrum Disorders*, some of the content of which is shared with material covered here. Kate played a central role in literature searches related to differential diagnoses between pediatric bipolar spectrum conditions and ADHD, disruptive mood dysregulation disorder, trauma, and disruptive behavior disorders.

My frequent collaborator, Jed Yalof, is also deserving of my deep thanks for his suggestions and support of my efforts to write the sections of the book more specific to neuropsychological assessment, as is my valued colleague, Ali Khadivi, who assisted me to better understand some of the nuanced diagnostic distinctions within the bipolar spectrum. I am grateful to Radhika Krishnamurthy for her generous consultation related to diversity sensitivity assessment. I acknowledge Mary Jo Peebles, my former Menninger Clinic supervisor, longtime assessment mentor, and coauthor of *Psychological Testing*

That Matters: Creating a Road Map for Effective Treatment (2014), for her guidance over many years in solidifying in my mind so many of the ideas contained in this book, especially with regard to systematic inference-making and the linking of diagnostic formulations with treatment implications. I also appreciate the assistance provided by Jennika Baines, acquisitions editor, Molly Gage, development editor, and Laurel Vincenty, copy editor, of the American Psychological Association's APA Books in shepherding this project as well as the three anonymous reviewers for their valuable suggestions.

Finally, I express my loving gratitude to my wife, Linda, children, Sophia and Jack, my mom, Vicki, and my sister, Julie, for their unwavering support. And extra appreciation to Linda for giving my various drafts the much-valued editorial "Lindy Eye."

PSYCHOLOGICAL ASSESSMENT OF **EMOTIONAL DYSREGULATION**

in Children and Adolescents

INTRODUCTION

A Way of Thinking About Psychological Assessment of Emotional Regulation and Dysregulation in Children and Adolescents

The transdiagnostic concepts of emotional regulation and emotional dysregulation have gained immense interest among researchers, clinicians, patients, families, and advocates over the past 2 decades.[1] Although numerous books on the topic—research summaries, treatment manuals, and self-help and parent-help guides—have been published in recent years, comparatively scant attention has been paid to clinical psychological assessment specific to emotional regulation/dysregulation, be it focused on child or adolescent and/or adult work. But challenges with emotional regulation are common in the complex patients of all ages who are referred for formal psychological assessment, and cultivating an understanding of the nature and severity of such challenges is crucial if evaluators are to elucidate accurate formulations and meaningful treatment implications.

[1]Based on a PsycInfo search, from 1981 to 2001, 183 articles, chapters, or dissertations contained these terms (i.e., "emotion regulation," "emotional regulation," "emotion dysregulation," or "emotional dysregulation") in the title. Between 2002 and 2022, 7,087 such titles appeared, an increase of more than 3,772%.

https://doi.org/10.1037/0000430-001
Psychological Assessment of Emotional Dysregulation in Children and Adolescents: The Bipolar Spectrum and Beyond, by A. D. Bram
Copyright © 2025 by the American Psychological Association. All rights reserved.

Overlapping the increased interest in emotional regulation/dysregulation but dating back a bit earlier to the mid-1990s has been both greater clinical focus on whether and in what form bipolar spectrum disorders are suffered by children and adolescents (Parry & Levin, 2012). *Bipolar conditions*, as defined by psychiatric taxonomies, such as the *Diagnostic and Statistical Manual of Mental Disorders* (5th ed., text rev.; *DSM-5-TR*; American Psychiatric Association, 2022), can be conceptualized as a genetically based, biologically driven special type of severe, episodic but persistent vulnerability to emotional dysregulation. The interest in pediatric bipolar conditions has been intertwined with the shift in psychiatry toward predominantly biomedical understanding of emotional difficulties and the associated growth of the pharmaceutical industry, which features ubiquitous direct-to-consumer advertising (Parry & Levin, 2012). A bipolar diagnosis points to both lifetime vulnerability as well as the likely use of potent psychotropic medication as a first-line intervention (McClellan et al., 2007).

Although it has been difficult to find published research studies addressing trends over time in child or adolescent assessment referral questions, clinically, I have noticed in recent years more and more referral questions specifically referencing the bipolar spectrum in evaluations of kids prone to various kinds of emotional dysregulation. This has been the case in both my private practice and as a supervisor in the child and adolescent outpatient department of a community safety net hospital. On occasion, I have had a sense that the two concepts were even being conflated: that for some referring colleagues and families, severe emotional dysregulation has immediately brought to mind concerns about and explanations involving possible bipolar illness.

Therefore, it has become imperative to approach psychological assessment in a manner that (a) exercises systematic due diligence in addressing this *DSM-5-TR* diagnostic question and that simultaneously (b) holds onto the idea that the range of challenges with emotional dysregulation subsumes but extends beyond the bipolar spectrum. Thinking beyond the bipolar spectrum means not only considering alternative or co-occurring nomothetic *DSM-5-TR* categories (e.g., various kinds of neurodevelopmental, regulatory, anxiety, and posttraumatic conditions) that fit our young patient's history and symptom constellation but, at least as importantly, also considering their functioning from a dimensional perspective as well as developing an idiographic understanding of their internal and interpersonal styles of regulating emotion, how these vary conditionally, and what the implications are for intervention. I have written this book for students, trainees, and practitioners of clinical psychological assessment with the aim of explicating such a model for evaluating kids prone to emotional dysregulation.

WHAT THIS BOOK DOES AND DOES NOT INCLUDE

In this book, I focus on formal, specialized psychological assessment in which a dysregulation-prone child or adolescent has typically been already seen by a frontline clinician—often a therapist or prescriber—who then refers for an in-depth comprehensive, multimethod evaluation involving psychological testing to clarify something that remains puzzling despite previous, more routine clinical encounters. The comprehensive approach to assessment described here is not necessary or even recommended as part of the intake process in various outpatient and inpatient settings.[2] The need for the kind of comprehensive, multimethod assessments addressed here arises when routine clinical assessment by interview and observation and/or efforts to embark on treatment of the young patient leaves clinicians or caregivers with a sense of impasse, confusion, or that something otherwise important about the child or adolescent is being missed. This could include a specific conundrum about differential diagnosis from a *DSM-5-TR* perspective, but not always. Often, our patient is referred for reasons related to having been seen by multiple therapists, having participated in multiple treatment modalities, or having tried various medications without appreciable benefit. This type of formal multimethod assessment is aimed at teasing out what has not been previously understood, what has gotten in the way, and what will facilitate therapeutic engagement and growth. Part of this process involves explicating in a nuanced way the nature and severity of challenges with emotional regulation with an eye on implications for more effective intervention.

Rooted in the framework of *evidence-based practice* as defined by the APA [American Psychological Association] Presidential Task Force on Evidence-Based Practice (2006)—the blend of attentiveness to research, clinical expertise, and patient characteristics—this book is intended to be primarily clinical and pragmatic. The emphasis is on ways of thinking and tools that assessment psychologists can apply in their work right now. Findings from nomothetic empirical research—especially on a multitude of measures as well as treatment outcome studies—are complemented by and integrated into the

[2]For an evidence-based approach to more routine assessment in frontline treatment settings (e.g., outpatient therapy or psychiatry clinics, inpatient or residential units), readers are directed to the work of Youngstrom and colleagues (e.g., Youngstrom, Choukas-Bradley, et al., 2015; Youngstrom et al., 2012; Youngstrom, Prinstein, et al., 2020). Many ideas from the work of Youngstrom and colleagues are applicable and integrated into the approach to formal psychological assessment described in this book. Also, some of the specific measures reviewed here (especially caregiver-report questionnaires; see Chapter 4), though, can be considered for inclusion in intake screenings and psychiatric evaluations.

idiographic, cross-theoretical conceptual framework of "treatment-centered diagnosis" as described by Bram and Peebles (2014, p. 18; see also Peebles, 2012).

As implied previously, this book is not just about arriving at *DSM-5-TR* diagnoses and matching with a treatment package that has been validated in randomized clinical trials for young patients meeting criteria for that diagnosis. To be sure, this is part of what is considered here in describing an emotionally dysregulated child or adolescent and thinking about what will be beneficial to them. But there is more to be taken into account regarding the idiographic formulation of the nature and severity of proneness to dysregulation and what the implications are for helping them. A few such factors are the patient's implicit style of regulating emotions, including what conditions are destabilizing versus facilitative; to what extent emotional dysregulation reflects underlying psychological underdevelopment, trauma, or emerging characterological difficulties; the patient's capacity for therapeutic alliance; treatment preferences; and realistic recognition that rigorously validated treatment packages are not always readily available in our patient's community. Because the vital connections among assessment findings, diagnostic formulation, and meaningful treatment implications are often elusive to or overlooked by assessors (Bram, 2013; Shectman & Smith, 1982), this is an emphasis here.

It is also important to clarify that this book is focused more on psychological assessment compared with neuropsychological assessment. The role of neuropsychological testing is highlighted most notably in the context of performance-based approaches to assessment (see Chapter 6), but specific neuropsychological measures are not reviewed. When questions surface about whether and how our young patient's emotional dysregulation might be intertwined with possible neurodevelopmental conditions (e.g., autism spectrum), challenges with attention and executive functioning, other learning differences/difficulties, or acquired brain injury, there is a crucial need for the assessor to integrate a neuropsychological perspective or refer to a neuropsychologist colleague to conduct their own complementary assessment. Readers interested in a more in-depth discussion of neuropsychological measures and their application with kids are referred to books, such as Reddy et al. (2013), D. C. Miller and Maricle (2019), and Reinstein and Burau (2014).

This volume is also clinically rather than forensically focused. It is hoped that many of the ideas and measures will be of value to forensic assessors, but it will be up to readers with forensic training to determine the extent of their applicability to such specialized work. Those interested in forensic psychological and neuropsychological assessment with kids are referred to the edited work by Sparta and Koocher (2006).

Although this book is about assessing children and adolescents, most of the measures reviewed are applicable to kids from about age 5 through 18 years. This means that measures specific to the assessment of infants, toddlers, and preschoolers are not covered here. Details about assessing emotional regulation and other key neurodevelopmental factors within this youngest age group can be found in edited volumes, such as those by Zeanah (2009) and DelCarmen-Wiggins and Carter (2019) as well as in guidelines published by U.S. Department of Health and Human Services (2010; see Appendix C of those guidelines for reviews of specific measures to consider). Additionally, although the principles of assessment presented in this book are applicable to the evaluation of emerging adults (Arnett, 2000; i.e., those older than 18 years and into their twenties), most of the measures described here are not designed and normed for people older than 18. For measures applicable more broadly in the assessment of adults—including emerging adults—readers are referred to handbooks by Groth-Marnat and Wright (2016) and Weiner and Greene (2017), and for assessment tools to aid with differential diagnosis related to the bipolar spectrum, see the volume edited by Kleiger and Weiner (2023).

The measures for assessing emotional dysregulation in children and adolescents presented in this book encompass collateral-report, self-report, and performance-based methods. Some are broadband symptom or personality measures, some are construct- or disorder-specific, and some involve stimulus attribution/performance-based measures (formerly referred to as projectives; see Bornstein, 2007; Meyer & Kurtz, 2006). Measures range from quick screeners to lengthy diagnostic interviews. Many of the broadband measures are likely to be familiar to most assessors, whereas many of the disorder-specific scales may not. I selected the measures included in this volume based on efforts to thoroughly review the child and adolescent assessment literature as well as on my own clinical training and experience and consultation with colleagues. Inevitably, I will have overlooked measures that some clinician-readers have found useful or even essential. Similarly, although I have done my best to cite the literature on racial/ethnic, gender, and other biases of the various measures, it is conceivable that I have missed some studies. I welcome emails about such oversights so I can consider them for inclusion in a potential subsequent edition.

ORGANIZATION OF THIS BOOK

The book is divided into five parts. Building on conceptual considerations for assessing emotional dysregulation broadly and the bipolar spectrum specifically (Part I), the book moves to pragmatics involving choice of measures

(Part II), differential diagnosis (Part III), and treatment implications (Part IV). The book concludes with a series of case examples (Part V).

Part I: Basic Considerations

Part I comprises two chapters. Chapter 1, "Emotional Regulation and Dysregulation in Children and Adolescents: What Are We Assessing?," begins with operational definitions related to emotional regulation/dysregulation as internal processes manifested behaviorally by children and adolescents in different ways. Central to this opening chapter is the premise that meaningful assessment of emotional dysregulation attends to but transcends *DSM-5-TR* diagnoses.

Chapter 2, "Emotional Dysregulation, the Bipolar Spectrum, and Assessment Considerations With Children and Adolescents," takes up the historical controversy about diagnosing bipolar spectrum conditions in children and adolescents and how the authors of the fifth edition of the *Diagnostic and Statistical Manual of Mental Disorders* (*DSM-5*; American Psychiatric Association, 2013) attempted to resolve it by introducing the disruptive mood dysregulation disorder (DMDD) diagnosis to subsume young patients prone to irritability and angry outbursts who previously were considered by some to exhibit a juvenile version of bipolar illness. Additionally, this second chapter addresses fundamental considerations in diagnosing or ruling out a bipolar condition in children and adolescents before any formal assessments are introduced: base rates, family history, previous reaction to medications, medical history, and course of illness.

Part II: Emotional Dysregulation and the Bipolar Spectrum: Multimethod, Dimensional, and Diversity-Sensitive Assessment

Part II opens with Chapter 3, "Basic Rationale for and Principles of Multimethod, Dimensional, and Diversity-Sensitive Assessment." This chapter introduces the premise of thoughtful integration of collateral-report, self-report, and performance-based measures, emphasizing the need to consider as ideographically meaningful the convergences and incongruities across methods. The third chapter also underscores the importance of complementing categorical diagnosis with assessing key variables (e.g., depression, hypomania, level of impairment) dimensionally as well as conducting evaluations that are sensitive to issues of diversity.[3]

[3]For additional considerations related to diversity-sensitive assessment, edited volumes by S. R. Smith and Krishnamurthy (2018a) and Brabender and Mihura (2016) are highly recommended.

Chapter 4, "Collateral-Report Measures to Assess Emotional Dysregulation," reviews a multitude of caregiver-report questionnaires that can be used to assess emotional dysregulation broadly and the bipolar spectrum more specifically. Also addressed are considerations related to the role and application of teacher-report versions of many of these collateral measures.

Chapter 5, "Self-Report Measures to Assess Emotional Dysregulation," is organized around reviews of various interviews and questionnaires for which the young patient themselves is the respondent. Among the questionnaires reviewed are disorder-specific scales as well as broadband symptom and personality measures.

Up front in Chapter 6, "Performance-Based Measures and Methods to Assess Emotional Dysregulation," is an acknowledgment that performance-based measures (i.e., in which inferences are based on what a person does or shows rather than reports in response to standardized stimuli) are generally not central to a bipolar spectrum or other *DSM-5-TR* diagnoses, which rely mainly on reports of history and symptoms. However, this chapter emphasizes that performance-based methods—neuropsychological tests, personality measures (e.g., Rorschach and narrative tasks like the Children's Apperception Test [Bellak & Bellak, 1949] or Thematic Apperception Test [Murray, 1943]) as well as attending to patient–examiner data—illuminate implicit processes of emotional dysregulation that deepen our idiographic understanding of the child's or adolescent's experience and expression of emotions and have valuable implications for treatment.

Part III: Emotional Dysregulation and the Bipolar Spectrum: *DSM-5-TR* Differential and Co-Occurring Diagnoses

Chapter 7, "Orienting to Differential Diagnosis Within and Beyond the Bipolar Spectrum," opens Part III and provides a framework for taxonomic considerations (a) locating a young patient along the bipolar spectrum (bipolar I vs. bipolar II vs. cyclothymia), (b) teasing out the bipolar spectrum from other *DSM-5-TR* conditions, and (c) identifying when the bipolar spectrum co-occurs with other conditions. The three chapters that follow in Part III go into depth to address considerations b and c, attending to collateral-report, self-report, and performance-based measures most relevant to differential diagnosis.

Chapter 8, "Either/Or: Diagnoses Mutually Exclusive With the Bipolar Spectrum" details two diagnostic *DSM-5-TR* categories. These are "either/or" alternatives to the bipolar spectrum: DMDD and the schizophrenia spectrum.

Chapter 9, "And/Or: Conditions to Differentiate From the Bipolar Spectrum or That Co-Occur," reviews taxonomic categories that include symptoms that overlap with the bipolar spectrum and that can potentially be diagnosed alongside the bipolar spectrum. These include attention-deficit/hyperactivity disorder, alcohol/substance use disorders, trauma/posttraumatic stress disorder, the autism spectrum, disruptive behavior disorders, reactive attachment, and borderline personality.

Part III concludes with Chapter 10, "Conditions More Readily Differentiated From the Bipolar Spectrum But Potentially Co-Occurring," which covers anxiety disorders (including obsessive-compulsive disorder), eating disorders, and learning disabilities. Although these conditions are less apt to be mistaken for the bipolar spectrum, they often co-occur.

Part IV: Treatment Implications and Other Considerations for Follow-Up

The emphasis in Part IV is on translating assessment findings into meaningful interventions and other next steps for our young patients and their families. Part IV opens with Chapter 11, "Treatment Implications: Broad Considerations and Level of Care," making the point that treatment implications derived from comprehensive psychological assessment includes but involves much more than the suggestion of a therapeutic modality (e.g., a particular brand of cognitive behavior therapy). Treatment implications also encompass thoughts about necessary level of care, factors affecting therapeutic engagement and collaboration, what findings mean for school, and follow-up evaluation and adjunctive interventions. The second part of Chapter 11 reviews the continuum of care available for children and adolescents vulnerable to emotional dysregulation and discusses matching the patient's severity with an appropriate level of care. Options discussed include inpatient, residential, partial/day hospital, intensive outpatient, wraparound, and conventional outpatient services.

Chapter 12, "Treatment Modalities," addresses a wide array of non–mutually exclusive potential therapeutic interventions: parent/caregiver- and family-focused treatments, individual therapy, group therapy, and pharmacotherapy. Individual therapy is addressed from perspectives of both (a) the *DSM-5-TR* (American Psychiatric Association, 2022) disorder-specific lens and (b) treatment-centered diagnosis, which includes the concept of underlying developmental disruption (i.e., structural weakness/deficit, maladaptive character patterns, and trauma; Bram & Peebles, 2014; Peebles, 2012).

Chapter 13, "Factors Affecting Therapeutic Engagement and Collaboration," focuses on factors, such as treatment-relevant variables like patient and parent preferences, cultural considerations, and capacity for—and conditions that facilitate versus impede—therapeutic alliance. Also highlighted are anticipated transference and countertransference paradigms, cognitive/learning style, proneness to shame, and factors potentially getting in the way of engagement and therapeutic progress.

Part IV continues with Chapter 14, "Implications for School," based on the premise that emotional dysregulation suffered by children and adolescents often affects engagement in school, including their social, emotional, and/or academic functioning. Here, an overview is offered about individualized education programs, or IEPs, and 504 plans, followed by discussion of a range of accommodations and special education interventions that can be considered for kids vulnerable to dysregulation at school. I offer suggestions for assessors in assisting parents to advocate for their children and navigate the educational system while, at the same time, mitigating the potential for an adversarial relationship with the school district.

Chapter 15, "Additional Considerations for Follow-Up Evaluation and Treatment Adjuncts," concludes Part IV. This chapter comprises two sections: The first focuses on possible further evaluation or consultation that the assessor might recommend: multidisciplinary evaluation by the school district; comprehensive or focused private neuropsychological assessment; consult with a neurologist or sleep specialist, with an occupational therapist or a speech-language therapist, or other specialty consultation (e.g., eating disorders, alcohol/substance abuse, threat assessment). The second section reviews a range of other interventions that could be helpful to a particular child or adolescent vulnerable to emotional dysregulation—depending on their strengths, interests, and preferences—such as music or art therapy, yoga, or martial arts. Support for siblings is also addressed.

Part V: Case Illustrations

Part V closes the book with five de-identified/disguised examples of emotionally dysregulated children and adolescents referred for psychological evaluation.[4] Presented separately in Chapters 16 to 20, each case illustration includes the context for referral, specific questions posed for the evaluation, discussion of major findings, excerpts from key sections of the respective reports to offer a flavor of how to translate findings into report language, and detailed discussion of treatment implications. Information about follow-up is included when it is available. Referrals for all five of the young patients, who vary in their overall level of functioning, included a question about the bipolar spectrum. As a collection, the cases are intended to demonstrate the central premise of this book that emotional dysregulation of children and

[4]All clinical examples offered throughout the book are also de-identified/disguised.

adolescents takes many forms, both in terms of manifest symptoms and underlying vulnerabilities, and thus requires assessors to be thoughtful in tailoring treatment implications.

Chapter 21, "Commentary on Cases and Concluding Thoughts," offers reflection on and comparisons and contrasts among the five illustrative evaluations. Included in the chapter is a discussion of how convergence and seeming incongruity among data points from different measures informed diagnostic conclusions, conditions-under-which inferences about implicit processes of emotional regulation, and formulation of treatment implications.

GOALS OF THE BOOK

Broadly, this book has two overlapping goals. The first is to provide an overview of a process by which assessment psychologists can evaluate and report the nature and severity of emotional dysregulation in their young patients. This includes—but is not limited to—conceptualizations and measures to aid in more accurately identifying when dysregulation is consistent with a bipolar spectrum picture and when it is not. The hope is that the methods presented do justice to taxonomic diagnostics while, at the same time, illuminate the enormous value of dimensional and idiographic narrative perspectives that are at the heart of depth-oriented, patient-, and treatment-centered psychological assessment.

The second, related goal is for this book to serve as a pragmatic resource to which assessors can continue to return as they seek to understand their young patients' proneness to dysregulation. Notably, the compendium of measures reviewed in Part II creates a menu from which assessors can select to customize and augment their test batteries depending on the young patient, the referral questions, and rule-outs and other hypotheses that emerge as the evaluation unfolds. Whenever possible, especially in the case of assessment tools with which assessors are less likely to be familiar, online links to access the specific measures themselves—or other details for accessing them—are referenced in the text. It is also hoped that assessors will return to relevant sections of the book as needed to find assistance in interpreting data, integrating findings across measures and methods, and thinking through a wide range of potential treatment implications to convey in the assessment report to caregivers, treaters, and educators.

PART I BASIC CONSIDERATIONS

In this opening section, I introduce foundational concepts relevant to the psychological assessment of emotional regulation/dysregulation in children and adolescents. Chapter 1 operationalizes emotional regulation and dysregulation and details the aims of assessment. Chapter 2 delves into controversies, challenges, and fundamentals related to diagnosing bipolar spectrum conditions in young people.

1 EMOTIONAL REGULATION AND DYSREGULATION IN CHILDREN AND ADOLESCENTS

What Are We Assessing?

When a young person is referred for comprehensive psychological assessment, it is typically the case that they are suffering from or demonstrating some kind of difficulty with emotional regulation. One child may be emotionally avoidant, constricted, shutdown, and withdrawn. Another may be easily frustrated and prone to explosiveness and violent rages. And a third may oscillate between avoidance and explosiveness depending on various conditions. Broadly, to elucidate meaningful treatment implications, the task of an assessor is to clarify the nature, severity, and variability of a child's capacity for emotional regulation under specific conditions. Before delving into considerations for the assessment of emotional regulation in children and adolescents, let's begin by orienting to some basic terms and concepts.

https://doi.org/10.1037/0000430-002
Psychological Assessment of Emotional Dysregulation in Children and Adolescents: The Bipolar Spectrum and Beyond, by A. D. Bram
Copyright © 2025 by the American Psychological Association. All rights reserved.

WHAT IS EMOTIONAL REGULATION, AND WHAT DOES IT MEAN TO BE DYSREGULATED?

The terms emotional regulation and dysregulation have become common not only in discourse among clinicians but also among patients, families, and mental health advocates in various online and offline forums. According to Gross (1998), *emotional regulation*

> refers to the *process* [emphasis added] by which individuals influence which emotions they have, when they have them, and how they experience and express their feelings. Emotional regulation can be automatic or controlled, conscious or unconscious, and may have effects at one or more points in the emotion producing process. (p. 275)

Jurist (2005) highlighted that emotional regulation "represents a convergence zone between cognition and affect, wherein the former is used to alter, but not eradicate, the latter" (p. 426). Bram and Peebles (2014) added that healthy emotional regulation "also allows affect to alter, but not eradicate, cognition" (p. 142).

Emotional regulation is conceptualized as a basic ego function[1] or psychological capacity necessary for adaptive functioning with significance for treatment planning (Bram, 2013; Bram & Peebles, 2014). Emotional regulation may be a treatment focus or objective, and it is essential to know something about emotional regulation to structure and pace the treatment itself. That is to say, for many patients, a primary task of psychotherapy might be to help them learn explicit skills to help them more effectively tune into, manage, and communicate their feelings. At the same time, it is also useful for treaters to have a sense of how the particular person is apt to tolerate, experience, and express their emotions within sessions. For example, it is valuable for a therapist to be aware of what kinds of themes are likely to be emotionally overwhelming and dysregulating, whether the child or adolescent is highly reactive to injuries to self-esteem, and what types of interventions lower the emotional temperature to facilitate transitions at the end of sessions.

A transdiagnostic concept (i.e., cutting across taxonomic categories of the fifth edition, text revision, of the *Diagnostic and Statistical Manual of Mental Disorders* [*DSM-5-TR*; American Psychiatric Association, 2022]; Sloan et al., 2017), emotional regulation is intertwined with other ego functions, such as sense of reality, logical reasoning, coherence of thinking, attention and executive functioning, sense of self, relatedness, and conscience among others

---

[1]*Ego functions* refer to processes through which a person tries to adapt their internal experience and needs to the reality of their environment (e.g., Marcus, 2017).

(Bram & Peebles, 2014). Neurologically, processes of emotion regulation are based in the interconnectivity between the prefrontal cortex and limbic system (Berboth & Morawetz, 2021). This interconnectivity is the neural level of Jurist's (2005) "convergence zone" (p. 426) between prefrontally based cognition and limbic-driven affect.

The capacity for emotional regulation unfolds developmentally as a function of the following: genetic/constitutional dispositions; safety, reliability, trust, and attunement in the child–caregiver attachment relationships; and subsequent direct and modeled experiences with and by others in one's environment (e.g., Bowlby, 1969; Brazelton & Cramer, 1991; Fonagy et al., 2002; Schore, 1994; Stern, 2004; Tronick, 2007; Winnicott, 1965). Moreover, recently, we have better appreciation that experiences with poverty (e.g., Kim et al., 2013; Raver et al., 2016) and racism (e.g., Lozada et al., 2022; Riley et al., 2021) have a deleterious effect on the development of emotional regulation. Although a neurotypical infant does not enter the world with a capacity for emotional regulation, they are typically born with potentials that can be realized if caregivers are attuned and responsive to their emotional needs and if they experience a safe and equitable environment. Over the course of development, the child gradually internalizes the ability for emotional soothing initially provided by caregivers as well as confidence and ability to seek out comfort adaptively and effectively from others when necessary.

When a child's emotional regulation potentials are compromised constitutionally and/or are thwarted by disruptions in attachment relationships or other environmental interactions and experiences (e.g., racism, genderism, homophobia), they are likely to exhibit behaviors such that the child is said to be dysregulated. *Dysregulation* refers to one's proneness or state of being unable to tolerate and express emotions in effective, adaptive, and socially acceptable ways. A child (or any person) who is prone to emotional dysregulation may be highly sensitive to certain feelings or bodily sensations, react to and experience them with heightened intensity, have difficulty tolerating them, be slow to return to emotional baseline, and/or cope with and communicate them in ways that are apt to unwittingly exacerbate whatever the emotional and interpersonal predicament (e.g., Carpenter & Trull, 2013; Mennin et al., 2007).

Emotional regulation/dysregulation is conceptualized as an internal psychological process. We do not directly observe this process, but it is typically inferred based on observations of manifest behaviors: the child in the throes of a tantrum or who is refusing to go to school, the adolescent who says they hate their parents and punches a hole in the wall, the young adult who is cutting themselves. We also can understand something about a person's dysregulation to the extent that they can verbally share aspects of their subjective experience during (less likely) or after (more likely) the episode "I was overwhelmed;" "I was so mad, couldn't think;" or "I wanted to kill him." This observational and retrospective self-report information is the kind of data yielded in a traditional psychiatric interview with a child or adolescent and their caregivers (Cepeda & Gotanco, 2017; Morrison & Flegel, 2016). Often times, this is sufficient to understand the nature and severity of the child's vulnerability to emotional dysregulation to contribute to effective psychosocial, educational, and/or pharmacological interventions. Sometimes, however, this is not the case if findings of the psychiatric assessment are inconclusive, later prove to be incomplete, and/or do not lead to effective intervention. Formal, multimethod psychological assessment (Hopwood & Bornstein, 2014) that integrates performance-based methods with self-report and collateral-report (i.e., observations of caregivers, teachers, or other adults) measures offers nuanced, meaningful, and useful understanding of a dysregulated child or adolescent when more common, straightforward psychiatric means of assessment (i.e., mostly clinical interviewing) have proven inconclusive or have not contributed to effective intervention.

AIMS IN THE ASSESSMENT OF EMOTIONAL REGULATION IN CHILDREN AND ADOLESCENTS

The task of assessing a child's or adolescent's emotional (dys)regulation—and comprehensive psychological assessment in general—can be considered so much more multifaceted and nuanced than arriving at or ruling out *DSM-5-TR* diagnoses (e.g., Bram & Peebles, 2014; Tuber, 2022; A. J. Wright, 2022). Although determining or ruling out *DSM-5-TR* diagnoses is often an aim of assessment, we are also interested in elucidating with nuance the dynamics associated with a child's or adolescent's processes of emotional regulation. This kind of dynamic assessment aims to answer questions, such as the eight that follow.

Question 1: In What Way Is the Child or Adolescent Dysregulated?

Some kids' dysregulation takes the form of behavioral disinhibition (e.g., explosiveness, impulsiveness), and others', more constriction (e.g., avoidance, withdrawal). Sometimes, the same child shifts between the two depending on various conditions (see Question 4). It is also possible to specify which emotions the child or adolescent is having the most difficulty managing: anger, sadness, depression, shame, guilt, and so on. Additionally, we try to clarify their characteristic means of self-protection (implicit defenses and conscious coping) and how effective those efforts are.

Question 2: How Severe and Pervasive Are Regressions Into Dysregulation? To What Degree Can the Functioning of the Child or Adolescent Be Considered to Be Impaired?

We clarify to what extent a child's or adolescent's dysregulation can be considered on dimensional continua from (a) mild to severe, (b) infrequent to pervasive, (c) transient versus long-lasting (i.e., with reference to how long it takes to return from dysregulation to baseline), and (d) relatively less to relatively more impairing.

Question 3: What Are Other Psychological Costs Associated With Dysregulation?

In other words, when a child or adolescent is dysregulated, to what extent is this experience associated with lapses in other psychological capacities (or ego functions)? For instance, we need to assess to what degree they also lose hold of their accurate sense of reality, coherence of thinking, logic of reasoning, soundness of judgment, creativity, or ability to trust.

Question 4: What Are the Functions Served by—or Even the Advantages to—Our Young Patient's Patterns of Emotional Dysregulation?

From a behavioral perspective, this question relates to ideas of motivational reinforcement and the need to understand factors that maintain problematic behaviors (e.g., Cipani, 2017). Psychodynamically, the concept of *secondary gain* (Freud, 1917/1953b) is relevant: that sometimes seemingly maladaptive behaviors can be motivated unconsciously to achieve some psychological or interpersonal benefit. Examples consistent with either theoretical perspective include kids whose dysregulation helps them to get their way with caregivers or avoid unpreferred activities. Regardless of theory, the key point for assessment is in anticipating what might potentially get in the way of treatment, that is, that change often requires relinquishment of experiences that are gratifying in some way.

All of this said, it is essential that assessors maintain their empathic stance and not default to oversimplified, blaming speculations that the patient's troubling behaviors can be boiled down to willful manipulativeness.[2] Greene's (2021) philosophy that kids do well if they can is a valuable guidepost.

[2]Clinical experience suggests that only in exceedingly rare instances can a child's ostensible emotional dysregulation be understood predominantly to be under conscious control and used intentionally for psychological and interpersonal gain. Such a conclusion would need to be firmly anchored in assessment data, not in the hypotheses of exasperated caregivers or the assessor's unreflective negative countertransference.

Question 5: Under What Conditions Are the Child or Adolescent Likely to Suffer Dysregulation? How Might the Form of Dysregulation Vary?

Even kids who are vulnerable to severe emotional dysregulation are apt to not be dysregulated 24/7. So, we aim to clarify with as much specificity as possible when they are—and when they are not—most prone. Some non-mutually exclusive examples of conditional variables include (a) physiological state (e.g., hunger, fatigue, sensory sensitivities), (b) interpersonal dynamics (e.g., separation or loss, competition, feeling one-downed in relation to an authority figure), (c) threats to self-esteem (e.g., rejection or failure, being challenged in an area of learning disability), (d) how generally emotionally evocative a situation is and if it stirs particular feelings (e.g., sadness, shame), and (e) the availability of clear guidelines and expectations and how much support by and feedback by others is available (i.e., the degree of external structure provided).

Question 6: What Helps the Child or Adolescent Recover From Dysregulation?

Consider whether and how the child or adolescent might regroup from moments of dysregulation as a function of shifting (e.g., narrowing, broadening, changing) focus or task, breaks, snacks, opportunities for movement, reduction of stimulation, certain types of support?

Question 7: What Strengths Do They Have That Mitigate Dysregulation and Aid With Recovery?

Here, we assess such factors as a child's or adolescent's facility with language—and, in particular, how developed and nuanced their emotional vocabulary is—to be able to put feelings into words instead of action. We can also assess their ability to collaborate and accept help and the associated conditions under which these vary. For some kids, their interest and abilities around physical activities (e.g., running, playing basketball, martial arts) provide outlets to reregulate or stay regulated.

Question 8: To What Extent Do Symptoms and Patterns of Dysregulation Map Onto Prototypes as Defined in the *DSM-5-TR*?

This question is broached in Chapter 2 and detailed in Part III. It is worth keeping in mind Holt's (1968) conceptualization that "[taxonomic] diagnoses are not addresses of buildings into which people may be put, but landmarks with respect to which people may be located" (p. 14). Shectman (1997) offered a similar metaphor: that a taxonomic diagnosis can identify what ballpark a person is in, but it does not locate their particular seat. Addressing the preceding seven questions reflects the effort to map their seat.

All the while considering these questions—and it may be that we cannot answer all of them with the data we have—we are also thinking about potential treatment implications because particular challenges with emotional regulation can inform treatment objectives and are important to hold in mind for how to optimally engage our young patients therapeutically (Bram, 2013; Bram & Peebles, 2014). Some *DSM-5-TR* diagnoses have more clear-cut treatment implications, and others less so. Part IV of this book takes up treatment implications in considerable detail.

From a conceptual standpoint, this kind of assessment—encompassing questions like this one and the aforementioned seven—values understanding in the form of (a) idiographic narrative (see Questions 1, 3, 4, 5, 6, and 7) and (b) dimensional considerations (Question 2) in addition to (c) conventional nomothetic, taxonomic categories (this question). Although this is not a new assessment framework for those trained in and practicing depth-oriented traditions, it is also consistent with the growing current zeitgeist in mainstream psychology and psychiatry to broaden the diagnostic endeavor beyond a purely categorical conceptualization (e.g., American Psychiatric Association, 2013, 2022; Hopwood, 2022).

2 EMOTIONAL DYSREGULATION, THE BIPOLAR SPECTRUM, AND ASSESSMENT CONSIDERATIONS WITH CHILDREN AND ADOLESCENTS

Bipolar spectrum conditions, as defined in the *Diagnostic and Statistical Manual of Mental Disorders* (5th ed., text rev.; *DSM-5-TR*; American Psychiatric Association, 2022), are specific, severe, and persistent kinds of patterns of emotional dysregulation that are understood to be primarily biologically driven. The bipolar spectrum encompasses bipolar I, bipolar II, and cyclothymic and other "related" disorders. If we conclude that a person meets categorical criteria for a bipolar spectrum illness, we are essentially saying that they suffer an affliction that will need to be managed—often primarily pharmacologically—over the course of their lifetime. It is not surprising, then, that the high-stakes question of diagnosing bipolar illness in children and adolescents has been controversial.

There have been two adversarial clinical perspectives on bipolar conditions in kids. The narrower perspective hews to the definition of *mania* as applied to adults: discrete episodes marked by elevated mood, irritability, grandiosity, excessive energy, and heightened activity levels of various kinds. The second perspective broadens the definition of mania in kids to also encompass an irritable disposition alongside vulnerabilities to prolonged rages and tantrums (e.g., Wozniak et al., 1995). With this broadened conceptualization

https://doi.org/10.1037/0000430-003
Psychological Assessment of Emotional Dysregulation in Children and Adolescents: The Bipolar Spectrum and Beyond, by A. D. Bram
Copyright © 2025 by the American Psychological Association. All rights reserved.

of what constitutes mania in young people, more kids suffering emotional dysregulation could be understood to be on the bipolar spectrum. Thus, disagreements within the field have revolved around the extent to which pediatric bipolar conditions might be over- or underdiagnosed (overdiagnosed: the position inherent in the first perspective; underdiagnosed: the position of the second). Since the fifth edition of the *Diagnostic and Statistical Manual of Mental Disorders* (*DSM*-5; American Psychiatric Association, 2013) introduced disruptive mood dysregulation disorder (DMDD) to more explicitly capture symptoms of irritability, tantrums, and rages in the absence of frankly manic indicators (American Psychiatric Association, 2013, 2022), the clinical controversy has been somewhat abated.

In this book, the perspective on diagnosing bipolar conditions in kids is consistent with the first, more restricted view of what constitutes mania and the one also articulated in the guidelines of the American Association of Child and Adolescent Psychiatry (McClellan et al., 2007) and the *DSM-5-TR*. This view is in large part informed by the fact that prospective research has shown that kids who primarily exhibit irritability, tantrums, and angry outbursts (in the absence of traditional symptoms of mania) typically do not meet bipolar criteria as adults (Duffy et al., 2020).

The assessment approach offered here is intended to be careful, humble, and rooted in the data. As assessors, we may feel pressure from our referring colleagues and the families of our patients—and our own ideals of what an assessor should be able to do—to peg with certainty whether or not a dysregulated child or adolescent is suffering a bipolar illness. We certainly do not want to miss a diagnosis of bipolar disorder because we recognize that doing so has costs in terms of trials of possibly contraindicated medications and delayed initiation of mood-stabilizing medication such that risks of various disruptions in functioning and well-being are heightened (T. Singh & Rajput, 2006). But in clinical practice, this differential diagnosis is not typically so clear and tidy. Not uncommonly, the data are mixed: some in support, others less so. Our tasks are to describe and weigh the data we have, make inferences accordingly, and communicate them in the written report and verbal feedback in language titrated to the level of confidence we have in our inferences (Weiner, 2000). When the data are equivocal, we describe in what ways the picture is consistent with the bipolar spectrum and ways that it is not. This is no different than a disciplined overall approach to inference-making (see Bram & Peebles, 2014), but it is highlighted here because of the serious, lifelong implications of concluding that a child has this type of severe and persistent mental illness (McClellan et al., 2007). We recognize that there is still much to unfold developmentally that we cannot predict; the younger the child, the more this is the case. So, to conclude that a child or adolescent meets criteria for a full-blown bipolar condition, we require repetition and convergence of data (Bram & Peebles, 2014; Peebles, 2012) pointing toward hypomania or mania. But even if we present findings that are equivocal regarding a bipolar diagnosis, we can offer understanding and implications that are clinically meaningful in addressing the child's emotional dysregulation.

VARYING PRESENTATIONS OF CHILDREN AND ADOLESCENTS ON THE BIPOLAR SPECTRUM

Kids whose emotional dysregulation is ultimately understood to be on the bipolar spectrum can present for evaluation and treatment in different ways. As Youngstrom, Morton, and Murray (2020) described evocatively, a young person with a bipolar condition

> might look like [a] wide-eyed, fast-talking person on a mission-to-save the world, with pacing, sleeplessness, psychosis (psychotic mania). It might be a wise-cracking, playful creative person experimenting with new things; or it might [be] one who is impulsive, risk-taking, irritable, and aggressive when challenged (both could be hypomania). It might also mean one is seriously and suicidally depressed; or the person might be fine, experiencing only ordinary ups and downs in a given week. All of these states may be experienced by the same individual at different times in the course of the same bipolar illness! (p. 193)

Thus, at the time of evaluation, the assessor may or may not have acute symptomatic clues as to the possibility of an underlying bipolar illness.

CONSIDERATION OF BASE RATES FOR BIPOLAR DISORDER IN CHILDREN AND ADOLESCENTS, AND SOME CAVEATS

Accurate diagnoses of a bipolar spectrum or any other condition involves taking into account base rates of that condition in the setting in which the assessor practices (Youngstrom, Choukas-Bradley, et al., 2015; Youngstrom et al., 2012). A *base rate* refers to the "naturally occurring frequency of a phenomenon in a population" (American Psychological Association, n.d.-a). In assessment, base rates are used as probabilities of encountering a person who meets criteria for a particular diagnostic category in a particular setting. Youngstrom et al. (2012) reported estimated base rates for pediatric bipolar disorder in various settings: 2% (4% for all bipolar spectrum conditions) in the general population; 5% to 10% in outpatient/community mental health; 11% of youths in a state foster care system; 2% to 22% of incarcerated adolescents; and 25% to 40% of psychiatrically hospitalized children and adolescents (see p. 18, Table 2, in Youngstrom et al. [2012] for references).[1] In general, the more intensive or acute the clinical setting, the higher the base rate of bipolar conditions. And the more specialized the setting is for evaluation and treatment of patients with mood disorders, the base rate can be expected to be higher.

Crucial to assessment, Youngstrom, Choukas-Bradley, et al. (2015) described that the lower the base rate, the greater the burden of proof—that is, more compelling and convergent evidence—required to support the diagnosis. It makes sense that in more intensive and specialized settings in which there is a higher frequency of bipolar spectrum diagnoses, it is likelier that the patient currently being assessed will also be found to have that diagnosis. Assessors working in such settings are encouraged to hold this in mind simultaneously with an awareness of some familiar diagnostic pitfalls: the confirmation bias and false dichotomy and reduction fallacies (e.g., Kahneman & Tversky, 1972). Some highly specialized clinics and programs (e.g., for bipolar disorders, attention-deficit/hyperactivity disorder [ADHD], autism, borderline personality) may be vulnerable to viewing complex patients through their own narrow diagnostic lens such that they (a) overlook, minimize, or otherwise fail to integrate data inconsistent with their diagnostic specialty and thus (b) do not adequately consider alternate or complementary conceptualizations and treatment modalities.

ACCOUNTING FOR DEVELOPMENTAL AND FAMILIAL FACTORS BEARING ON A POSSIBLE BIPOLAR SPECTRUM DIAGNOSIS

Assessment begins before the child or adolescent enters our office for one-to-one evaluation sessions. In addition to considerations about base rate, to clarify the context to address the referral questions, we want to have a handle on the child's family and developmental history elicited through some combination of questionnaires completed by parents or caregivers and/or interviews with parents or caregivers. Although what to inquire in a thorough developmental history is well beyond the scope of this chapter

[1]Note that these base rate data are based on criteria in the fourth edition of the *Diagnostic and Statistical Manual of Mental Disorders* (American Psychiatric Association, 1994), so also included were young patients who would now, based on *DSM-5-TR* criteria, meet criteria for DMDD rather than a bipolar spectrum condition. Thus, these prevalence rates for bipolar conditions are likely to now be overestimates, but by how much is currently uncertain.

(see Cepeda & Gotanco, 2017; Morrison & Flegel, 2016), four crucial points to highlight when there are questions about emotional regulation and a possible bipolar spectrum condition include whether (a) there is a family history of bipolar illness; (b) the child has had adverse reactions to selective serotonin reuptake inhibitor (SSRI) antidepressants or other medications; (c) the child has had a recent physical exam with laboratory work, ruling out other medical explanations; and (d) the course of symptoms is consistent with patterns more typically observed in children with bipolar illness. Most of these considerations involve identification of risk factors that can be integrated with what we know about base rates in our setting to inform the probability of a bipolar spectrum diagnosis (Youngstrom, Choukas-Bradley, et al., 2015; Youngstrom et al., 2012).

Family History of Bipolar Illness and Other Severe Psychiatric Conditions

Because there is a strong genetic component to bipolar conditions (McGuffin et al., 2003), with a confirmed diagnosis of bipolar disorder in at least one biological relative comes an increased likelihood that a child or adolescent will eventually meet criteria for the condition. Duffy et al. (2020) summarized:

> While specific estimates vary between families and studies, convergent evidence supports that first degree relatives of an adult with bipolar disorder have an 8–10-fold risk of developing bipolar disorder . . . compared to the general population or low-risk controls (Duffy et al., 2000). The risk is even higher for children with both parents affected (Gottesman et al., 2010). (para. 1, "Longitudinal High-Risk Studies" section)

Although the risk is lower when it is a second-degree or more distal biological relative who has had this diagnosis, it is still much higher than in the general population (Duffy et al., 2020). The key point here for assessment is that a familial diagnosis of bipolar disorder ought to be weighted and integrated with base rates and data from self-report, collateral-report, and performance-based data. For example, when such data are mixed, but there is a family history of a bipolar condition, the scale is tipped in this diagnostic direction; by how much is a function of the genetic proximity of the diagnosed relative(s). And even if the data do not allow us to go as far as a bipolar diagnosis, simply knowing about the family history has a potential treatment implication: M. K. Singh (2019) summarized research that in the general population, about 10% of kids get worse on antidepressant medication, but of those with a parent or first-degree relative, half get worse. Kowatch et al. (2005) recommended a three-generation genogram to inquire into family history of bipolar and other psychiatric illness (see McGoldrick et al., 2020).

A quick caregiver report screening measure that can facilitate assessment of a child's or adolescent's biological vulnerability to a bipolar spectrum condition is the Family Index of Risk for Mood (FIRM) checklist (Algorta et al., 2013). The FIRM allows a caregiver to check whether a biological parent, sibling, grandparent, aunt, uncle, or cousin has experienced any of the following: a bipolar or manic-depressive diagnosis, depression or dysthymia diagnosis, a nervous breakdown, admission to a psychiatric hospital, a diagnosis of alcoholism, a diagnosis of substance use disorder, a suicide attempt, or completed suicide. Two or fewer items checked reflect a low risk; 3 to 7 items, a moderate risk; and 8 or more, a high risk. Importantly, Algorta et al. highlighted that the risk index

> did not improve as a predictor of pediatric bipolar disorder when limited to family history of mania. This could be due to bipolar disorder resulting from the accumulation of multiple nonspecific risk factors (Tsuchiya et al., 2003), or else due to the inaccuracy with which bipolar disorder has been recognized in the past. (p. 21)

Thus, the inclusion of items involving family history of mood disorders, addictions, and other indicators of severe psychiatric illness (e.g., hospitalization, suicide) were shown to improve diagnostic accuracy above and beyond family history of diagnosed bipolar spectrum disorders. See The Family Index of Risk for Mood (FIRM; n.d.) for an online-administered version of the FIRM.

Adverse Reactions to SSRI Antidepressant Medication

Evidence from both observational studies and clinical trials suggests that the use of SSRI medications in some child and adult patients (especially in "monotherapy," i.e., prescribed in the absence of other psychotropics) is associated with triggering manic symptoms (a "manic switch"; see Allain et al., 2017; Bhowmik et al., 2014; and Fela-Thomas et al., 2018). One common explanation of this phenomenon, known as the *ignition hypothesis*, is that in such patients, the medication activates a latent genetic vulnerability to bipolar illness (Joseph et al., 2009). The aforementioned findings summarized by M. K. Singh (2019) lend some support to this hypothesis.

Among alternative explanations offered by Joseph et al. (2009) for the manic switch in children and adolescents are "medication as irrelevant" and "bipolar depression" hypotheses. The *medication as irrelevant* explanation is that the manic symptoms reflect "the natural course of the bipolar illness, not a response to the treatment" (Joseph et al., 2009, p. 90); the *bipolar depression* hypothesis is that "when treating youths for depression, we are often dealing with the depressed phase of what will prove to be a bipolar illness" (p. 91) so that the shift from depressive to manic symptoms is part and parcel of bipolarity that would have emerged in the absence of medication. Joseph et al. noted that studies supporting the ignition hypothesis tend to be weaker methodologically compared with those that do not. Although Joseph et al. cautioned that the empirical jury is still out on these various hypotheses, from an assessment standpoint, it is meaningful to know that a child or adolescent has had such an adverse reaction. Again, knowing this can lend at least some weight to other evidence pointing in the direction of a bipolar diagnosis.

Recent Medical Evaluation

Because numerous physical conditions can mimic bipolar/manic symptoms, we want to assure that these have been carefully ruled out by our physician colleagues. Among such conditions are hyperthyroidism, lupus, encephalitis, temporal lobe epilepsy, or head injuries (Kowatch et al., 2005). If medical explanations have not been addressed with physical examination and laboratory studies as part of the diagnostic and treatment process leading up to the child's psychological assessment, caregivers are urged to arrange for these to be undertaken in advance of or, at the very least, concurrently with our evaluation.

Course of Illness

Although there is variation in the course of a developing bipolar spectrum condition, the more the child's or adolescent's trajectory resembles a typical course, the more confident we can be that what they are suffering is consistent with a bipolar illness. Duffy et al. (2020) summarized what is now known from longitudinal research about the developmental course of bipolar conditions:

> Key findings in high-risk children include that (i) premorbid social and cognitive/academic functioning is comparable to the general population; (ii) childhood internalizing symptoms and disorders and sleep problems but not neurodevelopmental, cognitive or externalizing disorders predict for onset of mood disorder in adolescence and early adulthood; (iii) bipolar disorder typically debuts with depressive episodes with a recurrent illness course starting in adolescence; (iv) psychotic symptoms in depressive episodes predict for conversion to bipolar disorder; (v) clinically significant sub-threshold manic symptoms (often episodic) have a variable age of onset (typically not pre-adolescent), and predict for subsequent onset of bipolar disorder in emergent adulthood. (p. 5)

Duffy et al.'s (2020) description of risk factors highlighted that for kids who eventually meet criteria for a bipolar illness as adults, the trend is for an early childhood marked by anxiety and disrupted sleep and adolescence marked by episodic alternation between depressive and manic/hypomanic states. By contrast, kids who show early neurodevelopmental challenges, including symptoms of ADHD, and whose adolescence involves more chronic (rather than episodic) mood dysregulation, trend toward meeting criteria for DMDD and then depressive disorders as adults, rather than a bipolar spectrum condition. Of course, in clinical practice, there will always be exceptions to these nomothetic, longitudinal trends, but it is valuable for clinicians to weigh the developmental course of the child's or adolescent's symptoms as a consideration in the diagnostic process.

A CLINICIAN-RATED MEASURE TO AGGREGATE CONTEXTUAL RISK FACTORS: THE BIPOLARITY INDEX

The Bipolarity Index (Aiken et al., 2015) is a measure developed to aggregate and weight many of the contextual risk factors presented in this chapter. The Bipolarity Index can be rated by the assessor based on data gleaned from interviews with and/or questionnaires completed by caregivers. Kleiger (2023) summarized that this measure comprises

> five domains, which include (a) signs and symptoms, (b) family history, (c) age of onset, (d) course of illness and associated features, and (e) response to treatment. There are a total of 24 features [across the five domains] that are weighted within each domain from 2 to 20 points. A cutoff [total score] of 50 has good sensitivity and specificity for identifying bipolar spectrum disorders (Aiken et al., 2015). (p. 111)

Signs and symptoms captured by the Bipolarity Index relate to the nature, severity, and recurrence of (hypo)manic, depressive, and psychotic episodes. The *family history* domain accounts for various kinds of psychiatric illness in the immediate and extended family, and bipolar illness in a first-degree relative is weighted most heavily. *Age of onset* refers to the initial (hypo)manic or depressive episode and weights greatest risk between 15 and 19 years followed by younger than age 15 or ages 20 to 30 years; the later the onset, the lower the likelihood of bipolar illness. C*ourse of illness and associated features* takes into account such factors as distinct (hypo)manic episodes and periods of recovery, the presence of co-occurring psychiatric conditions, engagement in risky behaviors, and deleterious consequences of (hypo)mania (e.g., repeated or serious legal offenses). Specific to pharmacotherapy, the *response to treatment* domain considers the patient's reactions to mood stabilizers (e.g., the more rapid and complete the recovery, the greater likelihood of a bipolar condition) and antidepressants (e.g., patterns of serious side effects, poor responses to trials of more than three different medications, and apparent manic switch are differentially weighted).

PART II EMOTIONAL DYSREGULATION AND THE BIPOLAR SPECTRUM: MULTIMETHOD, DIMENSIONAL, AND DIVERSITY-SENSITIVE ASSESSMENT

Part II begins with Chapter 3, which makes the case that assessment of kids prone to emotional dysregulation is best served by a multimethod test battery and dimensional conceptualization and measurement, and is sensitive to diversity in both the selection of measures and interpretation. Subsequent chapters review specific measures among which assessors can choose to assess emotional dysregulation in a broad sense and bipolar spectrum conditions more narrowly. Consistent with the multimethod framework, collateral-report measures are presented in Chapter 4, self-report measures in Chapter 5, and performance-based measures in Chapter 6.

3 BASIC RATIONALE FOR AND PRINCIPLES OF MULTIMETHOD, DIMENSIONAL, AND DIVERSITY-SENSITIVE ASSESSMENT

Typically, when a dysregulation-prone child or adolescent is referred to us for a formal psychological evaluation, they have already been assessed by another clinician—such as a therapist, psychiatrist, or other physician—who has made use of clinical interview and observational methods. But something essential remains puzzling about their young patient and how to help them, leading the clinician to refer to us for a more specialized assessment. Central to what sets our evaluations apart from such more routine clinical assessments (Youngstrom et al., 2012; Youngstrom, Choukas-Bradley, et al., 2015) is our *multimethod approach,* that is, the systematic integration of self-report, collateral-report, and performance-based methods (e.g., Brabender, 2023; Bram & Peebles, 2014; Hopwood & Bornstein, 2014; Weiner & Greene, 2006; Yalof & Bram, 2021). Additionally, although we can still attend to taxonomic diagnostic categories, our evaluations aim to go beyond that to a more fine-tuned dimensional understanding of our young patients and their treatment needs.

https://doi.org/10.1037/0000430-004
Psychological Assessment of Emotional Dysregulation in Children and Adolescents: The Bipolar Spectrum and Beyond, by A. D. Bram
Copyright © 2025 by the American Psychological Association. All rights reserved.

To reiterate a crucial point from the Introduction, the intensive, multimethod, dimensional approach described here is generally not intended as a first line/intake assessment; rather, it is undertaken as a kind of follow-up consultation when primary clinicians are perplexed about something diagnostically (in the broader sense of the American Psychiatric Association's *Diagnostic and Statistical Manual of Mental Disorders*) or therapeutically. This chapter—which provides a broad orientation to multimethod, dimensional assessment—concludes with an emphasis on embedding this approach in sensitivity to and empathy for diversity among our young patients and their families.

MULTIMETHOD ASSESSMENT: CONVERGENCE AND DISCONTINUITY ACROSS METHODS

In subsequent chapters of Part II, an array of collateral-report, self-report, and performance-based measures are reviewed for assessors to consider as they tailor a battery to best clarify their young patient's emotional (dys)regulation, including the possibility of a bipolar spectrum condition. The greater convergence of findings across the various methods, the more confidence we have in them. When there is discontinuity or incongruity of findings across methods, we aim to be thoughtful about its meaning and, to the extent possible, make sense of it in a way that illuminates a more nuanced, idiographic understanding of the patient (Bram & Peebles, 2014).

In the subsections that follow, two different types of discontinuities are discussed. The first involves seeming discrepancies between findings from self-report and performance-based measures; the second, between self-report and collateral-report by a caregiver.

Discontinuities Between Self-Report and Performance-Based Measures

Because self-report and performance-based measures of the same or similar constructs tend not to be highly correlated with one other (e.g., Mihura et al., 2013), it is not unusual to find discontinuities across these methods in clinical psychological assessment. Our challenges involve considering possible meanings of such apparent discrepancies. Tools to aid us in meaningfully reconciling discontinuities include (a) appreciating differences between implicit (unconscious) and explicit (conscious, self-attributed) levels of functioning (e.g., Bornstein, 1998), (b) application of personality theory (Bram & Peebles, 2014), and/or (c) testing-of-limits interventions within the patient–examiner relationship (Bram, 2018a; Bram & Peebles, 2014).

Consider Brianna,[1] a depressed adolescent referred for evaluation following a brief hospitalization for a serious suicide attempt. Her responses to the performance-based Rorschach (Rorschach Performance Assessment System; Meyer et al., 2011) yielded a profile notable for high elevations in aggressive movement (AGM) and aggressive content (AGC). Further, configurational analyses (described in Chapter 6; see also Bram & Peebles, 2014, and Schafer, 1954) revealed that such aggressive themes were associated with lapses in logical reasoning (cognitive codes) and accurate reality sense (poor form quality). Thus, Rorschach data underscored Brianna's vulnerability to dysregulation when stirred by anger and aggressive impulses.

On the Beck Youth Inventories–Second Edition (Beck et al., 2005), however, Brianna's self-report resulted in low scores on the anger and disruptive behavior scales. In a testing-of-limits attempt to understand this incongruity, the examiner asked Brianna to reflect on her Rorschach responses, reading back to her those coded for AGC or AGM. She responded indignantly that the responses had "nothing to do with her"—because she was "not *at all* an angry person"—and simply were what the inkblots actually looked like. This intervention helped clarify Brianna's strong need to consciously disavow her anger, a disavowal that likely played some role in the aggressive act of her suicide attempt (Manning, 2015). This was a hypothesis that would be valuable for Brianna's new therapist to hold in mind as they worked together gradually to understand the emotional and interpersonal context associated with her suicidality.

Discontinuities Between Self-Report and Caregiver Collateral-Report Measures

When considering inconsistencies between the child's or adolescent's own self-report and collateral-report by their caregiver, it is important to appreciate that such discrepancies are also not unusual and are generally expected (e.g., Achenbach et al., 1987). The approach presented here emphasizes that both child and caregiver perspectives are valuable insofar as together they tell a story with treatment implications (elaborated in Chapter 5: See the section "Self-Report Measures Specific to Bipolar Disorders"). For example, self-report, caregiver-report, and teacher-report versions of the Behavior Assessment System for Children, Third Edition (BASC-3; Reynolds & Kamphaus, 2015; see Chapter 4, this volume) were administered in the evaluation of Jerome, an athletically and academically gifted, socially outgoing high school senior. Jerome had been referred for assessment because of concerns about slips

[1]Names have been changed and identifiers disguised to protect confidentiality.

in his grades as he was about to begin the process of college applications. Neither his parents' nor his teacher's BASC-3 reports yielded elevations on scales related to depression, anxiety, or other internalizing symptoms. Their reports, however, did elevate scales indicating Jerome's difficulties with attention and executive functioning, of which he did not have an earlier history. In his own BASC-3 self-report, though, Jerome not only acknowledged struggles with attention/executive functioning but also clinically significant levels of depression and anxiety.

Reflections on these discrepant findings with Jerome and his parents illuminated a story in which (a) Jerome's extroversion, appearance of physical strength, and continued success in sports and other extracurriculars masked to others how much he was struggling internally (which had manifested mainly in his difficulties keeping up with schoolwork) and (b) his family's emphasis on achievement and valuing a "growth mindset . . . try harder, work harder" had not created an atmosphere in which Jerome had felt it acceptable to directly express his vulnerability and ask for help. Making sense of this discontinuity in self-reports and collateral-reports set the stage for effective parent guidance and family therapy.

Although an example such as Jerome's underscores the rich, treatment-relevant meaning that can be gleaned by reconciling incongruous findings across methods, such incongruities can sometimes also be understood through the psychometric lens of response bias. Related to validity/accuracy of questionnaire and interview responses—whether self-report or collateral-report—*response bias* refers to the "systematic tendency to respond to a range of . . . items on some basis other than the specific item content" (Paulhus, 1991, p.17). With regard to self-report and caregiver-report measures of child psychopathology, Stokes et al. (2011) operationalized response bias in terms of scores on validity scales assessing defensiveness (underreporting of symptoms) and dissimulation (overreporting or exaggeration of symptoms). In their study of psychiatrically hospitalized preadolescents and their parents, Stokes et al. found that response bias for the children and parents were positively correlated, especially for defensiveness, raising the possibility that

> there might be a broader *shared* [emphasis added] parent–child view of the need to defend against problems or emphasize the most positive characteristics of a child that needs to be understood in the context of assessment and intervention planning. (p. 533)

Additionally, although it is not certain to what extent this pattern might generalize to outpatient settings and/or adolescent patients, Stokes et al. (2011) clarified that in their sample, rare was a parent–child dyad in which one was exaggerating and the other was defensive. Other notable findings by Stokes et al. were that (a) parent-reports and child-reports were more likely to be congruous for externalizing symptoms as opposed to internalizing symptoms and (b) support was not found for what has been referred to as the *depression-distortion hypothesis*, that is, the idea that a depressed parent will be more likely to exaggerate their child's problematic symptoms and behaviors. Stokes et al.'s findings were more nuanced than the depression-distortion hypothesis, discerning instead that parents reporting more depression themselves were apt to be lower in both defensiveness and exaggeration regarding their child's symptoms, suggesting "decreased tendencies for the parent to present an idealized image of the child as opposed to a tendency to interpret all behaviors as problematic" (p. 534).

THE VALUE OF DIMENSIONAL ASSESSMENT

When it comes to questions about the categorical bipolar diagnoses, it is important to acknowledge that even with our specialized, multimethod approach, this dichotomous yes–no differential is still often not clear-cut. Based on Weiner's (2000) invaluable suggestion to convey test findings with a level of confidence commensurate with evidence in the data, it is preferable to conclude that findings are mixed or equivocal, specifying in what ways as opposed to forcing a decision that is inadequately supported by the data.

Tempering such necessary humility about traditional categorical diagnoses, though, is knowledge that our assessments can contribute consistently to nomothetic dimensional understanding of important aspects of emotional (dys)regulation. A *dimensional perspective* is based on the premise that symptoms, traits, and motivations exist—and can oscillate—on a continuum from not present to mild to extreme/severe. Among other things, dimensional assessment (a) acknowledges variability and differentiates severity within a taxonomic category; (b) helps determine the urgency of treatment needs; (c) allows for identifying when a person might be subthreshold for a categorical diagnosis but is still in distress or is impaired and thus requires treatment; and (d) facilitates the idiographic assessment of change over time, fitting with the recent emphasis on measurement-based mental health care (American Psychiatric Association, 2013, 2022; Helzer et al., 2006; Hopwood, 2022; Jones, 2012; LeBeau et al., 2015; Lewis et al., 2019).

Dimensional Assessment of the Bipolar Spectrum: Depression and Mania

The subsequent chapters on collateral-report, self-report, and performance-based measures address considerations related to dimensionality in more detail. For now, it is worth highlighting that when referral questions involve the bipolar spectrum, two primary symptom dimensions to assess are depression and (hypo)mania (Youngstrom et al., 2009). As Youngstrom, Morton, and Murray (2020) elaborated,

> Counterintuitively, depression and mania do not appear to be opposite poles of a single dimension. Instead, they are two distinct sets of symptoms that can occur independently of each other or overlap. . . . A dimensional model resolves many of the problems . . . with the current categorical classification system, including the large number of cases with "mixed hypomanias" [simultaneous hypomanic and depressive symptoms] or "anger attacks" in the context of depression, or agitated depressive presentations. (p. 202)

In other words, this dimensional framework allows us to map our young patient's levels of depression and (hypo)mania on separate axes to capture their respective severities at a given point in time (as illustrated in Figure 8.1 in Youngstrom, Morton, & Murray, 2020).

Dimensional Assessment of Impairment

In addition to assessing depression and (hypo)mania on separate continua, it can be valuable to include a dimensional measure of functional impairment (Pan et al., 2019). To be clear, impairment is related to but different from symptoms. Barkley (2016) made the distinction that

> a symptom is a physical, cognitive, or behavioral manifestation of a disorder. . . . By contrast, impairment refers to the *adverse consequences* [emphasis added] that arise from functioning ineffectively in a major life activity due to the expression of those symptom(s) of a disorder. (p. 257)

For instance, in attention-deficit/hyperactivity disorder, hyperactivity is a symptom, but the resultant failure to complete schoolwork reflects impairment.

With kids, impairment can be assessed overall and across various domains, such as home/activities of daily living, school, and peer relationships. As Pan et al. (2019) suggested, "Impairment may help guide our judgment when we face the hard task of distinguishing manic symptoms from normative (and perhaps developmentally essential) exuberant and undercontrolled behavior in youth" (p. 104). Even if the symptom picture is murky enough to preclude a definitive rule-in or rule-out of the bipolar spectrum (or other condition in the fifth edition, text revision, of the *Diagnostic and Statistical Manual of Mental Disorders* [*DSM-5-TR*; American Psychiatric Association, 2022]), measures of impairment allow us to make—and document—a case for the appropriate degree of exigency for various treatment interventions. Moreover, assessing level of impairment is often essential in tracking change over time. For example, it is possible that a patient improves symptomatically with treatment, which can be misleading when it is also learned that they remain highly impaired in their functioning (Canino et al., 2013). This would have implications for decisions about discontinuing, continuing, modifying, or augmenting pharmacological, psychotherapeutic, in-home, or school-based interventions.

So, even if it is not possible with the data that we have to be conclusive about a categorical bipolar diagnosis, our dimensional and narrative idiographic descriptions of the patient and their processes of emotional regulation are valuable in (a) pointing toward meaningful interventions and (b) highlighting what to watch for over the course of ongoing development, especially if there are compelling bipolar signs but short of meriting a full-blown diagnosis. Within this framework, the next three chapters move to specific collateral-report, self-report, and performance-based measures.

CONSIDERATIONS FOR DIVERSITY-SENSITIVE ASSESSMENT

Multimethod and dimensional approaches go a long way toward individualizing and optimizing the assessment of complex kids vulnerable to emotional dysregulation, but in our multicultural world, also essential is sensitivity to the diversity of our young patients and their families. Sensitivity to diversity encompasses respect for, attunement to, and consideration of the effect on adaptation and presenting concerns of children and their families related to "race, ethnicity, language, sexual orientation, gender, age, disability, class status, education, religious/spiritual orientation, and other cultural dimensions" (American Psychological Association [APA], 2003, p. 380). Such variables are important for the assessor to take into account from (a) the time of referral when decisions are made about whether one has the training and competence to conduct the assessment (e.g., if the assessor does not speak the patient's first language, a colleague who does might be better suited) to (b) selection of the test battery to (c) test administration and other interactions with the patient and family (e.g., determining if the patient's physical disability necessitates accommodations in administration or if an interpreter is necessary) to (d) interpretation of data to (e) report writing and the feedback process (e.g., Brabender & Mihura, 2016; Dana, 2005; S. R. Smith & Krishnamurthy, 2018b).

Assessor Self-Awareness: Our Own Cultural Biases

Broadly, sensitivity to diversity requires commitment to the ongoing professional/developmental task of reflecting on and redressing our own cultural biases (Baca & Smith, 2018; Mihura & Brabender, 2016). When a patient is referred to us, and we learn specifics about their multicultural background, we carefully consider our own similarities to and difference from the patient/family on various dimensions of identity and anticipate how these might contribute to various kinds of countertransference biases, both negative and positive (see Hays, 2008). Moreover, at any point in the assessment process, we also hold in mind the potential need for supervision/consultation with mentors and other colleagues, especially those possessing greater familiarity and expertise with the cultural context of our patient and their family. In contemporary practice, access to professional LISTSERV™ systems makes networking to obtain appropriate consultation more pragmatic than ever.

More specifically, it is essential for assessors to be aware of and to counteract cultural biases toward—or away from—certain taxonomic diagnoses. Along similar lines, for patients from marginalized groups vulnerable to overt and more subtle forms of oppression, we can select measures that tap into particular types of traumatic stressors. Additionally, in some instances, it is important to recognize that the same test scores might be interpreted differently based on the patient's cultural context. Each of these considerations is addressed at various points in the remaining chapters of Part II as collateral-report, self-report, and performance-based measures are reviewed.

Accounting for Biases in Our Measures: The Concept of Measurement Invariance

Perhaps the most humbling challenge in diversity-sensitive assessment involves selecting measures that are not culturally biased against our patient. What makes this so daunting is that most of the measures available to us have been normed on primarily White, cisgender, heteronormative samples that are not representative of many of the patients who come to our offices and clinics for assessment. Psychometric determination that a measure is not biased against a person from a particular cultural group requires research demonstrating that it possesses measurement invariance across particular groups (e.g., Borsboom, 2006; Dimitrov, 2010; Stevanovic et al., 2017). A kind of internal validity, *measurement invariance* includes the instrument's possessing the same factor structure across different groups. Some aspects of measurement invariance include (a) *dimensional invariance*, meaning that the measure "consists of the same number of factors across groups" (Stevanovic et al., 2017, p. 143); (b) *configural invariance* in which each factor is "measured by the same set of items across groups" (Stevanovic et al., 2017, p. 143); and (c) lack of *differential item functioning* (DIF) across different cultural groups, which indicates that members of the respective groups are equally likely to respond a certain way to items.

When there is evidence of DIF and there are no known or expected differences in a symptom or trait across groups, the varying patterns of item endorsement between groups can be explained by factors, such as differences across the groups in understanding or interpretation of words or phrases within the item (Columbia University, Mailman School of Public Health, n.d.). It is also possible to demonstrate what has been called *partial measurement invariance* (Byrne & Watkins, 2003; Dimitrov, 2010; both cited in Stevanovic et al., 2017), meaning that although the instrument demonstrates the same factor structure across cultural groups, not all the same items load on the respective factors. In such instances, only the items that do load across groups should be used for comparison between them (e.g., Stevanovic et al., 2017).[2]

As the chapters that follow make clear, what is especially humbling is that most of the measures useful for assessing aspects of emotional dysregulation in children and adolescents do not have evidence of measurement invariance that would give us greater confidence for application across different multicultural groups.[3] In some instances, measures have been found to show the opposite, that is, *measurement noninvariance*. For the most part, though, the measures have not yet been evaluated for measurement invariance and cross-cultural suitability. Unfortunately, this scenario is not uncommon in the broader practice of contemporary psychological assessment. S. R. Smith and Krishnamurthy (2018b) grappled in a sophisticated way with the dilemma around whether to err on the side of either (a) proceeding with assessment's "not taking diversity into account," (p. 363) so, regardless of the patient, administering whatever

[2]For a more technical discussion of measurement invariance, see Putnick and Bornstein (2016) and Tay et al. (2015). Putnick and Bornstein (2016) address this from the perspective of structural equation modeling; Tay et al. (2015), from the perspective of item response theory. Also, because it has been challenging for researchers to demonstrate measurement invariance, Funder (2020) has made the case for an alternative to measurement invariance to demonstrate cross-cultural applicability. Funder shifted the focus from internal to external validity: that is, to what extent do the measure and its scales correlate with meaningful variables within the particular cultural group? Timbrook and Graham's (1994) research showing nonbias of the Minnesota Multiphasic Personality Inventory–2 (Butcher et al., 1989) across African American and White participants exemplifies this methodology.

[3]Based on my literature searches, when measurement invariance/nonbias has been researched in psychological assessment with children and adolescents, it has been most commonly, if not exclusively, in the context of comparing across racial/ethnic groups and traditional binary notions of gender.

measure and interpreting it traditionally versus (b) "viewing diversity factors as wholly explanatory" (p. 363) of the presenting concerns and thus not administering the measure (or perhaps any measure) at all. The authors elaborated:

> Complicating these decisions is the fact that identifying the various sources of pathological difficulty is usually not a simple either/or proposition. In essence, one . . . need[s] to consider both a pathology-centered hypothesis *and* a diversity-centered hypothesis (e.g., López, 2002), as well as the intersection of multiple variables with and across each domain. (S. R. Smith & Krishnamurthy, 2018b, pp. 363–364)

Mitigating Biases Through Principles of Evidence-Based Practice

To manage this complexity while holding the ethical "burden of conducting psychological assessments . . . appropriate for a given question with a particular population" (S. R. Smith & Krishnamurthy, 2018b, p. 365), S. R. Smith and Krishnamurthy described a process of adhering to principles of evidence-based practice involving thoughtful integration of relevant empirical research, clinical experience, and patient variables (APA Presidential Task Force on Evidence-Based Practice, 2006).

Role of Research

Among the recommendations by S. R. Smith and Krishnamurthy (2018b) for attending to research is the previously discussed concept of measurement invariance. S. R. Smith and Krishnamurthy acknowledged, however, that

> given that assessment research has not adequately sampled underrepresented populations in the past, it might be that clinicians will be left with little robust data on the validity of their tools with their clients. *In those cases, we urge clinicians to be cautious, consult when necessary, and acknowledge the limitations of the measures they have chosen* [emphasis added]. We also suggest that clinicians continue to remain abreast of the most updated literature on the populations they serve and the measures they choose. *However, there will be times when all of the published research will still come up short and clinician experience will be an even more important component of the assessment process* [emphasis added]. (p. 366)

Hopefully over time, published research on the measurement invariance/nonbias of collateral-report and self-report instruments assessing emotional dysregulation in children and adolescents will be increasingly available. Access to internet databases like PubMed and PsycInfo—entering the name of the measure alongside terms, such as "measurement invariance," "cultural bias," and "diversity"—are crucial tools for us to remain current.

Role of Clinical Experience

In instances in which research is less available and in tandem with seeking consultation from colleagues with more experience and expertise with certain measures or populations, we can mobilize clinical experience to guide "a cautious and informed use of hunches in the context of a larger hypothesis-testing approach" (S. R. Smith & Krishnamurthy, 2018b, p. 368). *Clinical experience* includes choosing measures and interpreting test data in the context of what we—or our consultants—know about the cultural context of our patient and their family. For example, consider an adolescent whose family immigrated from a non-English-speaking country 3 years before, and their therapist referred them for evaluation to clarify to what extent and under what conditions the patient's emotional dysregulation might be associated with cognitive disorganization. Although, this adolescent's speaking and comprehension of English had progressed since immigrating, it would have been optimal for them to be evaluated in their native language. However, no assessment clinicians speaking their native language were practicing in their community. The patient and family expressed that they felt comfortable proceeding with the evaluation in English and, based on the assessor's initial conversations with the patient, the dyad agreed to move forward in this way rather than using an interpreter. Given the referral question, administering the Rorschach made sense (Kleiger, 2017), but the assessor recognized the absence of a normative comparison group of patients the same age from their country of origin, acculturation status, and so forth.

It turned out that this youngster's Rorschach profile (Meyer et al., 2011) was marked by a small number of mild (Level 1) cognitive codes—deviant verbalizations and incongruous combinations—contributing to a slight elevation (standard score = 113) on the weighted sum of cognitive codes (WSumCog) variable, ostensibly a measure of disordered thinking. Lacking a normative comparison group, the assessor relied on clinical experience in the form of previous assessment of patients referred around questions of thought disorder. The assessor appreciated that the patient's idiosyncratic use of language that contributed to the cognitive codes and elevation of WSumCog were best explained by the patient's English as a second language rather than by reflecting clinically meaningful vulnerabilities in coherence of their thinking and logical reasoning.[4]

[4]Had the adolescent's Rorschach been coded for more bizarre (Level 2) lapses in thinking and logical reasoning, contributing to extreme elevations in WSumCog, there would be compelling evidence for a more psychopathological interpretation. However, clinical consultation, judgment, and humility would still be necessary to try to tease out the potential effect of the patient's English as a second language.

Role of Patient-Specific Variables

In terms of considering patient-specific variables in evidence-based assessment, S. R. Smith and Krishnamurthy (2018b) highlighted considerations related to the concept of *intersectionality* based on

> the notion that . . . that *identity* is a fluid construct in which our various identifiers (e.g., African American, woman, Christian, homosexual) are more or less salient depending on context. . . . As we see different aspects of our selfhood as discrepant from those in our surroundings, they become more salient and at the forefront of our minds. (pp. 368–369, italics in original)

The authors elaborated the value of direct discussions with our patients (and their caregivers) "about what aspects of their identities are important and relevant given their setting, context, and current circumstances" (S. R. Smith & Krishnamurthy, 2018b, p. 369). This can set the stage for being open and collaborative with them about selecting and interpreting measures. Especially with older children and adolescents as well as caregivers in general, it might be possible to share our own dilemmas about choice of measures and alternative interpretive hypotheses and attempt to engage their reflective input, which not only assists in our clinical decision making and informs our inferences but also can yield treatment-relevant data about their potential—and conditions under which—for therapeutic alliance (Bram, 2010; Bram & Peebles, 2014; see also the section on the patient–examiner relationship in Chapter 6 of the present volume).

Multimethod Assessment to Mitigate Potential Biases

Consistent with the case made by Mihura and Brabender (2016), S. R. Smith and Krishnamurthy (2018b) emphasized that a fundamental antidote to the potential for cultural insensitivity and bias is the application of a multimethod approach. Bringing us back to the initial focus of this chapter and setting the stage for the reviews of collateral-report, self-report, and performance-based measures that follow in the remainder of Part II, S. R. Smith and Krishnamurthy reiterated that we "should never rely on one measure in isolation" and that "by incorporating paper-and-pencil self-reports [and collateral-reports] with performance-based measurement, clinicians increase their perspectives and thus increase the likelihood that their data will be culturally sensitive and useful for the client [and their family]" (pp. 370–371).

4 COLLATERAL-REPORT MEASURES TO ASSESS EMOTIONAL DYSREGULATION

Typically, collateral-report[1] measures to assess emotional regulation in general and bipolar spectrum conditions in particular are completed by parents or other caregivers[2] because these ratings correlate most strongly—compared with self-reports and teacher-reports—with diagnoses based on structured interviews. Such interviews include the Kiddie Schedule for Affective Disorders and Schizophrenia for School Aged Children–Present and Lifetime Version for the fifth edition of the *Diagnostic and Statistical Manual of Mental Disorders* (K-SADS-PL *DSM-5*; Kaufman et al., 2016; described in Chapter 5 in this volume; see also American Psychiatric Association, 2013).

[1]Although many other authors—including many of those cited in this chapter—refer to these as "informant-reports" rather than "collateral-reports," I have chosen to eschew "informant-reports" because of its additional but also popular meaning related to secretly providing information to law enforcement or other investigative agencies, which is far afield from the collaborative spirit intended by the present approach to assessment.

[2]These measures are more typically referred to as "parent-report," but they are intended for administration to primary caregivers whether or not they are the parents of the child or adolescent. For the sake of inclusiveness, there is a case to be made that these measures should be called caregiver-reports.

https://doi.org/10.1037/0000430-005
Psychological Assessment of Emotional Dysregulation in Children and Adolescents: The Bipolar Spectrum and Beyond, by A. D. Bram
Copyright © 2025 by the American Psychological Association. All rights reserved.

But Duffy et al. (2020) reminded us of the value of making use of data from multiple vantage points (including the patient and others in their life):

> There has been *no consistent approach to manage information from multiple informants* [italics in original]. This is especially problematic in child psychiatry because diagnoses differ depending on whether everyone's positive symptoms are counted even if inconsistent versus counting only those where there is agreement between informants. Rather than trying to understand what the discrepancy tells us, the approach has been to count one or the other informant or combine everyone's positive symptoms. Such diagnostic approaches can be highly susceptible to confirmatory bias. . . . If teachers observe no evidence of irritability, hyperactivity, rapid speech etc. where parents rate the child as severely ill, *the discrepancy needs to be understood* [emphasis added]. Mania does not just occur at home. (p. 3)

The words of Duffy et al. (2020) are consistent with the emphases here on (a) efforts to make sense of seeming incongruities in the data and (b) assessing conditions under which a patient's functioning is variable (Bram & Peebles, 2014; Peebles, 2012). Youngstrom et al. (2012) suggested the value of multiple perspectives to appreciate more fully "the degree and contexts of impairment" even if doing so is "less helpful in differential [taxonomic] diagnosis" (p. 20). In other words, for the ruling in or out of the bipolar spectrum diagnosis, although caregiver-report is the most important crucial data point, self-report and teacher-report ratings potentially contribute to a more nuanced understanding of the child's or adolescent's functioning.

As is the case for the self-report measures discussed in Chapter 5, collateral-report measures of emotional dysregulation can be classified according to whether they are broadband or bipolar specific. Each is discussed in this chapter, sandwiching a discussion of collateral-report dimensional measures of functional impairment.

BROADBAND COLLATERAL-REPORT MEASURES OF EMOTIONAL REGULATION

Collateral-report broadband measures include caregiver-report and teacher-report forms of multiscale symptom measures, such as the Behavior Assessment System for Children, Third Edition (BASC-3; Reynolds & Kamphaus, 2015); Child Behavior Checklist (CBCL; Achenbach, 1999); or the *DSM-5*–referenced version of the Child & Adolescent Symptom Inventory-5 (CASI-5; Gadow & Sprafkin, 2013). Such broadband measures typically include scales illuminating aspects of a young patient's functioning, such as adaptive skills, level of impairment, internalizing (e.g., depression, anxiety, social withdrawal) and externalizing (e.g., anger, aggression, oppositionality, risk-taking, hyperactivity) symptoms, and attention and executive functioning. These types of broadband scales are used routinely by assessors who evaluate kids, so they are not detailed here. However, three considerations regarding broadband collateral-report measures bear emphasis: assessment of (a) depressive symptoms, (b) externalizing symptoms, and (c) functional impairment. Before delving into these three considerations, it is important to acknowledge that to date, currently available broadband caregiver-report and teacher-report measures have not yet been shown to meet standards of measurement invariance to indicate applicability across cultural groups: Only the parent-report CBCL and its companion Teacher Report Form (TRF; Achenbach & Rescorla, 2004) have been the focus of research on measurement invariance across various cultural groups,[3] but Stevanovic et al. (2017) concluded that of the six CBCL and TRF studies available for review, none revealed measurement invariance, thus not providing support for their cross-cultural validity. This is a reminder for us to remain cautious and humble in our interpretations of such broadband measures in the assessment of people from underrepresented cultural backgrounds (see Chapter 3).

Broadband Collateral-Report Measures and Depression

As noted in Chapter 3, assessing depression dimensionally is essential when there are specific questions about the bipolar spectrum. Really, assessing the level of depression—along with anxiety and anger/aggression—is fundamental when there are any concerns about emotional dysregulation. Inclusion of a broadband collateral-report measure builds in such a dimensional assessment of depression as well as items that screen for suicide and self-harm.

Broadband Collateral-Report Measures and Externalizing Symptoms

Youngstrom et al. (2012) alerted assessors to the value of attending to broadband collateral-report measures' scales that capture externalizing behaviors: "If Externalizing is extremely elevated the odds of [pediatric bipolar disorder] triple or quadruple. Conversely, low Externalizing scores make [pediatric

---

[3]Outside of the parameters of this book, there has been one published study on measurement invariance across the English and Spanish versions of the BASC-3 caregiver-report preschool forms (Edyburn et al., 2020). The authors concluded,

> Given that previously identified factor structures and full measurement invariance across languages were not supported, additional validity evidence is needed. The Spanish version of the Parent Preschool form should be used with caution and in conjunction with other data on children's behavioral and emotional functioning. (p. 307)

bipolar disorder] less likely, decreasing the odds by a factor of as much as 20" (p. 19, citing Youngstrom et al., 2004). Low externalizing scores are weighted heavily in helping to rule out bipolar disorder. Elevated externalizing scores flag the need to further assess with more specificity because such elevations, in and of themselves, are associated with a high risk of false positives.[4]

Broadband Collateral-Report Measures of Functional Impairment

Some, but not all, broadband collateral measures allow for ratings and include scales reflecting the young patient's overall degree of functional impairment. The BASC-3 (Reynolds & Kamphaus, 2015) is one such measure; it involves the aggregation of an observer's reports of disturbances in social/relational interactions, management of mood, and performance of school-rated and other age-expected tasks. The CASI-5 (Gadow & Sprafkin, 2013) yields both an overall Global Impairment Index as well as Impairment Severity Scores that are disorder specific. So, for instance, regarding the CASI-5 Global Impairment Index, in the context of rating their child's depression (or mania, conduct problems, social anxiety), a caregiver can indicate severity of impairment associated with that particular set of symptoms. These disorder-specific impairment ratings are helpful in operationalizing the fifth edition, text revision, of the *Diagnostic and Statistical Manual of Mental Disorders* (*DSM-5-TR*; American Psychiatric Association, 2022) impairment criterion for a given disorder (i.e., in that impairment is tied specifically to symptoms of a specific condition).

COLLATERAL-REPORT MEASURES SPECIFIC TO FUNCTIONAL IMPAIRMENT

If our selected broadband measure does not yield a measure of impairment, a separate collateral-report impairment scale can be added to the battery. The Brief Impairment Scale (BIS; Bird et al., 2005) is a 23-item caregiver-report

[4]Some of the aforementioned broadband collateral-report measures also have scales developed more specifically to detect bipolar conditions. For example, the CASI-5 (Gadow & Sprafkin, 2013) includes a mania scale. And for the CBCL, Papachristou et al. (2013) created a mania scale, the Child Behavior Checklist–Mania Scale (CBCL-MS), comprising items that capture factors of distractibility/disinhibition, psychosis, increased libido, and decreased sleep. Unfortunately, Youngstrom et al. (2012) summarized that, in general, broadband-derived subscales, such as the CBCL-MS, do not provide incremental validity over externalizing scales from the same broadband instruments.

measure to be administered in interview format, validated for ages 4 years to 17 years, that offers dimensional assessment of a child's or adolescent's impairment. Each item is rated on 0-to-3 scale with the following anchor points: 0 (*no problem*), 1 (*some problem*), 2 (*a considerable problem*), and 3 (*serious problem*); higher scores reflect greater impairment. The BIS assesses level of impairment across the three domains of interpersonal relating, self-care/self-fulfillment, and functioning at school or work. Based on analyses aimed at balancing specificity and sensitivity, the authors have recommended a cutoff score of at least 14 to determine impairment and need for clinical services. The BIS is disseminated by the American Academy of Pediatrics and is freely available to clinicians (to download the BIS, see American Academy of Pediatrics, n.d.).

Among commercially available options for norm-based caregiver-report instruments are the Rating Scale of Impairment (RSI; S. Goldstein & Naglieri, 2016a, 2016b)[5] and the Barkley Functional Impairment Scale–Children and Adolescent (BFIS-CA; Barkley, 2012; see also Barkley, 2016). The parent version of the RSI comprises 41 or 49 items (41 items for kids ages 5 years to 12 years; 49 items for kids ages 13 years to 18 years) covering five or six areas of functioning: school/work, social, mobility, domestic, family, and self-care (the area of self-care is only for the older age group). Each item is rated on a 6-point scale with the following anchor points: 0 (*never*), 1 (*rarely*), 2 (*sometimes*), 3 (*often*), 4 (*very often*), and 5 (*always*); higher scores denote more overall impairment. Raw scores for each domain and total score are readily converted to *T* scores and percentiles with classification ranges as follows: $T < 60$, no impairment; $T = 60–64$, mild impairment; $T = 65–69$, moderate impairment; $T > 69$, considerable impairment.

The BFIS-CA (Barkley, 2012; see also Barkley, 2016) is a 15-item caregiver-report scale whose items capture areas of a child's or adolescent's functioning, such as interactions within the family and with peers, school performance, participation in community and leisure activities, self-care, and completion of schoolwork and chores at home. All items (caregivers can also note if an item does not apply) are rated on 0-to-9 scale ranging from 0 (*not at all*) to 9 (*severe*); higher scores reflect more impairment. In addition to a total mean impairment score (across all of the rated items), the BFIS-CA yields scores on two factors—home-school and community-leisure—as well as a score for the number of items in which the child or adolescent was rated as impaired (i.e., defined as above the 93rd percentile). Scores on each scale can be compared to norms stratified according to age groups (6 to 11, 12 to 17).

[5]The RSI also offers a teacher-report version.

Among the collateral-report measures of impairment reviewed here, research on measurement invariance is not available. Thus, their multicultural application ought to proceed cautiously as discussed in Chapter 3.

COLLATERAL-REPORT MEASURES SPECIFIC TO BIPOLAR CONDITIONS

An early part of the evaluation often involves administration of collateral-report broadband measures, and if those yield elevations on scales associated with externalizing behaviors and bipolar characteristics, then caregiver-report bipolar-specific scales ought to be administered subsequently (Youngstrom et al., 2012). Alternatively—and as often is the case in clinical practice—if the referral question, symptoms, and/or risk factors point immediately to the need to rule out a bipolar spectrum condition, these collateral-report measures can be included from the evaluation's outset. Although as stated earlier, there is value in obtaining perspectives of multiple collaterals; from a *DSM-5-TR* differential diagnostic standpoint, the most essential is the report by the caregiver (Youngstrom et al., 2005). Thus, it is strongly recommended that any evaluation in which there is a question of bipolar illness include a caregiver-report scale that assesses for symptoms of mania.

Youngstrom et al. (2012) noted that "manic symptoms such as elated mood, grandiosity . . . and decreased need for sleep have fewer likely causes than irritability and aggression" (p. 19). Aggression and irritability are not mania-specific symptoms per se, so with bipolar-specific caregiver-report measures, we aim to zero in on symptoms that are unique to bipolar conditions. Here, four such bipolar-specific collateral scales are described for assessors to consider: (a) Child Mania Rating Scale–Parent version (CMRS-P; Pavuluri, Henry, et al., 2006), (b) the 10-item Parent General Behavior Inventory Mania scale (P-GBI-10M; Youngstrom, Frazier, et al., 2008), (c) parent version of the Young Mania Rating Scale (P-YMRS; Gracious et al., 2002), and (d) Parent-Report of the Mood Disorder Questionnaire-Adolescent Version (P-MDQ-A; Wagner et al., 2006). Elevations on any of these scales require follow-up with further, focused inquiry as described later in this chapter. Note that McDonnell (2010) investigated measurement invariance (see Chapter 3) of these bipolar-specific caregiver-report measures across patients in the United States (*N* = 758 families) who were (a) White and African American and (b) male and female, and found that for each measure,

> DIF [differential item functioning] was detected on specific items, indicating that the probability of a parent endorsing that item differs between equal groups

> due to group membership, rather than the construct (mania), which it is intended to measure. *However, most differences were small and unlikely to be clinically-meaningful or influence diagnostic or treatment decisions in research or clinical practice* [emphasis added]. (p. 7)[6]

CMRS-P

For caregivers of children ages 5 years and older, the CMRS-P (Pavuluri, Henry, et al., 2006) comprises 21 items that capture a range of (hypo)manic symptoms. Caregivers rate each item on a 0-to-3 scale with the following anchor points: 0 (*never/rarely*), 1 (*sometimes*), 2 (*often*), and 3 (*very often*) with instructions to "consider [the symptom] a problem if it is causing trouble and is beyond what is normal for your child's age." A cut score of at least 20 has been shown to help differentiate between kids with bipolar spectrum and those with attention-deficit/hyperactivity disorder (ADHD) with high sensitivity and specificity.

Recently, though, Duffy et al. (2020) critiqued the original CMRS-P study for being based on a sample of kids classified at the time on the bipolar spectrum, yet many of them would now be considered to meet *DSM-5-TR* criteria for disruptive mood dysregulation disorder instead. This is in large part because the CMRS-P also includes items related to irritable mood and aggression that are less specific to mania. Despite these criticisms, clinically, the CMRS-P is still valuable, but it is useful to informally weight elevated scores more heavily if they are driven by endorsements of specific manic symptoms, such as grandiosity, elevated mood, decreased need for sleep, hypersexuality, risk-taking, unusual thinking, and bizarre sensory-perceptual experiences. See Helping Give Away Psychological Science (n.d.) for an online-administered version of the CMRS-P (Pavuluri, Henry, et al., 2006).

P-GBI-10M

The 10-item P-GBI-10M (Youngstrom, Frazier, et al., 2008) is a screening measure focused mainly on symptoms of mania/hypomania (e.g., elated mood,

---

[6]With only McDonnell's (2010) study supporting measurement invariance, Stevanovic et al. (2017) concluded that there is only weak evidence overall for cross-cultural validity for each of the CMRS-P, P-GBI-10M, P-YMRS, and P-MDQ-A. Stevanovic et al. defined weak evidence as reflecting that in a single study, "2 ethnic/cultural groups . . . demonstrated full/partial strong measurement invariance or no/few DIF evident" (p. 131). Still, McDonnell's (2010) findings offer some confidence in the use of these caregiver-report measures with African American families in the United States.

psychomotor acceleration, excessive energy, emotional volatility, racing thoughts) but also on some related to irritability and depression. Youngstrom, Frazier, et al. (2008) developed this short form out of the original, 73-item version of the Parent General Behavior Inventory (Youngstrom et al., 2001) that itself comprises hypomania and depression/biphasic (mixed symptom) scales.

The P-GBI-10M yields a single scale. Caregivers of kids ages 5 years to 17 years rate each of the 10 items from 0-to-3 based on observations of their child over the past year; the anchor points are 0 (*never/hardly ever*), 1 (*sometimes*), 2 (*often*), and 3 (*very often/almost constant*). The rating scale is prefaced by detailed instructions for caregivers on how to account for aspects of frequency, duration, and changeability of symptoms to inform their ratings. For caregivers with lower reading ability or who are less fluent in the language the scale is presented in, the scale can be administered as an interview such that the instructions can be clarified. Interpretation of the P-GBI-10M is as follows, including implications for the likelihood (risk) of a bipolar spectrum diagnosis given the base rate: 0, minimal risk (decrease likelihood from base rate by a factor of about 100); 1 to 4, mild risk; 5 to 14, neutral risk (no change in likelihood from base rate); 15 to 17, high risk (nearly triples likelihood from base rate); and 18 to 30, very high risk (likelihood increases nearly seven from base rate; Youngstrom, Frazier, et al., 2008). See Mood Center (n.d.) to access the P-GBI-10M.

P-YMRS

Also for caregivers of kids at least 5 years of age, the P-YMRS (Gracious et al., 2002) has 11 items covering symptoms of mania (e.g., grandiosity, elevated mood, heightened energy level and sexual interest), irritability, aggression, unusual thinking, and hallucinations as well as changes in dress/grooming and insight into impairment. Of the 11 items, seven are rated on a 0-to-4 scale and four are rated on a 0-to-8 scale with anchors varying depending on the item; higher item and total scores reflect more severe psychiatric disturbance.

Based on their research in a community mental health sample, Marchand et al. (2005) proposed a cut score of 18 to reliably differentiate between kids with bipolar spectrum conditions and those with mood disorders, ADHD, and other psychiatric disorders. Methodologically, Marchand et al. described their modification of directions for administering the P-YMRS: “In cases where patients were already stabilized on medications or in a euthymic phase between mood episodes, parents were instructed to complete the instrument based on a past manic or hypomanic episode” (pp. 32–33). Their findings led them to conclude that their study suggests the P-YMRS can be used either to rate symptoms retrospectively or to rate current levels of symptomatology. This is an important characteristic of a bipolar diagnostic scale: Because bipolar disorder is a cycling disorder by definition, kids may often present for treatment when they are not currently having manic or hypomanic symptoms. Further, patients frequently present already on some psychotropic medications, which may result in symptom control; however, the need still exists to confirm the diagnosis. Copies of the P-YMRS can be found in an online search; see, for example, one such source: Tennessee State Government (n.d.).

P-MDQ-A

Validated with the caregivers of adolescents ages 12 years to 17 years, the P-MDQ-A (Wagner et al., 2006) presents the prompt: "Has there ever been a time for a week or more when your adolescent was not his/her usual self and. . . ." This is followed by 13 items tapping into symptoms, such as elevated mood, grandiosity, increased energy, decreased need for sleep, hypersexuality, and other erratic behaviors. Note that the P-MDQ-A also contains items about irritability and aggression that are nonspecific to mania. Caregivers are to check presence or absence (rated 1 or 0) of each symptom, and they then are to note (a) whether they have observed more than one symptom during the same period and then (b) the degree of impairment associated with the symptoms (*no problem, minor problem, moderate problem, serious problem*). A cut score of 5 was determined to be the threshold for differentiating adolescents with bipolar spectrum from those with other psychiatric conditions.

As with the CMRS-P (Pavuluri, Henry, et al., 2006), assessors can informally place more weight on scale elevations not driven by less manic-specific endorsements of irritability and aggression. Wagner et al. (2006) included in their appendix the items of the P-MDQ-A.

Considerations for Clinical Application of Collateral-Report Bipolar-Specific Scales

It is worth reiterating how essential obtaining collateral-report is in the assessment of a child's or adolescent's proneness to emotional dysregulation. To conclude the chapter on this topic, the following eight considerations are offered.

Consideration 1

This review of collateral-report bipolar-specific scales emphasized caregiver-report—as opposed to teacher-report—questionnaires. This is because research findings have been quite consistent that caregiver-reports are superior to teacher-reports (and self-reports) in correlating with bipolar diagnoses as determined by structured interviews, such as the K-SADS-P (Geller et al., 1998; Youngstrom et al., 2004; Youngstrom et al., 2005). As Youngstrom et al. (2012) noted, "Teachers do not observe some hallmark features of mania, such as decreased need for sleep; and they also tend to attribute many of the other symptoms to ADHD or oppositionality" (p. 20).

However, assessors who wish to administer teacher versions of the P-YMRS (Gracious et al., 2002) and CMRS-P (Pavuluri, Henry, et al., 2006) or the P-MDQ-A (Wagner et al., 2006) will learn more about how the child or adolescent functions under varying conditions (Youngstrom et al., 2009, 2012). Compared with caregiver-reports, those from teachers inform us about how dysregulated—or not—kids can become even under school's conditions of greater external structure (e.g., predictable routines, clear expectations, consequences) and need to save face in front of a peer group. Even if the assessor chooses not to administer these bipolar-specific scales to teachers, use of teacher versions of the broadband scales presented earlier, such as the BASC-3 (Reynolds & Kamphaus, 2015) or CBCL (Achenbach, 1999), expands an appreciation of the child's or adolescent's range of emotional functioning.

Consideration 2

For clinical applications of any of these collateral-report bipolar-specific measures, consider augmenting the instructions as Marchand et al. (2005) did with the P-YMRS (Gracious et al., 2002): If the patient is effectively medicated or otherwise stabilized at the time of evaluation, instruct the caregiver to complete ratings based on the child's or adolescent's functioning before stabilization. The assessor can also consider requesting that the respondent do two sets of ratings (e.g., in pens of two different colors): one current and the other retrospective before stabilization. This enables the assessor to comment on the nature and extent of changes associated with an intervention.

Consideration 3

Encourage caregivers (or other collateral observers) to make notes in the margins clarifying or qualifying their ratings. This provides context for interpreting the item endorsement or overall score. For example, a parent might note that a symptom was related to an adverse medication reaction, substance use, or a loss. This context can be further clarified with follow-up, focused queries by interview.

Consideration 4

On any of these collateral report measures, a total score that is well below the research-based diagnostic threshold is often meaningful. Specifically, such a low score can be strong evidence against a bipolar spectrum condition.

Consideration 5

If a total score for a scale reaches or exceeds the research-based diagnostic cut point, be mindful of the risk of a false positive determination (Miguez et al., 2013; Youngstrom et al., 2012). Note also if the scale elevation is largely attributable to endorsement of symptoms that are not specific to mania (e.g., irritable mood, aggressive behaviors, distractibility).

Consideration 6

When a caregiver has endorsed multiple symptoms on any of the questionnaires resulting in a score at or above the research-based threshold for differential diagnosis, the assessor needs to follow up with them with a focused interview to determine to what extent these symptoms cluster into discrete episodes (i.e., that the child or adolescent experienced multiple symptoms within the same period). Among the measures described earlier, a query like this is only explicitly built into the P-MDQ-A (Wagner et al., 2006) but is easily added. The assessor then strives to clarify with the caregiver the frequency, onset, duration, offset (and its conditions) of such episodes.

As Youngstrom, Morton, and Murray (2020) have recommended, ideally such follow-up inquiry involves, at minimum, a semistructured interview with the caregiver and patient (the patient is included, depending on age and amenability) guided concretely by lists of *DSM-5-TR* symptoms and criteria for episodes of mania, hypomania, and depression. Specifically, Youngstrom and colleagues offered that one option is to use as a guide the Kiddie Schedule for Affective Disorders and Schizophrenia Mania Rating Scale (K-SADS-MRS; Axelson et al., 2003; this scale is downloadable: see UPMC Western Psychiatric Hospital, Child & Adolescent Bipolar Spectrum Services, n.d.-b). Other possibilities include administering to the caregiver and/or child the three pages of the Mini International Neuropsychiatric Interview for Children and Adolescents (MINI-KID; Sheehan, 2016) focused on manic and hypomanic episodes or administering the mood disorders section of the Diagnostic Interview for Anxiety, Mood, and OCD [Obsessive-Compulsive Disorder] and Related Neuropsychiatric Disorders–Child and Adolescent Version (DIAMOND-KID; Tolin et al., 2023), especially the pages on manic/hypomanic episodes as well as those addressing criteria for bipolar I, bipolar II, and cyclothymia disorders. The K-SADS-PL *DSM-5* (Kaufman et al., 2016), MINI-KID, and DIAMOND-KID are elaborated on in the section on diagnostic interviews in Chapter 5, which focuses on self-report measures.

Consideration 7

When such structured interviews are administered to caregivers, it is useful to hold in mind qualitative research findings that families of different cultural backgrounds vary in the language used to describe their kids' emotional and behavioral struggles. Such findings by Carpenter-Song (2009) are summarized by Youngstrom, Morton, and Murray (2020):

> White middle-class families who had a child with bipolar disorder (per the research interview) were more likely to describe worries about "*mood swings* [emphasis added]," and intake clinicians were more likely to explore and confirm hypotheses about mood disorders. Black families, on the other hand, typically described the issues in terms of *behaviors* [emphasis added]—"Sometimes, he or she goes off the hook, and he or she is out of control. . . ." Even when the youth would meet full criteria for a bipolar disorder based on a semi-structured diagnostic interview, a clinician doing an unstructured interview was likely to frame the issue as a conduct problem, then confirm a diagnosis of ODD [oppositional defiant disorder] or conduct disorder, without ever exploring potential mood issues as a competing hypothesis. (p. 208)

Consideration 8

In addition to including collateral-report scales, such as those reviewed in this chapter, Kowatch et al. (2005) have reminded us also that

> it is helpful for families to keep daily logs for at least a 2-week period before their first visit. Ideally, families would track mood, energy, sleep, and unusual behavior. . . . Developing a timeline with the primary informant to establish onset, offset and duration of symptoms provides an efficient way to understand the unfolding of the bipolar phenomena, as well as the comorbid conditions over time. (p. 218)

Because the lead time between scheduling and the first appointment is often lengthy for the kinds of intensive, multimethod psychological evaluations described in this book, a case can be made to request that caregivers track these observations over a longer period (e.g., 4–6 weeks). Assessors can provide a template of such a log that includes simple Likert scales for daily rating of elevated mood, depression, anxiety, and energy level; hours slept; and space to record notes about manic and other unusual behaviors, sleep, medication, or stressors.

5 SELF-REPORT MEASURES TO ASSESS EMOTIONAL DYSREGULATION

Self-report measures encompass both interview and questionnaire formats. The first section of this chapter addresses diagnostic interviews, and the second focuses on questionnaires.

SELF-REPORT BY INTERVIEW

If the assessment objective is principally a hard-and-fast ruling in or out of a categorical bipolar spectrum condition, ideally a cornerstone assessment method would be a semistructured interview[1] anchored to the fifth edition, text revision, of the *Diagnostic and Statistical Manual of Mental Disorders* (*DSM-5-TR*; American Psychiatric Association, 2022)—or the latest psychiatric taxonomic system—criteria. Compared with the unstructured psychiatric

[1]Semistructured interviews are based on a standardized set of questions in a predetermined order but, unlike fully structured interviews, allow for clinical judgment in determining such things as pursuing further inquiry and skipping items deemed irrelevant and unnecessary.

https://doi.org/10.1037/0000430-006
Psychological Assessment of Emotional Dysregulation in Children and Adolescents: The Bipolar Spectrum and Beyond, by A. D. Bram
Copyright © 2025 by the American Psychological Association. All rights reserved.

diagnostic interviews preferred by many clinicians, more structured interviews have advantages in reliability, consistent coverage of relevant content, relative freedom from cognitive biases, and greater ability to discern co-occurring conditions (e.g., Croskerry, 2003; Jenkins & Youngstrom, 2016; Lauth et al., 2008; Rettew et al., 2009). The caveat to this is that such measures have largely been developed in and for research settings. As Kleiger and Khadivi (2015) wrote,

> Most of these instruments, despite their impressive psychometric properties and citation in the literature, are often too lengthy and time-consuming to be used routinely. Additionally, most require specialized training in order for the clinician to obtain an acceptable level of reliability as an interviewer and accuracy as a coder/rater. (p. 190)

Leffler et al. (2015) reviewed the accessibility and applicability for clinical practitioners of five structured or semistructured interviews for assessing psychiatric conditions in children and adolescents in the fourth edition of the *Diagnostic and Statistical Manual of Mental Disorders* (*DSM-IV*; American Psychiatric Association, 1994). Based on a literature search, it was not possible to verify that each of the interviews reviewed by Leffler et al. (2015) have been updated for the fifth edition of the *Diagnostic and Statistical Manual of Mental Disorders* (*DSM-5*; American Psychiatric Association, 2013) or the *DSM-5-TR*. But two that have been updated and stand out for their specificity to assessing bipolar spectrum conditions are (a) the Kiddie Schedule for Affective Disorders and Schizophrenia for School Aged Children–Present and Lifetime Version for the fifth edition of the *Diagnostic and Statistical Manual of Mental Disorders* (K-SADS-PL *DSM-5*; Kaufman et al., 2016; see also American Psychiatric Association, 2013), and (b) the Mini International Neuropsychiatric Interview for Children and Adolescents (MINI-KID; Sheehan, 2016). Both of these interviews are addressed here, followed by a description of the more recently published Diagnostic Interview for Anxiety, Mood, and OCD [Obsessive-Compulsive Disorder] and Related Neuropsychiatric Disorders–Child and Adolescent Version (DIAMOND-KID; Tolin et al., 2023).

K-SADS-PL *DSM-5*

The K-SADS-PL *DSM-5* (Kaufman et al., 2016) is a detailed, lengthy semistructured interview that queries about history and symptoms associated with a full range of *DSM-5-TR* conditions suffered by children and adolescents ages 6 years to 18 years. The authors instruct users to administer the interview separately to the child or adolescent and also to a parent/caregiver (i.e., about the child). Outside of nonprofit institutions, clinical use of the K-SADS-PL *DSM-5* screening interview and supplements requires permission from the authors. Information about permission and about the K-SADS-PL *DSM-5* interview itself, including supplements, is available online through the University of Pittsburgh Child & Adolescent Bipolar Spectrum Services (see UPMC Western Psychiatric Hospital, Child & Adolescent Bipolar Spectrum Services, n.d.-a). Computer-administered versions of the K-SADS-PL *DSM-5* are available commercially to clinicians (see KSADS-COMP, n.d.).

The K-SADS-PL *DSM-5* (Kaufman et al., 2016) involves first administering an extensive screening interview that covers *DSM-5-TR* categories most relevant to kids; then, any of the five supplements can be selected to follow up in domains shown to be of concern (i.e., mood disorders, psychotic disorders, anxiety/OCD/trauma, neurodevelopmental/disruptive behavior, and eating disorders). It is estimated that complete administration of the K-SADS-PL *DSM-5* to child and parent requires close to 3 hours total when administered by experienced clinicians (Leffler et al., 2015; Youngstrom et al., 2009). In clinical settings, in which time and cost are at a premium, assessors can be selective based on referral information and other data about whether to complete the screening interview or move directly to the relevant supplements, which themselves go into great detail about symptoms and their chronology. For similar pragmatic reasons, the assessor might consider interviewing the child or adolescent and parent simultaneously, noting when their perspectives do and do not align. To assess emotional regulation, any of the supplements could be of potential value depending on specific diagnostic differentials and rule-outs, but the most consistently relevant is Supplement I: Depressive and Bipolar Related Disorders (Kaufman et al., 2016). This supplement guides the assessor through queries, ratings anchors, and diagnostic decision trees. In addition to a section elucidating details of depressive episodes, this supplement structures the assessor in delving into presence and duration of manic symptoms of grandiosity, pressured speech, racing thoughts, increased goal-directed activity, psychomotor agitation, and the role of alcohol and substances, among other things.

Because of the time and associated cost, not to mention the sitting and attentional requirements required to completing such a detailed semistructured interview for a child or adolescent struggling with self-regulation, it makes sense to defer such a comprehensive interview or even specific supplements pending positive screens on disorder-specific caregiver-report questionnaires (Youngstrom et al., 2012). For instance, as noted Chapter 4, positive screens on such parent questionnaires specific to the bipolar spectrum can be followed up with semistructured interviews guided by the nine-plus pages of the Kiddie Schedule for Affective Disorders and Schizophrenia Mania Rating Scale (K-SADS-MRS; Axelson et al., 2003). The K-SADS-MRS is downloadable (see UPMC Western Psychiatric Hospital, Child & Adolescent Bipolar Spectrum Services, n.d.-b). Interviewing based on these scales is apt to be experienced by clinical assessors as less daunting than the corresponding supplements of the full K-SADS-PL *DSM-5* (Kaufman et al., 2016). Also, use of such scales does not require permission from the authors.

MINI-KID

According to Youngstrom, Morton, and Murray (2020), the MINI-KID (Sheehan, 2016) is likely the most commonly administered child/adolescent interview.[2] Intended for use with kids ages 6 years to 17 years, the MINI-KID has been updated for *DSM-5* (at the time of this writing, the most recent English version is 7.0.2; Sheehan, 2016). Accessing the MINI-KID for clinical assessment requires a process of obtaining permission and licensing from the author, and there is a cost per each administration licensed. See Mapi Research Trust (2010) for information about licensing and training.

Like the K-SADS-PL *DSM-5* (Kaufman et al., 2016), the MINI-KID covers a gamut of *DSM-5-TR* psychiatric conditions involving emotional dysregulation (e.g., bipolar spectrum, depressive disorders, anxiety/OCD, posttraumatic stress disorder [PTSD], attention-deficit/hyperactivity disorder [ADHD], alcohol and substance use, suicidality, conduct disorders, eating disorders, autism spectrum). Leffler et al. (2015) summarized that each of the categorical diagnostic modules in the MINI-KID begins with screening questions; if those questions are "positively endorsed, additional symptom questions are given for the particular disorder. All questions are presented in a yes–no format. The instrument can be given to parent and youth together or separately" (p. 7). Such explicit rules for skipping items and modules allow for more brevity in administration compared with the K-SADS-PL *DSM-5*: Leffler et al. (2015) reported that typical administration times range between 15 minutes and 50 minutes. It is reasonable to expect that MINI-KID administration time for the complex, emotionally dysregulated kids that come to us for comprehensive psychological assessment will often be on the longer end of this continuum.

For clinical purposes and expedience, depending on findings from caregiver-report screening measures (see Chapter 4), assessors can select particular

[2]It is unclear whether this refers to the MINI-KID's application in clinical and/or research settings.

modules of the MINI-KID for follow-up rather than administering the entire interview. For example, the module for current and past manic and hypomanic episodes is only three pages, and the module for depressive episodes is a page-and-a-half. Based on patient and caregiver responses to these modules, the MINI-KID facilitates assessors' application of *DSM-5* anchored algorithms to clarify bipolar I versus bipolar II versus other specified bipolar and related disorder.

DIAMOND-KID

A promising new option for a child/adolescent psychiatric interview linked to the *DSM-5-TR* is the DIAMOND-KID (Tolin et al., 2023). The DIAMOND-KID is intended for patients ages 6 years to 18 years with possible or previously established mood, anxiety, or OCD and related disorders. But sections also assist with differential diagnosis of psychotic conditions and other clinical presentations associated with emotional dysregulation, such as PTSD, ADHD, eating disorders, conduct problems, and somatization. The module for mood disorders is notable for its up-to-date comprehensiveness and specificity: Following items to clarify current and past manic and hypomanic episodes, this module includes lines of inquiry specific to bipolar I, bipolar II, and cyclothymic disorder as well as disruptive mood dysregulation disorder (DMDD).

The instructions for the DIAMOND-KID walk the assessor through considerations for when it is more important to include the perspective of caregivers instead of or in addition to the patient themselves (e.g., depending on age/developmental status, cognitive functioning, externalizing behaviors, internalizing versus externalizing symptoms, certain sensitive topics). These introductory instructions and the directions guiding assessors through the DIAMOND-KID—as well as the overall visual layout—are user friendly. The DIAMOND-KID also includes self-report and parent-report screening questionnaires, each comprising 35 items, that can be used to determine which modules of the full DIAMOND-KID should be administered, especially if time is limited. Each item of these screeners directs assessors to specific page numbers of the interview for the modules to be followed so this task can be undertaken expeditiously. This kind of convenience in various aspects of the interview's design—that the full interview is expected to require only an hour for most patients and that it is currently freely available and is intended to stay that way (D. Tolin, personal communication, March 16, 2023)—bodes well for its potential appeal to clinical assessors. See Hartford HealthCare (n.d.) for the DIAMOND-KID, the aforementioned screeners, and information about training.

Brief Commentary on Self-Report Interview Measures

Before concluding this section on self-report interviews, there are four points to emphasize about their application in clinical personality assessment. First, although more time-consuming to administer than self-report questionnaires, interviews offer the advantage of yielding data that encompass not only the content of the patient's responses but also the clinician's observations of the patient throughout the interview.

Second, although it might seem formidable to add a lengthy semistructured interview to an already crowded multimethod battery in a time-limited evaluation, judiciously selecting and administering the most relevant module(s) of such interviews can often be a pragmatic compromise. Decisions about such modules can be determined based on specific referral questions, findings from caregiver-report (see Chapter 4) and self-report screening measures (see the next section), and other hypotheses about taxonomic diagnoses emerging over the course of the evaluation.

The third point is a bit less sanguine. Based on their acceptance as gold standard for taxonomic diagnosis in empirical research and their strong psychometric properties, it is tempting to idealize semistructured interviews and expect more from them than they can deliver in clinical assessment, especially with the kinds of complex patients referred to us for comprehensive evaluation. Among other things, such interviews rely on patients' and caregivers' accurate, fine-tuned recall of onset and offset dates of specific symptoms and assessors' judgments about whether reports of particular experiences meet the threshold to meet a symptom criterion. This means that a semistructured interview ought not be expected to routinely deliver an infallible, objective diagnostic truth. Instead, at least sometimes, similar to other assessment modalities, the findings will be murky and indeterminate.

Consider the equivocal findings from the evaluation of an emotionally dysregulated older adolescent whose therapist and parents posed a referral question about a bipolar spectrum condition. The multimethod assessment included the following modules of the MINI-KID (Sheehan, 2016): Major Depressive Episode, Manic and Hypomanic Episodes, Psychotic Disorders and Mood Disorder With Psychotic Features, and Rule Out Medical Organic or Drug Causes for All Disorders. However, the Manic and Hypomanic Episodes module, administered separately to the patient and parents, yielded contradictory clusters of symptoms and duration of episodes: The adolescent reported that past episodes lasted longer than 7 days and were marked by elated mood; their parents recalled that irritability, not mood elevation, was prominent in episodes that lasted no longer than 4 days.

Moreover, in response to the MINI-KID query about the symptom of grandiosity, the parents noted that although the adolescent at their baseline expresses high, questionably unrealistic ambitions (e.g., to be a nationally ranked chess player), they did not observe increases in this behavior during the episodes when other hypomanic symptoms clustered. And although, the patient themselves did endorse the MINI-KID item about grandiosity during the phases they were reporting other symptoms of hypomania, the examples (e.g., "I can run so much faster than other kids") that they offered were actually not that compelling as crossing the line into manic-level grandiosity. Although there was meaning to be discerned about the discrepancy of reports—for example, that the adolescent subjectively experiences greater and more prolonged distress than their parents appreciate—the aim of including the MINI-KID was to rule in or out a bipolar spectrum diagnosis, but the findings remained confusing and uncertain. The idea here is not to disparage semistructured interviews or discourage their clinical application but to recognize that they are not diagnostic panaceas.

The fourth and final point is also cautionary: Although each of the interviews reviewed here has been translated into multiple languages for use with kids and families from a range of backgrounds, there is a surprising paucity of research published on diversity sensitivity and potential cultural bias specific to these and other child or adolescent (as well as adult) diagnostic interviews. This leaves us to rely more heavily on clinical expertise and attunement to patient-specific variables as we administer and interpret such instruments (S. R. Smith & Krishnamurthy, 2018b). Cimbora and Krishnamurthy (2018) summarized that this involves the assessor's fostering an atmosphere of curiosity, humility, and collaboration; balancing open-ended and close-ended questions; providing encouragement; and paraphrasing the patient's (or caregiver's) responses, reflecting back feelings, and offering intermittent summary statements, each in an iterative effort to clarify the accuracy of the assessor's evolving understanding of the patient and the internal and environmental factors affecting them. Amplifying principles of diversity sensitive assessment introduced in Chapter 3 of this book, Whitehead (2016) added the importance of affirmation of the patient and awareness of our stereotypes and other biases, emphasizing that interviewing "requires more than [asking] questions. . . . [Assessors] must consider how their own personal feelings, fears, hopes, biases, and conflicts shape their participation in the interview, and consequently the data that emerge" (p. 103).

SELF-REPORT BY QUESTIONNAIRE

Self-report questionnaires/scales are relatively time- and cost-effective methods (especially relative to semistructured interviews like the K-SADS-PL *DSM-5* [Kaufman et al., 2016]) that allow us to appreciate the child's or adolescent's own perspective on their emotional functioning. Depending on various developmental, cognitive, and emotional considerations (e.g., reading level, attention, impulse control, self-directedness, fatiguability), questionnaires can be administered orally in an interview format or given to the child or adolescent to complete independently in the assessor's office or at home between evaluation sessions.[3] Either way, the assessor is encouraged to be curious and use clinical discretion in follow-up inquiry into responses that potentially illuminate something important about elevated or unstable mood, suicide potential, style of handling emotions, unusual beliefs or sensory-perceptual experiences, or grandiose self-perception. Such inquiry provides contextual nuance that complements the contributions of self-report questionnaires in terms of their yielding scales assessing dimensional aspects of emotional (dys)regulation on a continuum and yielding data points that can inform decisions about categorical diagnoses.

To assess a child's or adolescent's subjective emotional experience, there is no shortage of options for self-report questionnaires or inventories to include in a multimethod battery. These measures encompass those related to the broader construct of emotional dysregulation, broadband personality measures, and symptom-specific and disorder-specific scales.

Self-Report Measures of the Emotional (Dys)Regulation Construct

In their evaluative review of more than 80 child and adolescent self-report and collateral-report measures operationalizing the construct of emotional regulation in various ways for research purposes,[4] Mazefsky, Conner, et al. (2021) identified two types of instruments: (a) those that assess the effectiveness of emotional regulation (or extent of dysregulation) and (b) those that assess strategies for emotional regulation. They evaluated each measure based on psychometric properties related to quality of norms, reliability, and validity. Among self-report measures of effectiveness of emotional (dys)regulation, these reviewers rated most highly the Emotion Dysregulation Inventory (EDI; Mazefsky et al., 2018; Mazefsky, Yu, & Pilkonis, 2021), a 24-item scale with 7-item short form. See REAACT Research Program (n.d.) to request access

[3]Historically, the exception to independently completing questionnaires at home has been copyrighted pencil-and-paper measures, such as the Minnesota Multiphasic Personality Inventory-Adolescent version (MMPI-A; Butcher et al., 1992), whose publishers restrict test materials from leaving the assessor's office. However, the recent development of remotely administered, computerized versions of such measures that can be completed at home has mitigated this limitation.

[4]These were a mixture of self-report and collateral-report measures.

to the self-report and collateral-report versions of the EDI. The EDI includes subscales for emotional reactivity and dysphoria.[5]

Mazefsky, Conner, et al. (2021) also highlighted the strong properties of an anger-specific scale, the 7-item Affective Reactivity Index (Stringaris et al., 2012). Among self-report measures of strategies for emotional regulation, Mazefsky, Conner, et al. (2021) rated highly the 10-item Emotion Regulation Questionnaire for Children and Adolescents (ERQ-CA; Gullone et al., 2010; Gullone & Taffe, 2012), which includes scales assessing the strategies of cognitive reappraisal and expressive suppression (see Gullone, n.d., to access the ERQ-CA online).[6] Although Mazefsky, Conner, et al. (2021) acknowledged limited, let alone systematic, study of clinical application of these kinds of research-based emotional regulation scales, such measures are useful for practitioners to be aware of—especially those for which normative data are available to facilitate interpretation. Although there does not yet appear to be much of a literature about measurement invariance/nonbias of self-report measures of emotional dysregulation, it is encouraging that Núñez et al. (2022) have a systematic review in progress to address such questions in measures for adolescents (and adults).

Self-Report Symptom- and Disorder-Specific Scales

A comprehensive review of self-report symptom-specific scales is beyond the scope of this book, and assessors are apt to already have a range of them in their testing toolkits for routine use. One example is the Beck Youth Inventories–Second Edition (BYI-2; Beck et al., 2005), which includes scales assessing depression, anxiety, anger, and disruptive behavior (as well as self-concept). There is not, however, published research on measurement invariance/nonbias with the BYI-2. Another popular instrument is the Youth Self-Report (YSR; ages 11 years to 18 years), part of the Child Behavior Checklist (CBCL; Achenbach, 1999) constellation of measures (Achenbach & Rescorla, 2004). Interestingly, although in their systematic review, Stevanovic et al. (2017) did not find support for the cross-cultural validity of the caregiver-report and teacher-report versions of the CBCL (see Chapter 4), they did

[5]The EDI also has a caregiver-report version of which Mazefsky et al. (2018) provided evidence for its lack of bias based on intellectual and verbal abilities in kids diagnosed on the autism spectrum.

[6]*Cognitive reappraisal* (an “antecedent-focused strategy”) refers to “redefining a potentially emotion eliciting situation in such a way that its emotional impact is changed,” and *expressive suppression* (a “response-focused strategy”) refers to “a form of response modulation involving the inhibition of ongoing emotion expressive behavior” (Gullone & Taffe, 2012, p. 2).

conclude moderate support for the YSR.[7] For example, among the studies reviewed by Stevanovic et al. (2017), O'Keefe et al. (2006) found measurement invariance for the YSR across Latine, African American, Asian American, and White participants in a school-based sample ($N = 938$) in the United States. But the BYI-2 and the YSR are just two of a multitude of options for broadband and specific self-report symptom scales of which Deighton et al. (2014) offered a comprehensive review.

Disorder-specific scales can be selected to help with differential diagnosis and identify co-occurring conditions (e.g., ADHD, trauma, OCD, behavior disorders, psychotic conditions, substance use). These scales are addressed later in Part III on differential *DSM-5-TR* diagnoses. The focus of the remainder of this chapter is on self-report measures that home in on specific characteristics of bipolar disorder. Broadband personality inventories are discussed first, followed by bipolar-specific questionnaires.

Self-Report Broadband Personality Inventories to Assess Bipolar Conditions

Broadband personality measures enable the assessment of a wide range of emotional and behavioral characteristics and problems. Self-report broadband inventories, which typically have hundreds of items, are more often designed for assessment of adolescents as opposed to younger children. Some adolescent measures to choose among include the MMPI-A (Butcher et al., 1992), the Minnesota Multiphasic Personality Inventory–Adolescent-Restructured Form (MMPI-A-RF; Archer et al., 2016), the Personality Assessment Inventory–Adolescent version (PAI-A; Morey, 2007), and the Millon® Adolescent Clinical Inventory, Second Edition (MACI®-II; Millon et al., 2020), as well as the self-report portion of the Behavior Assessment System for Children, Third Edition (BASC-3; Reynolds & Kamphaus, 2015; the collateral-report portion was discussed in Chapter 4 of this volume). The BASC-3 also allows for self-reports by younger children (ages 6 years to 12 years).[8] These measures' respective bipolar-relevant dimensional scales are as follows: MMPI-A Scale 9 plus subscales that include psychomotor acceleration and ego inflation; MMPI-A-RF Scale RC9 Hypomanic Activation; PAI-A Mania scale and its subscales of activity level, grandiosity, and irritability; and BASC-3 Mania

---

[7]Stevanovic et al. (2017) defined moderate evidence for cross-cultural validity thusly: "For 3–4 ethnic/cultural groups in 1 study or for 2 ethnic/cultural groups in multiple studies demonstrated full/partial strong measurement invariance and/or no or few DIF [differential item functioning] evident" (p. 131).

[8]For ages 6 years to 7 years, the BASC-3 involves self-report via interview rather than self-administered questionnaire.

scale. The MACI-II has a scale specific to disruptive mood dysregulation.[9] Endorsed critical items that elevate the bipolar-related scales ought to be clarified with subsequent inquiry. A compelling rationale for including one of the broadband self-report measures is their inclusion of validity scales, enabling us to account for response biases (see Chapter 3).

Note, though, that there is not an extensive literature on measurement invariance/nonbias for these self-report broadband measures. At the time of this writing, online searches in the PubMed and PsycInfo databases did not yield any hits for such research involving the PAI-A (Morey, 2007) or MACI-II (Millon et al., 2020). Some recent support exists for measurement invariance of the self-report version of the BASC-3 (Reynolds & Kamphaus, 2015) across race/ethnicity (i.e., Latine, African American/Black, and White) and male/female gender in a sample of fourth through eighth graders ($N = 601$) from Midwest urban areas of the United States (Basting et al., 2022). For the MMPI-A (Butcher et al., 1992) and MMPI-A-RF (Archer et al., 2016), the literature appears limited to a small number of dissertations. One example is Wilson's (2010) comparison of African American and White male adolescents in the juvenile justice system ($N = 281$) in terms of the predictive relationship between MMPI-A scores and caregiver-report of behavior on the CBCL (Achenbach, 1999). Wilson reported a pattern of statistically significant findings of various MMPI-A scores (including Scale 9 as well as content and supplemental scales related to anger, conduct problems, and immaturity) overpredicting psychopathology for the African American adolescents, but effects sizes were small. In the illustrations Wilson provided in her Discussion, such overpredictions amounted to only about 1 to 2 T score points on the MMPI-A, but Wilson noted that this can make an interpretative difference when scale scores are in the mildly elevated $T = 60–65$ range.

Self-Report Measures Specific to Bipolar Disorders

Few bipolar-specific self-report measures are designed for children and adolescents. In large part, this is the case because in research, child-report measures are inferior to parent-report measures in correlating with bipolar diagnoses as assessed by gold-standard structured interviews, such as the K-SADS-PL *DSM-5* (Kaufman et al., 2016; see Miguez et al., 2013; Wagner et al., 2006; Youngstrom et al., 2004; Youngstrom, Genzlinger, et al., 2015). Such studies have also shown that self-report and caregiver-report measures

[9]The Millon® Pre-Adolescent Clinical Inventory (Millon et al., 2005) does not have scales specific to bipolar disorder or DMDD.

tend not to be highly correlated with each other. So, the trend in research and assessment practice has been to deemphasize the child's or adolescent's self-report in this domain. Youngstrom et al. (2012) explained that "parent report is more accurate [than self-report] for the purpose of detecting pediatric bipolar disorder, possibly because hypomanic symptoms are not dystonic to the person experiencing them and because compromised insight is a feature of hypomania and mania" (p. 20). Nevertheless, if time and cost allow, there are potential benefits of including a self-report of manic symptoms in a multimethod battery, especially if a semistructured interview, such as the K-SADS-PL *DSM-5*, is not used.

If a child's or adolescent's own ratings are consistent with their caregivers', the convergence lends greater confidence to the diagnostic conclusion (Bram & Peebles, 2014; Peebles, 2012). Interestingly, G. A. Carlson and Youngstrom (2003) found that in such cases of congruence, patients show more severe impairment. But if the data from self-reports and caregiver-reports are incongruous, our curiosity is further piqued as we recognize that the incongruity might illuminate important treatment implications (Bram & Peebles, 2014; Peebles, 2012). For instance, when the caregiver's ratings are compelling that their child's pattern of dysregulation is consistent with a bipolar spectrum condition, but their child's report does not match up, we might anticipate greater challenges in forging a treatment alliance with the child (e.g., getting the child's buy-in for taking medication or attending therapy). As Youngstrom et al. (2009) reminded us, "Youth report adds data about the degree of insight into problems and motivation for treatment, both providing helpful prescriptive information to guide intervention" (p. 364).

For children 12 years and younger, a self-report tool is the Jeannie and Jeffrey Illustrated Interview for Children (J/J; Papolos, 2006). Administered either in online or paper-and-pencil formats, the J/J has 40 items, each accompanied by a cartoon of a child—Jeannie for girls, Jeffrey for boys—engaging in the behavior described in the item (e.g., irritability, bursts of energy, grandiosity, giddiness). For kids who identify as transgender, a case can be made that it is most empathic to administer the version that corresponds with their identified gender. For those who identify as gender nonbinary, it is up to the assessor based on their evolving clinical sense to determine whether to (a) broach with the child the dilemma about administering an imperfect but potentially helpful questionnaire (i.e., one that elicits their own perspective on symptoms) or (b) erring on the side of foregoing the J/J to not risk unnecessarily disrupting the assessment alliance by offending the child.

The items of the J/J (Papolos, 2006) involve the child's rating on a 4-point scale ranging from 1 (*never or hardly ever*) to 4 (*very often or almost constantly*) of their perception of the frequency with which they engage in each behavior. Items on the J/J tap into mania, grandiosity, hypersexuality, and psychotic symptoms, among other dimensions that are potentially helpful for differential diagnosis (e.g., attention and executive function deficits, sensory sensitivity). At present, there does not appear to be published research on psychometric properties of the J/J. Additionally, note that the premises on which the J/J scoring algorithms are based on the older *DSM-IV* formulation that includes as part of the bipolar spectrum (i.e., bipolar disorder not otherwise specified) behaviors that now would more likely be understood in the context of DMDD (e.g., irritability, poor frustration tolerance, regulation of aggressive impulses). Nevertheless, the J/J is unique and potentially useful method to obtain the perspective of a younger child on (hypo)manic and related symptoms. The yield of the J/J can illuminate symptoms in a way that informs categorical diagnosis related to the bipolar spectrum.

For adolescents, there is a self-report version of the Mood Disorder Questionnaire–Adolescent version (MDQ-A; Wagner et al., 2006).[10] The self-report MDQ-A has 13 items for the patient to mark the presence or absence of a range of symptoms. Compared with the parent version, the self-report MDQ-A is less sensitive in predicting a bipolar diagnosis on semistructured interview, such as the K-SADS-PL *DSM-5* (Kaufman et al., 2016; i.e., it is more associated with false negatives; see also Paterniti & Bisserbe, 2018). The value of including the self-report MDQ-A is as a comparison/contrast with collateral reports. Currently, there are no published studies on measurement invariance/nonbias bearing on interpretation of the self-report MDQ-A across different cultural groups.

[10]The items of the self-report MDQ-A are the same as the parent-report version (P-MDQ-A; Wagner et al., 2006; see Chapter 4 of this volume) with the exception that in the queries, the subject "your adolescent" is changed to "you" (K. D. Wagner, personal communication, May 2, 2023). The parent version can be found in the appendix of Wagner et al. (2006).

6 PERFORMANCE-BASED MEASURES AND METHODS TO ASSESS EMOTIONAL DYSREGULATION

Including performance-based methods in our battery enables us to sample a child's or adolescent's implicit processes of emotional (dys)regulation and related vulnerabilities in real time. Performance-based data complement what the child or adolescent and collaterals tell us explicitly about their feelings, mood, and behavior. Performance-based methods are also valuable because, compared to self-report, they are likely "more immune to the influences of gender roles [and gender differences] when assessing personality characteristics" (Mihura & Brabender, 2016, p. 663).

Of the eight broad aims of assessment of emotional (dys)regulation posited in Chapter 1, performance-based methods play a critical role in the first seven: in what way the patient is dysregulated; the severity or pervasiveness of dysregulation; the psychological costs of dysregulation; the possible functions served by dysregulation; the conditions of dysregulation; the conditions facilitating recovery from dysregulation; and strengths that mitigate dysregulation and facilitate recovery. Notice that these aspects are less related to categorical diagnoses. Instead, they involve idiographic and dimensional perspectives on the young patient's style and effectiveness of emotional regulation.

https://doi.org/10.1037/0000430-007
Psychological Assessment of Emotional Dysregulation in Children and Adolescents: The Bipolar Spectrum and Beyond, by A. D. Bram
Copyright © 2025 by the American Psychological Association. All rights reserved.

Here, the focus is first on performance-based neuropsychological assessment. The subsequent section in this chapter involves what can be learned about emotional regulation from performance-based personality methods, specifically the Rorschach Performance Assessment System (R-PAS; Meyer et al., 2011) and narrative tasks, such as the Thematic Apperception Test (TAT; Murray, 1943), Children's Apperception Test (CAT; Bellak & Bellak, 1949), Roberts–Second Edition (Roberts-2; Roberts & Gruber, 2005), or the Tell-Me-A-Story assessment (TEMAS; G. Constantino et al., 2007).[1] Embedded in this overview is the role—albeit limited—of these performance-based personality methods in assisting with the differential diagnosis of bipolar spectrum conditions (the eighth aim of assessment of emotional regulation listed in Chapter 1). Making use of data from the patient–examiner relationship (Bram, 2010; Bram & Peebles, 2014; Shectman & Harty, 1986) is addressed as another performance-based method.

PERFORMANCE-BASED NEUROPSYCHOLOGICAL ASSESSMENT AND EMOTIONAL DYSREGULATION

Challenges in emotional regulation are rooted neurologically in the brain's prefrontal cortex in coordination with the limbic system and other structures (Berboth & Morawetz, 2021). Although at present, performance-based neuropsychological assessment is not essential to taxonomic differential diagnoses among bipolar spectrum and other conditions in the fifth edition, text revision, of the *Diagnostic and Statistical Manual of Mental Disorders* (American Psychiatric Association, 2022) that feature emotional dysregulation (Youngstrom, Morton, & Murray, 2020), children and adolescents on the bipolar spectrum have been shown to have considerable weaknesses in verbal memory (Joseph et al., 2008) and moderate difficulties in "attention, executive function, working memory, visual memory, visual-perceptual skills and verbal fluency" (Joseph et al., 2008, cited in Horn et al., 2011, p. 434; see also Viapiana et al., 2022). Additionally, there is evidence that medication prescribed to address emotional dysregulation—most notably, traditional mood stabilizers (i.e., lithium and anticonvulsants)—can have deleterious effects on cognitive efficiency (e.g., DelBello et al., 2004; Henin et al., 2009). It is also well established that people of all ages with a range of neurodevelopmental and psychiatric conditions—whether on the

[1]Readers interested in a more comprehensive and in-depth discussion of Rorschach and narrative assessment of emotional regulation as described here are referred to Chapter 5 of Bram and Peebles (2014).

bipolar spectrum or not—are likely to have deficits in their neurocognitive functioning, most consistently in executive functioning and episodic memory (East-Richard et al., 2020). As it is a reasonable hypothesis that neuropsychological vulnerabilities will "have a larger impact in childhood than in adulthood, because they could strongly impact the [child's] academic performance and further development" (Pavuluri, O'Connor, et al., 2006, cited in Horn et al., 2011, p. 434), there is often a compelling case to be made to elucidate our young patient's neurocognitive profile so that caregivers, teachers, and treaters can optimally accommodate, remediate, and scaffold as well as be in the best position to help the patient access their strengths.

Comprehensive neuropsychological assessment involving performance-based measures[2] may or may not be high priority for every dysregulated child or adolescent presenting for evaluation. Priority will be a function of the extent that (a) the young person is struggling in any way with learning/academics and/or with school attendance and (b) the school has not done any recent testing and no individualized education program (IEP) is in place (or if the adequacy of a current IEP is questioned by a parent, treater, or other team member). Neuropsychological assessment is also more likely indicated in instances in which the patient is known or suspected to have suffered a head injury, especially if their dysregulation originated or exacerbated around the time of the injury. Similarly, when referral questions arise related to developmental conditions, such as the autism spectrum, intellectual disability, or learning disabilities, neuropsychological evaluation will also be essential. Depending on the circumstances, the neuropsychological component can be conducted by the primary assessor (assuming the requisite training and skill set), by a collaborating specialist colleague (if the primary assessor does not have the training), or by a neuropsychologist employed by the school district.

Performance-based neuropsychological testing involves standardized in vivo assessment—with reference to age-based norms—of aspects of neurocognitive functioning, many of which are associated with a person's capacities for emotional regulation. Such aspects include, but are not limited to, intellectual functioning, production of speech and accessing of language, various types of memory and attention, and executive functioning. Executive functioning is related to essential self-regulatory capacities, such as delay and

[2]In addition to performance-based measures, neuropsychological test batteries for kids typically include self-report, caregiver-report, and teacher-report measures and sometimes classroom observations. For an example, please see the section "Bipolar Spectrum and ADHD" in Chapter 9 on differential diagnostic assessment related to attention-deficit/hyperactivity disorder.

response inhibition, planful and organized problem-solving, cognitive flexibility and perspective-taking, and tolerance of unpleasant stimuli (e.g., Andrés et al., 2021; Blair, 2017; Diamond, 2013).

Even if a full neuropsychological evaluation does not appear to be indicated—or if this is not yet certain—the assessor can consider a neurocognitive screening in the form of a test of intellectual functioning, such as one of the Wechsler (2008, 2011, 2014) tests. At minimum, such performance-based screening can inform us about the child's or adolescent's learning style, which will have implications for optimizing their engagement in psychotherapy, psychoeducation, and other aspects of treatment (see Chapter 13). Findings from a test of intellectual functioning can also illuminate when adults'—and/or the child's own—academic expectations are unrealistically mismatched with the child's capacities in a way that dysregulation is, at least in part, a function of the pressure and sense of failure this incongruity creates. Moreover, uneven, anomalous, or unexpected patterns of scores can raise questions about previously unknown or unsuspected learning difficulties that might contribute to or exacerbate emotional dysregulation. Such findings can then be followed up with a more complete neuropsychological battery.

If a neuropsychological evaluation is undertaken beyond a test of intellectual functioning, the test battery for a child or adolescent prone to emotional dysregulation will often include a battery of performance-based measures assessing attention, executive function, learning and memory, language, perceptual–motor abilities, and social cognition (American Psychiatric Association, 2013). It will also often include performance-based measures assessing core academic skills (e.g., reading, writing, math; D. C. Miller & Maricle, 2019; Reddy et al., 2013; Reinstein & Burau, 2014). Because an abundance of tests exist to assess these various neuropsychological capacities, a detailed review of specific measures is beyond the present scope, and thus, readers are referred to summaries elsewhere (e.g., Bland et al., 2016; Braconnier & Siper, 2021; Horn et al., 2011; D. C. Miller & Maricle, 2019; Reinstein & Burau, 2014; Strauss et al., 2006). Along similar lines, the recent article by Malik and Norman (2023) is recommended for a thoughtful discussion of issues related to diversity sensitivity in research and practice of pediatric (and adult) neuropsychological assessment.

A crucial point here is that whatever the specific measures, neuropsychological assessors—where possible and relevant—connect findings back to their young patient's challenges with emotional regulation. For example, findings that an adolescent struggles with verbal memory as part of a language-based learning disability (Newhall, 2011) might bear not only on their academic learning (e.g., negative effect on listening, note-taking, rote memory and retention) but on the resultant frustration that eventuates in meltdowns and angry outbursts. Problems with verbal memory might also help explain their academic performance anxiety, lack of confidence socially, or struggles to label and communicate feelings in real time.[3] Related tasks in the test report and other feedback will be to clarify what such findings mean in terms of (a) tasks and conditions when the child or adolescent is most prone to dysregulation and what can be done to support their return to a state of relative calm; (b) implications for enhancing engagement academically, therapeutically, and at home; and (c) what can be done to accommodate and remediate underlying neurocognitive vulnerabilities. For the adolescent with weaknesses in verbal memory, the assessor might note that student is likely to be dysregulated by expectations for rapid note-taking and multistep directions with potential implications for being allowed a scribe and repetition and assistance with breaking down of directions. Such implications could be highlighted as relevant not only at school but if a psychoeducational group were to be recommended.

PERFORMANCE-BASED PERSONALITY MEASURES TO ASSESS EMOTIONAL DYSREGULATION

Performance-based personality measures facilitate assessment of implicit processes of emotional (dys)regulation. Toward this end, two valuable performance-based methods include (a) the Rorschach and (b) narrative techniques. Each of these methods is addressed in the sections that follow.

Rorschach Assessment of Emotional Dysregulation

Rorschach assessment of emotional (dys)regulation involves attending carefully, at both response and protocol levels, to (a) key determinants (in particular, Color, Achromatic Color, Shading, Inanimate Movement), (b) the degree of Form Dominance (whether Form is primary, secondary, or absent), (c) emotional thematic content scores (Morbid [MOR], Aggressive Movement [AGM], Aggressive Content [AGC], Oral Dependent Language [ODL]), (d) summary scores and ratios, (e) Cognitive Codes (thought disorder scores), and (f) sequence and configurational analyses. Because the complex and nuanced interpretive process has been detailed in depth in Bram and Peebles (2014), aspects are only summarized here.

[3]I thank Jed Yalof (personal communication, February 8, 2023) for assistance with this illustration.

Determinants, Form Dominance, Thematic Codes, and Summary Scores and Ratios

Briefly, *determinants,* that is, features of or attributed to the inkblot that justify one's percept, are empirically and conceptually linked to different types of emotional experiences. The *degree of Form Dominance* (primary, secondary, or no Form) captures how well contained and modulated in intensity the emotional experience is (Bram & Peebles, 2014; Kleiger, 1997; Schafer, 1954).[4] In addition to comparing to age-based norms sum totals of key determinant and thematic code scores, important summary scores and indices to tune into in R-PAS (Meyer et al., 2011) include R8910% (which tells us something about how constricted or reactive a person in response to heightened emotional stimulation), Critical Contents Percent (CritCont%; number of emotionally charged contents divided by total number of responses), and the Suicide Concern Composite (applicable to patients 14 years and older). In R-PAS, all such variables are dimensional and expressed in standard scores on a continuum ($M = 100$, $SD = 50$).

In the other major Rorschach system, the revised Comprehensive System (CS-R; Exner et al., 2022), the Affective Ratio is analogous to R8910%, and the Suicide Constellation, to the Suicide Concern Composite. The CHESSSS 2.0 scoring software program (International Rorschach Institute, n.d.) for the CS-R converts most raw scores to standard scores in a similar manner to which the R-PAS scoring program does. Note that at the time of this writing, the CS-R does not include norms for children and adolescents, only adults. Thus, relevant to the focus of this book, the CS-R can be used with 18-year-olds and emerging adults, but it is not yet recommended for younger patients until the CS-R authors publish norms for children and adolescents.

Cognitive Codes

Cognitive Codes inform us about the nature and severity of our patient's susceptibility to incoherent thinking and illogical reasoning, that is, about potential thought disorder. Cognitive scores are similar in R-PAS (Meyer et al., 2011)

---

[4]Although R-PAS (Meyer et al., 2011) requires coding Form Dominance for Color responses, unlike the Comprehensive System (CS; Exner, 2003), it does not include coding Form Dominance for Shading and Achromatic Color responses. (Note that the recently revised CS [Comprehensive System–Revised [CS-R]; Exner et al., 2022] includes coding Form Dominance for Color, Achromatic Color, and Diffuse Shading but not for Shading Texture or Shading Vista.) Because not coding Form Dominance for Shading and Achromatic Color sacrifices a more nuanced understanding of our patients' emotional regulation, R-PAS users can consider making these coding determinations supplementally (Bram & Yalof, 2018). To assist in making these challenging coding determinations, consider additional guidelines offered by Viglione (2010; see also Bram et al., 2023).

and the CS-R (Exner et al., 2022), although in the CS-R, they are referred to as *cognitive special scores*. In both R-PAS and the CS-R, aggregate weighted indices (i.e., Weighted Sum Cognitive Codes and Weighted Sum 6, respectively), also converted to standard scores, provide a dimensional perspective on degree of thought disorder. More about Cognitive Codes as they relate to emotional regulation is elaborated in the subsequent discussion about sequence and configurational analyses. Here, though, note that certain types of Cognitive Codes can be clues to a vulnerability to lapses into hypomanic states. In particular, attend to codes for (a) combinative thinking (Fabulized Combinations and Incongruous Combinations) that are associated with enlivened, playful, jocular content and/or delivery and (b) tangential, often excitable or flippant, responses (coded as Deviant Responses; Kleiger, 1999, 2017). Typically, such responses are more silly than bizarre and are thus coded at a lower level of severity (Level 1 rather than 2).[5] Consider the following three combinative responses, all offered in an energized way by a 9-year-old for whom a referral question involved the possibility of a bipolar spectrum condition:

> Card II. Two elephants high-fiving with their trunks. (Clarification Phase [CP]) Elephant shape, trunks here high-fiving. Weeee! (Fabulized Combination Level 1 [FAB1])
>
> Card III. Ooooh! Two monkeys dancing the jig. With music notes flying around them! (CP) Monkeys here, and top red are the notes. (FAB1)
>
> Card X. Two seals on a rock with chipmunks. (CP) You have the fish-shaped tail at the bottom, and here are the flippers. And here are two chipmunks, actually they look more like squirrels with some crazy hat on, floating. (hat?) It's a party hat [laughs]. . . ." (FAB1)

And here is an example of a tangential, excitable Deviant Response (DR) from the same child:

> Card II. Clowns celebratin' at a birthday party! When's your birthday? Mine is in June! I told my mom I want an Xbox. [laughing and singing] Happy birthday to me! Happy birthday to me!

Of course, we would never diagnose a bipolar spectrum condition based on a single—or even multiple—response(s) such as these. But these kinds of Rorschach responses can add weight to evidence of overt symptoms from collateral-report and self-report data. And when there is less evidence in

[5]Note that this research on taxonomic diagnostic implications of Cognitive Codes (summarized by Kleiger, 1999, 2017) has predominantly been conducted with adults. Based on the premise of continuity between childhood and adulthood versions of (hypo)mania, it is possible to extrapolate from this literature to our assessment of children and adolescents.

support of a bipolar condition from those other data sources, these playful, combinative or tangential Rorschach responses can alert treaters and parents/caregivers to a possible latent vulnerability to hypomania so that they can continue to watch for more overt signs and take this into account in considering medication options.

It bears extra emphasis that having Cognitive Codes with a hypomanic quality in a Rorschach protocol is not sufficient in and of itself to conclude a bipolar spectrum diagnosis. We need additional evidence from collateral-report and self-report symptom measures. Also, it is important to keep in mind that some combinative thinking is not unusual in the protocols of young children (Leichtman, 1996), so we need to compare our patient's scores against age-based norms (Exner et al., 2022; Meyer et al., 2007, 2011). It is when these scores are elevated and responses have the kind of hypomanic flavor as illustrated earlier that we have some evidence in the direction of a bipolar condition.

One final point about Cognitive Codes is that the presence of certain more severe indicators can signal us to consider that the child or adolescent might be better understood on the schizophrenic, rather than bipolar, spectrum (see Kleiger, 1999, 2017). These include bizarre neologisms (scored as Deviant Verbalization Level 2 [DV2]) and pathological condensation of ideas (scored as Contaminations [CON]).[6]

Configurational and Sequence Analyses

Arguably, the most nuanced and meaningful contribution that the Rorschach can make to the assessment of emotional regulation involves *configurational and sequence analyses* (Bram & Peebles, 2014; Peebles-Kleiger, 2002; Schafer, 1954; Weiner, 1998). This refers to a response-by-response tracking and sampling of how a person experiences and manages their emotions over the course of their Rorschach protocol. This approach facilitates the kinds of "conditions under which" inferences that we delineated earlier as central to the broad aims of an evaluation of emotional (dys)regulation. The "configurational" component involves attending to each response's unique constellation of structural scores (i.e., location, determinants, Form Dominance, Form Quality, Cognitive Codes), thematic content, and patient–examiner data (involving the patient's attitude and behavior during the response; see Bram, 2010; Bram & Peebles, 2014). The "sequence" element allows us to track the precursors, adaptations, and sequelae of the person's emotional experience.

[6]When making such coding determinations with potentially significant diagnostic implications, assessors with less Rorschach experience are encouraged to consult more expert colleagues to assure coding accuracy.

In configurational and sequence analyses, we look for patterns that inform us about such things as what conditions trigger different emotions, how intense and overwhelming the experience is, to what extent and how are other psychological capacities affected, how the patient tries to manage the emotions, and what helps the patient regroup. Say, for example, a child shows signs of dysregulation (Form Secondary or absent; Critical Contents) primarily when offering detail (D, Dd) but not whole (W) responses, especially on chromatic cards. An inference can be made that they are prone to dysregulation when they encounter greater emotional stimulation and lose appreciation for the bigger picture. Or, if another child dysregulates around responses coded for any Human content (Whole human [H], Imaginary human [(H)], Human detail [Hd], or Imaginary human detail [(Hd)]), Texture (T), and ODL, we would infer something about their vulnerability under conditions of attachment/dependent longings being stirred. If the Rorschach signs of emotional dysregulation of either child were also consistently accompanied by poor Form Quality and Cognitive Codes, we would consider inferences about emotional dysregulation being associated with lapses in the child's sense of reality and capacities for coherent thinking and logical reasoning. Consider this sequence for the child who exhibits dysregulation on responses with constellation of H, T, and ODL: They follow such responses with ones that are more emotionally constricted (pure Form) with nonhuman content, and those responses involve good Form Quality and no Cognitive Codes. Here, we would infer that the child recovers from such dysregulation and the associated lapses in functioning by distancing from interpersonal engagement that evokes their attaching longings. This helps us appreciate the psychological costs of their effort to cope. Hopefully, this offers a flavor for how the Rorschach's strengths are in elucidating *processes* of emotional regulation that transcend diagnostic categories in the American Psychiatric Association's (1994, 2013, 2022) *Diagnostic and Statistical Manual of Mental Disorders*.

Rorschach and Considerations for Diversity Sensitivity

Research on R-PAS (Meyer et al., 2011) and the original CS (Exner, 2003) has shown little meaningful differences in scores across ethnicities and the traditional binary concept of gender (Meyer, 2002; Meyer et al., 2015). Weiner (2000) has reminded us that although the basic interpretation of Rorschach scores is typically similar for people with different cultural backgrounds,

> cultural differences can lead to cross-cultural variation in modal personality characteristics, and there is good reason to believe that cultural demands and expectations often determine the implications and consequences of particular personality characteristics, especially with respect to how adaptive they are. (p. 172)

Consider, for example, "the role that cultural norms and display rules play in the expression of emotions in general and anger in particular" (González-Prendes, 2013, p. 236). There is evidence from a study of Asian American and European American college students that the association between anger suppression and depression (both self-reported) is moderated/attenuated by Asian American status and greater interdependent orientation (Cheung & Park, 2010). More specifically, anger suppression was less likely to be associated with depression for participants who were Asian American and/or whose interpersonal orientation was more interdependent. Knowledge of this finding can inform our interpretation of an adolescent's Rorschach marked by indicators of emotional constriction (elevated F%, low Sum of Color Responses [SumC], and low 8910%) and an absence of AGC and AGM: Inferences about the potential adaptiveness and costs of such a pattern would be a function of what we know about the adolescent's family and cultural context.

Narrative Assessment of Emotional Dysregulation

To assess emotional dysregulation using narrative methods—such as the TAT (Murray, 1943), CAT (Bellak & Bellak, 1949), Roberts-2 (Roberts & Gruber, 2005), or TEMAS (G. Constantino et al., 2007)—three strategies are offered. First, with administration instructions to tell stories that include what characters are thinking and feeling, we use such methods to sample our patient's emotional vocabulary. Second, we attend to implicit premises embedded within their stories about how emotions are dealt with. And third, we consider how the child or adolescent themselves respond to and cope with the emotional demands of the task. Primarily, each of these strategies contributes to idiographic descriptions of how a child or adolescent accesses and processes emotions.[7]

[7]In addition to these strategies, assessors may choose among various research-validated measures to code structural and thematic elements of narratives. Among the eight subscales of the Social Cognition and Object Relations Scale–Global (Stein & Slavin-Mulford, 2018), Experience and Management of Aggressive Impulses is particularly relevant for assessment of emotional regulation. Also relevant, the Defense Mechanism Manual (Cramer, 1991) allows coding of three developmental levels of defense (from lower to higher level of maturity: denial, projection, and identification). The manual for the Roberts-2 (Roberts & Gruber, 2005) includes details for coding expressions of anxiety, depression, and aggression. Similarly, the TEMAS (G. Constantino et al., 2007) builds in scales on which to code aggression, anxiety/depression, and avoidance (avoidance is labeled "Functions Not Pulled") and also enables each story to be coded for the following affects: happy, sad, angry, fearful, neutral, ambivalent, and inappropriate.

Before delving into to the three strategies, it is useful to acknowledge that, published more than 80 years ago, the visual stimuli in the TAT not only involve antiquated scenes but are limited to depictions of White people. For chronologically and developmentally younger kids, the CAT—involving cartoons of animals in humanlike behavior, albeit also involving anachronistic drawings—is a less culturally biased option. The Roberts-2 and TEMAS are more contemporary alternatives: picture-based narrative tools that have been validated multiculturally and include separate card sets designed specifically for kids of Black, Hispanic/Latine, Asian American, and European American backgrounds.[8]

Sampling Emotional Vocabulary

Emotionally dysregulated kids are prone to communicate their feelings in behavioral action (e.g., destructiveness, aggression, tantrums, avoidant behaviors) rather than words. Therefore, the emotional language that a child or adolescent is able to access on a narrative task informs us about how much and what kind of therapeutic focus will be necessary to help them identify and verbally express different feelings. For example, a child who responds to queries about characters' feelings with somatic states (e.g., tired, hungry, sick) or even vague, less differentiated emotions (e.g., upset, stressed, frustrated, bored) will require more help expanding their awareness of and ability to verbalize their internal experiences. A child or adolescent who, on the TAT (Murray, 1943), CAT (Bellak & Bellak, 1949), Roberts-2 (Roberts & Gruber, 2005), TEMAS (G. Constantino et al., 2007), or other narrative task, articulates a range of positive and negative emotions with some nuance can be identified as having strengths that can be built on psychotherapeutically so that they can better deploy this vocabulary in moments of heightened emotional stirring. Among kids who do possess relatively well-developed emotional vocabularies, we tune into any feelings that are conspicuous by their absence in their stories. Consider a bright, articulate teenager prone to occasional explosive outbursts who had experienced a series of painful losses and separations as a younger child. It was meaningful that their otherwise emotionally rich and varied TAT stories did not reference sadness, even on cards with strong dysphoric pulls. This led to an appreciation of their struggles to allow themselves to mourn and to allow themselves the illusion of power and control (as opposed to vulnerability) in moments of rageful aggression.

---

[8]At the time of this writing, the TEMAS (G. Constantino et al., 2007) appears to be out of print and not easily obtained.

Implicit Premises About How One Manages Emotions

Embedded in narratives are *implicit premises*—procedural knowledge—that a person holds about people, relationships, and how one manages emotions (Bram & Peebles, 2014). Here, the focus is on the management of emotions, keeping in mind that our inferences about emotional regulation are strengthened to the extent that there is repetition across stories (Bram & Peebles, 2014). One dysregulation-prone adolescent, for instance, responded thusly to TAT (Murray, 1943) card 3BM (an ambiguous image of a person huddled over a couch or bench): "The woman is very sad because her pet hamster died. So now she is crying. And she will smash her hamster cage to bits" (Bram, 2010, p. 94). The adolescent's implicit premise about emotional regulation is that sadness and loss are not readily contained and are reflexively transformed into rage and destructiveness. Not often, but on rare occasions, a patient's implicit premises have a hypomanic flavor; although far from pathognomonic for a bipolar spectrum diagnosis, similar to the aforementioned Rorschach signs of hypomania, these implicit premises potentially add weight to collateral-report and self-report evidence or raise questions of vulnerability that treaters can be encouraged to be watchful for.

Consider an emotionally volatile adolescent for whom the referring psychiatrist raised the question of a bipolar condition. This is the patient's response to Card 3BM, which pulls for depressive, hopeless, and sometimes suicidal themes:

> Before, her boyfriend broke up with her. She's sad . . . no, not sad anymore. This is after. Got invited to a party, danced all night, got drunk, hooked up with a hot guy! Here, she's passed out after a wild night. [laughs] She goes out again that night, finds another guy, and has even more fun.

The implicit premise is that sadness and loss are denied and covered over by hypomanic activity—frenzy, disinhibition, indiscretion, and hypersexuality. The adolescent told two other stories with similar qualities, and these TAT findings converged with evidence from the patient's (a) parents' ratings on the Child Mania Rating Scale–Parent version (Pavuluri, Henry, et al., 2006), including episodically clustered multiple mania-specific items, resulting in an above-research-threshold score and (b) the patient's Minnesota Multiphasic Personality Inventory–Adolescent (Butcher et al., 1992) scale elevations on Scale 9 and the psychomotor acceleration and ego inflation subscales. Follow-up interview guided by the Kiddie Schedule for Affective Disorders and Schizophrenia Mania Rating Scale (K-SADS-MRS; Axelson et al., 2003) clarified the patient's experience of hypomanic episodes and supported a bipolar II diagnosis.

How the Child or Adolescent Responds to and Manages Emotions Evoked by the Narrative Task

The visual stimuli of the TAT (Murray, 1943), CAT (Bellak & Bellak, 1949), Roberts-2 (Roberts & Gruber, 2005), TEMAS (G. Constantino et al., 2007), and other narrative methods are designed to be emotionally evocative. So, we learn about a person's style of emotional regulation not only by the underlying premises embedded in their stories but how they themselves respond to the task. A child who crawls under the desk, throws the cards, or bolts from the room shows us something about their limited emotional tolerance and how they cope through action. We would attend to whether there is a particular emotion (e.g., fear, sadness, anger) that has been stirred by the particular card or cards that led to such behavior. We also attune to the extent a patient is constricted (indicating self-protective efforts to ward off a painful feeling) or expansive/verbose (vulnerability to being reactive and overstimulated) and whether this is associated with emotions in general or with specific ones. Along similar lines, we map whether certain emotions are associated with stories that are more confusing and difficult to follow, indicating their cognitively disorganizing effect.

In terms of picking up on tendencies toward hypomania, there are occasional instances in which patients respond to the dark, dysphoric pictures with unusually bright and energized accounts. One teenager began their response to TAT Card 14 (silhouette of a figure in dark room against a bright window)—a card that pulls for stories of loneliness, depression, hopelessness, or suicide—with rapid speech: "This is a man who loves his house. He likes to play music and dance around his house. . . ." And to Card 18GF (woman with her hands around the throat of another woman, by a staircase), to which people typically respond with stories about aggression or illness/loss, this teenager began: "The daughter and the mom were walking up the stairs to the house and they were like 'Hee, hee, we're so happy. . . .'" The giddiness of the teenager's content and delivery were striking in their incongruity with the somber perceptual features of the drawings.

PATIENT-EXAMINER RELATIONSHIP DATA AND ASSESSING EMOTIONAL DYSREGULATION

The previous discussion about how a young patient engages with picture stimuli on a narrative task, such as the TAT (Murray, 1943), enters the realm of what has been called *patient–examiner relationship data*. The method of making use of experiences in the patient–examiner relationship as data is included in this chapter on performance-based assessment because it involves what a patient shows us rather than tells us (or what a parent/caregiver, teacher, or other observer tells us) about their capacity to regulate emotions. As Mary Jo Peebles and I have described,

> Patient–examiner relationship data transcend what is more commonly described as "behavioral observations." It refers to the nature, quality, and style of the way our patient approaches, connects with, and responds to us and the test materials that we present [them]. Such includes, but is not limited to, the way the patient greets us, the informal moments, [their] asides, the dynamics between us during asking and answering test question and inquiries, the patient's style of collaborating, our experience of [them], and the sudden unexpected reactions that reveal [their] preconceptions about who we are and how we view [them]. (Bram & Peebles, 2014, pp. 41–42)

Patent–examiner data encompass the patient's nonverbal behaviors and communication, attitude toward the testing experience, judicious hypothesis testing (about conditions fostering or impeding emotional regulation and collaboration), and the assessor's countertransference (see Bram & Peebles, 2014, pp. 43–45; see also Shectman & Harty, 1986).

The patient–examiner relationship is a window through which we learn more about how the patient expresses different kinds of distress—whether through words, physical symptoms, aggression, withdrawal, or other behavioral action. Patient–examiner data are also helpful in clarifying the conditions under which our young patient is more likely to become dysregulated and, importantly, to subsequently recover. For example, do they become dysregulated with us in response to a certain kind of cognitive task (e.g., a subtest on the Wechsler Intelligence Scale for Children–Fifth Edition [Wechsler, 2014] taxing a particular ability) or stirring of a traumatic or dynamic theme (e.g., as evoked on the Rorschach [e.g., R-PAS, Meyer et al., 2011] or TAT [Murray, 1943], or even by an item on a self-report questionnaire)? Or in the context of needing to separate from a parent/caregiver to begin the session and/or from the assessor to end the session? In such instances, we also note what the child's or adolescent's feelings are that can spiral out of control and how they spiral: Anxiety into helplessness? Frustration into despair? Shame into rage? Also meaningful is what the assessor does in an attempt to mitigate the patient's dysregulation and how effective such efforts are: Putting words to what is happening? Offering a break? Giving them some space? Setting a limit? Providing reassurance? Going for a walk or providing a snack? The idea is that it is possible to infer from these patient–examiner interactions something about the patient's vulnerability to emotional dysregulation and conditions of recovery outside of the assessment situation.

Additionally, the assessor's *countertransferences*, that is, their own emotional reaction to the patient, can serve as valuable data.[9] On occasion, the assessor's subjective sense of feeling overwhelmed and out of control—in response to the patient's pressured speech; whirlwind of movement about the office and with the assessment materials; and silly, jocular attitude—might be another data indicator pointing to hypomania. Khadivi (2023) observed that

> patients in a manic phase of bipolar disorder could evoke unique reactions in clinicians, different from those elicited by patients presenting with psychosis and schizophrenia spectrum disorders. . . . The elevated mood of a manic patient can be contagious, causing the clinician to have a similar emotional response. Manic patients with pressured speech and flight of ideas can confuse and frustrate the clinician's ability to connect with the patient. Manic patients with irritable moods and increased energy can invoke anxiety in the interviewer and be challenging to engage in assessment. (p. 43)

More broadly, though, the assessor's countertransference informs us about how the child's or adolescent's manner of dysregulation and style of engagement might affect others in their life and/or implicitly communicate a disowned feeling or unwanted aspect of the patient's self (i.e., a projective identification;[10] see Ogden, 1977). This might involve the assessor's feeling helpless, impotent, frightened, angry, or otherwise overwhelmed. And through the assessor's responses to these internal reactions, we might learn something about the kinds of interpersonal dynamics the child or adolescent is apt to evoke within and outside of treatment, for example, pulling a therapist or

---

[9]It is recommended that trainees and early career assessors exercise caution in making use of countertransference as a data source on their own. Supervision and consultation are crucial. Dynamically oriented personal psychotherapy and supervision over time are necessary to develop this method so it can be applied thoughtfully and with discipline. Related to this is the importance that assessors become aware of and work to mitigate their own stereotypes and biases (see Chapter 3).

[10]*Projective identification* is an implicit/unconscious interpersonal process in which a person experiences an unwanted feeling or aspect of oneself as existing in another person (the idea of externalizing or projecting) and acts in a way that pressures the other to actually experience the unwanted feeling themselves (Gabbard, 1995; Ogden, 1977). For instance, consider a preadolescent who has experienced severe abuse and neglect but acts self-assuredly with the assessor. Viewing the assessor as weak and ineffective, the child belittles and taunts the assessor such that the assessor feels impotent, useless, and helpless. This resultant painful subjective experience of the assessor can be understood as reflecting something of the disowned experience of a maltreated child, who has learned to cope through a consciously inflated sense of self and identification with the aggressor.

other adult into power struggles and acting punitively. Intense emotional reactions on the part of the assessor can be clues to alert treaters of the kinds of difficult but potentially meaningful dynamics (whether conceptualized as projective identification or enactment [Gabbard, 1995] or cyclical psychodynamics [Wachtel, 1997]) apt to play out and that need to be understood psychotherapeutically. The key point here is that the assessor can reflect on and conceptualize their own experience of the patient's in-session dysregulation as potentially meaningful data, not as simply a nuisance disrupting administration of the tests (for a detailed example, see Bram, 2010).

PART III EMOTIONAL DYSREGULATION AND THE BIPOLAR SPECTRUM: *DSM-5-TR* DIFFERENTIAL AND CO-OCCURRING DIAGNOSES

As introduced back in Chapter 1, one aim in the assessment of emotional dysregulation in children and adolescents involves mapping history and patterns of symptoms onto taxonomic diagnostic prototypes as defined by the fifth edition, text revision, of the *Diagnostic and Statistical Manual of Mental Disorders* (5th ed., text rev.; *DSM-5-TR*; American Psychiatric Association, 2022). Here in Part III, attention is turned to this challenging task of differential diagnosis. Specifically, Part III begins with an orientation to taxonomic diagnoses within and beyond the bipolar spectrum (Chapter 7). The three chapters that follow address categorical diagnoses that are mutually exclusive with the bipolar spectrum (Chapter 8); that either can be differentiated from the bipolar spectrum or that co-occur with it (Chapters 9); and that potentially co-occur but are more readily differentiated from the bipolar spectrum (Chapter 10).

7 ORIENTING TO DIFFERENTIAL DIAGNOSIS WITHIN AND BEYOND THE BIPOLAR SPECTRUM

This chapter addresses two aspects of descriptive, categorical differential diagnosis of kids vulnerable to emotional dysregulation. The first is relevant to patients for whom the evidence does point to a bipolar spectrum condition. Here, the task—with implications for prognosis, psychoeducation, and pharmacotherapy—is to try to locate where along that spectrum their symptoms can be considered to fall. The second involves differentiating bipolar conditions from other behavioral and symptomatic manifestations and identifying when more than one taxonomic category adds to meaningful understanding.

LOCATING THE PATIENT ALONG THE BIPOLAR SPECTRUM

To determine where the child or adolescent is located along the bipolar spectrum (if they appear to be at all), we rely most heavily on caregivers' reports of hypomanic/manic and depressive symptoms and their clustering, onset/offset, and frequency of recurrence. To orient to this challenging aspect of differential diagnosis, it is essential to review briefly some definitions related to manic,

https://doi.org/10.1037/0000430-008
Psychological Assessment of Emotional Dysregulation in Children and Adolescents: The Bipolar Spectrum and Beyond, by A. D. Bram
Copyright © 2025 by the American Psychological Association. All rights reserved.

hypomanic, and major depressive episodes in the fifth edition, text revision, of the *Diagnostic and Statistical Manual of Mental Disorders* (5th ed., text rev.; *DSM-5-TR*; American Psychiatric Association, 2022).

Clarifying What Constitutes Manic, Hypomanic, and Major Depressive Episodes

Mania and *hypomania* involve elevated or irritable mood marked by symptoms that include grandiosity/inflated sense of self, diminished need for sleep without fatigue and loss of energy, hypertalkativeness/pressured speech, racing thoughts, distractibility, heightened goal-directed activity, and engagement in high-risk activities (American Psychiatric Association, 2022). To qualify for a manic or hypomanic episode, such symptoms are not attributable to medical illness or substance use. A manic episode entails a week or longer of at least three of the aforementioned symptoms (four if mood is primarily irritable) and is associated with severe impairment in psychosocial functioning, psychotic features, or need for hospitalization. A hypomanic episode is marked by 4 or more days of at least three of the symptoms (four if mood is primarily irritable); represents a clear change in functioning that is observable to others; but does not involve psychotic symptoms or dramatic psychosocial impairment, or does not require hospitalization.[1]

To meet criteria for a *major depressive episode,* over at least a 2-week period, a person must experience a cluster of at least five of the following symptoms: depressed mood (or, for children and adolescents, mood can be irritable), loss of interest/pleasure, increased/loss of appetite or nondiet-related weight loss/gain, insomnia or hypersomnia, psychomotor slowing or agitation, fatigue/loss of energy, feeling worthless or excessive guilt, disrupted decisiveness or concentration, and suicidal thinking or behavior (American Psychiatric Association, 2022). At least one of the symptoms must be depressed mood or loss of interest/pleasure. Symptoms are associated with diminished psychosocial functioning or subjective distress and are not attributable to a medical condition or substance use. Clarifying the distinctions among manic, hypomanic, and depressive episodes enables locating a person's constellation of symptoms along the bipolar spectrum. Recall from Chapter 2 that a bipolar spectrum illness is not indicated when symptoms of mania, hypomania, and or depression are circumscribed around and attributable to substance use or a medical condition.

---

[1]The presence of psychotic symptoms and/or need for hospitalization during this time frame are indicative of a manic episode.

Differentiating Among Bipolar I, Bipolar II, Cyclothymia, and Other Bipolar-Related Conditions

For a *DSM-5-TR* diagnosis of bipolar I disorder, a patient must have experienced a full manic episode as defined in the previous section (American Psychiatric Association, 2022). A patient need not have had a full-blown major depressive episode to meet criteria for a bipolar I diagnosis (American Psychiatric Association, 2022), but depression is "often the first phase of the illness to come to clinical attention in teens (Hillegers et al., 2005)" (Youngstrom, Morton, & Murray, 2020, pp. 195–196). Also, for bipolar I disorder, another psychotic condition (e.g., schizophrenic spectrum) does not better account for the symptom presentation.

For bipolar II, one must have met criteria for a hypomanic episode (but never a full manic episode) as well as a separate full major depressive episode (American Psychiatric Association, 2022). Like with bipolar I disorder, symptoms are not better explained by a psychotic disorder.

Often overlooked by clinicians and understudied by researchers, cyclothymic disorder—sometimes informally referred to as bipolar III—is more challenging to diagnose (Van Meter & Youngstrom, 2012).[2] For a child or adolescent to be diagnosed with cyclothymic disorder, over the course of a year or longer, they must experience multiple periods of hypomanic symptoms that fall short of a hypomanic episode and depressive symptoms that fall short of a depressive episode. Further, during that year-plus period, a patient must experience the hypomanic or depressive symptoms at least 50% of the time and be free of these symptoms for a period of no more than 2 months (American Psychiatric Association, 2022). One can appreciate how challenging it could

[2]Outside of the framework of the *DSM-5-TR*, cyclothymia has been conceptualized and researched from a neurodevelopmental perspective as a temperamental disposition rather than a disorder per se (e.g., Kochman et al., 2005; Perugia et al., 2017; Pisano et al., 2020). A transdiagnostic construct (e.g., evident in attention-deficit/hyperactivity disorder [ADHD], autism, depression, bipolar spectrum, among others), cyclothymic temperament involves "emotional dysregulation, characterized by intense and rapid mood changes of both polarities [manic and depressive] to over-react to external stimuli, especially within the interpersonal field" (Perugia et al., 2017, p. 372). There is evidence that this temperament is a risk factor for depressed children and adolescents to later develop a full-blown bipolar condition (Kochman et al., 2005). For assessors to consider, the youth self-report Cyclothymic-Hypersensitive Temperament Questionnaire (CHTQ) has been developed (Kochman et al., 2005; 25 yes–no items) and revised (Pisano et al., 2020; 22 yes–no items). A cut score of 15 for females and 17 for males on the revised 22-item scale has been shown to optimize sensitivity and specificity to identify cyclothymic temperament in adolescents. The items composing both versions of the CHTQ can be found in Kochman et al. (2005) and Pisano et al. (2020).

be for caregivers to retrospectively report these kinds of complex and nuanced patterns in a way conducive to an accurate diagnosis of cyclothymia, so it requires considerable effort on the assessor's part to try to parse this out by interview. Detailed daily logs completed prospectively by caregivers (see Chapter 4; Kowatch et al., 2005) over an extended period are valuable in clarifying patterns of cyclothymia.

The *DSM-5-TR* also includes a diagnosis on the bipolar spectrum called "other specified bipolar and related disorder" (American Psychiatric Association, 2022). Abrams (2022) noted that this diagnosis can be considered when "manic symptoms . . . do not fit into the other [bipolar spectrum] diagnostic categories" and that this is a "common diagnosis for children and adolescents" (p. 41). The *DSM-5-TR* offers clinical scenarios that would fit in the category referred to as "other specified bipolar and related disorders," including: (a) criteria met for the count of hypomanic symptoms but over fewer than 4 days, alongside at least one episode of major depression; (b) at least 4 days of hypomanic symptoms but with symptom count subthreshold for episodic criteria, alongside at least one episode of major depression; (c) at least one hypomanic episode in the absence of any major depressive episode; and (d) a pattern of cyclothymia observed over period greater than 6 months but short of the 1-year criteria (American Psychiatric Association, 2022; see also Youngstrom, Morton, & Murray, 2020).

As noted elsewhere, given the lifelong implications of a bipolar spectrum diagnosis, the approach presented here is cautious: Unless the symptoms in question are unmistakably (hypo)manic in form and/or there are compelling nonmanic contextual markers (e.g., family history, course of illness, response to medication) as reflected in an elevated Bipolarity Index (see Chapter 2; Aiken et al., 2015), consider indicating a rule-out of a bipolar spectrum disorder rather than risk prematurely and perhaps erroneously concluding that the young patient merits a bipolar disorder through the backdoor of this "other" category. As long as the nature and severity of the patient's emotional dysregulation is captured in reports of our findings, deferring a bipolar diagnosis until there is more solid evidence ought not necessarily interfere with pharmacological and other interventions.

THE BIPOLAR SPECTRUM, DIFFERENTIAL DIAGNOSIS, AND CO-OCCURRING CONDITIONS

Challenges with emotional regulation can manifest in symptoms of various *DSM-5-TR* conditions besides or in addition to a bipolar spectrum condition. There is clinical value—and, in many cases, it is essential—to identify the *Diagnostic and Statistical Manual of Mental Disorders* (*DSM*) "ballpark" (Shectman, 1997) where our young patient is located. Many assessors make the mistake, though, of believing that arriving at the *DSM* diagnosis reflects an equivalence with—and end point of—understanding, such that more nuanced and individualized treatment implications are then not considered. Despite pressures from insurance companies, agencies, and regulatory bodies, our true assessment task is really not to force a patient into a *DSM* category. The tasks are to describe, understand, and consider what will help. It can be beneficial to describe in our report how a patient matches a categorical prototype and how they do not.

With this aforementioned caveat, alongside a reminder of the other broad aims of assessment offered earlier (see Chapter 1), the following chapters in Part III present synopses related to (a) differentiating other *DSM-5-TR* diagnoses from those on the bipolar spectrum and (b) recognizing *DSM-5-TR* diagnoses apt to co-occur (Tyrer, 2017) with bipolar diagnoses. "Co-occur" is used as an alternative to "comorbid" because the more commonly used term *comorbid* actually refers to "any *distinct* [emphasis added] additional clinical entity that has existed or that may occur during the clinical course of a patient who has the index disease under study" (Feinstein, 1970, pp. 456–457). By contrast, *co-occurrence* denotes "two or more conditions present together but there is insufficient evidence to regard them as separate or joined together" (Tyrer, 2017, p. 167). This leaves open the possibility that bipolar and other condition(s) are actually part of the same underlying—but as yet remaining to be clarified in contemporary taxonomies—syndrome. Along these lines, Youngstrom, Morton, and Murray (2020) noted that

> what are sometimes considered patterns of comorbidity may also prove to be useful "endophenotypes" (Hasler et al., 2006)—dimensions that cut across or underpin the recognized binary diagnoses—as they may reflect the activity of particular genes that are not uniformly present in all cases meeting DSM criteria for either disorder. For example, cases with bipolar and generalized anxiety disorder (GAD) may involve genes related to the behavioral inhibition system that are not present in other cases with [bipolar spectrum disorder], and they will also have genes affecting mood dysregulation that are not present in most individuals meeting criteria for GAD. (pp. 201–202)

So, for pragmatic purposes, the conservative preference here is to think of patients' symptoms as "meeting criteria" for multiple disorders as constructed in the *DSM-5-TR* rather than reifying the idea of a child or necessarily "having" multiple conditions, each of which may actually be manifestations of the coinciding underlying vulnerabilities.

The task of differentiating pediatric bipolar disorder from other *DSM-5-TR* categories begins with acknowledging its considerable challenge:

> Hallmark manic symptoms of grandiosity, psychomotor agitation, and reckless behavior must be differentiated from those of other more common childhood disorders such as hyperactivity, irritability, dangerous play, inappropriate sexualized activity, as well as from normal childhood phenomena such as boasting, imaginative play, and youthful indiscretion. (McClellan et al., 2007, p. 113)

In this context, bipolar disorders are addressed in Chapters 8, 9, and 10 as they relate to the following other conditions: disruptive mood dysregulation disorder, the schizophrenia spectrum, alcohol/substance use, ADHD, trauma/posttraumatic stress disorder, the autism spectrum, disruptive behavior disorders, reactive attachment disorder, borderline personality disorders, anxiety disorders, eating disorders, and learning disabilities. These synopses are not intended to be applied as substitutes for careful review of all *DSM-5-TR* criteria in the service of a final diagnosis but, rather, to offer a framework for assessors in thinking about some of the most salient features to consider. The subsequent chapters in this part of the book are organized according to (a) "either/or" differential diagnosis (see Chapter 8; i.e., bipolar spectrum versus another condition, but not both), (b) "and/or" diagnoses (see Chapter 9; bipolar vs. or co-occurring with another diagnosis), and (c) possible co-occurring conditions less likely to be mistaken for the bipolar spectrum (see Chapter 10).

8 EITHER/OR

Diagnoses Mutually Exclusive With the Bipolar Spectrum

Not uncommonly, children and adolescents struggling with emotional dysregulation meet criteria for more than one descriptive diagnosis in the fifth edition, text revision, of the *Diagnostic and Statistical Manual of Mental Disorders* (*DSM-5-TR*; American Psychiatric Association, 2022). Sometimes, there is a question of whether a young patient meets criteria for a bipolar spectrum condition versus another condition or in addition to that other condition. However, with children and adolescents, there are two categories for which the differential diagnosis is either the bipolar spectrum or the other, but it cannot be both: disruptive mood dysregulation disorder (DMDD) and schizophrenic spectrum conditions.

BIPOLAR SPECTRUM VERSUS DISRUPTIVE MOOD DYSREGULATION DISORDER

As described earlier (see Chapter 2), DMDD represents the attempt by the authors of the fifth edition of the *Diagnostic and Statistical Manual of Mental Disorders* (*DSM*-5; American Psychiatric Association, 2013) and the *DSM-5-TR*

https://doi.org/10.1037/0000430-009
Psychological Assessment of Emotional Dysregulation in Children and Adolescents: The Bipolar Spectrum and Beyond, by A. D. Bram
Copyright © 2025 by the American Psychological Association. All rights reserved.

to resolve the controversy surrounding pediatric bipolar disorder, specifically cases previously considered by many clinicians to be an ultradian (less than a day but longer than an hour) subtype of the disorder.[1] Both DMDD and pediatric bipolar disorders are marked by irritable and volatile mood. But the primary distinguishing features are the intertwined (a) chronicity of symptoms in DMDD versus the episodic course in pediatric bipolar disorder and (b) the specificity of elevated mood, grandiosity, and other features of mania or hypomania (mania if a duration of at least a week, associated with substantial impairment, psychosis, or hospitalization; hypomania if 4 or more days with observable behavioral change but no psychosis, hospitalization, or dramatic impairment) to bipolar conditions. In the instance in which the child or adolescent exhibits an episode of primarily irritable—as opposed to elevated or expansive—mood, they must also show unusually increased energy and goal-directed activity for at least 4 days (hypomania/bipolar II) or at least a week (mania/bipolar I if accompanied by psychosis, hospitalization, or substantial impairment) to meet criteria for a bipolar diagnosis (American Psychiatric Association, 2022).[2] Irritable mood in and of itself without excessive energy and goal-directed activity is more in the realm of DMDD.[3] The differential diagnosis between DMDD and bipolar disorder is either/or, but not both. Also, it is worth reiterating that children meeting DMDD criteria are rarely diagnosed with a bipolar spectrum illness later in life (Althoff et al., 2010;

[1]DMDD is one taxonomic entity for which there is divergence between the *DSM-5-TR* and the *International Classification of Disorders–11th Revision* (ICD-11; World Health Organization, 2019). The ICD-11 classifies the same set of symptoms as a subtype of oppositional defiant disorder (ODD with chronic irritability-anger). The ICD-11 based this classification on research findings suggesting that the symptoms of DMDD are better conceptualized and treated as externalizing in nature rather than internalizing (i.e., in the *DSM-5-TR*, DMDD is categorized as a form of unipolar depression). It would be informative to research how a caregiver's attitudes and clinician countertransference toward young patients varies depending on whether the same set of symptoms is framed in terms of challenges with self-regulation (i.e., DMDD) versus oppositionality/defiance (i.e., ODD). The hypothesis here is that a caregiver's attitudes and countertransference will be more negative and less empathic toward kids classified as ODD compared with DMDD.

[2]When mood is elevated or expansive, the same additional requirement for heightened energy and goal-directed behavior applies to meet criteria for a bipolar disorder. Irritable mood is emphasized in the text because when irritability is primary, it is more challenging to differentiate between bipolar disorder and DMDD.

[3]Assessment of irritability as a transdiagnostic symptom is addressed in Chapter 9 in the section on differentiating between the bipolar spectrum and attention-deficit/hyperactivity disorder (ADHD).

Copeland et al., 2015), further establishing the two conditions as having distinct symptom profiles. The multimethod approach to determining the presence of bipolar/manic characteristics presented in Part II is applicable to the differential diagnosis between the bipolar spectrum and DMDD, specifically in terms of ruling out bipolar disorder.

Recently, Mürner-Lavanchy et al. (2023) reviewed measures that have been used—primarily in research settings—to assess DMDD. Among disorder-specific measures used in research is the DMDD module of the Kiddie Schedule for Affective Disorders and Schizophrenia for School Aged Children–Present and Lifetime Version for the fifth edition of the *Diagnostic and Statistical Manual of Mental Disorders* (K-SADS-PL *DSM-5*; Kaufman et al., 2016; see also American Psychiatric Association, 2013). The more recently developed Diagnostic Interview for Anxiety, Mood, and OCD [Obsessive-Compulsive Disorder] and Related Neuropsychiatric Disorders–Child and Adolescent Version (DIAMOND-KID; Tolin et al., 2023) also includes a DMDD module. In terms of self-report measures for adolescents, the DMDD Questionnaire (Boudjerida et al., 2022; scale included in the article) is a 10-item questionnaire anchored to *DSM-5-TR* criteria. Along the same lines, a caregiver-report measure is the DMDD section of the Extended Strengths and Weaknesses Assessment of Normal Behavior (E-SWAN; Alexander et al., 2020). To download the DMDD section, see *Extended Strengths and Weaknesses Assessment of Normal Behavior (E-SWAN)* (n.d.). Also tied to *DSM-5-TR* criteria, the E-SWAN DMDD scale is designed for caregivers of kids ages 5 years to 17 years and covers 10 symptoms, enabling reports on each separately in the context of home, school, and with friends (so, there are 30 items, 10 symptoms rated across three settings). Each item is rated on a 7-point scale with reference to "how well your child handles emotions compared to other children of the same age": –3 (*far below average*), –2 (*below average*), –1 (*slightly below average*), 0 (*average*), 1 (*slightly above average*), 2 (*above average*), and 3 (*far above average*). Both the DMDD Questionnaire and the E-SWAN are relatively new, and there is not yet published literature on their measurement invariance/nonbias that would inform use with patients and families from commonly underrepresented groups.

BIPOLAR VERSUS SCHIZOPHRENIA SPECTRUM

When a young patient presents to us not only with symptoms of dysregulation but also with what sound like possible psychotic symptoms, it is important to consider the differential diagnosis between the schizophrenic and bipolar spectra. Bipolar and schizophrenic spectrum disorders[4] are both considered severe and persistent mental illnesses that affect functioning throughout one's lifetime. Psychotic symptoms, such as hallucinations, delusions, and disorganized thinking and speech, are a hallmark of schizophrenia but are also not uncommon during manic and depressive episodes in bipolar conditions (especially bipolar I; van Bergen et al., 2019).[5] Differential diagnosis between the two spectra has crucial implications for pharmacological, psychotherapeutic, psychoeducational, and family intervention.

Consideration of Base Rates

In the assessment of preadolescent children, it is useful to know that base rates for schizophrenia are exceedingly low (e.g., point prevalence[6] less than 1 in 10,000; Androutsos, 2012). Among adolescents, prevalence increases, but still is quite low: estimated around 0.23%. This alerts us to caution and the need for highly compelling evidence in concluding that an adolescent's, or especially a younger child's, dysregulation can be understood in the context of an emerging schizophrenic illness.

Contextual Considerations

Toward the differential diagnosis between bipolar and early onset schizophrenia spectra, we can attend to research contrasting family history, developmental courses, and prodromal profiles of symptoms associated with each. First and

[4]Bipolar and schizophrenia spectrum conditions are presented here as mutually exclusive because the bipolar type of schizoaffective disorder is considered part of the schizophrenic spectrum (American Psychiatric Association, 2022; Pagel et al., 2013). Broadly, to meet criteria for schizoaffective-bipolar type, one needs to exhibit symptoms of both mania and psychosis, but with the mania evident outside of episodes of psychosis. It is worth noting that diagnosis of schizoaffective conditions in kids has not been associated with good reliability (Werry et al., 1991; Salamon et al., 2018), and the schizoaffective bipolar type is likely extraordinarily rare in children and adolescents (extrapolated from American Psychiatric Association, 2022, p. 123). Among adults, there is less than 0.3% lifetime prevalence of schizoaffective disorder; diagnostic onset typically is in early adulthood. Because the bipolar type is then only a fraction of that in adults, the prevalence is likely minuscule among kids.

[5]It is essential for assessors to be aware that symptoms that might initially sound like signs of psychosis can also be associated with other conditions, such as a manifestation of OCD or trauma (i.e., posttraumatic stress disorder or trauma in a broad sense).

[6]*Point prevalence* refers to "the proportion of a population that has the characteristic at a specific point in time"; this is in contrast to *lifetime prevalence*, referring to "the proportion of a population who, at some point in life has ever had the characteristic" (National Institute of Mental Health, n.d., "How Is Prevalence Reported" section).

foremost, it is important to know that a history of schizophrenia in one's biological family is the most robust single predictor of schizophrenia (e.g., Mortensen et al., 2010). Thus, if a young person has a family member with schizophrenia, especially a first-degree relative, this becomes a crucial rule-out not only at the time of our evaluation but, if the patient continues to struggle, subsequently through early adulthood.

Other useful considerations for the bipolar/schizophrenia differential diagnosis come from Salagre et al.'s (2020) prospective, naturalistic study of patients experiencing a first-episode psychosis. Salagre et al. found that those with an ultimate bipolar diagnosis were more likely—compared with those later determined to meet criteria for schizophrenia—to have a family history of mood disorder, higher premorbid psychosocial functioning, greater cognitive flexibility (as displayed on the Wisconsin Cart Sort Test [Berg, 1948]), and fewer negative symptoms (e.g., loss of interest, pleasure, and motivation; flat affect; social withdrawal; paucity of speech). In another study, Kafali et al. (2019) determined symptoms of ADHD and subsyndromal manic symptoms (i.e., meeting some criteria but falling short of diagnostic threshold for a manic or hypomanic episode) to be more specific to the prodromal phase of bipolar illness than to early onset schizophrenia. Kafali et al. also reported that episodes of brief limited intermittent psychotic symptoms (BLIPS) are more specific to early onset schizophrenia than to bipolar illness.[7] In Arango et al.'s (2014) study, patients diagnosed with early onset schizophrenia showed greater premorbid social impairment than those with early onset bipolar illness; these researchers added that the patients with early onset schizophrenia showed poorer academic achievement and greater developmental difficulties (e.g., problems with language) compared with those diagnosed with early onset bipolar illness.

Multicultural Considerations

Broadly, the process of assessing for psychotic symptoms requires exquisite cultural and clinical sensitivity. For example, as B. L. Smith (2021) reminded us,

> African Americans, Latinxs, LGBTQ [lesbian, gay, bisexual transgender, and queer/questioning] individuals, religious minorities, and many immigrant groups have genuine experiences of persecution and victimization. At the same time . . . just because one is a member of one of these marginalized groups doesn't mean that they cannot have paranoid tendencies. (p. 290)

[7]*BLIPS* refer to "transient, non-serious psychotic symptoms lasting part of the day . . . [up to] one week" that remit spontaneously, that is, in the absence of antipsychotic medication (Montemagni et al., 2020, para. 8).

Similarly, members of some religious groups may hold beliefs and assumptions that the majority culture views as illogical or unrealistic and thus can be (mis)taken for delusions. Because the differentiation between cultural beliefs/experience and psychotic symptoms is often not easily teased out in practice, consultation with colleagues with backgrounds or expertise in the particular culture can be invaluable. Additionally, as is described later in this chapter, multimethod assessment that includes the performance-based Rorschach can also be helpful in that the absence, presence, and severity of Cognitive Codes (capturing impairments in coherent thinking and logical reasoning) can point away from or point toward the patient's vulnerability to psychotic states.

MEASURES TO AID DIFFERENTIAL DIAGNOSIS BETWEEN THE SCHIZOPHRENIC AND BIPOLAR SPECTRA

To differentiate between symptoms of schizophrenic and bipolar spectrum conditions, one primary task in assessment is to clarify the nature and severity of psychotic symptoms. Another is to determine to what extent such symptoms have been circumscribed to manic or depressive episodes. Measures to aid in these assessment tasks are discussed in the paragraphs that follow.

Semistructured Interviews

A semistructured interview aligned with *DSM-5-TR* criteria and involving reports from both patient and caregiver is valuable toward these ends. As noted in Chapter 5, the K-SADS-PL-*DSM-5* (Kaufman et al., 2016) is one such measure, including Supplement I: Depressive and Bipolar Related Disorders and Supplement II: Schizophrenia Spectrum and Other Psychotic Disorders. Analogous modules from the Mini International Neuropsychiatric Interview for Children and Adolescents (Sheehan, 2016) and DIAMOND-KID (Tolin et al., 2023) are other options.

Self-Report Inventories and Questionnaires

Self-report broadband personality inventories and symptom-specific questionnaires enable assessment of psychotic symptoms on dimensional continua. To assist with categorical, differential diagnosis, such self-report measures require follow-up queries of patient and caregiver to discern onset, course, severity, and offset of specific symptoms, especially relative to manic or depressive episodes. The aforementioned modules of semistructured interviews can be used in the service of following up elevations on psychosis-related self-report measures.

For adolescents, broadband personality inventories, such as the Minnesota Multiphasic Personality Inventory–Adolescent (MMPI-A; Butcher et al., 1992) and Personality Assessment Inventory–Adolescent version (PAI-A; Morey, 2007) have scales that help to differentiate between schizophrenic and bipolar spectrum profiles. Symptom-specific self-report tools, such as for children and adolescents, the Child Unusual Belief Scale (CUBEScale; Viglione & Senecal, 2014), and for adolescents and young adults, the Prodromal Questionnaire–Brief version (PQ-B; Loewy & Cannon, 2010; Loewy et al., 2011), can be administered as semistructured interviews with the kinds of follow-up queries described earlier. The CUBEScale comprises (a) 40 true–false primary items related to unusual beliefs and sensory-perceptual experiences followed by (b) three items that assess the child's or adolescent's insight into psychoticlike symptoms they endorsed. Although the CUBEScale's psychometric properties are not yet established, it can nonetheless be a useful method (if not a measure per se) to inquire into atypical and often difficult-to-talk-about experiences, beliefs, and concerns held by our young patients. Also, although measurement invariance/biases have not been investigated for the CUBEScale, its instructions explicitly encourage assessors to be cautious about scoring items that can be accounted for by cultural and religious beliefs.

The PQ-B (Loewy & Cannon, 2010; Loewy et al., 2011) is a 21-item version screener for psychosis risk, which includes scoring of both psychotic symptoms as well as the associated distress. Documentation accompanying the PQ-B includes thresholds that optimize diagnostic specificity and sensitivity related to psychosis risk. To access the PQ-B and its documentation, see University of California, San Francisco (2010).[8] There is not yet published research on measurement invariance/nonbias for the PQ-B with adolescents in clinical settings.[9] Sharma and McClellan (2020) have reviewed additional self-report and clinician-administered measures of psychosis proneness that assessors may consider.

[8]Also, note that a version of the PQ-B designed for school age children—the 21-item Prodromal Questionnaire–Brief Child version (PQ-BC; Karcher et al., 2018)—has been used in research. At the time of this writing, the PQ-BC is under development to establish clinical scoring thresholds (N. Karcher, personal communication, April 12, 2022).

[9]Lång et al. (2021) conducted such a study in nonclinical young adult samples (i.e., college undergraduates) within the United States. Among other things, Lång et al. investigated the measurement invariance in the PQ-B (Loewy & Cannon, 2010; Loewy et al., 2011) with respect to traditional binary gender, race/ethnicity (i.e., Caucasian or non-Caucasian), and level of self-reported depression. The authors summarized:

> The differences found in the measurement of PLEs [psychotic-like experiences] across different groups were overall rather small, and the items had similar measurement properties across groups. However, some larger differences in the measurement of PLEs were detected, especially between the high and low depression groups. (Lång et al., 2021, p. 6)

Performance-Based Measures

Further clues to aid in the differential diagnosis between the bipolar and schizophrenic spectra can be found in the nature and severity of Cognitive Codes from the performance-based Rorschach: either the Comprehensive System–Revised (CS-R)[10] (Exner et al., 2022) or Rorschach Performance Assessment System (R-PAS; Meyer et al., 2011). It is worth reiterating earlier caveats about using the Rorschach toward this diagnostic end (see Chapter 6): Rorschach data (a) ought not be used in the absence of self-report and caregiver-report of history and symptoms and (b) need to be interpreted relative to age-specific norms (Exner et al., 2022; Meyer et al., 2007, 2011). That said, indicators pointing more to the schizophrenic spectrum include unusual use of language (i.e., neologisms) and reasoning that is bizarre and highly confused; these include Level 2 (more severe) Deviant Verbalizations and combinative thinking (i.e., Incongruous Combinations [INCs] and Fabulized Combinations [FABs]) as well as Contaminations (CON; see Kleiger, 1999, 2017). Exceedingly rare and unlike other Cognitive Codes that are not uncommon in protocols of children (Leichtman, 1996), CON responses have high diagnostic specificity but low sensitivity for schizophrenia (Kleiger, 1999). This means that even though most patients with schizophrenia do not provide a CON response (low sensitivity), CON is barely ever coded in the protocols of patients without schizophrenia (i.e., high specificity).[11] In contrast, prototypical Cognitive Codes for patients on the bipolar spectrum are marked by more mild and less bizarre (Level 1) but more energized and playful combinative (i.e., INCs and FABs) and off-track thinking (Deviant Responses [DRs]). Examples of a 9-year-old's energized responses garnering such Cognitive Codes were presented in Chapter 6 in the section "Rorschach Assessment of Emotional Dysregulation." Although not formally scored in the CS-R or R-PAS, energized, playful, jocular embellishments along the lines of confabulations as defined by Rapaport et al. (1968; see also Chapter 4 of Bram & Peebles, 2014) point toward a vulnerability to hypomania (Kleiger, 1999, 2017). An example of a this kind of energized, playful embellishment/confabulation is this response to Card IX: "The middle part looks like an evil witch doing a square dance. . . . She had her dress like this and she was doe-see-doeing" (Johnston et al., 1986, p. 493).

---

[10]Recall from Chapter 6 that at the time of this writing, the CS-R has not published norms for children and adolescents but has done so for ages 18 and up.

[11]Because of this potential diagnostic implication for CON, errors of commission in this code are potentially costly. Therefore, it is recommended that when coding CON, assessors consult with an experienced colleague or supervisor to verify the accuracy of the coding decision.

One final caveat about use of the Rorschach in the assessment of the nature and severity of difficulties in thinking and reason is one that has been broached by Kleiger (2016), although there is not yet published corroborating research. It is this: For patients who identify as transgender or are struggling with their gender identity, it is useful to consider that combinative (e.g., INCs, FABs) and fluid thinking (DRs) on the Rorschach might be understood differently than as indicators of illogic and incoherence. Kleiger cautioned:

> We must consider the fact that the transgender individual's internal psychological experience *is* [italics in original] incongruous with [aspects of] biological reality. Life for the transgender person is an incongruous combination of critical details that are incompatible. Thus, we might view the Rorschach INCOMs [Incongruous Combinations], FABCOMs [Fabulized Combinations], or DRs given by these individuals as reflections of the discontinuities in self-experience as opposed to impairments in thinking. . . . (p. 244)

9 AND/OR

Conditions to Differentiate From the Bipolar Spectrum or That Co-Occur

Some of the most difficult differential diagnoses in the fifth edition, text revision, of the *Diagnostic and Statistical Manual of Mental Disorders* (*DSM-5-TR*; American Psychiatric Association, 2022) that relate to the bipolar spectrum involve conditions with overlapping symptoms in which there is a question about whether our young patient meets criteria for one versus the other, or both. Such conditions to be addressed in this chapter include attention-deficit/hyperactivity disorder (ADHD), alcohol/substance use disorders, trauma or posttraumatic stress disorder (PTSD), reactive attachment disorder (RAD), the autism spectrum, disruptive behavior disorders, and borderline personality disorder (BPD).

BIPOLAR SPECTRUM AND ADHD

A familiar but nonetheless challenging differential diagnosis when evaluating a child or adolescent prone to emotional dysregulation involves distinguishing between the bipolar spectrum and ADHD. Further complicating this differential is that bipolar spectrum and ADHD diagnoses not only can co-occur, but this

https://doi.org/10.1037/0000430-010
Psychological Assessment of Emotional Dysregulation in Children and Adolescents: The Bipolar Spectrum and Beyond, by A. D. Bram
Copyright © 2025 by the American Psychological Association. All rights reserved.

is relatively common. A recent meta-analysis examining the prevalence of ADHD in kids with bipolar spectrum disorder estimated such co-occurrence to be as high as 73% in childhood and 43% in adolescence (Sandstrom et al., 2021). The subsections that follow address (a) symptom overlap between the bipolar spectrum and ADHD, (b) features that distinguish between the two diagnostic categories, considerations related to (c) irritability and (d) executive functioning, (e) methods and measures to assess ADHD, (f) racial/ethnic biases in the assessment of ADHD, (g) screening of sleep symptoms, and (h) possible risks of stimulant medication for the onset of psychotic symptoms.

Overlap Between Symptoms of the Bipolar Spectrum and ADHD

The psychiatrist and researcher Gabrielle Carlson offered a conceptualization that can assist the assessment clinician to tease apart the confusingly overlapping characteristics of the two conditions. These four characteristics are as follows: (a) both involve distractibility and sleep problems, (b) manic activity of bipolar conditions and the hyperactivity of ADHD can mimic each other, (c) manic lapses in judgment can be confused with impulsivity of ADHD, and (d) bipolar irritability and the poor frustration tolerance of ADHD resemble each other (C. Miller, n.d.).

Features Distinguishing the Bipolar Spectrum From ADHD

It is again the episodic nature of bipolar manic symptoms in contrast to the chronicity of those of ADHD (American Psychiatric Association, 2013, 2022) that is a crucial distinguisher. For example, C. Miller (n.d.; based on her interview with G. A. Carlson) explained that "the low frustration tolerance of ADHD does not go away, while a child with bipolar disorder could be severely irritable for six months and then not have another episode for years" (para. 8). Related to this is the episodic grandiosity that is a hallmark of manic states in bipolar spectrum disorders but is not part of an ADHD picture (American Psychiatric Association, 2013, 2022). And along similar lines, impulsivity that is centered around excessive spending, sexual disinhibition, and substance use points more toward the bipolar spectrum than ADHD (Jensen et al., 2001).

In considering the chronicity of ADHD symptoms, however, it is also important to hold in mind that there can be situational exacerbation of irritability, impulsivity, restlessness, and fidgeting (Marangoni et al., 2015). For instance, hyperactive behaviors may increase as a function of task demand, such as in the classroom or when asked to engage in activities that require focus and prolonged effort. Also, note that in ADHD, mood lability may be observed within the same day but not over the 4-to-7-plus-day requirement for a hypomanic or manic episode (American Psychiatric Association, 2013, 2022). And if that same-day pattern of mood lability involves persistent irritability (elaborated in the next section) and frequent severe verbally and/or physically aggressive outbursts for at least a year, the possibility of disruptive mood dysregulation disorder (DMDD; see Chapter 8) ought to be considered instead of or in addition to ADHD.

Considerations Related to Irritability

Irritability refers to "the excessive physiological and negative affective reactivity to stimuli . . . and is characterized by subjective feelings of anger, short/bad temper, crankiness, resentment, or annoyance—sometimes resulting in aggressive behavior" (Pylypow et al., 2020, p. 2002). Irritability is a transdiagnostic symptom, a criterion for the bipolar spectrum and DMDD, among other *DSM-5-TR* diagnoses (Klein et al., 2021). Albeit not a defining feature of ADHD, recent research has indicated that a stable subtype of kids diagnosed with ADHD are prone to significant irritability (Karalunas et al., 2019). Empirical studies have also shown us that (a) irritability in children and adolescents is predictive of later mood and anxiety disorders as well as negative academic, employment, and relationship outcomes (summarized by Pylypow et al., 2020), and (b) psychosocial interventions can improve irritability (and aggression) in emotionally dysregulated kids diagnosed with ADHD (Vacher et al., 2020). So, for purposes of planning intervention, even if a child is diagnosed with ADHD but not a bipolar disorder or DMDD, it is still useful to specify whether they are characterized by a highly irritable disposition.

Therefore, it can often be helpful to include a measure of irritability, such as the six-item Affective Reactivity Index (ARI; Stringaris et al., 2012), which has strong psychometric properties (Evans et al., 2024) and includes caregiver-report, teacher-report, and self-report versions.[1] The items of the ARI are included in Table 1 of Stringaris et al. (2012) with instructions (to rate each item referable to the past 6 months) detailed in the "Method" section of that article. Research on measurement invariance/nonbias across multicultural groups is not yet part of the literature on the ARI.

[1]There is also a clinician-administered semistructured interview version of the ARI (Haller et al., 2020).

Considerations Related to Executive Functioning

Some research has shown that kids diagnosed with bipolar spectrum disorder, ADHD, or both all show weaknesses on a performance-based test of executive functioning (Passarotti et al., 2016). Interestingly, although the three groups (bipolar, ADHD, bipolar + ADHD) did not differ from each other on this performance-based measure, differences in the severity and nature of their executive functioning were evident based on the Brief Rating Inventory of Executive Function–Parent Report (BRIEF-PR; Gioia et al., 2015):

> While all three groups were impaired in General Executive Functioning and Metacognition only the two [pediatric bipolar] groups revealed more extensive [executive functioning] dysfunction, in both cognitive and emotional control domains, relative to the ADHD group. Conversely, the ADHD group exhibited selective deficits in cognitive domains such as working memory, planning/organization, monitoring, and metacognition. The two [pediatric bipolar] groups showed greater impairment than the ADHD group in the domains of Inhibition, Shifting, Monitoring and Emotional Control. (p. 185)

These findings have implications for considering a caregiver-report measure of executive functioning, such as the BRIEF-PR (Gioia et al., 2015), for inclusion in the test battery when this differential is salient. Elevated indicators of emotional dyscontrol point toward the bipolar spectrum or, in the absence of indicators of mania on other measures, perhaps toward DMDD.

Methods and Measures to Assess ADHD

When there is a question of ADHD—whether or not a bipolar spectrum condition is also suspected—it is necessary for assessors to query a thorough history of the onset, nature, severity, and duration of symptoms as well as to administer disorder-specific, norm-based self-report, caregiver-report, and teacher-report measures, such as the Conners, Third Edition (Conners, 2008); ADHD Rating Scale-5 (DuPaul et al., 2016); Vanderbilt Assessment Scales, Third Edition (Zurhellen et al., 2019); or Attention Deficit Disorder Evaluation Scale, Fifth Edition (McCarney & House, 2019). In more comprehensive evaluations, assessors also can make use of attention-specific computerized performance tests (e.g., Conners Continuous Performance Test, Third Edition [Conners, 2014b]; Conners Kiddie Continuous Performance Test [Conners, 2015]; Conners Continuous Auditory Test of Attention [Conners, 2014a]) alongside other neuropsychological and psychoeducational performance-based tests aimed at discerning the degree and type of executive dysfunction and other potential specific learning disabilities.

Racial/Ethnic Biases in the Diagnosis of ADHD

Slobodin and Masalha (2020) have alerted us to racial/ethnic biases in the diagnosis of ADHD. They summarized the findings of their review:

> Ethnic minority children were less likely than their nonminority counterparts to be diagnosed with ADHD and its comorbid conditions and less likely to be prescribed and adhere to stimulant drug treatment. These differences reflect cultural diversity in norms and attitudes towards mental health issues (e.g., fear of social stigma) as well as limited access to qualified health care. Paradoxically, cultural, racial, and language bias may also lead to the overidentification of ethnic minority children as disabled and to higher ratings of ADHD symptoms. (p. 468)

ADHD, Bipolar Spectrum, and Sleep

Assessors are encouraged to consider including a brief caregiver-report (or self-report for older adolescents) questionnaire to screen for sleep disorders (see Spruyt & Gozal, 2011, for options).[2] This is because untreated sleep disorders, such as sleep apnea and restless leg syndrome, which interfere with deep, restorative sleep, can manifest in daytime symptoms that look like ADHD, and when they are treated medically, the symptoms improve (e.g., Sedky et al., 2014). Moreover, screening of sleep helps us more fully appreciate and document the effect of bipolar conditions on our young patient's functioning. Comsa et al.'s (2022) review illuminated the following research findings about sleep and the bipolar spectrum, which are useful for assessors to be aware of:

> Robust adult data and preliminary data in young people suggests that sleep problems can be encountered in all phases of bipolar disorder, can be associated with psychosocial impairment and can play a role in predicting mania and depression. Sleep disturbances among adolescents with bipolar disorder can have an effect on the severity of depressive and manic symptoms, are associated with academic and social impairment during recovery, and can be a poor prognostic indicator. Young people with bipolar disorder show a range of sleep difficulties, including delayed sleep onset, insomnia, hypersomnia and difficulties waking up in the morning. They can also present with difficulties maintaining a regular rhythm, longer naps during the day, more night-time wakings, a greater total time awake during the night and nightmare disorder. Nightmares appear to augment the risk of suicide, and insufficient sleep duration has been associated with self-injurious behaviours. Mania has been associated with decreased need for sleep in young people; however, in adolescents, mania also appears to be linked to a broader sleep disturbance, including variable sleep duration and unstable morning routines. Sleep disturbance does not appear to differentiate

[2]If the child or adolescent has access to a wristwatchlike activity tracker (e.g., FitBit Charge HR; see Lee et al., 2017), this can potentially offer sleep data complementing caregiver-report and self-report.

> between types of bipolar disorders. . . . Depressed youth with bipolar disorder are significantly more likely to be affected by daytime sleepiness and hypersomnia than young people with unipolar depression. (p. 5; enumerated citations are provided in the original)

Although as assessment psychologists, typically we do not have the training and expertise to diagnose many sleep disorders ourselves, based our screening, we can suggest that the pediatrician consider a referral to a board-certified sleep clinician and possible sleep study (see also Chapter 15). Additionally, as discussed in Part IV, identification of specific difficulties with sleep can have treatment implications in terms of pharmacotherapy as well psychoeducation and family/behavioral interventions aimed at bolstering sleep hygiene.

ADHD and the Risk of Stimulant-Associated Onset of Psychotic Symptoms

Recent research has indicated that some of the newer stimulant medications—such as Adderall (amphetamine/dextroamphetamine) and Vyvanse (lisdexamfetamine)—compared with the older Ritalin (methylphenidate) are more likely associated with the onset of psychotic symptoms in adolescents and young adults with no prior history of psychosis (Moran et al., 2019). For kids diagnosed with ADHD, we can alert subsequent prescribers to potential contraindications when we find hints of latent vulnerabilities to psychosis that could be activated by amphetamines. Such vulnerabilities can be elucidated in our assessment by (a) clarifying to what extent there is a family history of psychosis, (b) screening the child or adolescent for psychotic symptoms that they may not have reported previously (e.g., Child Unusual Belief Scale [Viglione & Senecal, 2014] or the Prodromal Questionnaire–Brief version [Loewy & Cannon, 2010; Loewy et al., 2011]), and/or (c) Rorschach Performance Assessment System (R-PAS; Meyer et al., 2011) indicators of susceptibility to disordered thinking (Cognitive Codes) and lapses in accurate perceptions of reality (poor Form Quality; Kleiger, 1999, 2017).

BIPOLAR SPECTRUM AND ALCOHOL AND SUBSTANCE USE

Maniclike symptoms, such as overconfidence/grandiosity, euphoric mood, racing thoughts, and risk-taking behaviors, can be secondary to alcohol and recreational drug use (Quello et al., 2005). Especially with adolescents, it is valuable to tease out to what extent such symptoms are circumscribed or exacerbated around alcohol or substance (e.g., cannabis, amphetamines, hallucinogens) use. If mania is circumscribed around drug use, there is reason to conceptualize the symptoms as substance-induced rather than an incipient bipolar condition. But in many instances, drinking and drug use can be understood as misguided efforts to self-medicate extant emotional dysregulation, in which case the substances amplify manic symptoms and other manifestations of dysregulation. Indeed, Frías et al. (2015) found that 31% of youths with a bipolar diagnosis also met criteria for a substance use disorder.

To evaluate the possible role of alcohol and substance use in maniclike symptoms and other forms of emotional dysregulation of our young patient, we can implement screening and/or more in-depth assessment measures of addiction. Winters and Kaminer (2008) reviewed both types of assessment tools designed for adolescents, highlighting those deemed strong psychometrically and user friendly for administration and scoring.

The two self-report measures that Winters and Kaminer (2008) recommended are the six-item CRAFFT scale (Knight et al., 2002)—which derives its name from key words in each item: car, relax, alone, forget, friends, trouble—and 40-item Personal Experience Screening Questionnaire (PESQ; Winters, 1992), both of which have been shown to be effective screeners in a large (N = 1,573) racially/ethnically diverse urban sample of patients ages 12 years to 18 years receiving services in community health clinics in the United States (D'Amico et al., 2016). Free access to the most updated versions of the CRAFFT, including translations into many languages as well as a clinician-administered version, are available online (see https://crafft.org/). Commercially available, the PESQ elicits history and severity of substance use and associated psychosocial difficulties, and it includes validity scales and allows for norm-referenced interpretation. Two other quickly administered, psychometrically sound self-report measures published after the review by Winters and Kaminer (2008) include the Brief Screener for Tobacco, Alcohol, and other Drugs (Kelly et al., 2014) and the Screening to Brief Intervention scales (S. Levy et al., 2014). Both measures are freely available online from the National Institute on Drug Abuse (n.d.). Access to measures is available via a search on the Substance Abuse and Mental Health Services Administration (n.d.) resources webpage.

A positive screen on any of these measures merits further inquiry of patient and caregivers to parse out the temporal relationship between alcohol/substance use and the maniclike or other symptoms of emotional dysregulation. When a screening inventory and subsequent queries do not provide clarity about the association between dysregulation and substance use or the assessor otherwise judges it necessary to obtain a greater understanding of the role of substances, a more thorough assessment can be added to the test battery. Such an added assessment can take the form of a semistructured interview or more detailed self-report inventory (Winters & Kaminer, 2008).

One semistructured interview is the Teen-Addiction Severity Index (T-ASI; Kaminer et al., 1991) that yields both patient-rated and interviewer-rated severity scores. The T-ASI and its revision, the Teen Addiction Severity Index–Two (T-ASI-2; Brodey et al., 2008), not only facilitate a detailed history of alcohol and substance use, including context and sequelae, but also illuminate the young patient's attitudes toward their use and their motivation to change. There is not yet a literature on measurement invariance/nonbias with the T-ASI or T-ASI-2.

An alternative to such a semistructured interview is a comprehensive self-report addiction-specific questionnaire. Interestingly, not only are self-report measures typically more efficient and cost-effective in terms of direct time required of the assessor, but there is some evidence that adolescents are more likely to be honest in their disclosure of substance use on a self-report measure compared with a clinician-administered interview (Knight et al., 2007). An example of this kind of self-report tool is the Personal Experience Inventory (PEI; Winters & Henly, 1989), which assesses the adolescent's use of a wide range of substances and the nature and severity of psychosocial effect. The PEI includes validity scales and norms to guide interpretation. Responses to specific items on self-report measures like the PEI can be subsequently queried to elucidate the link between substance use and episodes of mania and other forms of emotional dysregulation.

When an adolescent is unwilling or hesitant to answer questions about or discuss their alcohol or substance use and how it is related to their emotional dysregulation, assessors can include a caregiver-report instrument, such as the Personal Experience Inventory–Parent Version (Winters et al., 2000). However, it is important to appreciate that reports by parents/caregivers are apt to underestimate the severity of their adolescent's use (Piehler et al., 2020). Still, though, "in situations when adolescents may be likely to inaccurately minimize or deny use due to potential negative consequences of acknowledging use, parents may more readily share any observed substance use behaviors" (Piehler et al., 2020, p. 15). Moreover, in some circumstances, an assessor might consider administering both self-report and caregiver-report measures of alcohol/substance because greater discrepancies between the two can illuminate problematic aspects in trust and communication within the caregiver–child relationship (Lippold et al., 2014; Piehler et al., 2020).

When we do determine that our patient's manic symptoms or other forms of emotional dysregulation are likely related to alcohol or substance use, a referral to more specialized addiction evaluation is often in order. This topic is discussed further in Chapter 15.

BIPOLAR SPECTRUM, TRAUMA, AND PTSD

Studies of adults with bipolar spectrum disorders illuminate how common—up to 98%—it is for members of this group to report a traumatic event sometime in their lifetime (Otto et al., 2004). This is compared to 70% of all adults in the United States (National Council for Mental Wellbeing, 2022). Further, Aas et al. (2016) cited findings that (a) adults diagnosed with bipolar disorders are more likely than controls to have experienced multiple childhood traumas (Bernstein et al., 1994) and (b) childhood trauma is associated with an earlier onset of bipolar symptoms and a more severe course of the illness, including rapid cycling, psychotic features, suicidality, and vulnerability to substance use (e.g., Álvarez et al., 2011; Bebbington et al., 2004; Garno et al., 2005; Olgiati & Serretti, 2022). Thus, when evaluating a child or adolescent exhibiting emotional dysregulation, it is crucial to consider the potential involvement and effect of trauma. After all, when trauma is salient in a patient's struggles, treatment that is not trauma informed, if not trauma focused, is less likely to be meaningfully accessed by and effective for the patient (e.g., Rice et al., 2021).

When assessing the role of trauma for an emotionally dysregulated child or adolescent, it is important to consider both trauma in a broad sense—as a potential underlying developmental disruption (Bram & Peebles, 2014; Peebles, 2012; see Chapter 12 of this volume)—and in the narrower *DSM-5-TR* sense of PTSD. A patient can experience emotional, behavioral, and interpersonal sequelae of trauma even if symptomatic manifestations fall short of *DSM-5-TR* PTSD criteria (Armstrong, 2011). To ascertain trauma as an underlying developmental disruption, we attend to caregiver-report and self-report data from interview, broadband personality inventories (e.g., Minnesota Multiphasic Personality Inventory–Adolescent [MMPI-A; Butcher et al., 1992], Personality Assessment Inventory–Adolescent version [PAI-A; Morey, 2007]) and trauma-specific questionnaires that point to posttraumatic stress reactions (discussed at the end of this section). And we also look for evidence on performance-based tests (e.g., R-PAS [Meyer et al., 2011], Thematic Apperception Test [TAT; Murray, 1943], and even the Wechsler tests [see Bram, 2017]).

On performance-based measures, specifically, we attune to "(a) jarring and disruptive intrusion of raw or inappropriately placed [trauma-themed] content, which is thematically repetitive, temporarily disorganizing, and sometimes difficult to shift from [and] (b) lapses around such traumatic content in *otherwise-adequate* focus, coherence, organization, reality sense, reasoning, and so forth" (Bram & Peebles, 2014, p. 291). For example, with R-PAS

(Meyer et al., 2011), we might find that poor Form Quality and more Cognitive Codes are circumscribed or exacerbated around a child's responses marked by traumatic content (e.g., a person being beaten, a house on fire, a slaughtered animal; see also Brand et al. [2006] for a description of their Trauma Content Index and Meyer et al. [2011] for discussion of the R-PAS Critical Contents summary score).

Turning to the narrower *DSM-5-TR* differential diagnosis between a bipolar spectrum disorder and full-blown PTSD, we begin with recognition that the two categories are not mutually exclusive. With the caveat that this was based on the older criteria in the fourth edition of *the Diagnostic and Statistical Manual of Mental Disorders* (*DSM-IV*; American Psychiatric Association, 1994), Joshi and Wilens (2009) found that significantly more adolescents with bipolar disorder also met criteria for PTSD (16%) compared with controls having nonmood disordered diagnoses (4%).

To conclude a PTSD diagnosis in the presence or absence of a bipolar picture requires the requisite constellation of symptoms of hypervigilance, hyperarousal, avoidance, and negative alteration in cognitions and mood (American Psychiatric Association, 2013). But complicating this differential diagnosis—and determination of their co-occurrence—is that their respective criteria and characteristics overlap: irritability, mood lability, distractibility, increased risk-taking, emotional outbursts, and sleep disruption (Aguirre, 2021; Cogan et al., 2021). Aguirre (2021) noted that young patients and their families identifying "mood swings" as a symptom may more often be describing a child who is easily angered or upset, is prone to dissociation, engages in self-destructive behaviors, has nightmares, or is hypervigilant, which are common in PTSD. The key for diagnosticians, though, is to further clarify what the patient or family is referring to as mood swings. A word of caution is this: Avoid jumping to a conclusion that such symptoms must be or are even likely to be posttraumatic in the absence of more specific data about trauma and its effect. As described earlier, chronic irritability, aggression, and volatile mood in the absence of more specific indicators and episodes of (hypo)mania can be captured by *DSM-5-TR* DMDD, which itself is permissible to be diagnosed alongside PTSD if criteria for both are met (American Psychiatric Association, 2022).

Two other overlapping symptoms can be challenging to tease out to what extent they are more indicative of a bipolar spectrum condition versus PTSD: sleep disruption and sexual preoccupations. Regarding sleep disruption, the decreased need for sleep associated with an episode of (hypo)mania can be confused with insomnia (disruption in sleep onset and maintenance) common in PTSD (Cogan et al., 2021). Part of the diagnostic task is to discern whether the child's or adolescent's decreased hours of sleep are episodic, accompanied by no changes—or even increases in—daytime energy level, and cluster with other (hypo)manic symptoms (e.g., grandiosity, elevated mood, increased goal-directed behavior). In contrast, PTSD-related insomnia is apt to be associated with daytime grogginess and reduced energy and focus (Cogan et al., 2021). Moreover, such loss of sleep for a child or adolescent can manifest in irritability, which, as noted previously, can be difficult to tease out from the mood volatility of bipolar conditions. This is another reason to recommend that formal screening of sleep patterns and symptoms be included in a thorough evaluation of a child or adolescent struggling with emotional dysregulation (see earlier section "Bipolar Spectrum and ADHD" in this chapter).

Sexual preoccupations and disinhibitions can be symptomatic of trauma/PTSD in kids who have been sexually abused or otherwise sexually overstimulated or hypo(mania) in those suffering a bipolar condition. When a child or adolescent exhibits a heightening of such sexual interest or behaviors in circumscribed episodes that are part of a constellation of other symptoms of (hypo)mania, this points us toward the bipolar spectrum. However, for kids who have experienced sexual trauma, they can experience periodic exacerbations of hypersexuality as a function of triggers, such as media exposure, contact with the perpetrator, or anniversaries. These exacerbations can appear to be episodic—waxing and waning as a function of the temporal proximity and duration of the trigger—in which case the crucial diagnostic consideration is the extent to which their hypersexuality co-occurs with core (hypo)manic indicators.

To assess the role of trauma, including the possibility of full blown PTSD, it is suggested that diagnosticians include in their battery (a) trauma-specific measures—self-report and caregiver-report questionnaires that can be administered or followed up in an interview format so that responses can be queried for additional detail, (b) broadband personality measures (e.g., MMPI-A [Butcher et al., 1992], PAI-A [Morey, 2007], Millon® Pre-Adolescent Clinical Inventory [Millon et al., 2005]) containing trauma scales, and (c) performance-based measures that can elicit traumatic themes and thus facilitate in vivo assessment of how such thematic intrusion affects various aspects of psychological functioning (e.g., reasoning, sense of reality, emotional (dys)regulation, relatedness; see Bram & Peebles, 2014). When time and cost of the evaluation are at a premium, the assessor may choose to begin with the broadband personality inventory, and then only if trauma scales are elevated, follow up with a trauma-specific questionnaire/interview.

Assessors can choose among a plethora of trauma-specific self-report and caregiver-report screeners; some are available freely online, and others are for purchase from the publisher (see review by Eklund et al., 2018). Positive screens on such measures merit follow-up query by interview. One such measure is the Child and Adolescent Trauma Screen 2 (CATS-2; Sachser et al., 2022), which has self-report and caregiver-report versions and is in the public domain; the self-report version of the CATS-2 can be downloaded (see *Child and Adolescent Trauma Screen-2 [CATS-2]: Self-Report [7–17 Years],* n.d.). The CATS-2 queries about a range of possible traumatic events and assesses the degree of presence of core PTSD symptoms as well as domains of functional interference. This measure includes guidelines for scoring PTSD symptoms both dimensionally and categorically. There is not yet published research on measurement invariance/nonbias in the CATS-2. A similar but briefer trauma screener is the 16-item Life Incidents of Traumatic Experiences questionnaire (LITE; Greenwald & Rubin, 1999), of which there are self-report and caregiver-report versions but also no published research on measurement invariance/nonbias. The LITE is available for purchase from the Trauma Institute & Child Trauma Institute (n.d.). One can access other self-report and caregiver-report measures of trauma experienced by children and adolescents through the International Society for Traumatic Stress Studies (n.d.).

More recently, as awareness has grown about the potential traumatic effect of systemic racism, we can consider including a new semistructured interview when assessing adolescent patients from cultural backgrounds that have been historically marginalized and disadvantaged: the University of Connecticut Racial/Ethnic Stress & Trauma Scale (UnRESTS; Williams et al., 2018; see Cultural and Mental Health Disparities [n.d.] to download this measure). The UnRESTS elicits both qualitative (subjective experiences of racism and discrimination) and quantitative (related to ethnic identity and presence of specific PTSD symptoms) data. Along similar lines, the self-report adolescent version of the Gender Minority Stress and Resilience Measure (GMSR-A; Hidalgo et al., 2019; measure available online: see *Gender Minority Stress and Resilience Measure for Adolescents (GMSR-A)* [n.d.]) can be administered to patients who are gender nonconforming and thus also vulnerable to trauma associated with marginalization and mistreatment.[3]

In instances in which data point to the role of trauma in the child's or adolescent's emotional dysregulation—and especially when there are indicators of attentional problems and/or uncharacteristic behaviors—a measure of dissociation can be added. For younger children, the self-report and parent/caregiver-report Child Dissociative Checklist–Version 3 (Putnam et al., 1993)

[3]The GMSR-A is based on Testa et al.'s (2015) Gender Minority Stress and Resilience (GMSR) measure for adults.

is useful; for adolescents, the self-report Adolescent Dissociative Experiences Scale-II (Armstrong et al., n.d.).[4] A study of the original version of the Adolescent Dissociative Experiences Scale (Armstrong et al., 1997) in a large sample of adolescents in Finland (N = 4,072) showed measurement invariance/nonbias with respect to traditional binary categories of gender as well as with transgender identification, among other variables (Lindfors et al., 2022).

BIPOLAR SPECTRUM AND RAD

Also related to trauma is the *DSM-5-TR* category of RAD, which can be considered for emotionally dysregulated children and adolescents who suffered an early history of inconsistent and disrupted caregiving—including institutional placement, foster care, or adoption. A child's development of the capacity for emotional regulation is inextricably intertwined with the safety, emotional attunement, and responsiveness of early caregivers (e.g., Bowlby, 1969; Fonagy et al., 2002). Thus, disruptions in caregiving relationships in the form of abandonment, neglect, and various forms of abuse interfere with the maturation in the regulation of emotion.

Behavioral indicators of RAD are evident before age 5 years. In addition to difficulties seeking comfort from caregivers when distressed or being comforted by caregivers' efforts to soothe, RAD is marked by "episodes of unexplained irritability, sadness, or fearfulness" (American Psychiatric Association, 2013, p. 265). Ellis et al. (2022) elaborated the clinical presentation of kids meeting criteria for RAD:

> Affected children have difficulty forming emotional attachments to others, show a decreased ability to experience positive emotion, cannot seek or accept physical or emotional closeness, and may react violently when held, cuddled, or comforted. Behaviorally, affected children are unpredictable, difficult to console, and difficult to discipline. Moods fluctuate erratically, and children may seem to live in a fight, flight, or freeze mode. Most have a strong desire to control their environment and make their own decisions. (para. 1)

The prevalence of RAD is not well established, let alone its co-occurrence with bipolar spectrum conditions. However, it is useful for assessors to know that base rates are understood to be quite low, even in populations of children who have suffered severe neglect (under 10%; American Psychiatric Association, 2022). In terms of the relationship between RAD and the bipolar spectrum in kids, based on decades of clinical experience with children

[4]Both measures can be found by entering their names into an internet search engine.

suffering disordered attachment, John F. Alston (cited in M. Myers, 2021) considered RAD to involve a posttraumatic early history manifested in mixed hypomanic and dysphoric symptoms, which are best treated pharmacologically with mood stabilizers (as opposed to stimulants and antidepressants). Alston (2007) emphasized that such medications are "helpful for moderating arousal symptoms associated with oversensitivity, overreactivity, irritability, opposition and defiance, rage reactions, grandiosity, and dysphoria (what I believe to be the bipolar piece of the diagnostic puzzle)" ("Correct Diagnosis as the Key to Treatment Planning" section, para. 5).

To assess whether a young patient's emotional dysregulation can be conceptualized in terms of RAD, it is valuable to add a disorder-specific, caregiver-report scale to the battery. For a quick screen, one such measure is the 10-item Relationship Problems Questionnaire (RPQ; Vervoort et al., 2013), which homes in on observations of the child's attachment-related behaviors associated with interactions with caregivers and strangers (see *Relationship Problems Questionnaire*, n.d., to download this measure). A more comprehensive caregiver-report scale that is synched to *DSM-5-TR* criteria for RAD and has strong psychometric properties is the 42-item Early TRAuma-Related Disorders Questionnaire (ETRADQ; Monette et al., 2022). The RAD scale of the ETRADQ comprises three subscales: (a) low selective attachment, (b) low social and emotional responsiveness, and (c) emotional unpredictability.[5] Monette et al. cautioned that the ETRADQ has thus far been developed and validated with adoptive and foster parents who were not the maltreating caregivers. Therefore, it is possible that if administered to maltreating parents/caregivers, reports of the child's attachment behaviors on the ETRADQ could be less reliable for reasons of self-protection and misattunement. The ETRADQ and associated documentation including norms to guide interpretation are being finalized for clinical application (S. Monette, personal communication, March 28, 2022); as they become available, such details can be found on the Laboratoire Psychopathologie et Maltraitance (Psychopathology and Maltreatment Laboratory) website (see https://sebastienmonette.ca/). There are not yet published findings regarding measurement invariance/nonbias for the ETRADQ.

---

[5]The ETRADQ includes a second scale, one that assesses indicators of a second *DSM-5-TR* defined attachment disorder: disinhibited social engagement disorder (DSED; American Psychiatric Association, 2013). DSED involves a more indiscriminate style of attachment marked by a lack of anxiety and inhibition around strangers. The aforementioned RPQ screener items about strangers also tap into this style. Because emotional dysregulation is not considered a defining feature of DSED in the way it is for RAD (American Psychiatric Association, 2022), it is not highlighted in this chapter.

THE BIPOLAR AND AUTISM SPECTRA

Autism is a neurodevelopmental condition marked by underdevelopment of social communication, relatedness, and self-regulation. Among self-regulatory challenges are difficulties with emotional regulation as well as with sensory integration, attentional and executive control, and motoric coordination. In clinical assessment practice, two principal scenarios are often related to kids on the autism spectrum. In the first, a child or adolescent already has been diagnosed with an autism spectrum disorder [ASD], and their social and emotional difficulties are not responding to current interventions so require greater understanding. In such contexts, formal assessment is valuable to clarify the conditions-under-which of emotional destabilization/recovery and implications for intervention. And given that close to 7% of individuals with autism also meet criteria for the bipolar spectrum (close to three times the rate in the general population; Skokauskas & Frodl, 2015), there is reason to include formal assessment for this possibility through the methodology detailed earlier. If the child is nonverbal and/or has a severe intellectual disability, evaluation would rely on the caregiver-report and other collateral-report measures to determine to what extent specific symptoms cluster in a way pointing to hypomanic or manic episodes.

In the second scenario, the child or adolescent has not been previously diagnosed with autism. But they are experiencing profound struggles socially and emotionally such that a rule-out of the autism spectrum makes sense as part of a comprehensive evaluation. Sometimes the patient has already been diagnosed with a bipolar condition. Joshi et al.'s (2013) finding that nearly 30% of kids diagnosed with bipolar I disorder also met criteria for the autism spectrum suggests a high enough base-rate overlap to routinely consider whether, at minimum, a screen for autism is indicated. This would especially be the case if the child or adolescent is reported to not only be prone to emotional dysregulation but also to be socially unaware and awkward and to have few friends. Beyond the initial screening, thorough assessment would involve a detailed developmental history and norm-based, disorder-specific caregiver-report and performance-based measures. Comprehensive reviews of measures for the assessment of autism are offered by Chahin et al. (2020); Frazier, Whitehouse, et al. (2023); and Payakachat et al. (2012).

Collateral-Report Measures to Assess for the Autism Spectrum

Examples of caregiver-report measures include the Social Responsiveness Scale-2 (SRS-2; J. N. Constantino & Gruber, 2012) and the Autism Spectrum Rating Scales (ASRS; S. Goldstein & Naglieri, 2010), both of which allow for teacher-report as well. Although there is not yet research published on measurement invariance/nonbias with the SRS-2, McClain et al. (2020, 2021) have made vital contributions investigating such questions with the ASRS and its three subscales of Social Communication, Unusual Behaviors, and Self-Regulation. McClain et al. (2020) rooted their research in known disparities in identification of kids with autism spectrum conditions among different racial/ethnic groups (White, Black, Hispanic, and Asian American) in the United States (Baio et al., 2018; Centers for Disease Control and Prevention, 2006; Mandell et al., 2002, 2007; Sullivan, 2013, summarized by McClain et al., 2020).

Specifically, McClain et al. (2020, 2021) studied measurement invariance in the ASRS parent/caregiver-report version across nonclinical groups of self-identified Black, Latine, and White families of kids ages 6 years to 18 years ($N = 806$). McClain et al. (2021) found that (a) the ASRS's three subscales were invariant and thus not biased across the Black, Latine, and White groups, but (b) five items on the Self-Regulation subscale showed differential item functioning (DIF; i.e., noninvariance) across the three groups. McClain et al. (2021) were pragmatic and explicit in delineating the clinical implications of their findings:

> The ASRS interpretative guidelines recommend that clinicians first look at scale scores followed by item-level scores ([S.] Goldstein & Naglieri, 2010). Given our findings, it is recommended that when using the ASRS with Black and Latinx families, clinicians carefully consider whether to conduct item-level analyses with Items 1, 16, 30, 52, and 66. If these items are evaluated, clinicians should be mindful that these items may be over- or under-endorsed and evaluate how that may inform their interpretation. Furthermore, as noted in both our previous (McClain et al., 2019 [McClain et al., 2020]) and the present studies, Items 4 and 5 are problematic and prevented statistical analysis due to their reverse or weak correlations across racial/ethnic groups. As a result, we recommend that clinicians refrain from conducting item-level analysis with Black and Latinx families for Items 4 and 5. This is particularly critical, given known disparities in ASD identification among Latinx and Black populations.
>
> [S.] Goldstein and Naglieri (2010) also noted that examination of the ASRS subscales in addition to the ASRS total score is critical and provides a broader picture of the child. Results from this study and our prior examination of the ASRS factor structure across racial/ethnic groups indicate that examination of the three subscales separately may be more appropriate. Thus, clinicians may consider placing more emphasis on the SC [Social Communication], SR [Self-Regulation], and UB [Unusual Behaviors] subscale scores over the ASRS total score when using the measure with Black and Latinx families. In addition to the aforementioned suggestions when using the ASRS with Black and Latinx parents, clinicians should ensure families are extensively involved in the assessment process as practitioners need to integrate cultural expectations and

> beliefs into data collection, use multiple data sources, and obtain more information regarding ASD symptoms measured by the noninvariant ASRS items. (pp. 252–253)

Performance-Based Measures to Assess for the Autism Spectrum

A well-regarded standardized performance-based measure for in vivo assessment of a child's or adolescent's (or adult's) social communication, social interaction, play, and repetitive and restricted behaviors (RRB) is the Autism Diagnostic Observation Schedule, Second Edition (ADOS-2; Lord et al., 2012). The ADOS-2 consists of four potential modules for administration depending on the age and capacity for communication of the patient. The ADOS-2 has been found to have two primary factors: social affect (SA) and RRB. Considered by many to be the gold standard in assessing for the autism spectrum, the ADOS-2 has recently been researched for measurement invariance/nonbias with regard to race/ethnicity (White and Black children) and the traditional male/female binary (N = 6,269; Kalb et al., 2022). Kalb et al.'s (2022) findings included that

> when comparing ADOS-2 DIF for Black/African American children compared with White children, minimal DIF was observed. When DIF did occur, estimated effect sizes were small for all items but repetitive interests. There are 2 patterns worth considering, however. First, when DIF was present, it was most frequently observed in the SA domain. Second, the direction of bias . . . result[ed] in underestimation of ASD severity for Black/African American children. Discrimination was poorer as well, suggesting these items do not detect ASD as effectively in Black/African American children. . . .
>
> A different pattern of DIF emerged for sex. Sex-related DIF was equally split between RRB and SA. However, RRB-related DIF was solely confined to hand mannerisms. . . . SA, on the other hand, was split across 4 separate items across modules. . . . This finding is somewhat consistent with the literature of underdetection [of ASD in female children and adults]. (pp. 8–9)

Reminder About Dimensional and Idiographic Assessment of Autism as a Spectrum

Although autism is understood as a distinct category, it is crucial to hold in mind the *spectrum* component—that is, the vast heterogeneity—within it (Frazier, Chetcuti, et al., 2023). This underscores the importance that assessors attend and speak to idiographic and dimensional aspects related to symptom presentation, personality, and strengths as well as level of impairment. As Steven Shore, the autism advocate and person with autism, famously asserted, "If you've met one person with autism, you've met one person with autism" (quoted in Flannery & Wisner-Carlson, 2020, p. 319).

BIPOLAR SPECTRUM AND DISRUPTIVE BEHAVIOR DISORDERS

Not uncommonly, kids prone to emotional dysregulation engage in behaviors apt to get them in trouble with adults/authority figures. So, part of the *Diagnostic and Statistical Manual of Mental Disorders* (*DSM*) diagnostic process involves parsing out from the bipolar spectrum primary problems of disruptive behavior—encompassing oppositional defiant disorder (ODD) and conduct disorder (CD). Briefly, compared with ODD, CD involves more malevolent patterns of disruptive behavior, such as physical aggression toward people or animals, vandalism, lying, and stealing (American Psychiatric Association, 2022).[6] ODD is not diagnosed if the patient meets criteria for DMDD[7] or if their angry/irritable mood, argumentativeness, and vindictiveness are circumscribed to episodes of (hypo)mania, depression, psychosis, or substance use. CD can be diagnosed in addition to a bipolar (or depressive) disorder if behavioral criteria are met outside of (hypo)manic or depressive episodes.[8] Biederman et al. (2018) found that for kids who meet criteria for both, (a) (hypo)manic symptoms amplify CD-related behaviors (and those of antisocial personality disorder [ASPD]) and (b) the remission of (hypo)manic symptoms is associated with the waning of those specific to CD (and ASPD). Biederman et al. concluded that kids with symptoms of CD ought to be thoroughly assessed for mania/bipolar illness, especially if there is a family history of either disorder. Biederman et al. (1996, 1999) also found that rates of psychiatric hospitalization in kids with CD in the absence of a bipolar I diagnosis were low and indistinguishable from those diagnosed with ADHD, suggesting that the presence of full-blown mania (as in bipolar I) often drives the need for psychiatric hospitalization in children with CD. The implication is that especially in a psychiatric *inpatient setting*, a child or adolescent showing CD symptoms ought to be carefully assessed for mania as well.

---

[6]With a focus on identifying underlying psychopathic traits, Masi et al. (2018) reviewed measures that differentiate among disruptive behavior disorders.

[7]Recall from Chapter 8 that in the *International Classification of Disorders–11th Revision* (World Health Organization, 2019), there is no DMDD category, so patients with the same constellation of symptoms are diagnosed with a subtype of ODD.

[8]Prevalence rates for children and adolescents who meet criteria for both a bipolar spectrum disorder and disruptive behavior disorders are not reported here because the only published research identified (e.g., Joshi & Wilens, 2009) predated the *DSM-5*. In those studies, the rates of kids meeting criteria for bipolar and a disruptive behavior disorder were likely overestimated because many of those considered to have a bipolar illness at the time would now be understood instead as meeting criteria for DMDD according the to the *DSM-5-TR* (American Psychiatric Association, 2022).

To reiterate a principle central to all differential diagnostic questions involving bipolar disorder, to meet criteria, a child or adolescent needs to show episodic clustering and remission of (hypo)manic symptoms. In the instance of differentiating CD from bipolar symptoms, Youngstrom, Birmaher, and Findling (2008) have reminded us, for example, that inflated grandiosity is characteristic of both conditions, but it is the episodic inflation of self-esteem, in tandem with other symptoms of (hypo)mania, that points toward the bipolar spectrum. By contrast, patients with CD exhibit grandiosity that is more traitlike and thus unwavering. As described earlier, it is possible to meet criteria for both conditions, so we would look for other symptoms of mania alongside possible exacerbation of baseline grandiosity (that is perhaps increasingly delusional).

Another consideration to highlight regarding differentiating between bipolar and disruptive behavior disorders involves the need to recognize the risks of racial biases in the diagnostic process. Specifically, DelBello et al. (2001) alerted us that adolescents of color are likely to be overdiagnosed with CD (as well as schizophrenia) compared with their White counterparts (who were more likely to be diagnosed with mood and alcohol use disorders). This is a cautionary tale for assessors in working with patients of any age.

The assessment of disruptive behavior disorders, including differentiating them from bipolar and other conditions of emotional dysregulation, relies heavily on reports from collaterals in the child's or adolescent's life, typically caregivers and teachers (for a thorough review, see Walker et al., 2020). Broadband inventories that include scales specific to disruptive behavior that serve this function include the previously discussed Behavior Assessment System for Children, Third Edition (BASC-3; Reynolds & Kamphaus, 2015) and Child Behavior Checklist (CBCL; Achenbach, 1999). The BASC-3 includes subscales tapping conduct problems, anger control, and bullying. The CBCL has rule-breaking and aggressive behavior syndrome scales and *DSM*-specific scales for oppositional defiant problems and conduct problems. Although the caregiver and teacher versions of these and other broadband measures have been emphasized, both the BASC-3 and CBCL come with self-report versions that allow us—potentially with follow-up interview queries—to learn about the child's or adolescent's own attitude toward the behaviors that adults have identified as problematic. To what extent are they able to (a) acknowledge such behaviors, recognize the effect on others, experience remorse and guilt versus (b) deny, minimize, rationalize, and externalize blame for them and experience their attitude and behaviors as ego-syntonic? Answers to such questions clarify to what degree there might be an emerging characterological component to their emotional and behavioral dysregulation with implications for the aims, pace, and length of treatment (discussed further in Chapter 12; see also Bram & Peebles, 2014).

Although the aim of all good multimethod personality assessment is to paint a three-dimensional portrait of a person, it bears emphasis that this is particularly essential when an emotionally dysregulated child or adolescent has been or is diagnosed with ODD or CD, lest they be viewed only by parents/caregivers, treaters, and other adults through the lens of "bad kid." This means, when possible, illuminating areas of strength, the function of symptoms, and conditions under which they are prone to more prosocial versus problematic behavior.

BIPOLAR SPECTRUM AND BPD

Like bipolar spectrum conditions, BPD centrally involves vulnerability to severe emotional dysregulation and impulsivity (Eskander et al., 2020; Henry et al., 2001). BPD is also marked by an enduring pattern (at least 1 year for a person younger than 18 years) of relationship instability associated with fears of abandonment, identity disturbance, anger dyscontrol, stress-related paranoia or dissociation, and self-harm and suicidality (American Psychiatric Association, 2022). Some researchers have proposed that BPD be conceptualized as part of the bipolar spectrum (Akiskal, 2004), but this remains controversial (Zimmerman et al., 2021). Among adolescents,[9] BPD is prevalent in about 3% of the general population, 11% in outpatient clinics, and up to 78% of suicidal patients presenting to an emergency department (Guilé et al., 2018). It is difficult to find published data on the percentages of adolescents estimated to meet criteria for both bipolar spectrum disorder and borderline personality disorders, but among adults, Zimmerman and Morgan (2013) summarized that about (a) 20% of patients diagnosed with BPD were diagnosed with a bipolar spectrum disorder and (b) 10% of patients diagnosed with bipolar I and 20% of those diagnosed with bipolar II were also diagnosed with BPD. Adults meeting criteria for both BPD and bipolar spectrum disorder are more likely to suffer other severe psychiatric symptoms (e.g., obsessive-compulsive disorder, PTSD, somatoform disorders) and be at-risk for substance

[9]According to the *DSM-5-TR* (American Psychiatric Association, 2022), technically BPD and other personality disorders can be diagnosed in people under age 18, which presumably includes preadolescents, as long as the symptoms persist for at least a year. However, it is rare for clinicians to diagnose prepubertal children with BPD; although when clusters of associated traits *are* identified, it is reasonable for assessors to highlight when a child is at risk.

abuse, unemployment, hospitalization, and suicide (Frías et al., 2016; Zimmerman et al., 2021). It is reasonable to posit that adolescents meeting criteria for both also have a more guarded prognosis and thus require more intensive treatment at a higher level of care (see Chapter 11).

To differentiate BPD from the bipolar spectrum, the *DSM-5-TR* (American Psychiatric Association, 2022) specifies that a person must exhibit emotional lability and impulsivity that endure in the absence of a full-blown mood episode (of [hypo]mania or depression). Additionally, mood swings, including shifts to depressive states, in BPD are usually triggered by events and last for hours or, rarely, days compared with bipolar disorders, in which depressive or (hypo)manic swings are more random and last multiple days (Bayes et al., 2014; Sanches, 2019). Further, those meeting criteria for BPD are more prone to shame and guilt, confusion around identity, and a sense of emptiness (Bayes et al., 2014; Frías et al., 2016; Mneimne et al., 2018). Also, dynamically, BPD is marked by preoccupations with abandonment fears and with tumultuous relational patterns. The second preoccupation is associated with alternating patterns of idealization and devaluation, that is, *splitting*. Along similar lines, those meeting criteria for BPD are more apt to externalize blame and experience their anger as justified, whereas those diagnosed on the bipolar spectrum, when outside of a mood episode, are more likely to experience guilt looking back at their negative interpersonal effect (Bayes et al., 2014). By contrast, those with a bipolar condition are more likely to exhibit relational stability when not in the throes of a mood episode (Bayes et al., 2014; Kernberg & Yeomans, 2013).

To diagnose a bipolar disorder, unlike in BPD, emotional lability and impulsivity must represent a distinctive and episodic increase over baseline (American Psychiatric Association, 2022). Moreover, patterns of heightened and prolonged goal-directed activity (e.g., spending all day and night working on a creative project) are unique to bipolar conditions and not to BPD (Fulford et al., 2015). Although people diagnosed with BPD can experience elated mood states, in contrast to those on the bipolar spectrum, these states tend to last less than 48 hours and can be mixed with anxiety; this is in contrast to (hypo)manic episodes that are more prolonged and associated with attenuation of anxiety (Bayes et al., 2014).

Broadband assessment measures, such as the previously discussed PAI-A (Morey, 2007; e.g., Morey & Meyer, 2014) and MMPI-A (Butcher et al., 1992; see Sellbom & Jarrett, 2014), are valuable in differentiating between BPD and borderline spectrum and other psychiatric conditions in adolescents. Not only does the PAI-A include the mania scale and subscales described earlier, but it includes an overall borderline personality scale with subscales specific to affective instability, identity problems, negative relationships, and self-harm. Stokes et al. (2019) demonstrated how certain constellations of the MMPI-A's Personality Psychopathology Five (Harkness & McNulty, 1994) scales can point toward a BPD picture in adolescents.

B. A. Palmer et al.'s (2021) research suggests that patterns across disorder-specific scales for assessing bipolar spectrum and BPD conditions can also be helpful in distinguishing between the two. Although this research involved adults, conceptually and because of the face validity of the particular measures, findings can at least cautiously be extrapolated to adolescents. B. A. Palmer et al. administered the bipolar-specific self-report Mood Disorder Questionnaire (MDQ; Hirschfeld et al., 2000) and the self-report McLean Screening Instrument for Borderline Personality Disorder (MSI-BPD; Zanarini et al., 2003; measure included in the article's appendix) in a psychiatric inpatient setting to determine to what extent particular items differentiated the two conditions. The self-report MDQ is very similar in content to the adolescent versions (both caregiver-report and self-report) described in Chapters 4 and 5, and the MSI-BPD includes 10 items explicitly linked to BPD criteria in the fifth edition of the *Diagnostic and Statistical Manual of Mental Disorders* (*DSM*-5; American Psychiatric Association, 2013).

B. A. Palmer et al. (2021) found that endorsement of elevated mood, grandiosity, increased energy, pressured speech, decreased need for sleep, and hyperactivity on the MDQ (Hirschfeld et al., 2000) were predictors of both the presence of bipolar spectrum diagnosis and the absence of BPD. And based on the MSI-BPD (Zanarini et al., 2003) items, self-harm (e.g., punching oneself, cutting, burning) and/or previous suicide attempts as well as feeling distrustful predicted a BPD diagnosis. As a time- and cost-effective clinical method, the combination of the Mood Disorder Questionnaire–Adolescent version (Wagner et al., 2006) and the MSI-BPD holds potential to contribute to this important differential diagnosis. Because BPD is more frequently diagnosed in women, Martin et al. (2023) investigated possible bias of the MSI-BPD along binary male/female gender in a large sample of adults and concluded that "despite DIF in some items, ultimately, the effect sizes of these differences were small, however, and likely do not impact the individual's overall outcome on the measure" (p. 462). A longer alternative to the MSI-BPD, albeit one designed for and validated with adolescents, is the Life Problems Inventory (LPI; Rathus et al., 2015; see *Life Problems Inventory (LPI)*, n.d., to download), a 60-item self-report measure with subscales homing in on confusion about self, impulsivity, emotional dysregulation, and interpersonal chaos. Research has not yet been published on measurement invariance/nonbias with LPI.

Performance-based personality measures offer another vantage point to help clarify the bipolar-versus-BPD differential. On the TAT (Murray, 1943) and R-PAS (Meyer et al., 2011), for example, splitting in the representations of people (good versus evil, idealized versus devalued) points in the direction of BPD (S. H. Cooper et al., 1988; Lerner, 1990; Westen et al., 1990). And with the Rorschach (i.e., R-PAS), we can attend to patterns of Cognitive Codes and to what extent they are consistent with those identified in research as distinguishing between the bipolar and borderline flavors of thought disorder. As described in Chapter 6, the bipolar flavor is marked by silly, playful, jocular, and flippant (but nonbizarre) combinative (Incongruous Combination Level 1 or Fabulized Combination Level 1) and confabulatory (i.e., overembellishment, reading undue meaning into things, or going beyond what is justified by the inkblot itself) thinking (Kleiger, 1999, 2017; see also Bram & Peebles, 2014). The borderline type is characterized by confabulations, often with malevolent content (e.g., Card IX: "Two witches *making a potion to poison this guy* [emphasis added]"), but associated with good Form Quality (i.e., accurate reality testing; Kleiger, 2017). It is important to stress, though, that we would never arrive at a bipolar spectrum or BPD (or other *DSM-5* diagnosis based solely on such performance-based personality measures). Data from such measures allow a window into a patient's internal processes and offer evidence that can provide support for or raise questions about inferences based on history and symptoms illuminated by self-report and collateral-report measures.

10 CONDITIONS MORE READILY DIFFERENTIATED FROM THE BIPOLAR SPECTRUM BUT POTENTIALLY CO-OCCURRING

A child's or adolescent's emotional dysregulation can also manifest in anxiety disorders and/or eating disorders. Although the symptoms of such conditions do not overlap with the bipolar spectrum as do those described in Chapter 9 and are more easily disentangled diagnostically, they can co-occur with bipolar spectrum conditions. Thus, anxiety disorders and eating disorders are discussed in this chapter, along with learning disabilities. Possible learning disabilities are essential to identify because emotionally dysregulated young people—whether or not conceptualized on the bipolar spectrum—can also have unrecognized neurocognitive challenges that affect them academically, socially, emotionally, and behaviorally.

BIPOLAR SPECTRUM AND ANXIETY DISORDERS (INCLUDING OBSESSIVE-COMPULSIVE DISORDER)

When a child or adolescent is vulnerable to emotional dysregulation, clarifying the nature, severity, and role of anxiety is essential to consideration of psychotherapeutic and psychopharmacological interventions. Especially

https://doi.org/10.1037/0000430-011
Psychological Assessment of Emotional Dysregulation in Children and Adolescents: The Bipolar Spectrum and Beyond, by A. D. Bram
Copyright © 2025 by the American Psychological Association. All rights reserved.

when questions arise about a possible bipolar spectrum condition, it is important that assessors appreciate how vulnerabilities in emotional regulation can manifest in symptoms of both (hypo)mania and anxiety. Kids diagnosed with a bipolar disorder also meet criteria for an anxiety disorder more frequently than any other *Diagnostic and Statistical Manual of Mental Disorders* (*DSM*)–defined condition, including attention-deficit/hyperactivity disorder (ADHD; Frías et al., 2015). In a meta-analytic review, Yapıcı Eser et al. (2020) found that children and adolescents diagnosed with a bipolar disorder had a 44.7% lifetime prevalence (at the time of assessment) of meeting criteria for any anxiety disorder, 12.7% specific to panic disorder, 2.1% for social anxiety, 27.4% for generalized anxiety, 26.1% for separation anxiety, and 16.7% for obsessive-compulsive disorder (OCD).

Clearly, then, multimethod evaluations of emotionally dysregulated kids—even when the primary referral question is focused on the bipolar spectrum—should include systematic and thorough screening/assessment for different types of anxiety. Optimally, this includes self-report and caregiver-report inventories. Two measures to consider that offer both vantage points on a range of specific forms of anxiety are the Multidimensional Anxiety Scale for Children–Second Edition (MASC-2; March, 2012) and the Screen for Child Anxiety Related Disorders (SCARED; Birmaher et al., 1999). The MASC-2 is available commercially (see Multi-Health Systems, n.d.), and the SCARED is freely downloadable (see *Screen for Child Anxiety Related Disorders [SCARED]: Child Version*, n.d.). Although there is not yet research published on measurement invariance/nonbias for the MASC-2, Stevanovic et al. (2017) concluded in their review moderate evidence in support for the suitability of the original Multidimensional Anxiety Scale for Children (March et al., 1997) across racial/ethnic groups.[1] For the SCARED, Stevanovic et al. (2017) findings were conflicting for multicultural application.[2]

Subscale elevations on measures like the MASC-2 (March, 2012) or SCARED (Birmaher et al., 1999) warrant follow-up with focused interviewing and application of disorder-specific scales. For example, screening indicators of OCD can be explored in more detail by an interview guided by the Children's Yale-Brown Obsessive Compulsive Scale (CY-BOCS; Scahill et al., 1997) and its associated symptom checklist, social anxiety by the Liebowitz Social Anxiety Scale for Children and Adolescents (LSAS-CA; Masia-Warner

[1]Stevanovic et al. (2017) defined *moderate evidence* as follows: "For 3–4 ethnic/cultural groups in 1 study or for 2 ethnic/cultural groups in multiple studies demonstrated full/partial strong measurement invariance and/or no or few DIF [differential item functioning] evident" (p. 131).

[2]Stevanovic et al. (2017) defined *conflicting evidence* as follows: "In 2 or more samples/studies conflicting findings exist on measurement invariance" (p. 131).

et al., 2003) or the Kutcher Generalized Social Anxiety Disorder Scale for Adolescents (K-GSADS-A; Brooks & Kutcher, 2004), and panic by the Panic Disorder Severity Scale for Children and Adolescents (PDSS-C; Elkins et al., 2014).[3] Such measures assist in the clarification of the extent to which a child's or adolescent's dysregulation can be understood to involve symptoms of (hypo)mania and/or anxiety. A full range of measures available to assess anxiety disorders in general and OCD in particular are reviewed by Fleischer et al. (2020) and Abramowitz and Bucholz (2020), respectively. At the time of this writing, there is not yet published literature on measurement invariance/nonbias for the aforementioned disorder-specific scales.

In terms of clinical conceptualization beyond the particular taxonomic diagnoses, it is useful to keep in mind that a child's or adolescent's behavioral manifestations of emotional dysregulation—such as angry outbursts, tantrums, or self-harm—can be rooted in anxiety and their desperate efforts to manage it. For example, a child suffering intense separation anxiety might melt down emotionally, maybe even act aggressively, in anticipation of or in moments of actual separation from their caregivers (e.g., dropped off at school or camp). In Chapter 18, a case example of Jillian illustrates the process by which struggles with social anxiety, unbeknownst to her parents, who were pressuring her to be more socially active, resulted in moments of Jillian's intense anger that had her parents worried about a severe mood disorder. This example serves as a reminder that, as assessors, our focus on diagnoses in the fifth edition, text revision, of the *Diagnostic and Statistical Manual of Mental Disorders* (*DSM-5-TR*; American Psychiatric Association, 2022) should not be in and of itself an end point explanation and overshadow the equally—or arguably more—important task of conceptualizing the dynamics contributing to one's proneness to emotional dysregulation.

BIPOLAR SPECTRUM AND EATING DISORDERS

Eating disorders have been understood as another kind of symptomatic manifestation of emotional dysregulation (e.g., Brustenghi et al., 2019; Trompeter et al., 2022). Epidemiological research is not yet available regarding the

[3]See *Children's Yale-Brown Obsessive Compulsive Scale (CY-BOCS)* (n.d.) to download the CY-BOCS. Items from the LSAS-CA and a description of the scale can be found in Olivares et al. (2009; items in Table 2). A description of and items composing the K-GSADS-A can be found in Brooks and Kutcher (2004; items in Table 2). The PDSS-C is accessible in the online supplemental materials (Appendix A) of Elkins et al. (2014).

co-occurrence of bipolar spectrum and eating disorders in children and adolescents. There is some evidence, though, that avoidant/restrictive food intake disorder (ARFID),[4] specifically the variant involving sensory sensitivity,[5] is associated with a broad diagnostic category, namely, depressive and bipolar-related disorders (Kambanis et al., 2020).[6] In addition, McElroy et al.'s (2005) review has alerted us that in community samples of adolescents (as well as adults), associations have been found between symptoms of bipolar and eating disorders, whether or not formal criteria are met for either or each (what the authors referred to as "subsyndromal" [p. 108] to the particular diagnosis; for a discussion of subsyndromal bipolarity, see Nusslock & Frank, 2011). As assessors, this illuminates the importance—even short of a full-blown *DSM* diagnosis—of identifying vulnerabilities and symptomatic trends that need to be monitored clinically over the course of our young patient's development.

Given the paucity of data on co-occurrence of bipolar and eating disorders in kids, there is a benefit to orienting to findings in adults so we have some context, as long as we are careful not to overextrapolate: Among adults diagnosed with a bipolar spectrum illness, binge eating disorder is the most common type (prevalence found to be between 8.8% to 28.8%), followed by bulimia (4.8% to 10.0%), and then anorexia (1.0% to 7.4%; Craba et al., 2021). And among adults diagnosed with eating disorders, the prevalence rates of co-occurring bipolar conditions have ranged between 11.5% and 68.1% in various studies (Craba et al., 2021). McElroy et al. (2005) concluded that "bipolar disorder and eating disorders share important phenomenological similarities regarding impaired regulation in eating behavior, weight maintenance, mood, and control of activity and impulses" (p. 115). The authors acknowledged, however, ongoing uncertainty regarding whether these similarities are best understood as chance occurrence, separate but related disorders, or sharing common pathophysiology.

[4]Similar to individuals with anorexia, those with ARFID "limit the volume and/or variety of foods they consume, but unlike the other eating disorders, food avoidance or restriction is not related to fears of fatness or distress about body shape, size or weight" (National Eating Disorders Association, n.d., para. 1).

[5]Three profiles are associated with child and adolescent ARFID: In addition to avoidance of eating because of sensory sensitivity, these include fear of aversive consequences of eating (e.g., choking, nausea, vomiting) and restricted eating associated with lack of interest in food or eating (American Psychiatric Association, 2013).

[6]This category included mood disorder with psychotic features, disruptive mood dysregulation disorder (DMDD), bipolar I and II disorders, cyclothymic disorder, and unspecified/other specified bipolar and related disorder (Kambanis et al., 2020).

When assessing a young patient with known eating disorder symptoms, we want to better understand the nature and severity of their emotional dysregulation (see Chapter 1). To the extent possible, we aim to elucidate environmental, interpersonal, and emotional conditions associated with exacerbation—and attenuation—of negative preoccupations about body image and proneness to engage in maladaptive eating and body-focused behaviors.

And when assessing a dysregulated child or adolescent, we want to rule out an eating disorder. We can administer a brief self-report measure, such as the Eating Disorder-15 for Youth (ED-15-Y; Accurso & Waller, 2021; see the article's "Supporting Information" section to download the measure). Developed for ages 8 years to 18 years, the ED-15-Y includes 15 items that screen for symptoms such as restricted eating, binging, purging, compulsive exercise, and concerns about weight and body shape. If the patient reports restricted eating in the absence of concerns about weight and body shape, further screening can be conducted for ARFID and its subtypes using a self-report measure, such as the Eating Disorders in Youth–Questionnaire (EDY-Q; Hilbert & van Dyck, 2016). Designed for kids ages 8 years to 13 years, the 14-item EDY-Q can be accessed freely (see *Eating Disorders in Youth–Questionnaire: English Version*, n.d.). With a positive screen on the ED-15-Y or EDY-Q or previous reports of eating disorder symptoms, more thorough assessment can be pursued as part of our evaluation. An example of this kind of self-report measure is the 36-item Eating Disorder Examination of Adolescents (EDE-A; Carter et al., 2001); to download this measure, see *Eating Questionnaire–A (EDE-A)* (n.d.). There is not yet published research on measurement invariance/bias for the EDY-15-Y, EDY-Q, or EDE-A.[7]

When our patient is hesitant to acknowledge or elaborate specifics of eating disorder symptoms, an option is to administer a caregiver-report adaptation of the EDE-A (Lydecker & Grilo, 2017; available from the authors). A full complement of measures to assess eating disorders in children and adolescents is presented in Bardone-Cone and von Ranson (2020). In our role as assessor, positive findings with self-report and/or caregiver-report

[7]Using other versions of the Eating Disorder Examination (EDE; Bryant-Waugh et al., 1996; Fairburn & Cooper, 1993), Burke et al. (2017) conducted research on measurement invariance/nonbias across non-Hispanic White and non-Hispanic Black children and adolescents who were participants in various studies of obesity—so, not involving samples representing those with eating disorders, such as anorexia or bulimia. Burke et al. found measurement noninvariance (thus bias) with the 23-item, four-factor version of the EDE being studied but determined a nonbiased seven-item, three-factor alternate version, the three factors being: dietary restraint, shape/weight overvaluation, and body dissatisfaction.

measures carry implications of (a) communicating the findings (directly or via the parents) to the patient's pediatrician, so they can follow up on what can be a medically precarious condition; and, unless we possess expertise in eating disorders ourselves, (b) referring for further assessment by a specialist who can affirm or modify our understanding and offer their perspective on more specific treatment recommendations. Treatment implications in terms of level of care are broadly addressed in the next chapter, but with eating disorders, it is useful to know that about 20% to 30% of adolescents diagnosed with anorexia require more intensive treatment (e.g., inpatient, residential, day hospital) than is offered on a more standard outpatient basis (Herpertz-Dahlmann, 2021).

Assessors are encouraged to be cognizant of and try to mitigate a more general bias to overlook eating disorders in young patients of racial/ethnic minority identities (Moreno et al., 2023). Along similar lines, there is clinical value in acknowledging that, to date, there has been limited recognition and understanding of eating disorders as experienced by male patients as well as people who identify as lesbian, gay, bisexual, transgender, and queer/questioning (Breton et al., 2023).

BIPOLAR SPECTRUM, EMOTIONAL DYSREGULATION, AND LEARNING DISABILITIES

Surprisingly, aside from research showing that kids meeting criteria for ADHD are more likely to struggle with learning disabilities (e.g., Soto et al., 2021; Yulaf et al., 2018), the literature is sparse regarding the prevalence of learning disabilities for children and adolescents prone to emotional dysregulation in a broad sense and specifically to those exhibiting symptoms of bipolar spectrum conditions. What we do know, though, is that (a) across the lifespan, people experiencing a range of neurodevelopmental and psychiatric conditions—including bipolar spectrum disorders—are apt to suffer neurocognitive deficits, most notably in executive function and episodic memory (East-Richard et al., 2020); and (b) in one study of students with learning disabilities, more than 60% met criteria for a neurodevelopmental and/or psychiatric condition (Margari et al., 2013). Importantly, we also know that kids with learning disabilities are more likely to be suspended from school for disciplinary/behavioral problems (Brobbey, 2018). And from clinical experience, we appreciate that kids whose learning style and needs are not well understood can exhibit emotional dysregulation when their neurocognitive vulnerabilities are taxed at school and/or in response to homework demands.

Consider a fifth grader referred for psychotherapy because of nightly emotional outbursts and aggression toward their parents. They had been diagnosed with DMDD with a rule-out of bipolar disorder in a recent neuropsychological evaluation, which also corroborated their long-standing diagnosis of dyslexia alongside executive function weaknesses. The patient's new therapist clarified that their outbursts were circumscribed to evenings when their parents tried to help them with a daily homework writing assignment that the patient found frustrating; this had not been emphasized in the neuropsychologist's report. It also came to light that this child's new private school was not adhering to recommendations in their individualized education program to modify written assignments and provide in-school support to scaffold completion of such tasks. The therapist's consultation with the school led to implementation of these accommodations, and, in turn, the patient's nightly tantrums and aggression resolved.

This clinical vignette underscores (a) the overarching point about the importance of clarifying the conditions-under-which of emotional dysregulation and, more specifically, (b) that in assessing a child or adolescent prone to dysregulation, screening for the possibility of learning difficulties is warranted. Screening can include a tool, such as the one by the National Center for Learning Disabilities (n.d.) that is offered online, and/or inquiring about attitude and performance in different academic domains (e.g., reading, writing, math, processing speed), functioning around homework, as well as family history of learning difficulties. The assessor might then determine that formal neuropsychological/psychoeducational measures should be folded into their evaluation or, in instances in which the assessor does not have pediatric neuropsychological training themselves, they should refer the patient to such a specialist for complementary evaluation. Another option, not mutually exclusive and less costly to the family, is to support caregivers to request an evaluation by the school district. It can be recommended that the caregivers seek the school evaluation first, and if findings are equivocal or incomplete, follow up with a more thorough private neuropsychological/psychoeducational evaluation. Considerations related to an evaluation by the school district are discussed further in Chapter 14.

PART IV TREATMENT IMPLICATIONS AND OTHER CONSIDERATIONS FOR FOLLOW-UP

The ultimate value of a psychological assessment is, in large part, a function of the extent to which the assessor is able to translate the findings into meaningful implications for the patient's treatment and other aspects of their life (Bram, 2013). This is the focus of Part IV, which begins with some overarching considerations and then moves into a discussion of matching the appropriate level of care (Chapter 11). Subsequent to a review of a range of treatment modalities to consider for kids prone to emotional dysregulation (Chapter 12), the remaining chapters of Part IV focus on variables that bear on our young patient's capacity to engage/collaborate in treatment (Chapter 13), implications for school (Chapter 14), and considerations for various potential follow-up evaluations and adjuncts to treatment (Chapter 15).

11 TREATMENT IMPLICATIONS

Broad Considerations and Level of Care

Depending on the nature and severity of a child's or adolescent's vulnerability to emotional dysregulation—whether or not their vulnerabilities are understood to be on the bipolar spectrum—there is much to consider in terms of tailoring an effective treatment plan. Broadly, considerations relate to level of care, selection among a range of potential interventions, factors apt to affect the patient's ability to engage, and treaters' experience of working with them (Bram, 2013; Bram & Peebles, 2014). This includes explicating what findings mean for school, further evaluation, and adjuncts to treatment. All of these topics are addressed here in Part IV, beginning in this chapter with considerations involving level of care.

The menu of potential modalities and other interventions is expansive: pharmacological, parent/caregiver or family work, various kinds of individual and group psychotherapies, school-based services, and adjunct treatments. Therefore, one of the main tasks in report writing and verbal feedback is to prioritize for the family and treaters what treatment modalities make the most sense and are realistic for this patient presently and, when possible, in subsequent steps of treatment. This does not mean cutting and pasting

https://doi.org/10.1037/0000430-012
Psychological Assessment of Emotional Dysregulation in Children and Adolescents: The Bipolar Spectrum and Beyond, by A. D. Bram
Copyright © 2025 by the American Psychological Association. All rights reserved.

a generic, voluminous list of recommendations. Instead, it requires careful thought about what to include—and exclude—and what is more and less important among them. It involves taking into account what options are available in the community and are realistic given the family's means. If a modality is optimal (e.g., a self-pay specialty program in another part of the country) yet likely not accessible, it is okay to mention it, but it is more important to address viable alternatives.

The treatment-related ideas that follow in this and subsequent chapters of Part IV are offered in the spirit of the APA [American Psychological Association] Presidential Task Force on Evidence-Based Practice's (2006) principles of evidence-based practice in which research, clinical expertise, and patient characteristics, culture, and preferences are all valued in the equation. Also, note that what follows is focused primarily on treating our young patient's emotional dysregulation. In practice, there will likely be other treatment foci (e.g., social skills, relational patterns, learning disability) that need to be given similar consideration and integrated into the plan but are not as explicitly and comprehensively addressed here.

LEVEL OF CARE

The more severe a child's or adolescent's emotional dysregulation, the more intensive the level of care to be considered. The most intensive levels of care, roughly in order of intensity and external structure, are inpatient hospitalization, residential, partial/day hospital, and intensive outpatient (i.e., multiple individual and/or group sessions along with pharmacotherapy). Community-based wraparound care is also an option along the more intensive end of the treatment continuum. In this conceptualization, conventional outpatient (individual, group, and/or family) psychotherapy, parent guidance, and medication management are considered to be on the less intensive end of the continuum.

Indicators of greater severity are well known to clinicians, including acute suicidality; self-harm and other impulsive, self-destructive behaviors; danger to others; psychosis; and significant difficulties with age-appropriate self-care, activities of daily living, and attendance of school. In considering severity and level of care, it is also valuable to take into account past experiences of treatment. The more the patient has not responded to repeated efforts at lower intensity and more conventional treatments (e.g., weekly therapy along with intermittent medication checks), the more the need to consider these more intensive and structured interventions. Because it makes sense that kids are best served when they are at home, with their family, and participating in treatment and life in their community (American Academy of Child & Adolescent Psychiatry [AACAP], 2010), consideration of these kinds of intensive interventions ought not be taken lightly. If it is apparent, however, that a family is essentially—and often heroically—trying to run their own version of an inpatient unit in the home (e.g., making efforts to mitigate explosiveness, protecting siblings, making sure the child does not run away or have access to dangerous objects), a task is to help them recognize the need for and contemplate a more intensive level of care.

Inpatient Level of Care

In the contemporary landscape of mental health in the United States, inpatient psychiatric hospitalization is a relatively brief (typically a few days and rarely over a month)[1] intervention reserved for patients who are an imminent danger to themselves or others, are actively psychotic, or are experiencing severe sequelae of alcohol/substance abuse/withdrawal. Inpatient programs aim to secure safety and stabilization in the context of crisis; reinstate daily structure; allow for medication assessment and adjustments; offer a time-out for the young patient and their family; and allow for the family, inpatient team, and existing treaters to understand better what is going on for the child and within the family system in the service of a discharge plan. Inpatient programs may also provide group therapies and psychoeducation, but the limited time of hospital care means that these more psychotherapeutic interventions are unlikely to have much lasting effect on a severely dysregulated child unless followed up with a sound postdischarge treatment plan (Fontanella, 2008).

Residential Level of Care

Residential programs are appropriate for consideration for a patient who does not meet (or no longer meets) criteria for inpatient hospitalization, and the "clinician has considered less restrictive resources and determined that they are either unavailable or not appropriate for the patient's needs" (AACAP, 2010, p. 1). Then, "it might be necessary for a child or adolescent to receive treatment in a psychiatric residential treatment center. In other cases, the patient may have already received services in a less restrictive setting and they have not been successful" (AACAP, 2010, p. 1).

---

[1]A recent estimate of average length of inpatient stay was 7.2 days (*SE* = 0.5; Torio et al., 2015).

Two types of residential programs for children and adolescents are generally available in the United States. The first is relatively newer; in some states, it is referred to as community-based acute treatment in which the average length of stay is 7 days to 10 days and for which health insurance is more likely to reimburse. Such programs are similar to inpatient programs but are unlocked, and as patients make progress, they are able to leave with their family on passes to prepare for discharge back home. The second type is the more traditional residential program in which the length of stay can be several months or more, but accessibility often depends on the family's having generous health insurance and/or the financial resources to self-pay or having low enough income to qualify for public health insurance (i.e., Medicaid; Herbell & Banks, 2020). More of these programs are available for adolescents compared with younger children. But it bears emphasis that many financial and systemic barriers to access exist, even for highly dysregulated adolescents who have exhausted a full range of outpatient services, so families often must advocate fiercely to gain access to these longer term residential programs (Herbell & Banks, 2020).

Besides offering careful medication monitoring, residential (and inpatient) programs offer treatment through the *milieu*, which broadly refers to "how aspects of the physical environment, relationships between and within staff and patients, and general . . . 'atmosphere', play a significant role in clinical outcomes" (Banks & Priebe, 2020, p. 44). In residential programs for kids, the milieu often includes a level system for behavior management (e.g., earning privileges) as well as a school component so the patient can be assisted to reengage academically. Residential programs also offer opportunities for individual, group, and family therapies. Some of these programs are tailored for special populations, such as kids with neurodevelopmental disorders, bipolar spectrum conditions, eating disorders, reactive attachment disorder, substance use, disruptive behavior disorders, and emerging borderline personality (AACAP, 2010). One variant of residential program is *wilderness treatment*, which combines the aforementioned intervention with fresh air, prolonged exposure to nature, exercise, and challenging physical tasks requiring teamwork. Many such treatments have proven effective for adolescents with complex clinical profiles (DeMille et al., 2018; Hoag et al., 2014; Larivière et al., 2012). Wilderness programs can be considered for kids with difficulties in basic trust, conduct problems, or alcohol or substance misuse, or for those whose emotional dysregulation and underfunctioning are intertwined with an unhealthy relationship with technology.

Because it is challenging to identify a residential or wilderness program that is an optimal fit for a particular child or adolescent, it can be useful to recommend that the parents/caregivers work with an educational consultant toward this end. Information about educational consultants and their role in identifying potential residential programs can be obtained from the Independent Educational Consultants Association (n.d.). A caveat, though, is that educational consultants can be expensive on top of the aforementioned hefty costs of longer term residential programs that health insurance is unlikely to cover, if it covers any of those costs at all. This means a reality, unfortunately, that access to such intensive treatments is a function of socioeconomic privilege. It is useful, though, for assessors to know that if the child's or adolescent's emotional dysregulation (or other psychiatric difficulty) is interfering with their ability to access the curriculum at school, a case can be made sometimes that it is appropriate for the school district to fund their placement at a therapeutic residential (or day) program. However, such placements seldom occur expeditiously and are less likely to be made in the absence of costly legal advocacy. The potential role of the school district is discussed further in Chapter 14, "Implications for School."

When making a recommendation for intervention at the inpatient or residential/wilderness level or care such that the young patient would be participating in treatment outside their home and community, it is crucial for assessors to explicate two key considerations in their formal test report and other feedback to parents/caregivers. The first is, at minimum, to offer preliminary ideas about what levels of care and types of treatment might follow the intensive intervention after the child or adolescent returns home. Second and relatedly, as assessors, we do well to encourage families to be proactive in advocating with the inpatient/residential/wilderness team to collaborate around developing a realistic and meaningful discharge plan so that the treatment can continue when the patient returns home. More specifically, it is useful for families to be aware that the process of discharge planning ought to begin well in advance of their child's or adolescent's date of discharge and involve assisting the family to identify and connect with specific local programs and clinicians.

Partial/Day Hospital Level of Care

Contemporary partial or day hospital programs often meet 5 days per week, 4 to 5 hours a day, and are completed in a week or two. The child or adolescent attends the intensive program but lives and sleeps at home. Alongside medication monitoring and family meetings, therapies in partial programs are primarily group based and are focused on skill-building and psychoeducation. Such programs can offer a useful step-down from inpatient or acute residential care.

Intensive Outpatient Level of Care

Intensive outpatient programs can be either formal (i.e., multiple modalities integrated within a single setting, often with length of stay of under a month) or multiple modalities pieced together across different treaters and settings in which treatment length is more flexible. Care at the intensive outpatient level involves a mix of pharmacotherapy and individual, group, and family therapies.

Wraparound Level of Care

Offered and funded by government-run (e.g., a state's department of developmental disabilities or department of mental health) or community-based or private agencies, wraparound care includes such features as in-home family therapy (often solution focused and with an emphasis on behavioral management), case management, and access to a mobile crisis team to assure safety and reduce risk of hospitalization. Wraparound programs are alternatives to—but not necessarily mutually exclusive from—partial or intensive outpatient programs or conventional outpatient treatment. For kids whose emotional dysregulation is entwined with conduct/antisocial behaviors resulting in involvement in the legal system, a specialized community-funded wraparound model is multisystemic therapy that includes intensive interventions at the level of patient, caregiver, school, neighborhood, and community (Zajac et al., 2015).

Conventional Outpatient Level of Care

Conventional outpatient treatment consists of caregiver or parent guidance/family work, individual therapy and, if indicated, pharmacotherapy but can also entail groups and other adjunctive interventions. The line between what might be considered traditional outpatient versus intensive outpatient is often blurry. What to call it is less important, however, than tailoring treatment to what we believe a child needs to develop better capacities for emotional regulation.

12 TREATMENT MODALITIES

A vast range of therapeutic modalities exists for the assessor to contemplate in tailoring a treatment plan for a child or adolescent vulnerable to emotional dysregulation. These include parent/caregiver interventions (i.e., parent guidance, psychoeducation, and traditional family therapy), individual therapy, group therapy, and pharmacotherapy. Each of these modalities is reviewed in this chapter, and assessors can keep in mind that (a) these options are not mutually exclusive, (b) not necessarily every modality need be recommended for each patient, (c) it is essential to clarify the relative priority and rationale for each modality suggested, and (d) it is possible to recommend some modalities as more immediately indicated and others as worth considering at a later point after the patient has made progress. As assessors, we do not want to overwhelm parents and patients with more recommendations than they can realistically implement. This means that often less is more—better to offer fewer well-thought-out recommendations than rotely copying and pasting the same voluminous list for every patient.

https://doi.org/10.1037/0000430-013
Psychological Assessment of Emotional Dysregulation in Children and Adolescents: The Bipolar Spectrum and Beyond, by A. D. Bram
Copyright © 2025 by the American Psychological Association. All rights reserved.

PARENT/CAREGIVER INTERVENTIONS

With children and adolescents who are more severely dysregulated, parent/caregiver or family work will often be a high—if not the highest—priority to consider. This is not related to any premise that caregivers are necessarily to blame for their child's struggles and thus need remediation themselves. In some instances, in fact, the parents have provided more than "good-enough" caregiving (Winnicott, 1958; see Chapter 24); even the best of parents would be challenged under the circumstances. Parent/caregiver or family work is often a treatment of choice because home is the environment in which the child or adolescent typically lives (or will return to after a more intensive phase of treatment). Caregivers are often in a better position in the short- and medium-term to make adjustments in their style of interactions with and responses to the child compared with the child's own ability to generalize and apply at home what they are learning in individual treatment. Moreover, unlike outpatient treaters who at best are able to work with a child a few hours a week, caregivers have continual opportunities to intervene therapeutically throughout the day. It is important, though, to be attuned to when caregivers are overwhelmed and beleaguered by the depth of their child's needs, a clue to consider a higher level of care.

Parent/Caregiver Guidance

For kids prone to angry, aggressive outbursts, rigid thinking, and defiant behavior, parent/caregiver guidance is often a valuable recommendation. A common approach to parent/caregiver guidance, and one with considerable research evidence, involves a behavioral, reinforcement-based approach, as articulated by Kazdin (2009) and Barkley and Benton (2013), for example. Although parent/caregiver self-help books are available on these and similar methods, to be able to effectively implement the methods, caregivers of kids who are significantly dysregulated often require expert coaching by a professional.

An alternative guidance approach tailored specifically for caregivers of dysregulated kids is collaborative problem-solving (CPS; e.g., Greene, 2021; Greene & Ablon, 2005; see Pollastri & Wang, 2019, and Greene & Winkler, 2019, for its evidence base). The underpinnings of CPS are different than those from the aforementioned behavioral approaches in that in CPS difficult behaviors are understood as manifestations of delays or deficits in cognitive and emotional capacities, akin to learning disabilities. The authors of CPS operate from the perspective that many emotionally dysregulated kids do not respond to reward and punishment as favorably as behavioral approaches predict. Therefore, instead of focusing on reinforcement, CPS aims to build a child's or adolescent's skills in emotional regulation. In CPS, caregivers are taught ways of intervening with their kids to anticipate meltdowns and outbursts, proactively problem-solving with them, and then using particular methods to debrief with the child after and between such episodes. The aim is for caregivers to help their kids develop and practice such skills. Again, although self-help books on this method are available, implementation is easier said than done, so coaching by a specialist is often necessary to augment such literature, especially when the child or adolescent is vulnerable to more severe dysregulation.

Regardless of whether a formal model of parent/caregiver guidance like CPS or a behavioral one such as Kazdin's (2009) is accessible through a clinician in the community, it is important to encourage caregivers to connect with a thoughtful professional who routinely does caregiver work by offering support, psychoeducation, problem-solving, and understanding of complex kids. And although the emphasis here has been on caregiver guidance as a first-line intervention in a treatment plan for emotionally dysregulated children and adolescents, it is worth emphasizing that even if an individual psychotherapy is recommended as a primary intervention, the need for at least intermittent caregiver work can be explicated in the assessor's report. As Midgley and Kennedy (2011) highlighted in their review of child and adolescent psychotherapy research, outcomes are consistently improved when there is a caregiver component to individual treatment. Whether or not parent/caregiver guidance is offered by the individual therapist or another clinician will be a function of the age and developmental level of the child or adolescent, preferences of the individual therapist (e.g., based on their areas of expertise) and caregivers, and availability of another professional with the necessary specialty and expertise. If there are separate clinicians, it bears emphasizing the importance of their communication and collaboration.

Psychoeducation for Parents/Caregivers

When a child's or adolescent's difficulty with emotional regulation is meaningfully captured by a diagnosis in the fifth edition, text revision, of the *Diagnostic and Statistical Manual of Mental Disorders* (*DSM-5-TR*; American Psychiatric Association, 2022; see Part III, Chapters 7 through 10 of this volume), it is often beneficial for caregivers to learn more about the condition, how it is treated, the prognosis, and the implications for the family. For example, there is evidence that multifamily psychoeducational groups for caregivers (that also include simultaneous psychoeducational group sessions for the child) have been associated with reduction in their children's manic symptoms (Fristad et al., 2009). Particularly when a young patient meets criteria for a bipolar spectrum condition, it is crucial that psychoeducation for parents/caregivers (as well was the patient themselves) covers the importance of sleep hygiene, behavioral scheduling, and relapse prevention (Fristad & MacPherson, 2014; Youngstrom, Morton, & Murray, 2020).

Such highly specialized groups, however, are often not available in the family's community, so parent/caregiver psychoeducation can be offered by the assessor, current treaters, and/or other experts in the community. Parents/caregivers can also be directed toward relevant literature and videos. Of course, an (over)abundance of information can be found in online searches from sources of variable reputability and reliability. So, as assessors, we do well to provide specific references to books, online resources, parent/caregiver support and psychoeducational groups, and specialists known to be reputable. But we aim to be selective and not overwhelm parents/caregivers with copious lists.

In addition to disorder-specific psychoeducation, caregivers can benefit from psychoeducation about emotional regulation in a broad, transdiagnostic sense. For example, Salem et al. (2021) described their model of parent psychoeducation (paired with skill-building for the kids) that emphasizes mood and symptom recognition; the role of "negative family cycles" (p. 616); improving caregiver–child communication; problem-solving strategies, understanding the connection among thoughts, feelings, and behavior; and how to navigate systems of mental health and special education.

Family Therapy

In some evaluations, it becomes evident that the young patient's emotional dysregulation is embedded in and is an outgrowth of a family system that has been dysregulated, perhaps related to substance use, intergenerational transmission of trauma, confused boundaries, or other complex dynamics. In such cases, it is reasonable to suggest consideration of a more traditional family therapy that addresses systemic and dynamic patterns of family interaction that are problematic (e.g., Bowen, 1993; Buehler & Welsh, 2009; Minuchin et al., 2021; Slesnick et al., 2013). Along similar lines, this kind of traditional family therapy is valuable when parents/caregivers (a) disagree with each other about the nature and severity of their child's difficulties and what kinds of caregiving and treatment interventions are necessary and/or (b) experience and treat their child in ways imbued by the parent/caregiver's projections originating in their own previous relationships. One example of such projections would be a parent/caregiver whose own intense, dysregulated responses to the child stem from viewing them as being "exactly like" the hated ex-spouse.

INDIVIDUAL PSYCHOTHERAPY

There are two, nonmutually exclusive lenses through which assessors can view possible individual interventions for kids prone to emotional dysregulation. The first, narrower and more concrete, is focused on disorder-specific modalities. Recall that *DSM-5-TR* disorders are based on history and manifest symptoms. The second lens, broader and more nuanced, is related to our understanding of factors underlying the patient's manifest symptoms. This is what Peebles (2012) referred to as "underlying developmental disruption" (pp. 139–140; see also Bram, 2010, 2013, 2015, 2017, 2021; Bram & Peebles, 2014). Each lens is discussed in the sections that follow.

Considerations for Individual Psychotherapy: The Disorder-Specific Lens

If there are practitioners or clinics in the community offering a specialized, empirically supported therapy tailored to the patient's *DSM-5-TR* diagnosis (again, assuming that this meaningfully captures the nature of their dysregulation), it makes sense to seriously consider such a recommendation. For instance, if an adolescent's dysregulation fits the criteria of borderline personality disorder, recommendations can be considered for dialectical behavior therapy (DBT; Linehan, 2014; Rathus et al., 2015) or mentalization-based treatment (Roussouw et al., 2021). Or if a child's emotional outbursts and meltdowns are understood in the context of environmental demands that tax their obsessive-compulsive disorder (OCD), a suggestion of specialized cognitive behavior therapy (CBT) with exposure and response prevention can be offered (Franklin et al., 2019). Similarly, for kids meeting criteria for a disruptive behavior or other externalizing disorder, regulation-focused psychotherapy (Hoffman et al., 2016) or specially tailored CBT (Lochman et al., 2011) would be a strong option. If the young patient does meet criteria for a bipolar spectrum condition, and bipolar-specific therapy, such as interpersonal and social rhythm therapy (Hlastala et al., 2010) or child- and family-focused CBT (A. E. West et al., 2014), is available, by all means, this is worth strong consideration as a recommendation.

It is important, though, that assessors recognize the reality that despite the proliferation of these kinds of manual-based, disorder-specific therapies from university and medical center research settings, many have not yet been widely disseminated so may not be practiced by clinicians in the patient's community. Another crucial caveat is that these types of (typically time-limited) therapies, tested in randomized clinical trial (RCT) designs, are aiming for or have achieved narrowly defined evidence-based treatment status (e.g., Society of Clinical Psychology, n.d., Division 12 of the American Psychological Association) and are often based on stringent exclusionary criteria in the original research studies (Shedler, 2018; Wachtel, 2010; Westen & Morrison, 2001; Westen et al., 2004; see also Rosenfeld, 2008). This means that many of the complex young patients who come to our clinical practices for evaluation would have been excluded from the RCTs, so the findings are less generalizable. Additionally, although many of these treatments have received the evidence-based imprimatur, closer examination of the research indicates that their superiority over other treatments is either not clinically meaningful and/or gains are not maintained at follow-up (Shedler, 2018).

Therefore, assessors need to be more thoughtful than reflexively recommending a particular brand of therapy based on the *DSM-5-TR* diagnosis alone, that is, without taking into account (a) its realistic availability in the community, (b) to what extent the patient resembles research participants in the RCTs, and (c) whether its purported evidence-base status holds up to scrutiny. Taking these factors into account is consistent with what Stricker and Trierweiler (1995) referred to as being a "local clinical scientist" (p. 995; see also Stricker, 2006). Failing to consider these factors risks forcing patients in a *procrustean bed*[1]—"a scheme or pattern into which someone or something is arbitrarily forced" (Merriam-Webster, n.d.)—which psychotherapy research tells us is associated with higher likelihood of dropout and poor outcome (Norcross & Wampold, 2011; Owen & Hilsenroth, 2014). Attending to underlying developmental disruption (next subsection) and factors affecting therapeutic engagement and collaboration (Chapter 13) mitigates this risk.

Considerations for Individual Psychotherapy: The Lens of Underlying Developmental Disruption

In addition to thinking in terms of disorder-specific treatments, it is also useful to conceptualize the patient's underlying development disruption(s) that

[1]The term *procrustean bed* comes from Greek mythology: Procrustes was a bandit and innkeeper, among other things, who

> lived in Attica on the road to Athens, and there he waylaid travelers, forcing them to sleep in his iron bed. The difficulty was that the traveler was forced to fit his bed exactly. If they were too tall he would cut off their legs and if too short he would stretch them on his rack. (Janson & Vavra, 2017, p. e53)

account for manifest symptoms (which themselves are the primary basis of *DSM-5-TR* diagnoses). Formulating the underlying developmental disruption(s) illuminates implications for treatment (Bram & Peebles, 2014; Peebles, 2012). The four models of underlying developmental disruption are (a) structural weakness, (b) maladaptive character patterns, (c) trauma, and (d) conflicts and splits. In clinical practice, the first three of these models are most applicable to kids prone to profound emotional dysregulation, so those are the focus here. Multimethod psychological assessment is particularly suited to elucidating underlying developmental disruption, and strategies for doing so are detailed in Bram and Peebles (2014; see Chapters 8 and 9 in particular).

Structural Weakness

Structural weakness refers to underdevelopment (or deterioration) of essential psychological and neurocognitive capacities. Emotional regulation is one such essential capacity, alongside others, such as logical thinking, accurate attunement to reality, social pragmatics capacity for relatedness, sense of morality, attention and executive functioning, and other neurocognitive abilities.[2] Each of these capacities can be conceptualized as core "foundations" or "structures" required for adaptation, so insufficient maturation in any is referred to as a "structural weakness" (Peebles, 2012, p. 140). In clarifying domains of structural weakness, we also map (a) conditions under which they are apt to manifest and exacerbate as well as (b) mitigating strengths and environmental factors (Bram & Peebles, 2014).

Identifying and mapping structural weakness in emotional regulation has implications for suggestions about how a therapist might engage with the patient. In some instances, for example, we might alert the therapist about the need to actively regulate the pace of discussing more emotionally intense themes. And when troublesome symptoms are understood to stem from structural weakness, broad implications for treatment interventions include the need for stabilization, strengthening/compensating, and repairing/building (Bram & Peebles, 2014; Peebles, 2012).

It is typically not a major revelation when an evaluation corroborates that a child or adolescent exhibiting problematic externalizing behaviors suffers a structural weakness in emotional regulation. But such explicit conceptualization underscores the need to consider the possibility of certain kinds of

[2]Kids with neurodevelopmental conditions, such as those on the autism spectrum, are understood as having structural weakness in multiple domains (e.g., social pragmatics, management of sensory input, emotional regulation, flexibility of thinking).

interventions, notably, medication (stabilizing), psychoeducation (stabilizing, repairing/building), and skill-building (repairing/building). For skill-building, there are an abundance of CBT therapies, including DBT, that the assessor can recommend if the evaluation findings indicate that the patient has the potential to tolerate and engage (see Chapter 13). Such treatments do not necessarily have to be disorder specific, but the idea is that they target the particular type of underlying weakness in emotional regulation. In the test report, the assessor aims to specify as much as possible what kinds of emotion-regulatory skill-building are indicated (e.g., anger management techniques, addressing cognitive distortions, exposure-based work, relaxation or mindfulness, acceptance strategies).

Maladaptive Character Patterns

The term *maladaptive character patterns* refers to patterns of thinking, feeling, relating, and behaving that are ultimately unhelpful (to oneself and/or to others); ingrained; rigid; experienced and expressed automatically, largely outside awareness; and ego syntonic (i.e., not distressing to oneself; Bram & Peebles, 2014; Peebles, 2012). This is what is meant by saying that a person's difficulties are "characterological." A person begins developing maladaptive character patterns early in life and reflect their best efforts at the time to adapt to, compensate for, and cope with internal or environmental challenges. With age, such patterns can crystallize, so they are less and less malleable, unwittingly contributing to interpersonal and emotional difficulties.

Although we assessors appreciate that children and adolescents are far from fully formed psychologically, on evaluation, sometimes we find that they show signs of solidifying characterological difficulties. For kids found to suffer a structural weakness in emotional regulation, identifying a characterological component raises complications to treatment that need to be addressed in terms of treatment implication. Specific in-session therapeutic interventions to consider when a patient exhibits maladaptive character patterns include limit-setting; confrontation (in the psychodynamic sense of persistent, respectful efforts to help the patient recognize their patterns and experience them as more ego dystonic); education about reasons they are in treatment; and enhancement of curiosity and collaborative reflection on the patterns, their etiology, and the functions served (Bram & Peebles, 2014; Peebles, 2012).

When a patient's struggles are understood to be, in part, characterological, the assessor can clarify that treatment will require a slower pace and likely take longer than would probably be the case otherwise. Imagine two adolescents, each with similar manifestations of their weakness/underdevelopment in emotional regulation: Multiple times each week, when frustrated or angry, they are prone to destructiveness and aggression at home. Outside of those episodes, the first adolescent takes ownership for their behavior, expresses regret and remorse, and exhibits some openness to figuring out more healthy ways of managing distress. The second adolescent, in contrast, externalizes blame for their behavior; shows no regret, let alone remorse; and implicitly experiences the suggestion of needing or receiving help as a threat to self-esteem. For the second patient, we note the rigid and ego-syntonic attitude toward their behaviors that are conceptualized as being more characterological. All else being equal, likely the first adolescent will be sooner amenable to skill-building interventions around emotional regulation, whereas the second will require more energy toward building a therapeutic alliance (see Chapter 13), other relational interventions, limit-setting, education, and confrontation before being ready to more fully participate in skill-building.

Trauma

As previewed in Chapter 9, trauma as an underlying developmental disruption is a broader construct than posttraumatic stress disorder (PTSD) as defined in the *DSM-5-TR* (American Psychiatric Association, 2022). Specifically, *trauma* in this sense refers to when manifest symptoms are understood as attributable to "external events [having] overwhelm[ed] our patient to the point that [their] body, brain, and mind are disrupted in their ability to process, regulate, and intercommunicate adaptively" (Peebles, 2012, p. 169). It is conceivable that even if they do not meet symptomatic criteria for PTSD, a child or adolescent who struggles with emotional regulation (and other aspects of psychological functioning, e.g., attunement to reality, sense of self, experience of relationships) can still be understood in terms of trauma as underlying developmental disruption. This is more apt to be the case when we know that the child or adolescent has suffered *complex trauma*, that is, repeated traumatic experiences, especially in the context of caregiving relationships. At the very least, such a finding means calling attention to the importance of a trauma-informed treatment approach, which entails a premium on cultivation of safety and trust, encouragement of collaboration, recognition and enlistment of the patient's strengths, respect for their treatment preferences, and appreciation of the pervasive and lasting effect of trauma and the risk of retraumatization (Menschner & Maul, 2016).

Treatment implications for trauma also involve an accumulating sequence involving stabilization (i.e., restoration of safety; a therapeutic relationship; and scaffolding/repairing areas of structural weakness, including emotional regulation), reprocessing (i.e., safe, paced exposure to traumatic memories), and integration of traumatic memories into revised experiences of self and relationships (Bram & Peebles, 2014; J. D. Ford & Cloitre, 2009; Peebles,

2012). These ideas are consistent with those of the child psychiatrist, neuroscientist, and trauma expert Bruce Perry, who has illuminated the healing benefits of safe, nurturing, consistent, and affirming relationships; promotion of self-regulation skills; and safety and space to communicate and process experiences of trauma at one's own pace in whatever modalities are conducive (e.g., talk, various kinds of art, play; see Perry & Szalavitz, 2006; Perry & Winfrey, 2021). In the "Diagnostic Summary and Treatment Implications" section of the test report, assessors can highlight the salience of these basic but crucial psychotherapeutic tasks.[3] Many forms of trauma-focused cognitive behavior therapy (e.g., Cohen et al., 2012)—and eye-movement desensitization and reprocessing (e.g., Tufnell, 2005)—the psychotherapeutic modalities with the most evidence from RCT research with kids—systematize application of these crucial ingredients (Mavranezouli et al., 2020). If such treatments are accessible in the patient's community, they can be specifically recommended.

GROUP THERAPY

Group therapy is another modality worth considering for kids vulnerable to emotional dysregulation. For children and adolescents who have difficulty trusting and collaborating with adults—such as in an individual therapy in which it could take some time to cultivate a solid alliance—but who are open to or hungry for peer interaction, group could be a more appealing and valuable treatment component. Understanding of underlying developmental disruption(s) and/or symptom presentation/*DSM-5-TR* diagnosis can be taken into account to determine which available groups are the best match for a given patient.

To the extent that the evaluation has corroborated that our young patient possesses an underdeveloped capacity for (i.e., structural weakness in) emotional regulation, it makes intuitive clinical sense to recommend a group with a didactic/skill-building emphasis, such as DBT and other forms of CBT and psychoeducation. As noted earlier in the section on parent/caregiver psychoeducation, there is some evidence that children with symptoms of bipolar disorder (as defined in the fourth edition of the *Diagnostic and Statistical Manual of Mental Disorders* [*DSM-IV*; American Psychiatric Association,

[3]Perry also emphasized the benefits of these kinds of interventions outside of formal psychotherapy, such as in caregiving, mentoring, and educational contexts (Perry & Winfrey, 2021).

1994]) who participated in a psychoeducational group (that ran parallel with their caregiver(s)' participation in multifamily psychoeducational groups of their own) showed decreased symptoms of mania (Fristad et al., 2009).

Additionally, for adolescents exhibiting symptoms of borderline personality disorders whose emotional dysregulation is marked by self-injury and suicidality, DBT groups have shown to be effective (Kothgassner et al., 2021). Group DBT and other group CBT show promise for treating adolescents with symptoms of bipolar and other conditions associated with emotional dysregulation (Gill et al., 2018; Groves et al., 2012). However, RCTs of time-limited skill-building/psychoeducational therapies with adolescents having symptoms of attention-deficit/hyperactivity disorder (ADHD) and disruptive mood dysregulation disorder (DMDD; Waxmonsky et al., 2016), subclinical mania (Leopold et al., 2020), and full-blown bipolar disorder (as defined in the *DSM-IV*; T. R. Goldstein et al., 2015) show mixed findings. For kids meeting criteria for ADHD or DMDD, findings revealed reduction in parent/caregiver-reported irritability, but this was not maintained at follow-up (Waxmonsky et al., 2016). Adolescents and young adults at risk for bipolar illness had a reduction in manic symptoms and improvement in psychosocial functioning, but these changes were not statistically or meaningfully different from those experienced by patients in a nontherapeutic control group (Leopold et al., 2020). Additionally, among adolescents meeting criteria for a *DSM-IV* bipolar disorder, DBT compared with a treatment-as-usual condition was associated with lessened depression and suicidal ideation but not a reduction in manic and other emotionally dysregulated symptoms per se (T. R. Goldstein et al., 2015).

Because there are only a handful of such studies, some involving small sample sizes and others relying on outdated diagnostic criteria, there is considerable room for further refinement and empirical testing of these kinds of skill-building groups. Interestingly, the finding by Leopold et al. (2020) that patients at risk for bipolar illness reported similar reduction in manic symptoms and improvement in functioning in both the highly structured CBT/psychoeducation group and the control group, an intentionally nontherapeutic, relatively unstructured discussion group led by a therapist that matched the active treatment in frequency and length of sessions. This raises the potential stabilizing, nonspecific therapeutic benefits offered by group participation, CBT/DBT or otherwise: validation, peer connection and social support, the structure of meeting consistently at the same time and place with the same leader(s), and possible reduction of stigma of help-seeking. Clinician-led groups also inherently foster emotionally evocative conditions—by virtue of the need to interact with a diverse group of peers—affording continual in vivo opportunities to practice and receive feedback on coping skills. These are all things for assessors to keep in mind as they consider the range of therapeutic options available in the community: realizing that there could be a good enough group out there.

PHARMACOTHERAPY

As psychologists who generally do not have training and credentials to prescribe medications,[4] assessors do not make recommendations for specific medications. What we can offer respectfully and humbly in our report and other communications with prescribers, though, are ideas for consideration and to be weighed alongside findings from their own assessments of the patient. Five general types of pharmacotherapeutic considerations are offered here.

First, we can raise whether a current medication regimen appears to be effective. For example, if a child or adolescent previously known to have OCD is on an antidepressant targeting those symptoms, and that patient is found on evaluation to still be exhibiting a severe level of OCD, we can raise the possibility that the current medication or dose is less than optimally effective.

Second, we might raise possible contraindications to current or prospective medications. Recall from Chapter 2 that there is some evidence (albeit not unequivocal and uncontroversial) that selective serotonin reuptake inhibitor antidepressants can ignite latent vulnerabilities to hypomania. Therefore, should we find data that point to such a vulnerability (e.g., a pattern of Rorschach thought disorder scores), we can call the prescriber's attention to this matter, so they can take it into account in their decision-making. Along similar lines, given some research that stimulant medications can exacerbate psychosis and thought disorder (D. L. Levy et al., 1993), we would offer a heads-up about a child who meets criteria for ADHD but who also exhibited signs of disordered thinking on testing.

Third, we can raise for consideration possible *classes* of medication (but, again, not specific medications) for the prescriber to contemplate. These could include, for instance, mood stabilizers for certain kinds of severe emotional dysregulation; antipsychotics for vulnerability to lapses in logical reasoning, coherent thinking, and attunement to reality; and stimulant versus nonstimulant medication for ADHD symptoms.

[4]There are relatively rare exceptions in some states and other jurisdictions, where psychologists can seek training to obtain limited prescription privileges.

Fourth, in some cases, when a pediatrician is managing the medication for a patient whom we find to be highly complex, we can respectfully suggest that the patient be evaluated and followed by a child and adolescent psychiatrist. And fifth, we can call attention to dynamics apt to affect the young patient's ability to ally with the prescribing clinician, which is associated with better outcomes, even in pharmacotherapy (De Nadai et al., 2017; Peterson, 2019). The topic of therapeutic alliance is addressed further in the next chapter, which focuses on factors affecting engagement and collaboration.

13 FACTORS AFFECTING THERAPEUTIC ENGAGEMENT AND COLLABORATION

Beyond recommending specific treatment modalities in their reports (described in Chapter 12), assessors offer added value addressing implications for optimizing therapeutic engagement and collaboration. This is part of the process of treatment-centered diagnosis (Bram & Peebles, 2014; Peebles, 2012). Implications along these lines include taking into account patient and family preferences, variables bearing on therapeutic alliance, cultural factors, the patient's cognitive profile/learning style, narcissistic vulnerability/shame proneness, and potential sources of resistance. Each of these considerations is briefly summarized here, although details on how to assess them are elaborated elsewhere (see Bram, 2013; Bram & Peebles, 2014). Note, though, that it is not expected that each of these areas necessarily be addressed in every test report. Rather, that depends on the nature of the data—what information is most relevant to the patient and will be potentially useful to their treaters.

https://doi.org/10.1037/0000430-014
Psychological Assessment of Emotional Dysregulation in Children and Adolescents: The Bipolar Spectrum and Beyond, by A. D. Bram
Copyright © 2025 by the American Psychological Association. All rights reserved.

PATIENT AND PARENT PREFERENCES

Taking into account patient preferences in treatment planning is a pillar of evidence-based practice for psychologists (APA [American Psychological Association] Presidential Task Force on Evidence-Based Practice, 2006). This respectful, collaborative, and humane premise has voluminous empirical support for adults in psychotherapy: Meta-analytic research has indicated that psychotherapeutic treatments that adhere to patients' own preferences are associated with fewer dropouts and are more favorable outcome (Swift et al., 2018). Preferences encompass activity level of the therapist, characteristics of the therapist (e.g., age, ethnicity, gender identity), and modality of therapy (e.g., individual versus group; cognitive behavior therapy [CBT] versus psychodynamic; Swift et al., 2018). There is not yet an equivalent literature on the effect of kids' psychotherapy preferences on engagement and outcome. However, tuning into this variable for patients of any age—including children and adolescents—is consistent with the contemporary zeitgeist valuing patient-centered care (Langer et al., 2021). Langer et al. have offered one version of a brief, youth self-report preference questionnaire, this one specific to the treatment of depression (see Appendix B in their article).

Although there is also less of a literature on parent/caregiver preferences for child and adolescent treatment, it makes clinical sense that caregivers will be more likely to engage in and/or support their children's participation in a treatment approach that they find compelling (He et al., 2018; Langer et al., 2021; Lewin et al., 2014). Depending on the child's or adolescent's age and developmental level, caregiver preferences may be especially important to consider. Langer et al. (2021) also have shared the parent-report version of their preference measure referable to treatment of depression (see Appendix A in their article).

In a psychological assessment, the assessor can incorporate patient and parent preferences in two nonmutually exclusive ways. First, preferences can be queried as part of the evaluation. However, unlike psychotherapy for adults for whom a measure of patient preferences exists (i.e., Cooper-Norcross Inventory of Preferences; M. Cooper & Norcross, 2016), no validated, clinically applicable tools are available to assess treatment preference of children and adolescents and their parents/caregivers. Therefore, this aspect of assessment is informal, such as inquiring into past and ongoing experiences of treatment, asking what was helpful, and inquiring what they wish would be different. Focused questions can be asked about therapist activity level, therapist characteristics, and different treatment modalities. Second, even if preferences are not addressed as part of the evaluation, in the "Diagnostic

Summary and Treatment Implications" section of the test report, the assessor can look for opportunities to describe competing treatment pathways, allowing the patient and their caregivers and current treaters to consider and pursue their preferences.

An example of offering competing treatment pathways comes from the case of Jillian, an adolescent referred for evaluation to better understand factors related to reported intense, angry conflict with her parents, which the parents wondered might be an indicator of depression or even a bipolar condition.[1] The assessment revealed (a) that arguments and outbursts with her parents were typically elicited by their pushing her toward greater social involvement with peers, not recognizing her previously undiagnosed severe social anxiety; (b) her internal conflict about the developmental task of separation-individuation (Mahler et al., 1975); and (c) underdevelopment of particular aspects of emotional regulation, that is, the abilities to effectively notice, acknowledge, and communicate her anxiety, anger, and other aversive feelings. In addition to recommending parent guidance to help them better understand and navigate their daughter's social anxiety and developmental concerns, I highlighted possible directions for the individual therapy, allowing the patient to exert her own preferences.

In the "Diagnostic Summary and Treatment Implications" section of the test report, I wrote,

> There are two levels of psychological work, not mutually exclusive, that could benefit Jillian. The first would involve teaching her about social anxiety and providing her with cognitive (modifying thoughts that fuel anxiety) and behavioral (e.g., how to approach avoided situations; ways of being more assertive) strategies. This is a more educational, directed, time-limited approach which would require less emotional opening up and relational commitment compared to the second level.
>
> Working at the second level would involve providing Jillian with an opportunity to more fully access, accept, and express her emotions. It would aim to help her better understand and gradually modify how her mind works, how she manages feelings and solves problems, and her patterns of interpersonal interactions. This approach is more open-ended timewise but would allow greater opportunity to think carefully about and reflect on her experience growing up, what kind of person she would like to be, what kinds of relationships she would like to have, and how she is similar and different from her family, among other such things. Although working at this second level is likely to be more challenging than the first, the data from this evaluation suggest that Jillian has the intellectual, verbal, and emotional strengths to make productive use of such an approach.

[1]Jillian's evaluation is discussed further in Chapter 18.

> As noted above, the two approaches are not mutually exclusive. One possibility, for example, might be to begin with the first on a time-limited basis, see what it feels like and whether it benefits her, and later consider whether to continue and delve deeper into the second level. Other possibilities of sequencing or integration, depending on her preferences, can also be considered.

As it turned out, Jillian chose the first alternative involving the CBT approach to her social anxiety. She made excellent use of that treatment over the course of about 2 years, and she was able to transition to college with much more social confidence and competence and development of greater emotional awareness and expressiveness. The combination of (a) a brief course of parent guidance providing psychoeducation about social anxiety and developmental tasks of adolescents and (b) her engagement in weekly therapy fairly quickly mitigated the volatile parent–child interactions. Interestingly, a few years later, as college graduation approached, when Jillian was experiencing anxiety and uncertainty about the direction of her life, she returned to therapy, wishing to work at the deeper, relational level that had also been broached in the test report.

THERAPEUTIC ALLIANCE

Often overlooked in psychological assessment are implications for the therapeutic alliance, that is, the patient's capacity to collaborate with the therapist (and other treaters) toward shared goals (Bram, 2010, 2013; Bram & Peebles, 2014). But assessing capacity for therapeutic alliance—including elucidating conditions under which it is variable—is crucial because a strong alliance mitigates dropout/premature termination and is among the most robust predictors of psychotherapeutic outcome regardless of modality (Flückiger et al., 2018). This holds true for child and adolescent treatment (Gergov et al., 2021; Karver et al., 2018, 2019; van Benthem et al., 2020). Importantly, alliance has also been shown to be a predictor of treatment adherence and/or outcome in pharmacotherapy (e.g., De Nadai et al., 2017; Krupnick et al., 1996; Lohse et al., 2021).

As detailed elsewhere (Bram, 2010, 2012, 2013, 2018b; Chapter 6 of Bram & Peebles, 2014), the patient–examiner relationship in assessment can be conceptualized as a "screen test" for psychotherapy (Shectman & Harty, 1986, p. 281), rife with data about conditions under which collaboration is facilitated or impeded. Additionally, data about implicit relational paradigms from performance-based measures, such as the Rorschach (e.g., Rorschach Performance Assessment System [R-PAS]; Meyer et al., 2011) and Thematic Apperception Test (TAT; Murray, 1943), Children's Apperception Test (CAT; Bellak

& Bellak, 1949), or other narrative task, can be used for inference-making about conditions associated with more or less trust, curiosity, and acceptance of help (Bram & Peebles, 2014). For an elaborated case illustration of how such findings from assessment were instrumental to subsequent therapeutic engagement of a highly dysregulated and mistrustful adolescent, see Bram (2010). An edited volume by Castro-Blanco and Karver (2010) is less focused on assessment per se but details strategies for fostering collaborative alliances with dysregulation-prone adolescents who are otherwise challenging to engage therapeutically.

When the assessment data indicate that our young patient is not inclined to readily collaborate and engage in needed treatment, it is important that in our test report and verbal feedback to caregivers and treaters, we do not gloss over this finding. In contemporary clinical practice, it is not uncommon for assessors and other practitioners to reflexively recommend a particular evidence-based psychoeducational/skill-building package of treatment because the patient meets criteria for a certain category in the fifth edition, text revision, of the *Diagnostic and Statistical Manual of Mental Disorders* (*DSM-5-TR*; American Psychiatric Association, 2022). However, without acknowledging the patient's readiness to engage in that treatment risks not only overpromising but missing an opportunity to clarify that the initial treatment task will likely need to focus on gradually developing trust and safety within the therapeutic relationship, something that itself can take time.

Data from the patient–examiner relationship and performance-based personality measures can be valuable in our alerting therapists and other treaters about conditions and interventions apt to cultivate versus impede our young patient's willingness to accept help, trust, be curious, play, and share about their lives. To name just a few, such conditions and interventions might include asking or not asking direct questions, being curious and opening discussions about their interests and strengths, providing various kinds of reinforcement, offering opportunities for expression through art or music, or allowing for more physical movement in sessions. Explicating in our test report what worked and what did not in fostering the collaboration necessary to complete—and hopefully also deepen—the evaluation can provide treaters with a blueprint for their work with our young patient. This topic of engaging children and adolescents who are not initially ready to engage collaboratively in an otherwise recommended kind of treatment is further addressed later this chapter in the section "Narcissistic Vulnerabilities/Shame Proneness."

Depending on the patient's age and the frequency, severity, and impairment associated with their emotional dysregulation, assessment findings of significant barriers to a therapeutic alliance can point to a treatment plan that emphasizes (a) parent/caregiver interventions rather than direct work with the child or adolescent (see Chapter 12); (b) group interventions (see Chapter 12); and/or (c) therapeutic interventions folded into the child's services at school (see Chapter 14), so they are not required to see an outside therapist as well.

Another treatment consideration for adolescents for whom the assessment data portend difficulties engaging and collaborating in treatment involves motivational interviewing (Naar & Suarez, 2021). *Motivational interviewing* is

> a client-centered yet directive approach for facilitating change by helping people to resolve ambivalence and find intrinsic reasons for making needed behavior change. . . . It is particularly applicable when low intrinsic motivation for change is an obstacle. Rather than advocating for and suggesting methods for change, this approach seeks to elicit the client's own goals, values, and motivation for change and to negotiate appropriate methods for achieving it. (APA, n.d.-b)

Recent research has shown motivational interviewing as a pretreatment, preparatory intervention to be a promising approach to enhance treatment engagement and outcome with adolescents. For example, motivational interviewing has been demonstrated to improve adolescents' self-reported readiness for and subsequent attendance of an outpatient CBT group (Dean et al., 2016), attendance of outpatient sessions following discharge from inpatient psychiatric hospitalization (Chiappetta et al., 2018), and outpatient adherence to antidepressant and mood-stabilizing medications (Hamrin & Iennaco, 2017). Note that it is not clear yet from the published research, though, how effective motivational interviewing is in reaching adolescents who have profound struggles with basic trust. Additionally, as framed at the outset of Chapter 11 regarding any intervention that assessors formally recommend, we need to be sure that in our patient's community, there are available clinicians with training and experience in motivational interviewing with challenging-to-engage adolescents.[2]

In some instances, such as when an adolescent is prone to severe and impairing dysregulation, major impediments to trust and collaboration with a therapist—particularly when the anticipated effect of parent/caregiver

[2]There does not appear to be a literature on the integration of psychological assessment feedback and motivational interviewing, and I have not known of assessment colleagues trained in motivational interviewing, but this could be an interesting integration for assessors to develop. Gorske and Smith (2009) and Suarez and Martinez-Kaig (2022) have written about neuropsychological assessment feedback and motivational interviewing with adults.

and school-based interventions is less hopeful—may mean that outpatient treatment is apt to be insufficient to reach them in any kind of meaningful and timely way. Instead, the assessor might recommend a more intensive level of care involving immersion with a peer group in a therapeutic milieu (i.e., inpatient, residential, wilderness, and day hospital treatments described in Chapter 11; also see Crouch, 1998, for discussion of therapeutic milieu).

TRANSFERENCE AND COUNTERTRANSFERENCE PARADIGMS

Beyond commenting on capacity for and conditions-under-which associated with therapeutic alliance, we can also use test findings to explicate specific challenges in emotional and relational dynamics anticipated to unfold in how our young patient and their treaters experience and interact with one another. This is the realm of transference and countertransference, which I have previously described thusly:

> Transferences reflect the unique lenses through which a patient is inclined to implicitly view the therapist. Such individualized "spin" on perceptions and expectations of the therapist is based on the patient's (actual and fantasied) experiences with early caregivers and other important figures throughout life. Countertransference is conceptualized broadly as the therapist's total emotional reaction to the patient (Kernberg, 1965), included but not limited to the responses to the patient's transferences. . . . Even in ostensibly non-psychodynamic treatments that do not emphasize understanding transference–countertransference dynamics (e.g., CBT), recognizing what might play out emotionally and interpersonally between patient and therapist can guide clinical decision making. (Bram, 2013, p. 327)

Clues to likely possible transference and countertransference patterns can often be found in patient–examiner and other performance-based data. Consider, for example, Charlie, a young adolescent referred for evaluation because of significant emotional dysregulation manifested in intense outbursts, impulsivity, and aggression. Although Charlie was actually compliant with the evaluator, his Rorschach responses included "people kicking each other and hitting each other"; "people being executed . . . with a guillotine . . . as if they were misunderstood"; "people falling . . . as if they'd been pushed over"; "animal being knocked over . . . as if it's been hunted"; "someone running . . . as if they were being chased"; "bad-intentioned people trying to stop a truck . . . as if they were going to use it for something they shouldn't use it for"; and "a chain holding down the innocent . . . as if they've been wrongly imprisoned." It was possible to infer that even if Charlie initially interacted pleasantly and cooperatively with his new therapist, he would bring these implicit relational expectations of hostility and control to his experience of his new therapist. Without some awareness of this underlying transference disposition, the therapist might feel blindsided and personally attacked when Charlie expresses with intensity feeling misunderstood and mistreated by the therapist. Although awareness and anticipation of this transference–countertransference dynamic will not necessarily mitigate its enactment in treatment, the heads-up of its possibility offered in the test report enables the therapist to sooner recognize it, take it less personally, and regain their own ability to reflect rather than purely enact.

COGNITIVE PROFILE/LEARNING STYLE

Commonly, the evaluation of an emotionally dysregulated child or adolescent involves some neurocognitive—if not a full neuropsychological—assessment. Seldom, though, do assessors extrapolate in the report from (a) findings relating to learning style and cognitive strengths and weaknesses to (b) how a therapist might tailor their psychotherapeutic interventions.

For example, an adolescent with a well-developed capacity for abstract reasoning can be reached with metaphor, whereas a patient who does not will benefit from more concrete explanations. A young patient with slower processing speed will benefit from being allowed ample time to take in and respond to the therapist. A clinician working with child or adolescent who displays challenges in attention, working memory, and executive function may need to make accommodations (e.g., repetition, writing down key points for them, assisting with organization of handouts, movement breaks, making modifications to between-session assignments), especially if the modality is a more psychoeducational and skill-building one. Because therapy of all kinds involves learning, to the extent that assessors spell out how clinicians can deliver their interventions in ways that account for their patient's learning style, the better the chance of effective therapeutic engagement and internalization (Bram & Peebles, 2014).

NARCISSISTIC VULNERABILITIES/SHAME PRONENESS

A patient's ability to engage in treatment is often a function of the degree of shame they experience about their struggles and need for help (Black et al., 2013; see Chapter 7 in Bram & Peebles, 2014). To the extent that a person prone to emotional dysregulation has suffered early relational trauma, they are apt to be more vulnerable to experiencing shame (Fowke et al., 2012).

But one does not have had to experienced “capital T” trauma to be shame-prone. An accumulation of wounds to self-esteem—narcissistic injuries—of various kinds over the course of development can also contribute. Clinical experience indicates that young (and older) patients who are prone to shame have a more difficult time readily engaging in skill-building treatments, especially if those treatments typically involve naming the *Diagnostic and Statistical Manual of Mental Disorders* (*DSM*) diagnosis for the patient (e.g., “You have . . . [bipolar disorder, oppositional defiant disorder, borderline personality disorder, obsessive-compulsive disorder, etc.]).”[3]

Many highly dysregulated youngsters are—based on symptoms and *DSM* diagnosis—ostensibly textbook candidates for various kinds of CBT protocols. Yet being told so directly that they “have a problem” and that the clinician possesses knowledge that they do not and thus has something to offer them activates self-consciousness, humiliation, and sensitivity to feeling one-downed. Thus, when assessment points to the child’s or adolescent’s vulnerability in this way, it can be valuable to suggest that therapy begin with a more relational focus, affirming strengths, promoting face-saving, and attending carefully to the therapeutic alliance, particularly the need to repair inevitable ruptures in the alliance (Safran et al., 2011). Often, but not always, the patient may be more amenable to psychoeducation about their condition and associated skill-building later, that is, after cultivating comfort and trust in the therapeutic relationship.

Data from the patient–examiner interaction and performance-based measures (e.g., Rorschach [R-PAS; Meyer et al., 2011], TAT [Murray, 1943] or

[3]Although little has been written on the subject, it is not uncommon for assessors—as well as for therapists and prescribers—to experience dilemmas about whether—and if so, when—to share *DSM* diagnoses with kids. Because we have no hard-and-fast rules for resolving such dilemmas, decisions need to be case-by-case in thoughtful collaboration with parents/caregivers and current treaters.

Based on clinical experience, I offer the following considerations to guide such decision making, each of which can be evaluated in terms of pros and cons: (a) the patient’s age/developmental maturity and the extent to which naming the *DSM* diagnosis for them (b) furthers the aims of treatment; (c) is important to the patient themselves (although it is useful to learn what it means to them to know the diagnosis); (d) is apt to evoke shame, self-criticism, and shutting down; and (e) risks contributing to their oversimplified, incurious, and unreflective way of thinking about and understanding themselves (e.g., “because I have ADHD” as a reflexive explanation for all kinds of interpersonal difficulties). If the decision is ultimately to disclose a diagnosis, assessors can aim to present and describe it with age-appropriate psychoeducation tailored to the patient’s learning style (see section “Cognitive Profile/Learning Style” earlier this chapter) and embedded in acknowledgment of their strengths. Also crucial is allowing the child or adolescent opportunities to ask questions and share their emotional reaction during or after the formal feedback session.

CAT [Bellak & Bellak, 1949], and Wechsler tests [see Chapter 6]) are useful in illuminating a child's or adolescent's vulnerability to experience shame as well as conditions under which it is exacerbated versus mitigated (addressed in Chapter 6; also see Bram & Peebles, 2014, Chapter 7). There are also both self-report (Novin & Rieffe, 2015; Simonds et al., 2016) and narrative/performance-based measures (Cradock O'Leary et al., 2020; Thurston & Cradock O'Leary, 2009) to assess shame that can potentially be incorporated into our test battery.

CULTURAL FACTORS

In formulating and offering implications for treatment, it is also a tenet of nuanced evidence-based practice to consider how cultural factors might inform the recommendations themselves or how they are understood and received by treaters, caregivers, and the patient (APA Presidential Task Force, 2006). Because the focus here is on evaluation and treatment of emotional dysregulation, it is useful to recognize that there is cultural variability in attitudes toward whether and how emotions are acknowledged and expressed (Ford & Mauss, 2015). For instance, research has shown that (a) in cultures that place a premium on independence, such as those of North America and Western Europe, emotional expression is associated with well-being and thus valued; whereas (b) in those favoring interdependence, such as many countries in East Asia, emotional suppression is psychologically adaptive and valued (summarized by B. Q. Ford & Mauss, 2015; Tsai, 2022). Ford and Mauss (2015) have cautioned us, though, that

> it is not simply membership in a cultural group that should shape whether someone is motivated to regulate their emotions. Rather, it is the *extent to which an individual is oriented toward a particular culture's values* [emphasis added] that should predict their emotion regulation. (p. 2)

Also helpful for assessors to hold in mind are research findings indicating that people who have immigrated from one culture to another "report patterns of emotional experience that were more similar to those reported by members of the host cultures" (De Leersnyder et al., 2013, p. 2).

Imagine, for example, that we have evaluated an otherwise quiet and emotionally constricted young adolescent who, in response to frustration and perceived failure, is prone to intermittent aggressive outbursts at school and home. Through the testing, we have clarified that they not only possess an underdeveloped emotional vocabulary but that they are reactive to feelings that do not register in their conscious awareness. A seemingly obvious treatment implication involves interventions to help the adolescent become more emotionally aware and verbally emotive. But think about what this suggestion might mean in the context of a family's adhering to cultural values that do not look so favorably on emotional expressiveness. In the role of assessor, at the very least, in the report and other feedback, our task is to explicate and empathize with the dilemma: On the one hand, there is reason to expect that enhancing the adolescent's emotional awareness and communication will mitigate the potential for outbursts because they will be better to articulate their frustrations and ask for help before reaching the point of explosiveness; on the other, bolstering and encouraging the adolescent's ongoing emotional expressiveness might be experienced as unsettling and unwelcome at home. Although we may not have a solution to the dilemma, having spelled it out, the referring treater and family are in a proactive position to think through and problem-solve how to navigate it together.

POTENTIAL SOURCES OF RESISTANCE: WHAT MIGHT GET IN THE WAY?

Even when a patient or family has strong conscious intentions and motivation to change, inevitably, some factors make such change challenging. This is just an expectable part of human nature, not in itself pathological. Broadly speaking, resistances to change can be normalized and conceptualized as anything that gets in the way of progress (Bram, 2013; Freud, 1900/1953a). Among other sources, resistances can involve competing conscious or unconscious motivations on the part of patient and/or caregiver(s), dynamics within the family system, influences of the peer group, and variables at school and within the broader culture. Based on our assessment data, if we identify likely sources of resistance, we can explicate this in the "Diagnostic Summary and Treatment Implications" section of the test report so that treaters and patient can anticipate and address them proactively and/or when it becomes apparent.

For example, we may find evidence that an adolescent may be reluctant, consciously or unconsciously, to relinquish their aggressive outbursts because of the sense of power and control it provides them when they otherwise feel ineffectual or helpless. Or that our young patient's emotional dysregulation serves some function in the family system, such as keeping the focus off of the parents' otherwise fragile marital relationship and uniting them through crisis. Or that accepting help to ameliorate their dysregulation and unhealthy ways of coping (e.g., through addictive behaviors, eating disorder, other self-harm) risks losing a peer group that is based on such difficulties in common.

14 IMPLICATIONS FOR SCHOOL

The emotional dysregulation suffered by children and adolescents is apt to affect their engagement in school socially, emotionally, and/or academically. After all, aside from sleep, children and adolescents spend more time at school than in any other activity (Hall & Nielsen, 2020). So, there is a good chance that if emotional dysregulation is a concern, it will play out in some way at school, in completing homework, or getting ready for or anticipating the next school day. Among the assessor's tasks are clarifying (a) to what extent—and, if so, the ways in which—emotional dysregulation disrupts such engagement and (b) how and under what conditions experiences in school exacerbate or mitigate dysregulation. This understanding can then be translated into implications for school to be taken into account in an individualized education program (IEP) or 504 Plan.[1] This chapter addresses

[1]Based in the Individuals with Disabilities Education Act (IDEA; 1990), an IEP allows a child identified with a disability to receive special instruction and accommodations in school. Based in Section 504 of the Rehabilitation Act of 1973 (as amended, 2008), a 504 plan allows a child with a disability to receive in-school accommodations (see *IDEA: Individuals with Disabilities Education Act*, n.d., for details on these U.S. federal laws).

https://doi.org/10.1037/0000430-015
Psychological Assessment of Emotional Dysregulation in Children and Adolescents: The Bipolar Spectrum and Beyond, by A. D. Bram
Copyright © 2025 by the American Psychological Association. All rights reserved.

(a) a range of specific school-based accommodations and services that an assessor might recommend; (b) the value of being familiar with special education law; and (c) anticipating the patient/student's experience of the recommendations and teachers', school clinicians', and special educators' experience of the patient/student.

CONSIDERATIONS FOR SCHOOL-BASED ACCOMMODATIONS AND SERVICES

Some young patients who come to us for evaluation will already have an IEP or 504 plan, so based on our findings, we can recommend specific modifications or suggest intensifying interventions from a 504 plan to an IEP. Other patients will not have such a formal plan in place, and, if applicable, we can support parents/caregivers' and treaters' advocacy for the appropriate plan, including specifying the kinds of services to seek. To consider an IEP, school districts are required to complete their own multidisciplinary evaluations, often involving some combination of psychological, psychoeducational, speech-language, occupational therapy, functional behavior, and/or other assessments. In our role as an outside evaluator, if we believe that our patient requires accommodations or services provided by the school, we can encourage the parents/caregivers to make a formal written request that the school district initiate such an evaluation. Our findings complement those of the district, and with appropriate consent, we can collaborate with the school psychologist to coordinate what tests are considered for administration by the district, which disciplines to enlist for their evaluation, and what kinds of services are needed by the student.

We might recommend a wide range of accommodations (in an IEP or 504 plan) and services (in an IEP) for a school district to offer a child or adolescent prone to emotional dysregulation. Some examples of accommodations include preferential seating in class for a distractible child apt to get overly silly, loud, and disruptive when trying to impress nearby friends; modification of or reduction in homework assignments for a student who becomes frustrated and angry when it is time to complete them at home; or extended time to complete exams and standardized tests for students whose performance anxiety, obsessional style, or slow processing speed contributes to high levels of emotional distress and physical self-punishment when they are unable to complete such tasks.

Above and beyond accommodations, examples of special education services—roughly from less to more intensive—include the child's or adolescent's regular meetings with the school counselor, psychologist, or social worker; participation in a coping skills or social skills group; opportunities to complete homework assignments with support in a resource room during the school day; meeting with (or consultation for staff by) a speech therapist and/or occupational therapist; a 1:1 aide in the classroom or on the playground; or placement in a therapeutic classroom within or outside of the district.

It is encouraging that in recent years, schools have been placing greater emphasis on integrating social–emotional learning (SEL) into curricula spanning the preschool to high school years. A meta-analysis by Durlak et al. (2022) involving an estimated 1 million students across grade levels showed that "[SEL] programs have consistent, positive impacts on a broad range of student outcomes including increased SEL skills, attitudes, prosocial behaviors, and academic achievement and decreased conduct problems and emotional distress" (p. 765). So, it is now more common than in the past for classroom teachers, special educators, and school clinicians, to be attuned to students' vulnerabilities to emotional dysregulation and to have some training in how to embed appropriate skill-building interventions within the school day.

The Zones of Regulation™ (Kuypers, 2011; see also https://zonesofregulation.com/) is one popular example of an empirically supported SEL curriculum that emphasizes helping children and adolescents develop emotional regulation skills. Although many schools have been applying this kind of SEL program within the regular classroom, when our evaluation points to our young patient's strong need for intervention to bolster their capacity for emotional regulation, we can advocate that it be delivered more intensively by special educators or school clinicians in small group and/or individual formats.

Especially for our child and adolescent patients whose proneness to emotional dysregulation results in frequent disciplinary consequences, we can also recommend that the school consider training staff in collaborative problem-solving (CPS; Greene, 2021). CPS was discussed previously in the context of parent/caregiver interventions in Chapter 12, and school-based application of CPS in schools is detailed in Greene (2016) and Greene and Haynes (2021). Encouraging preliminary research support is cited in Greene and Winkler (2019). For additional information about the application of CPS in school settings, see the Lost at School website (https://lostatschool.org). Recall that CPS conceptualizes emotional dysregulation as a skills deficit to be understood and remediated rather than as willful disobedience to be corrected through reward and punishment. This reframing is of particular appeal given the alarming pattern that students from marginalized and socioeconomically disadvantaged backgrounds are more often subjected to harsh, countertherapeutic punishment than their White, cisgender, and otherwise more privileged counterparts (e.g., Amemiya et al., 2020; Lehmann et al.,

2022; N. A. Palmer & Greytak, 2017; Sabol et al., 2022). Advocating for an understanding of and approach to a student's problematic dysregulation through CPS holds the potential to help ameliorate a discouraging narrative about that student.[2]

Another potential recommendation is for our patient to participate in a school-based mentoring program (Herrera & Karcher, 2014). School-based mentoring involves an adult volunteer who receives training and supervision to meet weekly with the student at school during or after school hours. There is often flexibility in mentoring meetings to focus academically and/or social–emotionally. Ben-Eliyahu (2018) described specific ways that a mentor can support a young person who is struggling with emotional regulation, including helping them make healthy choices, more effectively focus their attention, reframe situations more adaptively, and access more healthy ways of coping. That said, for kids vulnerable to frequent and severe dysregulation or other clinically significant psychological/psychiatric/neurodevelopmental difficulties, school-based mentoring ought to be considered at most an adjunct to rather than a substitute for services provided by professional clinicians and special educators. Additionally, assessors would do well to be aware that meta-analytic studies of school-based mentorship programs show only small effect sizes for academic, behavioral, and social–emotional outcomes (summarized in Lyons & McQuillin, 2019). Of note, though, Lyons and

[2]Although less likely to be a recommendation included in our test report about an individual patient, it is useful for assessors to be aware that many schools in the United States have been adopting a federally funded, systemwide, research-supported, data-driven program as an alternative to a traditional punitive approach to students' problematic behaviors. Referred to as Positive Behavioral Interventions and Supports (PBIS; e.g., Harlacher & Rodriguez, 2017; see the PBIS website: https://www.pbis.org), this program has been shown reduce to racial inequities in school discipline (McIntosh et al., 2021). The foundation of PBIS includes clear behavioral expectations; building trusting teacher–student relationships; systematic reinforcement of appropriate behavior; and teaching strategies to bolster adaptive interpersonal, social problem-solving, conflict prevention/resolution, and emotional coping skills.

The program comprises three tiers: Tier 1 is universal, supporting all students by creating a safe, consistent, respectful, and affirming milieu for learning. Tier 2 provides support, typically in small groups, for students noted to be at risk of academic, social, or emotional struggles. Tier 3 offers intensive, individualized intervention for students who are having more profound difficulties. The young patients prone to emotional dysregulation whom we evaluate often benefit from interventions at Tier 3. So, if such a patient attends a school with a formal PBIS program in place, we can advocate for the necessity of Tier 3 interventions if they are not already in place. Students do not necessarily have to have an IEP to qualify for Tier 3. However, if our patient is receiving Tier 3 services but does not have an IEP, we can make the case that the student be formally assessed by the district for IEP eligibility. Optimally, PBIS and IEPs can be implemented synergistically (Farmer, n.d.).

McQuillin's (2019) own meta-analyses clarify that outcomes of mentorship programs improve with the student-rated quality of the student–mentor relationship, and this is more so the case for behavioral compared to academic outcomes. Thus, if we do suggest a school-based mentorship program, we can emphasize the importance of the school's making a thoughtful student–mentor match and continuing to monitor the patient/student's subjective experience of their relationship with the mentor.

PROVIDING CONTEXT FOR ASSESSORS: FAMILIARITY WITH SPECIAL EDUCATION LAW

Although details are beyond the scope of this book, it is valuable that assessors who evaluate children and adolescents have some familiarity with special education law (e.g., Laviano & Swanson, 2017; P. W. P. Wright & Wright, 2006, 2007). We can be more effective translating our assessment findings into implications for supporting our young patient at school to the extent we are aware of the rights and services to which our patient is entitled. For example, according to the Individuals With Disabilities Education Act (IDEA; 1990), services provided by the school district do not have to occur at school (P. W. P. Wright & Wright, 2007). In one instance, based on the assessor's recommendation, a special education team added to an IEP a plan to send the school social worker to the home of an elementary school–aged child who regularly suffered tantrums in the morning associated with anxiety, panic, and incipient school refusal. Daily for several weeks, the social worker provided guidance to the parents and helped problem-solve, deescalate the child, listen to the child's concerns, and help them leave the house and physically enter the school building.

Some school districts convey to parents/caregivers that if the student is performing academically at grade level, regardless of their social, or emotional, or learning challenges, they are ineligible for consideration for an IEP and sometimes not even a 504 plan. Or if a student's disability is not manifesting severely at school—such as the clinically familiar scenario of a child who holds it together emotionally during the school day but rages in the evening when it is time to complete homework—they are ineligible. These and similar dismissive tropes are not true. In fact, a child or adolescent is eligible if they are identified as having any kind of *disability*, defined as "impairment that substantially affects one or more major life activities" (P. W. P. Wright & Wright, 2002, p. 353). This is where including dimensional measures of level of impairment—as described in Chapter 4—can be vital to advocacy. Students struggling with emotional regulation are potentially eligible under the official categories of emotional disturbance, autism, or other health impaired (other health impaired includes students diagnosed with attention-deficit/hyperactivity disorder, depression, or an anxiety disorder). This is, of course, in addition to eligibility that the same student might have for a physical disability or specific learning disability.

Thus, especially if the parents/caregivers have already received pushback from the district or anticipate this, one recommendation to consider including in the test report is for the parents/caregivers to reach out to their state's disability rights center for advice and advocacy support (see National Disability Rights Network, n.d., for an online list of such agencies in each state of the United States). Along similar lines, books and online resources about parental advocacy can also be suggested in the report, such as P. W. P. Wright and Wright's (2006) second edition of *From Emotions to Advocacy: The Special Education Advocacy Survival Guide* or Laviano and Swanson's (2017) *Your Special Education Rights: What Your School District Isn't Telling You*. And depending on complexities of the case, receptivity of the district, and other factors, the assessor might also, or instead, suggest consultation with a special education advocate or attorney. In many instances, though, the assessor may choose to convey these types of suggestions verbally to the parents/caregivers rather than include them in the report that will be shared with the district. Placing these recommendations explicitly in the report version to be viewed by the district risks potentially igniting an unnecessarily adversarial relationship between the private assessor and the district's team, which may not help the family in making their case.

Clinically and legally (in accordance with the Americans with Disabilities Act of 1990), students benefit from provision of services in the *least restrictive environment*, which refers to "the requirement to educate [children with disabilities] with children who are not disabled *to the maximum extent possible* [emphasis added]" (P. W. P. Wright & Wright, 2002, p. 355). Our challenge as assessors is to use our findings to ascertain implications that are consistent with our patient's abilities and needs and meet the criteria of being least restrictive. Although it is not routine to recommend that a student be placed in a separate, specialized therapeutic setting (especially at the residential level), and we do not do this without considerable thought and the weighing of various options, there are instances in which such a recommendation may be necessary. Because of the expense of funding therapeutic placements, especially those outside the district, school districts do not often readily agreed to them. So, the findings from our evaluation, the clarity of our report, and our subsequent advocacy are often critical pieces of the family's making the case to the school district for such a clinical/educational need.

ANTICIPATING THE STUDENT'S EXPERIENCE OF SCHOOL-BASED RECOMMENDATIONS AND THE SCHOOL STAFF'S EXPERIENCE OF THE STUDENT

Another important way that assessors can speak to implications for school is by using the evaluation findings to anticipate how the child or adolescent will experience the suggestion and implementation of accommodations and services. Knowing something in-depth about the young person's self-perception and self-esteem as well as their attitude toward receiving help will inform how the recommendations and interventions can be presented to and will be received by them. To the extent possible, such implications ought to be explicated both in the report and in communications with parents/caregivers and the team at school.

Consider the evaluation of 15-year-old Marcus over the summer before the start of his freshman year of high school. Marcus had an early history of attachment trauma and was referred for psychological assessment because of more frequent aggressive outbursts at home and having failed most of his classes the previous academic year. Before that, his grades had been mostly Bs and Cs, and he never had formal academic support at school. Among other things, the test findings underscored Marcus's uneven cognitive functioning, significant attentional and executive functioning weakness, and, as I wrote in the "Sense of Self" section, "Self-esteem more tenuous than he is apt to acknowledge. . . . In general, Marcus is apt to cover over, try to justify, and externalize areas of insecurity, such as when he is wrong or does not know something." Thus, in the "Diagnostic Summary and Treatment Implications" section in the paragraph specific to school, I highlighted the importance of the school district's following up with their own assessment of Marcus's eligibility for an IEP while also emphasizing that

> in the event that the district's evaluations do point to the need for an IEP, it will be crucial that interventions are presented to Marcus and applied in a manner aiming to minimize his shame and optimize his ability to save face among his peers.

There is value in anticipating how teachers, school clinicians, and special educators are apt to experience our patient, and when possible, help them to reframe their understanding in a more accurate and empathic way. An example comes from the evaluation of 9-year-old Heather. Patient–examiner data (see Chapter 6) included (a) her repeatedly grabbing a book out of her backpack to read while I attempted to transition from one Rorschach card to the next and (b) my efforts to refocus her on the task. Heather's Rorschach structural scores indicated her meaningful engagement (e.g., average range Rorschach Performance Assessment System [Meyer et al., 2011] Complexity score) while her responses themselves were laden with traumatic imagery. My inference was reflected in the "Diagnostic Summary and Treatment Implications" section of the report thusly: "It is useful to highlight for teachers and others working with Heather at school that behaviors that can appear disrespectful and off-task often reflect her desperate efforts to self-regulate as opposed to willful defiance."

15 ADDITIONAL CONSIDERATIONS FOR FOLLOW-UP EVALUATIONS AND TREATMENT ADJUNCTS

The findings from our psychological assessment can illuminate the need for follow-up evaluations from specialists in other disciplines as well as implications for interventions adjunctive to the primary treatments recommended. Whether or not and to what extent such considerations are included in the "Diagnostic Summary and Treatment Implications" section of the test report depends on the particular child or adolescent.

FOLLOW-UP EVALUATIONS

Assessors might suggest a myriad of potential follow-up evaluations, but it is imperative that we home in on what our specific patient and family needs and make such recommendations judiciously. In doing so, we highlight just how high priority each need is, from urgent to something to hold in mind over the next year or two; the timing of an acute need depends on the unfolding of various contingencies. Again, we want to be cautious about not inundating what is already likely to be a beleaguered family with expectations that they embark on what could ultimately be experienced as multiple goose chases.

https://doi.org/10.1037/0000430-016
Psychological Assessment of Emotional Dysregulation in Children and Adolescents: The Bipolar Spectrum and Beyond, by A. D. Bram
Copyright © 2025 by the American Psychological Association. All rights reserved.

Although far from exhaustive, the following sections contain examples of types of follow-up evaluations.

School District's Multidisciplinary Evaluation

As noted in Chapter 14, we might recommend that the school district follow up with their own multidisciplinary evaluation to assess for the appropriateness of an individualized education program (IEP). There is often some urgency to this, especially if the student is really struggling to function at school or is on the verge of school refusal or expulsion. We can alert caregivers of the legal necessity to put this request to the district in writing and the value of delivering this request in person and obtaining a time-stamped receipt.

Neuropsychological Assessment

We may also highlight the need for a thorough or focused neuropsychological evaluation, especially if the assessor is not trained as a neuropsychologist themselves. This might be the case, for instance, if our data on the Wechsler Intelligence Scale for Children–Fifth Edition (Wechsler, 2014) point to previously unrecognized cognitive unevenness, distractibility, or memory dysfunction, any or all of which raise questions about some kind of learning disability. If the school district's evaluation is in process, it may be advantageous to deferring the private neuropsychological evaluation until the school's report are complete, so the private evaluation can further clarify or expand on findings highlighted by or unelaborated by the district's evaluation.

Neurology Consultation

Occasionally, our exploration of conditions under which our young patient is apt to become dysregulated reveals seemingly anomalous symptoms, such a severe headache, dizziness, or memory lapse. Although we can test hypotheses ourselves about these symptoms—such as by administering scales to assess for dissociation (see Chapter 9)—it also behooves us to retain alternative hypotheses that can only be evaluated by other, more qualified professionals. With the symptoms described here, we can recommend referral to a pediatric neurologist to determine whether the dysregulation might be, at least in part, associated with seizure activity.

Consultation With a Sleep Specialist

As described in Chapter 9, especially in regard to assessing emotional dysregulation that looks like attention-deficit/hyperactivity disorder (ADHD), it is useful for us to undertake some screening about sleep characteristics (e.g., bedtime, latency to fall asleep, snoring, limb movements, nighttime awakening, restfulness of sleep). Such screening can reveal possible indicators of a sleep disorder, which could account for the daytime distractibility and dysregulation, which we realize would need to be more rigorously evaluated by a pediatric sleep specialist, often a physician who is a pulmonologist.[1] This physician would make a determination of the necessity of an overnight sleep study.

Evaluations by a Occupational Therapist and/or Speech-Language Pathologist

In our evaluation, we may learn that conditions of the child's or adolescent's dysregulation are linked to sensory overload (e.g., loud noises, noxious smells, unfamiliar tastes, uncomfortable textures) or frustration related to fine motor tasks (e.g., difficulty tying their shoes, difficulty putting together small toys, handwriting). In such cases, an occupational therapist (OT) colleague will be able to better clarify what the nature of the struggle is and to generate a plan for accommodation or remediation. Similarly, we may find that our young patient's outbursts often occur in the context of trying to communicate with peers and teachers. We wonder whether there might be something about their speech articulation, receptive language, or social pragmatics that is getting in the way. At this point, it occurs to us that a speech–language pathologist (SLP) can help further clarify the nature and severity of such potential problems with communication and offer a plan to address them.

Evaluations by an OT and/or an SLP are commonly included in a school district's multidisciplinary evaluation (and if they are not, but we deem them relevant, we can advocate for their inclusion), but sometimes it can be valuable to encourage private assessment in these domains as well. Often, it makes sense to do this after the school's evaluation, so the private OT or SLP can offer a second opinion on those findings and generate other hypotheses to explore. In many instances, though, the parents/caregivers and team will be satisfied with the school's findings and recommendations so the private consultations can be deferred until there is any indication they are needed.

Functional Behavioral Assessment

Although, as assessors, we aim to clarify as best we can—with the data we work with—the conditions under which our young patient is prone to emotional dysregulation and those under which they are apt to recover and stabilize (see Chapter 1), in some instances, there is a need for greater specification of such interpersonal and other environmental conditions. Conducted by

---

[1]I am grateful to my late friend and colleague Dr. Bill Leeds for all I learned from him about the evaluation and treatment of sleep disorders.

board-certified behavioral analysts (BCBAs), a functional behavioral assessment (FBA) is one method to elucidate these kinds of conditions. Among other things, an FBA involves (a) careful observation, data collection, and analysis of antecedents and consequences of concerning behaviors and (b) conceptualization of reinforcement patterns eliciting and maintaining such behaviors. An FBA results in formulation, implementation, and evaluation of a behavior plan that alters reinforcement contingencies to redress the problematic behavior.

Consider the psychological assessment of 7-year-old Tommy, whose parents divorced when he was 2 years old. When frustrated and angry, Tommy was prone to prolonged tantrums, hitting and biting siblings and classmates, and oppositional refusal of seemingly routine academic and household tasks. Tommy's vulnerability to such severe regulation varied depending on which parent's home he was living in at a given time: With one parent, he was considerably more challenging than with the other. At school, where he had a 504 plan (Section 504 of the Rehabilitation Act of 1973 [as amended, 2008]; see Chapter 14 in this volume), based on a previous ADHD diagnosis by his pediatrician, his dysregulation was more likely in some contexts—specials like art, music, and physical education as well as recess—compared with classroom activities overseen by his experienced second grade teacher.

The combined psychological and neuropsychological evaluation of Tommy ruled out the autism and bipolar spectra (both referral questions) and highlighted his tenuous self-esteem, perfectionism that did not quite meet criteria for obsessive-compulsive disorder, and uneven cognitive functioning understood in terms of a language-based learning disability. The combined evaluation also illuminated that Tommy was more likely to become emotionally dysregulated, misperceive situations and people, and reason illogically under conditions of being more on his own with less external structure (when guidelines, expectation, feedback, monitoring and support are less available) and when being stirred by feelings of inadequacy, anger, and need for caretaking and fear of abandonment. It was clear from the evaluation that he would benefit from greater and more consistent external structure at home and school; special education interventions (by way of an IEP) to address his difficulties with verbal processing and fluency; and therapeutic attention to his self-esteem, worries about abandonment, and difficulties adaptively containing and expressing his anger. However, there was still much room to clarify specific modifications his parents and teachers might make to stabilize his emotional regulation across households and other settings and activities. Thus, the evaluator recommended an FBA, which was conducted by the school district's BCBA in each parent's home and across Tommy's school day. The BCBA proved to be a valuable consultant/coach to his parents and teachers.

Other Specialty Consultations

Recognizing the limits of our own training and expertise, we may wish to recommend follow-up evaluations with colleagues who have specialties that we do not and thus are able to assess our patient in certain areas with greater depth and nuance and who better know the array of treatment options. Such areas of specialty consultation might involve assessment of alcohol and substance use, eating disorders, or threat/dangerousness, to name a few.

ADJUNCTS TO TREATMENT

Besides considerations related to pharmacotherapy and family, individual, and group therapeutic interventions (see Chapter 12), we can offer ideas about complementary activities to cultivate a child's or adolescent's emotional regulation. Aligning such suggestions with the patient's interests and learning style optimizes the likelihood of their buy-in. Along these lines, art therapy—especially when it is integrated with principles of dialectical behavior therapy—is one option (Haeyen, 2018; Heckwolf et al., 2014; LaForce, 2021), and music therapy is another (Hou et al., 2017). Yoga not only has intuitive appeal for building emotional regulation but also has recently garnered empirical support as having this benefit (Janjhua et al., 2020; McMahon et al., 2021). Participation in martial arts as a means to enhance self-discipline and self-control over emotions and impulses has anecdotal support and also makes sense conceptually (e.g., Bell et al., 2016). Interestingly, though, the limited research conducted in this area thus far has suggested that martial arts training in and of itself is not associated with kids' enhanced emotional regulation (Strayhorn & Strayhorn, 2009), but it is if also linked with interventions to bolster moral reasoning (Fung & Lee, 2018).

To conclude this chapter and Part IV, one additional treatment adjunct is offered for consideration—but it is not focused directly on the identified patient. Regardless of the diagnosis in the fifth edition, text revision, of the *Diagnostic and Statistical Manual of Mental Disorders* (*DSM-5-TR*; American Psychiatric Association, 2022) and other conceptual understanding, a child or adolescent vulnerable to frequent and severe emotional dysregulation is apt to have a profound, sometimes even traumatic, effect on their siblings. This is especially the case to the extent that the patient is prone to physical and verbal aggression, self-harm, and suicidality. In such instances, siblings often witness or are direct recipients of frightening and disturbing behaviors, and this is on top of experiencing their parents/caregivers as less emotionally available because of needs to tend to the dysregulated child. So, as a piece of the evaluation, we can inquire with caregivers about effects on siblings. If this leaves us with concerns, we can add recommendations for psychoeducation and support for the siblings (Feriante et al., 2022). Such groups are offered through local (e.g., Massachusetts Sibling Support Network, n.d.) or national agencies (e.g., Sibling Support Project; see https://siblingsupport.org).

PART V CASE ILLUSTRATIONS

In this final part of the book, I offer five case illustrations[1] of emotionally dysregulated children and adolescents referred for psychological evaluation. Each illustration includes the context for referral, specific questions posed for the evaluation, excerpts from key sections of the respective reports (to offer a flavor of how I translate findings into the language of the report), and discussion of treatment implications. Information about follow-up is included when it is available. This set of case examples (Chapters 16 through 20) is followed by a final chapter of commentary (Chapter 21) organized by central themes of this book, including clarification of different aspects of emotional regulation, the role of *Diagnostic and Statistical Manual of Mental Disorders* (*DSM*) and treatment-centered diagnoses, and the value of multimethod assessment.

---

[1]It bears a reminder that to protect confidentiality, identifying information has been disguised in all of the case illustrations in this book, including those presented here in Part V.

16 CASE 1

Denny

I begin with Denny,[1] an Asian American, cisgender adolescent. At the time of the evaluation, Denny was a 13-year-old seventh grader who had been in outpatient psychotherapy to address a range of long-standing problematic behaviors, including volatile moods, emotional outbursts involving aggression toward others and destruction of objects, inattention and disorganization, difficulties getting along with peers, and oppositionality toward adults. His transition to middle school the previous year had been marked by heightened academic struggles and poor grades as well as frequent disruptiveness in the classroom. Recent neuropsychological testing revealed his uneven cognitive functioning with superior verbal capacities, "characteristics of a nonverbal learning disability," and a primary disorder of attention and executive functioning (i.e., attention-deficit/hyperactivity disorder [ADHD], predominantly inattentive type).

Denny was the youngest of three siblings whose parents separated 4 years prior, divorcing a year later. He and his siblings lived with their mother and had regular overnight visits with their father every other weekend. There was a family history of depression, anxiety, and attentional/executive functioning

[1]To protect confidentiality, identifying information has been disguised.

https://doi.org/10.1037/0000430-017
Psychological Assessment of Emotional Dysregulation in Children and Adolescents: The Bipolar Spectrum and Beyond, by A. D. Bram
Copyright © 2025 by the American Psychological Association. All rights reserved.

problems. Developmentally, no significant delays in speech/language or motor development were reported by his parents, but they did note that Denny had behavioral problems as early as preschool, including trouble following directions, responding to social cues, and getting along with peers. According to his mother, these chronic behavioral problems had exacerbated since his parents' separation; his father, though, did not see such a correlation. A recent physical examination suggested that Denny was medically healthy, and there was no evidence or reason to suspect that Denny was abusing alcohol or other substances.

Although over the previous 2 years, Denny had been on various stimulant medications, had weekly therapy sessions with a behaviorally oriented therapist, and had a 504 plan (Section 504 of the Rehabilitation Act of 1973, as amended 2008) at school, his problematic behaviors at home and school persisted. The main reason that Denny's therapist referred for present psychological assessment was to better understand the nature and severity of his emotional dysregulation, including clarification about whether to understand it as consistent with a bipolar spectrum condition.[2] To address these questions, the measures and methods included collateral-report (Child Mania Rating Scale–Parent version [CMRS-P; Pavuluri, Henry, et al., 2006], detailed developmental history forms completed by each of Denny's parents), self-report (Beck Youth Inventories–Second Edition [BYI-2; Beck et al., 2005]; Millon® Adolescent Clinical Inventory, Second Edition [MACI®-II; Millon et al., 2020]) and performance-based (Rorschach Performance Assessment System [Meyer et al., 2011]; Thematic Apperception Test [TAT; Murray, 1943]) instruments.

Regarding the more specific question about a bipolar spectrum illness, I took into account that (a) there was no reported family history of bipolar spectrum illness, (b) the base rate for bipolar conditions in the outpatient setting was low, and (c) Denny's course of illness was inconsistent with the typical longitudinal course typical of people who exhibit signs of bipolar

[2]At the outset of the initial testing session, after orienting Denny to what we would be doing together, I asked him what he might want to learn about himself from our evaluation. He politely said he did not think he needed another evaluation and did not have any questions but that he would go along with it. I responded that I would welcome his sharing any questions that he might think of during or between our two scheduled sessions.

At the beginning of our second session, I asked Denny again if any questions had occurred to him, and he shrugged indifferently and then requested clarification that he would be done with the testing that day. I recognize that in formal therapeutic assessment (Finn et al., 2012; Tharinger et al., 2022), additional time and effort would have been invested to support Denny to formulate his own questions.

illness. These factors contributed to a greater "burden of proof" (Youngstrom, Choukas-Bradley et al., 2015) to justify a bipolar diagnosis. Note that I conducted this psychological assessment in coordination with a child psychiatrist who would be interviewing the patient and his parents.

As the psychologist/assessor, my findings were to be integrated by the psychiatrist in drawing their own diagnostic conclusions and offering pharmacological options to Denny and his family. What follows is an excerpt from the "Emotional Regulation" section of the test report. The first paragraph addresses the style and effectiveness of Denny's emotional regulation more broadly; the second, the question of bipolar spectrum:

> Testing corroborates that Denny has a profound weakness in his capacity for emotional regulation. He is easily overwhelmed by his feelings and has difficulty bringing to bear his strong verbal skills to make sense of, de-intensify, and communicate them in words. Although on the BYI-2 and MACI-II he did not self-report high levels of depression, anxiety, or anger, data from the performance-based tests indicate that under the surface he is more dysphoric, anxious, and angry than he is apt to acknowledge or even realize himself. There is evidence that temporally removed from the situations that upset him, Denny is inclined to minimize and deny his troublesome emotions and their extent. Nevertheless, the data are compelling that he is largely bereft of reliably effective strategies to cope with the emotions stirred within him. Other than giving in to the feeling and expressing it—often in explosive or other provocative ways (breaking things; he says, "It feels good just to get your anger out")—he tries to distance from the source of the emotion either by trying to get away from the situation, narrowing his focus, or "trying not to think about it." At best, this only provides temporary relief, but it does not buffer him against re-intensification of the feelings, nor does it lead to any learning about and sense of mastery over his emotional experience. Denny's TAT stories, for example, were remarkable for his description of characters' getting over their emotional and interpersonal challenges but his having little or no idea *how* they were able to do so. This speaks to his own lack of understanding of what to do with what goes on inside and a naïve and magical expectation/wish that difficult feelings and situations just go away without his playing a role in their resolution. It was also notable, based on his responses to TAT inquiries, that he has little understanding of how to differentiate between thoughts and feelings; when queried for characters' thoughts, he consistently responded with descriptions of their feelings. This suggests that he does not comprehend an essential way that his own and others' minds work—that thoughts and feelings are different from one another yet are mutually influential in a way that contextualizes and regulates emotions and motivates overt behavior.
>
> Based on his parents' independent reports on the CMRS-P, there was a reasonable likelihood that Denny's severe weakness in emotional regulation is manifested in a fashion consistent with a bipolar spectrum condition. Before presenting the evidence, though, it is crucial that these findings be weighed alongside and integrated with those from a comprehensive assessment by the consulting psychiatrist before a bipolar diagnosis is concluded. The score on his

> mother's report of the CMRS-P exceeded the cutoff score that in research has reliably differentiated among children and adolescents with a bipolar disorder from those with ADHD and other psychiatric conditions; the score from his father's report was close to but did not exceed this differential diagnostic threshold. His mother described that there are "two Dennys" depending on his mood and that his mood can switch suddenly: He can be pleasant, cooperative, and loving for a stretch and then there are episodes, as long as 3 to 4 days at a time, marked by rageful oppositionality; slamming, banging, and breaking things; and shredding his homework and drawings. His mother also noted that these periods involve spikes in his energy and activity level, hyper-talkativeness, his own reports of his mind racing ("Like in fast forward," he reportedly explained to her), and acting sillier. She did not report, though, his decreased need for sleep, hypersociality, or increased productive and creative activities. On the CMRS-P, Denny's father also highlighted his son's proneness to mood swings, rage attacks, and periods of excessive energy and silliness, but his father was less certain that these behaviors cluster episodically. In contrast to the mother's report, Denny's father did not report frequent observations of his son's talking too much or racing thoughts. Denny's own self-report on the [MACI-II] did not point to elevated mood, although he did acknowledge his own wishes to stir up excitement, get silly, and get people laughing (particularly in the classroom). It is also worth highlighting that on the Rorschach, Denny did not show the style of illogical reasoning that is often associated with bipolar conditions. To summarize, although the present data were mixed overall regarding a bipolar spectrum condition, his parents' CMRS-P reports of his mood volatility are compelling and merit consideration in the concurrent psychiatric assessment. Clearly, Denny's struggles with emotional dysregulation exceed what can be explained solely by his previous ADHD diagnosis. But because bipolar disorder is considered a severe and persistent mental illness with implications across the lifespan, and there is no reported family history of this disorder (which tends to run in families), a thoughtful, conservative approach to this diagnostic endeavor is recommended. Regardless of what it ends up being called, the present findings underscore that Denny's underdeveloped capacities for emotional regulation are severe and are a treatment priority.

Based on the collaborating psychiatrist's own evaluation and taking into account this psychological assessment, they agreed that there were compelling reasons to suspect a bipolar condition but also that there was enough uncertainty (the parents' somewhat conflicting perspectives; the absence of family history of bipolar illness) and other intervening stressors (the acutely tense relationship between his parents) to defer concluding more definitively that Denny was suffering what would be a lifelong affliction. Nevertheless, the psychiatrist did recommend a trial of mood stabilizers and steered away from selective serotonin reuptake inhibitor antidepressants suspected of possibly exacerbating vulnerabilities to mania.

One of the recommendations coming from the psychological assessment was parent coaching/guidance with a method, such as collaborative problem-solving (Greene & Ablon, 2005; see Chapter 12), an evidence-based, caregiving approach that conceptualizes emotional dysregulation as akin to a learning disability and thus offers caregivers alternatives to traditional reinforcement-based frameworks. Another recommendation involved pursuing an individualized education program (IEP) at school to provide special education interventions aimed at scaffolding Denny to better manage his mood and behavior at school. Because Denny's parents were reluctant to pursue the parent coaching,[3] and the mood stabilizers were only partially effective in mitigating his dysregulation at home and school, it was ultimately placement at an out-of-district special education day school as part of his IEP—in which he was immersed in a therapeutic setting with a small teacher-to-student ratio and an intensive social–emotional skill-building curriculum—that was associated with the greatest improvement in the stabilization and improvement of Denny's functioning.

[3]In retrospect, I wonder to what extent the recommendation for parent coaching in CPS may not have been the most attuned to the culturally rooted values held by Denny's second-generation Asian American parents (Yim, 2022). By contrast, Wang et al. (2021) described the effectiveness of a culturally responsive school-based parenting intervention tailored to Asian American parents.

17 CASE 2

Stevie

At the time of this evaluation, Stevie,[1] a White, cisgender child, was a 9-year-old third grader referred for psychological assessment by the child psychiatrist with whom his parents had recently consulted for treatment of Stevie's symptoms of anxiety, insomnia, angry outbursts and tantrums, dangerously impulsive behaviors (e.g., opening the car door while it was in motion; jumping in front of traffic), and difficulties with peer interactions and social skills. Of further concern was that on occasion, he had reported hearing voices (e.g., more than a year prior, involving a man's voice imploring him to jump out of his bedroom window) as well as urges to hurt a pet or himself, which he acted on twice (trying to choke the family cat; another time, himself). Stevie was living with his parents as well as an older sister and younger brother.

Developmentally, Stevie suffered an array of social, speech/language, and motor delays and regressions such that he received early intervention and was diagnosed with an autism spectrum condition right after his third birthday. Medically, he had a history of recurrent ear infections, tonsillectomy, and various allergies. His parents reported a multigenerational history

[1]To protect confidentiality, identifying information has been disguised.

https://doi.org/10.1037/0000430-018
Psychological Assessment of Emotional Dysregulation in Children and Adolescents: The Bipolar Spectrum and Beyond, by A. D. Bram
Copyright © 2025 by the American Psychological Association. All rights reserved.

within the extended family of attention-deficit/hyperactivity disorder (ADHD), substance misuse and alcoholism, depression, and bipolar illness. A neuropsychological evaluation completed the year before affirmed his autism spectrum diagnosis but also illuminated his average-to-high-average overall intellectual capacities with strengths in the verbal realm. Highlighting Stevie's difficulties with attention, executive functioning, and slow processing speed, that evaluator added a diagnosis of ADHD along with a rule-out of disruptive mood dysregulation disorder.

In school, Stevie had been in a general education classroom with an individualized education program (IEP) providing academic support, occupational therapy, speech/language, social skills group, and counseling. During the evaluation highlighted here, he was reported to be doing well in school with academic/executive functioning support; at school, he was having greater success regulating behavior compared with at home. His parents noted, however, that he was highly self-conscious and often angry about his need to be pulled out of the classroom as required by his IEP.

In addition to the intensive interventions at school and medically over the years, Stevie had been followed at a local autism center, where he was involved in a program of applied behavior analysis, individual and family therapy, and pharmacotherapy. Medications at the time of this evaluation referral included the antihypertensive Tenex (guanfacine) to help with attention, impulsivity, and anxiety as well as melatonin for sleep. Despite all of such diligent efforts to understand and help Stevie, his parents remained concerned that there was something more severe going on with him emotionally than had been identified to date. His parents and his new psychiatrist were especially worried and puzzled about Stevie's report of the voices and urges to hurt himself or his siblings on which he had sometimes acted. In addition, they noted how difficult and confusing Stevie's speech could be to follow, and, thus, they wondered whether this might reflect a disturbance in his thinking and reasoning that transcended the expressive language/syntactic difficulties that had been conceptualized as part of his autism spectrum condition. The psychological testing, then, aimed to clarify to what extent these symptoms reflected an underlying, emerging thought disorder or psychotic illness, including a possible bipolar condition and/or other psychological factors above and beyond Stevie's known neurodevelopmental conditions.

To address these questions, the test battery included, among other measures, the Child Mania Rating Scale–Parent version (CMRS-P; Pavuluri, Henry, et al., 2006), Rorschach Performance Assessment System (Meyer et al., 2011), Thematic Apperception Test (TAT; Murray, 1943), Beck Youth Inventories–Second Edition (BYI-2; Beck et al., 2005), and Child Unusual Belief Scale (CUBEScale; Viglione & Senecal, 2014) as well as a detailed developmental questionnaire completed by Stevie's parents. Module C (Manic Episode, Hypomanic Episode, Bipolar I, Bipolar II) of the Mini International Neuropsychiatric Interview for Children and Adolescents (MINI-KID; Sheehan, 2016) was administered to follow up the CMRS-P. The following is an excerpt from the "Emotional Regulation" section of the report:

> A potentially encouraging finding is that Stevie did not self-report elevated levels of depression or anxiety on the BYI-2, suggesting improvement in his subjective mood compared to 10 months ago, when the same measure was administered in his neuropsychological evaluation and both scales were elevated (see Dr. Hartley's June report). It is reasonable to speculate that he is now feeling more settled with the support added as part of his revised IEP this academic year. The reason that this finding was qualified above as "potentially encouraging" is that it is also possible (and not necessarily mutually exclusive), that his healthier conscious self-report at this time reflects his self-protective efforts to convince himself and others that he is okay and "normal" (important to him, as described in the "Sense of Self" section of this report[2]). Independent of Stevie's subjective self-report of his mood, the performance-based test data underscore just how acutely flooded and overwhelmed by anxiety and other emotions Stevie is apt to become, especially in situations that are less routine and predictable and where external guidance, support, and feedback not so accessible. In such moments of emotional stirring, Stevie is vulnerable to experience his feelings with a certain rawness and intensity because he does not readily bring to bear his reasoning and language skills to make sense of, put into context, and effectively communicate what he is feeling. This means that it is difficult for Stevie to keep his emotions contained and to disinhibit the associated impulses toward action. Currently, Stevie requires considerable scaffolding by adults to help him manage his anxieties, frustrations, and other feelings and impulses, as was necessary during the evaluation: To stay emotionally regulated and focused during the evaluation, he required such proactive interventions as previewing expectations, attentiveness to pacing, frequent movement breaks, active encouragement, and positive reinforcements.
>
> It is promising that there is some evidence from his TAT stories that Stevie has developed at least a rudimentary emotional vocabulary (e.g., happy, sad, bored, surprised). But what is more challenging for him—and ought to be an ongoing therapeutic objective—involves abilities to tune into and identify his own intense emotional state in real time and to access the appropriate feeling words to be able to cognitively mitigate the rawness of his emotions and convey his experience to others in a more age-appropriate way.
>
> For a child Stevie's age, there are good reasons to be conservative with making this psychiatric diagnosis that has lifelong implications, but especially given his family history of bipolar illness, the data here do point to conceptualizing his struggles with emotional regulation on the bipolar spectrum. First, his parents'

[2]This cross-referenced section of report is not included as part of the present chapter.

> report on the CMRS-P yielded a score far exceeding the threshold that in research has differentiated children with a bipolar condition from those with ADHD. Specifically, his parents endorsed CMRS-P items highlighting their frequent observation of Stevie's patterns of inflated sense of self (e.g., convinced that he would soon be a hip-hop star and also the youngest NBA [National Basketball Association] player), excitability, high energy, elevated mood, racing thoughts, and jumping topic to topic; proneness to mood swings, angry outbursts, and irritable moods; and his having unusual thoughts and occasionally hearing voices. Follow-up interview administering the MINI-KID to his parents clarified that such symptoms have clustered episodically over periods of 4 to 5 days, consistent with hypomania. In addition to the CMRS-P and MINI-KID data, another piece of evidence comes from the performance-based Rorschach in which Stevie's pattern of putting ideas together in illogical ways sometimes had a playful, whimsical, energized quality that is often characteristic of people with bipolar conditions (e.g., "giraffes doing handstands," "a buffalo shooting out of a rocket," and "monkeys holding up the Eiffel Tower").

Treatment implications of these findings included parent guidance and psychoeducation as well as wraparound care through a state agency—care that would include access to a mobile crisis team (in response to aggressive/dangerous threats or acts) and respite care. Recommended parent guidance involved collaborative problem-solving (CPS; see Chapter 12), which was available through a local specialty clinic. This CPS model would help his parents further clarify Stevie's triggers and lagging emotional problem-solving skills, better anticipate his outbursts, learn to interact with him in a way that strengthens his coping skills, and sensitively and productively debrief with him after the difficult moments have passed.

Pharmacologically, I suggested primarily targeting Stevie's severe emotional dysregulation and associated vulnerabilities in capacities for logical reasoning and sense of reality. My report included a note of caution about future consideration of stimulants aimed at his attentional difficulties and selective serotonin reuptake inhibitor (SSRI) antidepressant medications aimed at his anxiety because these hold the potential for exacerbation of thought disorder and hypomania. The report was worded carefully—not telling the psychiatrist not to prescribe stimulants or SSRIs but to take into account the present findings and possible contraindications that they pose.

As noted previously, Stevie already had an IEP at school, and the test report highlighted the value of the kinds of environmentally based interventions that had been effective in helping him stay regulated during the evaluation. These interventions included previews of activities and expectations, opportunities for breaks and physical movement, affirmation of his strengths, and positive reinforcements. Also encouraged was Stevie's continued work with the school counselor individually and in small groups using The Zones of

Regulation™ (Kuypers, 2011; see Chapter 14) as well as a social thinking curriculum (Winner, 2006). The emphasis on social thinking was particularly important given Stevie's autism-related interpersonal challenges.[3]

Individual psychotherapy was not presented as a primary intervention that would likely have a major effect on Stevie's most concerning symptoms in the short term or even medium term because as it was expected that it would take time to cultivate an alliance. In large part, this was related to his immense self-consciousness and shame and understandable self-protective need to disavow experiences that make him feel or appear to others as atypical. This was most evident during administration of the CUBEScale, when he tried to avoid my efforts to sensitively inquire around his experiences of hearing voices and having impulsive urges: Stevie initially repudiated having ever had such symptoms, and he shushed and threatened his mother—"You're dead meat!"—when she tried to clarify what he had reported to her in the past. In the report, I highlighted the broad point that "a continual challenge for Stevie's parents, teachers, and treaters will be to walk the line between (a) providing him with developmental support and remediation that is necessary and (b) cultivating and reinforcing his areas of strength and whenever possible helping him save face."

Individual therapy was, however, raised as something that the parents might consider as an intervention that could help Stevie—a boy suffering both complex neurodevelopmental and psychiatric conditions—over time. The assessment data did not suggest that he would be readily amenable to an explicit psychoeducational/skill-building approach in which he would be expected to own and address directly his areas of emotional struggle. Thus, I wrote in the "Diagnostic Summary and Treatment Implications" section:

> Stevie would likely benefit from a supportive, relationally oriented therapy over the long-term. Mitigating his shame by recognizing and affirming his strengths will be an important element in cultivating a therapeutic alliance. It would be optimal if the therapist could see Stevie through various developmental stages. This would offer Stevie an opportunity to build trust and experience a safe space to gradually learn to tune into, identify, and communicate his feelings and other internal states. A task of the therapist will also be to help Stevie begin to consider the thoughts and feelings of other people. As important, the opportunity for a therapist to get to know Stevie in depth over time would put the therapist in the best position to advocate for his needs at school, in the community, and elsewhere. It is crucial to highlight that therapy itself will likely appear to be slow moving with growth gradual and in fits and starts. The format of the therapy

[3]The school-based interventions suggested for Stevie are applicable to many kids on the autism spectrum.

will need to accommodate Stevie's need for physical movement and make use of verbal communication that is not too complex.[4] Although it is recommended that the therapy be relationally oriented, there is room to judiciously (and not for prolonged periods that stretch the limits of his attention, at least at this point in his development) offer skill-building. This might include strategies, such as self-calming techniques, tips for anger management, and identifying and challenging the black-and-white thinking often leading to his outsized emotional reactions.

[4]These suggestions were extrapolated from findings from Stevie's prior neuropsychological evaluation about his learning style.

18 CASE 3

Jillian

An only child, Jillian,[1] a White, cisgender adolescent, was, at the time of assessment, a 16-year-old high school junior whose parents requested an evaluation to address their concerns that she was becoming increasingly depressed, isolated, and angry while rejecting their suggestions that she see a therapist. Jillian had been previously considered high functioning, excelling academically and in the performing arts. Now, though, her parents were noticing her preference for spending more time alone rather than with friends, losing interest in her typically preferred activities (e.g., deciding for the first time not to audition for the school musical), and a modest drop in grades (from As to Bs) along with unwillingness to seek help from her teachers. Jillian's parents reported that when they expressed their concerns to her and encouraged her to "be more social," talk to her teachers, or participate in extracurricular activities, the conversation quickly became heated because Jillian often erupted angrily, screaming and sometimes slamming doors. Jillian herself expressed her belief that there was nothing really wrong except that her parents worry

[1]Jillian is also discussed in Chapter 13 on factors affecting therapeutic engagement, specifically in the context of taking into account patient preferences. To protect confidentiality, identifying information has been disguised.

https://doi.org/10.1037/0000430-019
Psychological Assessment of Emotional Dysregulation in Children and Adolescents: The Bipolar Spectrum and Beyond, by A. D. Bram
Copyright © 2025 by the American Psychological Association. All rights reserved.

and nag her too much. She added her belief that her socially outgoing, high-achieving parents did not understand and respect that she is more of an introvert and thus held unrealistic social and academic expectations for her.

Her parents reported that Jillian had not exhibited delays in speech/language, cognitive, or motor development. Further, she had no reported history of trauma, was physically in good health, and there were no concerns about possible alcohol or drug involvement. Her parents did recall that from a young age, Jillian had been uneasy with separations from family and that she had always preferred a small group of friends rather than being in larger groups. Jillian's parents reported an extended family history of attentional problems, anxiety, and depression, and possible bipolar illness (a distant relative they suspected might be undiagnosed).

Although Jillian was against her parents' push for psychotherapy, she agreed reluctantly to make the short-term commitment for an evaluation to assist her parents and her to more systematically examine to what extent her parents' concerns warranted her consideration of the possible need for intervention. More specifically, might her parents' perception of her inhibitions and isolation reflect underlying depression, anxieties, or other psychological factors above and beyond her self-described temperamental introversion? Her parents also asked whether Jillian's recent angry outbursts might portend a bipolar spectrum condition, a concern not only because of the possible family history but because the adult child of close family friends had recently been diagnosed.

Primary instruments to assess Jillian's capacity for emotional regulation included the Minnesota Multiphasic Personality Inventory–Adolescent (Butcher et al., 1992), Beck Youth Inventories–Second Edition (Beck et al., 2005), Rorschach Performance Assessment System (Meyer et al., 2011), Thematic Apperception Test (TAT; Murray, 1943), Kutcher Generalized Social Anxiety Disorder Scale for Adolescents (Brooks & Kutcher, 2004), and Life Incidents of Traumatic Experiences (Greenwald & Rubin, 1999) questionnaire. I also administered the Wechsler Intelligence Scale for Children–Fifth Edition (WISC-V; Wechsler, 2014) as a screen of her cognitive profile that might offer clues about her recent academic dip and help determine whether a follow-up neuropsychological evaluation ought to be considered. Jillian's parents completed a developmental questionnaire as well as these parent versions: Child Mania Rating Scale–Parent version (Pavuluri, Henry, et al., 2006), the Screen for Child Anxiety Related Disorders–Parent Report (Birmaher et al., 1999), the Attention Deficit Disorders Evaluation Scale, Fifth Edition–Parent Report (McCarney & House, 2019), and an executive functioning questionnaire (Dawson & Guare, 2018). A teacher also completed the Attention Deficit

Disorders Evaluation Scale, Fifth Edition–Teacher Report, the school version of the scale (McCarney & House, 2019). These measures were selected to test hypotheses about the changes in Jillian's functioning not only about depression (including her parents' concerns about a bipolar condition) but different forms of anxiety, previously unreported trauma, and neurocognitive factors. Here is an excerpt from the "Emotional Regulation" section of Jillian's report:

> The self-report and parent-report data indicate that Jillian struggles with moderate levels of social anxiety, that is, anticipation/fear of negative evaluation by others that fuels her avoidance of some types of interpersonal interaction, most notably, those involving authority figures, such as teachers and counselors. Jillian's social anxiety is also evoked in unfamiliar interpersonal situations, including walking in on a group and going to parties. She also acknowledged that in the past few months, her self-conscious worries about being criticized or about embarrassing herself on stage has contributed to her pulling back from performing arts (including not trying out for the school musical) and spending time with her theatre and dance friends.
>
> Part of the reason Jillian did not self-report higher levels of anxiety is that she self-regulates through avoidance, so she does not have to often deal directly with the dreaded situations. Jillian is accurate when she views herself as shy and introverted by temperament. Nevertheless, there are ways that her social anxiety can hold her back from asking for or achieving things that are important to her, and that is why this is conceptualized here as more than mere shyness. Note there was not, though, compelling evidence from Jillian's self-reports, implicit themes in her responses to performance-based tasks, or her parents' reports that would point to clinical depression, let alone an emerging bipolar spectrum condition.
>
> In terms of her underlying capacity for emotional regulation, testing shows Jillian to have a mixture of strengths and vulnerabilities. To her credit, Jillian's excellent verbal skills (see "Intellectual/Cognitive Functioning" section[2]) extend to her ability to understand and articulate a wide range of emotions. For example, on the storytelling TAT, she was able to describe characters as having feelings both basic (e.g., happy, sad, angry) and more nuanced (e.g., disappointed, intimidated, regretful) as well as positive (e.g., happy, excited) and aversive (e.g., sad, scared). Moreover, Jillian also exhibited some sophistication and complexity in recognizing that people can hold seemingly contradictory emotions simultaneously (e.g., characters excited about their reunion but also sad about their inevitable separation).
>
> The aforementioned findings point to a conceptualization that Jillian is a young woman who is emotionally aware and capable of expressing her feelings but is inhibited about communicating them to others. Other data suggest, however, that this is only part of the picture. Specifically, there was evidence that—especially in

[2]The "Intellectual/Cognitive Functioning" section of the test report is not excerpted here, but Jillian's WISC-V Verbal Comprehension Index was in the Extremely High range.

> unfamiliar situations in which she senses herself as more on her own to cope—Jillian is vulnerable to being impacted by emotions that she does not consciously register but that can evoke a sense of helplessness and lack of felt control. Such unregistered emotions can disrupt Jillian's usually intact abilities to size up situations accurately and make sense of her experience. The additional finding is not surprising, then, that Jillian often attempts (not necessarily consciously) to steer away from situations and interpersonal interactions that are apt to evoke strong emotions and disrupt her functioning. Also, despite her potential for emotional expressiveness, in moments that heightened feelings do break through to awareness, Jillian is prone to minimizing and even disavowing feelings both to herself and others.
>
> There is some evidence too that Jillian is particularly uneasy when angry feelings or aggressive impulses are evoked, whether in her awareness or not. In such instances, she is inclined automatically to turn the aversive feelings into something less forceful and threatening. This was most notable in her Rorschach responses when she clarified that (a) the percept that she initially saw as "pincers clamping onto something" were actually doing so "tenderly . . . like gentle . . ." and that (b) the initial percept of "people [who are] arguing . . . having a disagreement" were actually "interested in what the other side has to offer." Notice here Jillian's care and effort to undo and make nice of emotional experiences that are essentially relationally tense and conflictual. Although there is a strength embedded here insofar as she may be inclined to be a peacemaker and respond in ways that do not perpetuate interpersonal conflict, there are also potential costs involving muting her own assertiveness and other necessary, adaptive expressions of aggression. Despite Jillian's habitual style of muting her anger, it is reasonable to speculate that her parents press a hot button when they persistently confront her social anxiety–related avoidance, resulting in her otherwise uncharacteristic outbursts.

Before a discussion of implications for treatment for Jillian (addressed in part previously in Chapter 13), it is useful to excerpt findings from the "Sense of Self" section of the test report:

> One aspect of Jillian's sense of self in which she struggles involves feelings and expectations associated with the adolescent developmental tasks of psychological separation from her family. These involve the challenging, interrelated, and gradual processes of (a) beginning to face and accept inevitable losses associated with growing up, (b) redefining herself in more adultlike terms and in ways that differentiate her from her family, (c) oscillating between wishes to still be attended to and taken care of in a more childlike way *and* strivings for greater autonomy, and (d) renegotiating her relationships within her family and being able to form new and more mature relationships. The most prevalent theme in Jillian's TAT stories entailed characters' suffering uncontrollable losses, separations, and short-lived reunions, suggesting that such concerns are impacting her, whether she is aware of them or not. In a similar but even more evocative way, her Rorschach percepts were marked by sequences of objects alternatively pulling toward and then away from one another, or vice versa, all with great intensity. One such sequence within the

> same inkblot was first "sea animals . . . trying to get the attention of whatever's at the top . . ." followed by "or they [sea animals] are all going in the opposite direction, trying to get away from it [the object on the top] . . . as if they don't like it." Notice the sudden oscillation between longing for and then disavowal of the same thing, which parallels an aspect of the developmental process of separation (metaphorically, the "same thing" being the care and support provided by caregivers). Impressively, Jillian was open to reflecting on these responses and what they might mean for her, especially in her relationship with her parents. She described a subjective sense of internal and external pressure to be and act more like an adult. She elaborated that her internal pressure to be more adult-like is one factor in wanting to figure things out on her own rather than seek and accept professional help.

Thus, Jillian's emotionally dysregulated behaviors—most prominently her angry reactions to her experience of parental pressure to be more active socially—were reactions to her misunderstood social anxiety as well as conflict (both internally and in her relationships with her parents) around the adolescent developmental task of psychological separation. As detailed in Chapter 13 to illustrate the role of patient preferences in treatment planning, these findings contributed to two possible treatment paths, should she decide to give therapy a try: (a) either a skill-building/psychoeducational cognitive behavior therapy (CBT)-oriented therapy or (b) a more traditional relationally oriented, expressive dynamic therapy. When Jillian was presented with test feedback along with the two options for therapy and their respective rationales, she chose to pursue the symptom-focused CBT. She was relieved to learn that this kind of therapy could address her anxiety and avoidance while not risking anything too intense or self-revealing, that is, without feared pressure to go deep into her feelings and relationships. Jillian made excellent use of the psychoeducation, cognitive restructuring, and gradual, hierarchical exposure to reduce her social anxiety and avoidance.

Complementing the individual CBT, feedback to her parents and follow-up parent guidance (i.e., about social anxiety, the way Jillian's temperament was different from theirs, and developmental needs and tasks associated with adolescence) helped attenuate the tension and conflict at home. It is worth reiterating from Chapter 13 that years later, as college graduation was approaching and Jillian would be encountering new developmental challenges, she returned to therapy to pursue the more relationally oriented, reflective kind of therapy for which she had not felt ready as a teenager.

19 CASE 4

Nicole

When the evaluation highlighted here occurred, Nicole,[1] a 16-year-old, White, cisgender adolescent, was a high school sophomore who had participated in outpatient, in-home, day hospital, and short-term residential treatments to address explosive and aggressive behavior (toward her parents, siblings, and pets); high levels of anxiety and depression; and reported auditory, visual, and tactile hallucinations. Although most of these symptoms had been chronic, she had experienced an exacerbation in the previous 6 months, which, on two occasions, briefly necessitated residential level of care for stabilization following violent and threatening behavior. She seldom attended school during this period because she was either too distressed or outright refused to attend. The worsening of her symptoms occurred not long after the retirement of her therapist of the previous 5 years. Importantly, Nicole had a history of disrupted attachments, having been removed from her biological parents' care by the state at age 2½ years because of neglect and possible physical and sexual abuse. She had multiple foster care placements—including one in which she reportedly suffered additional physical and emotional

[1]To protect confidentiality, identifying information has been disguised.

https://doi.org/10.1037/0000430-020
Psychological Assessment of Emotional Dysregulation in Children and Adolescents: The Bipolar Spectrum and Beyond, by A. D. Bram
Copyright © 2025 by the American Psychological Association. All rights reserved.

abuse—before her current family adopted her at age 6. At the time of evaluation, Nicole lived with her adoptive parents and an older brother, biological to her adoptive parents.[2]

Records from child protective services indicated that Nicole's earliest years were marked by domestic violence between her biological parents and by poverty and neglect. Her biological parents were suspected of alcohol and substance use, and her mother was also suspected of drinking and smoking during the pregnancy. There was reportedly history in her biological family of anxiety, depression, trauma, and schizophrenic spectrum illness. Nicole's aggressive behavior and difficulties being soothed were observed from the time she entered foster care, and they continued following adoption. Also noted were some speech and gross and fine motor delays, which gradually improved with speech/language and occupational therapies and more stable care. Aside from seasonal allergies, Nicole was in good physical health.

Academically, Nicole had been on an individualized education program (IEP) to address her challenges with attention and executive functioning. Because Nicole's emotional and behavioral difficulties had been disrupting her consistent attendance and engagement in school, her placement—including whether she required an out-of-district or even residential setting—was pending. The school district's evaluation a year prior estimated her overall intellectual functioning to be in the average range (47th percentile) but marked by unevenness with notable weaknesses in working memory and visual–motor processing speed (both below the 10th percentile). Previous neuropsychological evaluators had highlighted Nicole's solid verbal skills alongside significant challenges with attention, impulse control, and executive functioning that met criteria for attention-deficit/hyperactivity disorder (ADHD).

Despite a range of intensive interventions—pharmacological, psychotherapeutic, in-home, outpatient, inpatient/residential, educational, among others—over the course of her development, Nicole's concerning symptoms had not only persisted but worsened. Most troubling were her increased threats of and actual aggression toward her family and pets as well as her reported hallucinations, some of which sounded to be linked with her aggressive urges. For example, her mother reported that Nicole told her, "I can't help that voices in my head tell me to kill you"; but Nicole subsequently walked back this connection and insisted that the voices she hears are unintelligible. Thus, there remained questions about the role of possible psychosis in her ongoing

[2]For assessors and other clinicians interested in furthering their understanding of and therapeutic implications for adopted children and their families, the edited volume by Brabender and Fallon (2013) is highly recommended.

emotional and behavioral challenges. Previously, her psychiatric difficulties had been reportedly understood primarily in *Diagnostic and Statistical Manual of Mental Disorders* (*DSM*) terms of reactive attachment disorder, posttraumatic stress disorder (PTSD), and ADHD. When Nicole's parents reached out to me for an initial consultation, they expressed that the *DSM*-based formulations were of limited help in understanding their daughter and her needs. I shared with them that I was curious to learn through the evaluation what Nicole was experiencing underneath her manifest symptoms with an eye toward what will make a difference treatment-wise.

In discussions with Nicole's parents, application of models of underlying developmental disruption (Bram & Peebles, 2014; Peebles, 2012; see Chapter 12 in this volume) to understand their complex child was essential in generating referral questions. My back-and-forth with her parents clarified that testing would be aimed at better understanding (a) the nature and severity of weaknesses in her abilities to reason logically and perceive reality accurately, bearing on the question of psychosis; (b) her difficulties with emotional regulation, including the possibility of the bipolar spectrum; (c) the ongoing role of trauma; and (d) the possible emergence of a characterological component to her symptoms, that is, to what extent might her aggressive behaviors be becoming automatic, unquestioned, and less troubling to her. Conducted in coordination with an updated neuropsychological evaluation, this assessment was also aimed at clarifying her needs for educational placement and treatment. At the time of evaluation, Nicole's psychotropic medications included a mood stabilizer/antipsychotic, an antihypertensive aimed at reducing impulsivity, and a selective serotonin reuptake inhibitor (SSRI) antidepressant.

Beyond the developmental data gleaned from the earlier reports and questionnaire completed by—and followed up in an interview with—her parents, key assessment tools for Nicole's evaluation included the Rorschach Performance Assessment System (Meyer et al., 2011), Thematic Apperception Test (Murray, 1943), Minnesota Multiphasic Personality Inventory–Adolescent (MMPI-A; Butcher et al., 1992), Kinetic Family Drawings (KFD; Burns & Kaufman, 1970; see also D. V. Myers, 1978), Beck Youth Inventories–Second Edition (Beck et al., 2005), Child Mania Rating Scale–Parent version (Pavuluri, Henry, et al., 2006), Child and Adolescent Trauma Screen 2 (Sachser et al., 2022), Adolescent Dissociative Experiences Scale-II (Armstrong et al., n.d.), and Child Unusual Belief Scale (Viglione & Senecal, 2014). The parent-report Brief Impairment Scale (BIS; Bird et al., 2005) was also included to document the level of severity of Nicole's needs for services as the parents worked with the school district around placement. I later added the Children's Yale-Brown

Obsessive-Compulsive Scale (Scahill et al., 1997) to better understand her elevation on MMPI-A scales (Scale 7 [Psychasthenia; Pt] and content scale A-Obs [Obsessiveness]) suggestive of persistent, intrusive worries. The following excerpt from the concluding "Diagnostic Summary and Treatment Implications" section of the test report aimed to capture the complexity of the findings:

> The present data do not provide sufficient evidence that Nicole's most alarming symptoms—her violent outburst and reports of hallucinations—are manifestations of an emerging schizophrenic or bipolar spectrum condition. Because she was taking an antipsychotic at the time of the evaluation, a caveat is that this medication could have attenuated more severe test-based signs of thought disorder (impairments in coherence of her thinking and logic of her reasoning). Given her biological family history of schizophrenia and the present findings suggesting some unusual use of language, there is a need to continue close clinical monitoring of her symptoms and consideration of periodic formal reassessments. Testing does underscore that Nicole remains at risk for transient psychotic regressions when emotionally overwhelmed, marked by breakdowns in her ability to perceive situations and people accurately (i.e., lapses in her attunement to reality). Although Nicole's weaknesses in emotional regulation are severe, the data do not fit patterns suggestive of bipolar illness; from a *DSM-5-TR* [fifth edition, text revision, of the *Diagnostic and Statistical Manual of Mental Disorders* (*DSM-5-TR*; American Psychiatric Association, 2022)] perspective, disruptive mood dysregulation disorder is a more appropriate descriptor, alongside significant depression and anxiety. Her anxiety does have some circumscribed elements of OCD [obsessive-compulsive disorder], but at this time the latter is not deemed central. The concurrent neuropsychological evaluation indicated that Nicole continues to meet behavioral criteria for ADHD, but her challenges with emotional regulation far transcend this diagnostic category.
>
> Although Nicole did not report a full complement of PTSD symptoms, it is difficult to imagine that her early attachment disruptions and traumas have not played a significant role in the development and maintenance of ongoing emotion dysregulation, her sense of herself as deficient and inadequate, and her vulnerability to regress to states in which she perceives heightened interpersonal threats. The past descriptive diagnosis of reactive attachment disorder remains relevant. Nicole's relational challenges rooted in her attachment traumas are entwined with and exacerbated by often subtle yet significant weaknesses in social awareness, understanding, and nonverbal communication. According to the concurrent neuropsychological evaluation, Nicole meets *DSM-5-TR* criteria for a social pragmatic communication disorder (see Dr. Hartley's report).
>
> Encouragingly, the data here overall do not indicate that Nicole's aggressive behaviors emanate from a burgeoning antisocial/psychopathic character structure in which she is fundamentally callous, lacks concern for others, and experiences an absence of remorse. However, Nicole acknowledged moments when she is in the throes of her dysregulation that she takes a certain sadistic pleasure in hurting or angering her loved ones. Although she is at continued risk for aggression, it is hopeful that her sadistic impulses trouble and puzzle her and are associated with regret, making them potentially more malleable psychotherapeutically.

> This evaluation has highlighted areas of psychological vulnerability and risk, but it is also important to acknowledge that Nicole has some significant strengths that will be assets in her treatment. Nicole possesses solid verbal capacities, including a developing emotional vocabulary; has interest and talent in art (a modality through which she showed potential to cultivate self-awareness and more adaptive emotional expression[3]); and shows signs of having a conscience. Also hopeful is that with all that she has been through, she remains interested in people, at least at times is able to feel concern for others, and she has begun to internalize some sense that relationships can be the source of safety, caring, and nurturing. The latter (her internalized sense that relationships can be benevolent and sustaining) she is more apt to access outside of episodes of acute dysregulation and regression.

The treatment implications subsequently addressed in the report emphasized the continued need for a coordinated, multimodal educational/treatment plan conceptualized over the long term. Although it was hoped that these services could be implemented on an outpatient basis, I noted that if Nicole's behaviors at home were to prove unsafe to herself or her family and/or she was unable to reengage and learn in school, strong consideration ought to be given to an ongoing placement in a residential/therapeutic boarding school program that could provide greater safety while meeting her complex constellation of neurocognitive-social-emotional needs. I added that to give an outpatient plan the best chance for success, it would be essential to designate a clinician to serve as treatment coordinator/case manager to facilitate and synthesize communication among the various team members at school and in the community. In addition to continuing the in-home family therapy and crisis management services, a crucial recommendation was to step up interventions through the school district because her emotional difficulties were interfering with her ability to engage academically. Nicole's parents' report on the dimensional BIS—which yielded a highly elevated score, documenting her impairment across self-care, interpersonal, and academic domains—helped make the case to the school district to consider more intensive services. I wrote this in the "Diagnostic Summary and Treatment Implications" section:

> The present findings underscore how essential it is that Nicole's IEP and academic placement take into account the salience and severity of her social-emotional

[3]During the evaluation, a rare moment when Nicole conveyed curiosity and self-reflection occurred in the context of the KFD (Burns & Kaufman, 1970), which required her to draw a picture of herself doing something with her family. I wondered with her about the facial expression with which she depicted herself in the drawing. She examined the picture carefully, and with surprise and self-revelation, she observed that "it looks like I'm angry in this," although it was not her intention to depict herself as such. Her willingness and ability to engage psychologically around her art offered promise as a therapeutic tool to enhance her self-understanding and adaptive emotional expression.

> challenges. The findings of Nicole's underlying weaknesses in social pragmatics (diagnosed by Dr. Hartley as manifesting in *DSM-5-TR* social pragmatic communication disorder) indicate that these should be reflected in specific IEP goals and appropriate individual and group interventions around social thinking/ social skills. Nicole's IEP also ought to address her weaknesses in emotional regulation and provide a skills-based curriculum involving principles and techniques from dialectical behavior therapy (DBT) and cognitive behavior therapy (CBT).

To the extent that the school district might ultimately be unable or unwilling to provide the aforementioned skill-building groups in a timely way (or at all), such services would need to be accessed through community-based agencies or private clinicians. Importantly, her parents noted that Nicole had previously been most receptive to interventions that involve more concrete coping strategies and are offered in the context of a peer group in which she feels less alone and different in her struggles. Considering what is known about patient preferences and treatment outcome, the need to connect her with skill-building groups was especially highlighted in the report.

Parent guidance with a specialist in collaborative problem-solving (CPS; described in Chapter 12) was also recommended, particularly because her parents reported limited success with previous attempts using more traditional reinforcement-based behavioral management programs to help Nicole manage her emotional outbursts and regulate her behavior at home. In terms of pharmacotherapy, the findings from the evaluation suggested that the current pharmacological approach targeting Nicole's emotional dysregulation and impulsivity was on the right track, and no potential contraindication was raised about the use of SSRIs. Although individual psychotherapy was not viewed as likely to yield significant benefits in the short term, I made the following pitch at the end of the section on "Diagnostic Summary and Treatment Implications":

> As her previous therapist of 5 years retired from practice in the middle of last year, Nicole currently does not have an individual therapist. Her parents shared their observation that Nicole's processing challenges and limited capacity for insight have made it difficult for her to make optimal use of psychotherapy. Nonetheless, given her history of disrupted attachments and trauma, ongoing interpersonal struggles and profound difficulties with self-esteem, and at least a streak of underlying sadism activated when she is dysregulated, there remains a significant role for a carefully paced, relationally oriented therapy aimed at helping her to better understand her internal experience and her patterns in relationships (including consideration of her own and others' thoughts, feelings, and motivations).
>
> Although there is room for her therapist to offer skill-building CBT/DBT interventions (reinforcing and expanding on the emotional regulation strategies she would learn in school and other groups), the core task will be to listen to her

and assist her to articulate and reflect on how she experiences herself (including concerns about intimacy and sexuality, hinted at in her MMPI-A responses) and her interpersonal interactions, especially those in which she feels vulnerable or angry. Because it will likely be difficult for Nicole to put these experiences into words consistently, encouraging her drawing and artwork—which showed some promise as a mode of emotional expression during the evaluation—and attending to the here-and-now relationship with the therapist will be important elements of the therapeutic process. Regarding the latter, working together with Nicole to understand and repair inevitable misunderstandings, slights, or rejections experienced in the relationship with the therapist will be vitally therapeutic. Similarly, the therapist would do well to attend to and address sensitively Nicole's reactions, even seemingly minor ones, around interruptions in meetings (e.g., her own or the therapist's vacations). As implied here, connecting Nicole with a therapist well-versed in attachment theory and early trauma would be of immense value. It is reasonable to speculate that Nicole's needing to end with her previous therapist, likely reevoking early experiences of separation and loss, has been somewhere in the mix of her intensified dysregulation over the past 6+ months. Thus, one task as she begins with her new therapist will be to facilitate Nicole's sharing and reflecting on her feelings and attributions about the ending of that long-term relationship.

20 CASE 5

Pedro

Pedro,[1] a Hispanic, cisgender adolescent, was, at the time of the evaluation highlighted in this case study, a high school freshman who had recently begun psychotherapy to address his lack of interest, engagement, underperformance in school (failing most of his classes), frequent use of marijuana, and other behaviors that concerned his school's counseling staff. Most notably, there was at least one incident in which he reportedly texted inappropriate sexual content to classmates (leading to investigation by the police), raising concerns about his potential for more disruptive or aggressive behaviors.

Pedro was adopted from a Latin American country shortly after his birth, and he grew up with his adoptive White parents in the United States as the middle of three children (his siblings were biological offspring of his parents). Little was known about the psychiatric history of his biological family. Pedro was not reported to have experienced significant early delays in his speech, motor, or social development, and his adoptive mother recalled him to be an easy baby and toddler. There was no reported history of trauma. Physically, he was not only medically healthy but was considered an outstanding baseball

[1]To protect confidentiality, identifying information has been disguised.

https://doi.org/10.1037/0000430-021
Psychological Assessment of Emotional Dysregulation in Children and Adolescents: The Bipolar Spectrum and Beyond, by A. D. Bram
Copyright © 2025 by the American Psychological Association. All rights reserved.

and basketball player as well as cross-country athlete and dancer. And by all accounts, Pedro was socially outgoing and popular among his peers.

Pedro's difficulties engaging and performing academically dated back to early middle school, when challenges with attention and executive functioning, of which there were more than hints in earlier grades, began to interfere with meeting the increased academic demands. Evaluations at that time determined Pedro's intellectual capacities to be consistently at or above the average range (with above-average verbal skills), no specific learning disabilities (although subjectively, he reported being a slow reader and to have difficulties writing), and no concerns about his speech/language skills. Based on a diagnosis of attention-deficit/hyperactivity disorder (ADHD), Pedro qualified for an individualized education program (IEP) that over the years involved various interventions to address his struggles with attention and organization and other aspects of executive functioning. Throughout middle school, he was viewed by his parents and teachers as putting in less than optimal effort and underachieving (typical grades were low Bs and Cs), but it was not until beginning high school that he refused to complete most of his work and received failing grades. Also notable during those years was that brief trials of both stimulant and nonstimulant medications targeting his inattention were reportedly not helpful and were discontinued because of side effects.

Because of the seriousness of Pedro's academic difficulties alongside his marijuana use and the more recent behavioral concerns raised by the school counselor, Pedro's new outpatient therapist recommended the psychological evaluation to clarify the nature and severity of his difficulties with emotional regulation, possibly manifested in some form of anxiety, depressive, or bipolar spectrum condition. Another referral question involved the possibility that Pedro's troublesome behaviors were undergirded by an emerging maladaptive character style (i.e., an ingrained, rigid, automatic pattern of thinking, feeling, and relating largely outside awareness), in particular, a psychopathic/antisocial one. I had indicated to his parents that my findings would likely be more reliable if Pedro were to abstain from marijuana use for 6 weeks before the evaluation (Tapert et al., 2008)[2] and recommended

[2]Tapert et al.'s (2008) review summarized neurocognitive research findings that adolescents who are heavy users of cannabis "have . . . impairments in learning and working memory up to six weeks after cessation, suggesting persisting effects, yet raise the possibility that abnormalities may remit with a longer duration of abstinence" (p. 99). Although there is not yet published research on the relationship between length of marijuana abstinence and thought disorder–associated Cognitive Codes and other scores on the Rorschach (i.e., Rorschach Performance Assessment System [R-PAS; Meyer et al., 2011] or the Comprehensive System–Revised [Exner et al., 2022]), we do know that marijuana use increases vulnerability to psychotic

that they discuss this with him and have him drug tested. They did have this discussion with him and were confident that he had cut back on his use because they instituted more restrictions on his social activities outside of school, but they chose not to push formal drug testing with him.

The evaluation consisted of the following measures and methods: Similarities and Comprehension subtests of the Wechsler Intelligence Scale for Children–Fourth Edition (WISC-IV; Wechsler, 2003),[3] R-PAS (Meyer et al., 2011), Thematic Apperception Test (TAT; Murray, 1943), Minnesota Multiphasic Personality Inventory–Adolescent (MMPI-A; Butcher et al., 1992), Beck Youth Inventories–Second Edition (BYI-2; Beck et al., 2005), Child Mania Rating Scale–Parent version (CMRS-P; Pavuluri, Henry, et al., 2006), Children's Yale-Brown Obsessive Compulsive Scale (CY-BOCS; Scahill et al., 1997), Life Incidence of Traumatic Experiences questionnaire (Greenwald & Rubin, 1999), Adolescent Dissociative Experiences Scale-II (Armstrong et al., n.d.), Child Unusual Belief Scale (Viglione & Senecal, 2014), Kinetic Family Drawing (KFD; Burns & Kaufman, 1970), Animal Preference Test (Rojas & Tuber, 1991), alcohol/drug screening questionnaire, Drug Abuse Screening Test (Skinner, 1982), and a developmental questionnaire completed by his parents. Patient–examiner data (Bram, 2010; Bram & Peebles, 2014; Schafer, 1954; see Chapter 6 of this book) were also crucial, as reflected in the following passage from the "Emotional Regulation" section of the test report:

> The present data indicate that Pedro is considerably more anxious than he self-reports or than is typically visible to an observer. During the evaluation, this only became apparent when I inquired about his extended bathroom breaks during the Rorschach and storytelling TAT task. Pedro had exhibited some mild indicators of anxiety (e.g., shaking his leg), and it was notable that the most prevalent internal states that he attributed to his TAT characters were "nervous" and "worried." But it was when I asked him about his bathroom breaks (exceeding 20 minutes), he revealed that he was needing respite from the "emotions running through me," which, in response to my inquiry, he clarified involved fear and anxiety. Pedro was not able to elaborate on what it was about the tasks

---

experiences (M. L. West & Sharif, 2023). My suggestion of a minimum 6-week abstinence period—consistent with local norms of my neuropsychologist colleagues—was aimed at obtaining a cleaner read on Rorschach (i.e., R-PAS) indicators of thought disorder, although there is no way to know with certainty whether this would be of sufficient duration.

[3]Subtests from this earlier version of the Wechsler Intelligence Scale for Children (WISC) were administered because the questions for this evaluation did not require a full readministration of the WISC, and these subtests were deemed useful to addressing the referral questions. This decision considered the possibility of practice effects should Pedro be administered a full Wechsler Intelligence Scale for Children–Fifth Edition (Wechsler, 2014) as part of a future reevaluation by his school district.

that evoked those feelings, but in the case of the TAT, it is reasonable to speculate it had something to do with the interpersonal themes and dark quality of the TAT cards and/or the task requirements to think about the internal states of the characters.

In trying to discern what was happening during Pedro's extended bathroom breaks, I wondered about the possibility of washing or similar rituals that sometimes contribute to difficulties leaving the restroom. Thus, I administered the CY-BOCS as an interview to rule out the possibility of obsessive-compulsive disorder (OCD), which could potentially also explain some of his difficulty completing schoolwork. Pedro's self-report on the CY-BOCS did not reveal obsessions (unwanted, intrusive thoughts associated with increased anxiety) or compulsions (rituals aimed at neutralizing obsessions and reducing anxiety) related to contamination and washing (thus did not explain his extended time in the bathroom). However, he did report superstitious obsessions (aversion to certain numbers and colors) and, more notably, some "just so" perfectionistic obsessions associated with needing to reread, rewrite (also evident on the KFD when he repeatedly erased his drawing), and line objects up in a certain order. When I discussed with him how these thoughts and behaviors might affect his experience and avoidance of schoolwork, he shared his experience that reading and writing are so arduous, repetitive, and time consuming that he has settled on a solution that it is preferable to avoid these tasks all together. Thus, it became clear that OCD is indeed a significant driver of his avoidance, although his avoidance masks visible signs of OCD.

Neither the self-report nor performance-based data paint a picture that Pedro is currently depressed or struggling with underlying dysphoria. It is plausible, though, that he was working to consciously avoid acknowledging more depressive preoccupations, such as on the TAT, which led to the aforementioned distress and need for extended breaks from the task. There is also the possibility that his regular marijuana use has self-medicated and muted feelings of sadness and despair.

The data here underscore that Pedro suffers weakness/underdevelopment in his capacity for emotional regulation. It is difficult for him to sit with and tolerate his anxiety and a range of negative and even positive feelings. Pedro is inclined to be overwhelmed and respond impulsively to the welling of emotion. To prevent this, he relies heavily on efforts to minimize or deny distress, to turn painful and other aversive feelings into something happier and more exciting, and to avoid situations that are apt to evoke distress. As he so astutely self-reflected, "I am Mr. Ignore." His use of marijuana is understood, at least in part, as an effort to enhance this self-protective avoidant function. When I inquired into what he was doing during his aforementioned lengthy bathroom breaks, Pedro described "zoning out," involving staring at the wall and losing track of time passing. It is not possible to know to what extent this was an accurate account because Pedro did have his cell phone with him, so it is possible that he was actually texting, watching videos, or otherwise engaged on social media or the internet. He did not come back smelling of marijuana. But it is encouraging that the validity scales of Pedro's MMPI-A profile suggest that his orientation to self-report was an open and honest one. Pedro's report of this kind of zoning out raised questions about his propensity to dissociate (an extreme form of

> detachment from oneself and reality), but his responses to the A-DES-II were not consistent with a pattern of dissociation. Pedro's affinity for marijuana use—in which he sees no harm—can be understood in the context of his self-protective efforts to blot out and reverse unsettling feelings.
>
> Pedro's challenges around emotional regulation are significant and require treatment focus, but the present data do not converge in the direction of an emerging bipolar spectrum condition. His self-report on the MMPI-A did not elevate scales indicating proneness to mania, and his mother's report on CMRS-P fell far short of the threshold that in research has differentiated between kids with bipolar and ADHD conditions. Pedro did exhibit on the Rorschach, however, some mildly playful, jocular, energized combining of ideas consistent with what is seen with people who are vulnerable to (hypo)mania. It was difficult to know, though, whether this pattern of thinking could be associated with his ongoing (albeit reduced) marijuana use. Along similar lines, Pedro described a craving of exhilaration that has been satisfied through risk-taking behaviors. The possibility of an unfolding bipolar spectrum condition will need to be monitored clinically over time.
>
> Alongside his challenges with emotional regulation, Pedro displayed some hopeful signs of his potential for learning to better tolerate and more adaptively express his emotions. Most notably, his responses to the TAT indicated that he actually has a fairly well-developed emotional vocabulary, much more sophisticated than most teenage boys with emotional regulation and behavioral difficulties whom I have evaluated. That is, not only could he identify and attribute a range of positive (e.g., happy, excited, relief) and negative (e.g., worried, scared, angry, confused, regret) emotions, but he was able to appreciate that it is possible to experience mixed feelings ("angry . . . yet confused," "weary . . . yet excited"). Although, at this point, Pedro is likely not inclined to sit with his own distressed feelings long enough to process and verbalize them in this way, the fact that he possesses this language offers promise that through his therapy, he will be able to learn and practice applying it to himself in the moment. The hope is that being able to identify and communicate his feelings—and finding people like his therapist with whom he feels safe to do so—will contribute to detoxifying them psychologically, thus making them more tolerable and discussable.

The referral question related to the possibility that Pedro's texting inappropriate sexual content to classmates was a symptom of an emerging psychopathic character style was addressed most directly in sections of the report subtitled "Capacity for Relatedness" and "Development of Conscience." The following is an excerpt from the "Capacity for Relatedness" section:

> Encouragingly, the data overall do not point to Pedro as dismissive, callous, or exploitive in his orientation to relationships. Rather, he has strong longings for connection and caretaking, and he holds implicit expectations that relationships can be the source of nurturance, comfort, and mutuality. This suggests that he has been able to take in the love and care offered by his adoptive family. Also hopeful is that his responses to the TAT—in which he could speak to the internal experiences of multiple characters in the same story—suggest that he has the ability, at least in some situations, to consider the thoughts and feelings of others and to take their perspective. At the same time that he

is hungry for interpersonal connection, though, there are indicators of Pedro's subtle hypervigilance and mistrust that could impede (a) his sense of safety to share more vulnerability and thus also (b) greater closeness. Moreover, because of his own baseline discomfort with vulnerability, his preference to identify with a position of strength, and his challenges sitting with feelings (see earlier "Emotional Regulation" section) in moments when he is more emotionally stirred and he is on his own, he is more apt to lose access to his aforementioned ability for perspective-taking and to respond to others in impulsive, hostile ways. Related to this is another area of complication as Pedro navigates adolescent relationships: that is, the extent to which his physical maturity far exceeds his emotional maturity. Most notably, feelings and impulses around sexuality as well as peers' attraction to him may entangle him in relational situations involving intense feelings and confusing dynamics that he is not quite ready to manage on his own. Any or all of these factors may well have contributed to what transpired when he was accused of sexting by classmates.

And from the "Development of Conscience" section:

The data suggest that Pedro has developed a basic sense of right and wrong and, at this point, he does not show signs of a callous, exploitive orientation to his interactions and relationships with others as would someone consolidating a more psychopathic/antisocial character style. As described earlier (see "Capacity for Relatedness" section), Pedro has a strong longing for interpersonal connection and is able to experience relationships with some sense of mutuality. Another positive sign was his bristling in response to a BYI-2 disruptive behavior scale item about cruelty to animals, which suggested this as something he could not relate to or imagine. That said, there were indications that there is still much room for growth of sense of morality and his ability to apply it to guide his behavior. Specifically, there are times when he knows what he is supposed to do, but this can be overridden by his difficulty tolerating distressing emotions and proneness to impulsivity. This scenario was captured most tellingly in his responses to a WISC-IV item about what one should do when provoked by a younger child: "My first instinct would be to fight back." When asked to reflect on what one is *supposed to* do, he was able to identify the correct, more measured and restrained response, even though he acknowledged that he would be less likely to act in this more prosocial manner when his anger is acute.

Also of concern is some evidence that even when Pedro knows an action is wrong, he revels in the associated exhilaration and the process of avoiding getting caught. In response to an extended inquiry around another WISC-IV response, he shared an example of an incident at a concert in which he and friends snuck into a roped-off area, stole some candy, and "ran from a cop." Elsewhere in the data, he showed signs that at this point, although he cognitively knows right from wrong, he is often more motivated by avoiding punishment than any internalized sense of guilt. Thus, he still requires adults to serve as more active external regulators of his behavior.

Although the data as a whole do not point to Pedro's being at high risk for major premeditated antisocial or destructive acts, they do suggest that he remains vulnerable to poor judgment and impulsive behaviors apt to get him into trouble. Conditions more likely to be associated with such behaviors include being more on his own and less supervised, the presence of peers whom he is trying to connect

> with and impress, drug use that is disinhibiting, and when he is angry or craving exhilaration. Because the present evaluation was not a forensic one, if his team at school or others remain concerned about his level of risk, they are encouraged to pursue such an assessment.

The "Diagnostic Summary and Treatment Implications" section of the test report highlighted two potential challenges to deeper engagement and more successful outcome. First, the finding that Pedro still required a fair amount of external structure, supervision, and monitoring to regulate his behavior bumps up against his natural, developmental thrust toward greater independence in adolescence. Second, in light of current cultural views more favorable for the use of marijuana for recreational and medical purposes, it would likely be a difficult sell to convince Pedro of the need to address concerns about his marijuana use. Such concerns include the risks of harmful effects on his still-developing brain, not to mention that marijuana can exacerbate problems of apathy, judgment, impulse control, and hostility, all of which risk getting him in deeper trouble academically and otherwise. My recommendations included consultation with a certified addictions counselor to assess the priority and urgency of more intensive treatment of his marijuana use.

Pending the findings of the addictions consultation, the primary interventions detailed in the report were for (a) structured, group-oriented summer programming along the lines of an Outward Bound–type program; (b) parent guidance using a model such as collaborative problem-solving; and (c) outpatient individual and group psychotherapies with strong relationally oriented and skill-building/cognitive behavior therapy (CBT) elements. The intensive summer program was recommended because it would offer him more immediate and immersive opportunities for prosocial peer interaction and relationship-building—but under supervision; meet his cravings for excitement in healthier ways; create an extended break from marijuana use; and assist him to develop frustration tolerance, judgment, and impulse control. Regarding the outpatient treatment, group interventions were emphasized because Pedro was so drawn and receptive to peer connection and interaction. It would be important that between the combination of individual and group modalities, the CBT include both OCD-specific treatment (i.e., psychoeducation, exposure/response prevention, and acceptance strategies) and teaching dialectical behavior therapy skills, especially those related to distress tolerance. It was also recommended that the CBT clinician with expertise in treatment of OCD consult/collaborate with the team at school to revise Pedro's IEP to address the ways in which OCD interferes with his reading and written output (e.g., Adams, 2011; Chansky, 2001; March & Mulle, 1998).

The finding that mistrust was layered beneath Pedro's overt sociability underscored that a therapeutic alliance, a prerequisite for the aforementioned skill-building work, was not a given. Therefore, in the "Diagnostic Summary and Treatment Implications" section of the test report, I emphasized the importance of taking time and care to tend to the therapeutic alliance. Additionally, the hope was that as he developed more trust and was able make use of the skills to mitigate his covert anxiety/OCD, there might be opportunities to shift therapy in a more expressive/reflective direction to address such things as dynamics in close relationships, the meaning to him of his adoption and cultural identity as Latino in a White family (which he had minimized when I had directly inquired about it), and concerns around his moral decision making.

In terms of pharmacotherapy, although Pedro had negative experiences with medications aimed at helping with his inattention, it was reasonable to consult with a psychiatrist about the possibility of medication to reduce his OCD and anxiety symptoms. However, in the report, it was spelled out for the consultant that although there was no evidence for a bipolar spectrum condition, Pedro did show signs of vulnerability to a playful, energized style of thinking that can be associated with (hypo)mania, which could have implications for medications believed to activate latent vulnerabilities to (hypo)mania. I concluded the discussion of treatment implications by underscoring that to the extent that the recommended outpatient intervention did not prove effective over the subsequent 6 months to 12 months in helping Pedro improve his capacity to regulate his emotions, increase his academic engagement, and reduce his reliance on marijuana—and/or if he were to get into more serious trouble again at school or in the community—a more intensive and long-term treatment program in a residential or wilderness setting would require strong consideration.

21 COMMENTARY ON CASES AND CONCLUDING THOUGHTS

As a collection, the five cases presented in Chapters 16 through 20 demonstrate the central premise of this book that emotional dysregulation of children and adolescents takes many forms, both in terms of manifest symptoms and underlying vulnerabilities, and thus requires assessors to be thoughtful in tailoring treatment implications. These illustrations also underscore an approach to the assessment of emotional dysregulation that (a) attends to and respects taxonomic diagnosis, including the possibility of a bipolar spectrum condition, but also transcends it and (b) the value of multimethod assessment, particularly in the context of complex patients.

THE ROLE OF BIPOLAR SPECTRUM AND OTHER *DSM-5-TR* DIAGNOSTIC CATEGORIES AS WELL AS TREATMENT-CENTERED DIAGNOSIS

In each of the five cases, there was an explicit or implicit question of whether the patient's proneness to dysregulation might be understood as consistent with a bipolar spectrum condition. In only one of the five cases—Stevie's

https://doi.org/10.1037/0000430-022
Psychological Assessment of Emotional Dysregulation in Children and Adolescents: The Bipolar Spectrum and Beyond, by A. D. Bram
Copyright © 2025 by the American Psychological Association. All rights reserved.

(see Chapter 17)—did the data (e.g., family history, caregiver-report, performance-based measures) converge strongly in the direction of a bipolar spectrum diagnosis. But even in Stevie's evaluation, the assessment clarified beyond this important diagnosis in the fifth edition, text revision, of the *Diagnostic and Statistical Manual of Mental Disorders* (*DSM-5-TR*; American Psychiatric Association, 2022): Among other treatment-relevant variables, we learned about the rawness and intensity of his internal experience of emotions and his inability to contain them, his vulnerability to shame, conditions associated with his better and more regressed emotional regulation, and his strength involving a burgeoning emotional vocabulary. All of this made for an empathic, multidimensional understanding of Stevie that translated into a meaningful, individualized way of thinking about his treatment needs.

It is important to acknowledge that the account of Denny's evaluation (see Chapter 16) underscores that the approach presented here to the differential diagnosis of bipolar spectrum in young people leans conservatively. It is not difficult to imagine that other diagnosticians would be more confident than I was to conclude, based on the same data, that Denny suffered a bipolar spectrum disorder. After all, his mother—the primary caregiver—reported that Denny's hypomanic symptoms clustered over 4-day stretches, which would be enough to tick the necessary *DSM-5-TR* boxes to put him over the diagnostic line. Nevertheless, even though I believed my weighing of the mixed data (e.g., the father's less severe report on the Child Mania Rating Scale–Parent version [CMRS-P; Pavuluri, Henry, et al., 2006]; absence of bipolar-type thought disorder signs on the Rorschach [Rorschach Performance Assessment System; i.e., R-PAS; Meyer et al., 2011]; no self-report of elevated mood on the Millon® Adolescent Clinical Inventory, Second Edition [MACI®-II; Millon et al., 2020]; no family history of bipolar illness) justified equivocating on the diagnosis, I believe that the nuanced descriptions of Denny's processes of emotional regulation and how the findings did and did not fit with a bipolar prototype were facilitative of effective pharmacological, psychotherapeutic, and educational/behavioral interventions associated with his stabilization. In my view and that of the consulting psychiatrist, because Denny was barely a teenager at the time of evaluation, there would be time to determine whether his development unfolded in a manner that would lead to greater certainty that he and his family should be prepared for a lifetime of disruptions by (hypo)manic episodes and a possible indefinite need for powerful but risky psychotropics. But, in the meantime, Denny was understood well enough so that his treatment needs were met during a crucial developmental phase. In many real-world cases such as this one, a sound diagnostic understanding involves clarifying the patient's underlying makeup and treatment needs while not prematurely foreclosing on other possible developmental outcomes. Future treaters and evaluators would be able to take the present findings into account as they continued to monitor the trajectory of Denny's symptoms, functioning, and needs.

Thinking about Denny's evaluation also illuminates that sometimes nailing definitively the *Diagnostic and Statistical Manual of Mental Disorders* diagnoses is crucial, and sometimes it is less so. In Denny's case, cautiously deferring the bipolar spectrum diagnosis was not a hindrance to a meaningful formulation and treatment plan. Similarly, for Nicole (see Chapter 19), corroborating that she met *DSM-5-TR* criteria for reactive attachment disorder and adding a disruptive mood dysregulation disorder diagnosis (while ruling out the bipolar spectrum) was less valuable to her family and treaters' understanding of her than the clarifying of her: internalized sense of herself as damaged, propensity to implicitly anticipate threat and danger in her interpersonal interactions, her vulnerability to brief psychotic regression, struggles against partially ego-dystonic sadistic impulses, potential to make use of expressive arts in the service of self-reflection, and her needs for intensive educational and therapeutic interventions. On the other hand, identifying the role of social anxiety for Jillian (see Chapter 18) and obsessive-compulsive disorder (OCD) for Pedro (see Chapter 20) had clear-cut and vital treatment implications in terms of the specific variants of cognitive behavior therapy (CBT) that would be most beneficial. At the same time, though, for both Jillian and Pedro, those *DSM-5-TR* diagnoses were only one piece of a more complex picture.

For Jillian, the assessment also clarified strengths and weaknesses in her efforts at emotional regulation, her challenges acknowledging and expressing anger/assertiveness, and struggles in the developmental task of psychological separation. Her struggles with psychological separation were particularly important in informing the subsequent parent guidance component of treatment. For Pedro, diagnosing the OCD was important insofar as it was crucial in explaining his difficulty engaging in school, but the test data also highlighted his proneness to mistrust that would present potential challenges in engaging him in CBT and other potential modalities; his self-protective style strongly marked by minimization, denial, and avoidance; that although not interpersonally callous, he showed other signs of underdevelopment in his moral conscience; and the dilemmas apt to be posed by his need for external structure/supervision bumping up against his natural developmental thrust toward greater separation and independence.

THE VALUE OF MULTIMETHOD ASSESSMENT

This concluding set of cases also underscores the value of multimethod assessment (Brabender, 2023; Bram & Peebles, 2014; Hopwood & Bornstein, 2014; Weiner & Greene, 2006, 2017; Yalof & Bram, 2021). Although in the development of a new measure it is essential to establish incremental validity over existing measures in predicting relevant criterion variables (Hunsley & Meyer, 2003), in the clinical practice of assessment, we typically do not know in advance which measures will add the most value in understanding a given patient and illuminating meaningful treatment implications. Additionally, it is in the integration of findings from self-report, collateral-report, and performance-based measures that we are able to ascertain richer and more nuanced understandings. Not uncommonly, too, we can be surprised by the value added by a particular measure. In Denny's evaluation, it was the contrast between (a) his minimal self-report of concerns on the Beck Youth Inventories–Second Edition (Beck et al., 2005) and MACI-II (Millon et al., 2020) and (b) indicators of dysphoria, anxiety, and anger on the performance-based Rorschach (i.e., R-PAS; Meyer et al., 2011) and Thematic Apperception Test (TAT; Murray, 1943) that conveyed something important about his self-protective style and his limited access to his internal experience. The TAT in particular contributed to an appreciation of how little of a realistic sense Denny had about effectively addressing emotional and interpersonal challenges. Meanwhile, the caregiver-report CMRS-P (Pavuluri, Henry, et al., 2006) and its follow-up interview were crucial in teasing out the possibility of a bipolar spectrum condition (even if, ultimately, the findings were deemed equivocal).

With Stevie for whom a bipolar spectrum diagnosis was ascertained, the CMRS-P (Pavuluri, Henry, et al., 2006) and follow-up Mini International Neuropsychiatric Interview for Children and Adolescents (Sheehan, 2016) were also essential, but the convergent findings of (hypo)manic flavor of thought disorder on Stevie's Rorschach (i.e., R-PAS; Meyer et al., 2011) lent further confidence to that diagnosis and offered a window into his style of reasoning. In Jillian's evaluation, the disorder-specific self-report Kutcher Generalized Social Anxiety Disorder Scale for Adolescents (Brooks & Kutcher, 2004) was key to pinpointing the role of her social anxiety and why she was so reactive to her parents' prodding her to be more socially active; at the same time, without the Rorschach, we would not appreciate her developmental struggles around separation, another factor contributing to her intense aversion to her parents' nudging.

For Pedro, the self-report Children's Yale-Brown Obsessive Compulsive Scale (Scahill et al., 1997) that illuminated his OCD would not even have been administered were it not for the patient–examiner data involving the discussion of his prolonged bathroom breaks. Further, his responses to some Wechsler Intelligence Scale for Children–Fourth Edition (Wechsler, 2003) comprehension items pointed to lags in his moral development. At the same time, his Rorschach (i.e., R-PAS; Meyer et al., 2011) and TAT (Murray, 1943) responses did not show callous interpersonal attitudes suggestive of budding psychopathy. My excerpted summary of the findings from Nicole's evaluation did not detail specific findings from different measures, but the Rorschach (i.e., R-PAS; Meyer et al., 2011) was crucial in showing that her pattern of disordered thinking was not suggestive of an emerging schizophrenic spectrum despite reports of transient psychotic symptoms; the caregiver-report CMRS-P (Pavuluri, Henry, et al., 2006; e.g., no endorsement of manic symptoms) was crucial in ruling out the bipolar spectrum; and the performance-based TAT and Kinetic Family Drawing (Burns & Kaufman, 1970) were valuable in highlighting areas of treatment-relevant psychological strengths (e.g., her burgeoning emotional vocabulary, artwork as a means of not only self-expression but self-reflection) otherwise easily overlooked amid the seriousness of her symptoms.

CONCLUDING THOUGHTS

My hope is that this book has offered assessors both pragmatic and conceptual assistance in the assessment of children and adolescents vulnerable to emotional dysregulation. Pragmatically, I have reviewed a wide range of specific measures—self-report, collateral-report, and performance-based—for assessors to consider in individualizing their test batteries. This has involved attention to selecting and interpreting measures with a mindset sensitive to issues of diversity. The approach to assessment presented here has included methods for systematically addressing referral questions about the bipolar spectrum, but it has not been limited to such taxonomic differential diagnosis. Conceptually, attention has been devoted to thinking broadly about assessing emotional dysregulation with particular focus on translating findings into meaningful treatment implications.

I emphasize that not every emotionally dysregulated child or adolescent who presents for treatment requires the kind of comprehensive, in-depth assessment as described in this book and illustrated in Part V. However, when a young person has not responded well to previous efforts at treatment and/or when families and treaters remain puzzled about how to help, this nuanced approach can be a vital investment toward deeper understanding and consideration of what kinds of interventions—not only the principal modality but also how to engage the patient—will make a difference.

References

Aas, M., Henry, C., Andreassen, O. A., Bellivier, F., Melle, I., & Etain, B. (2016). The role of childhood trauma in bipolar disorders. *International Journal of Bipolar Disorders, 4*(1), Article 2. https://doi.org/10.1186/s40345-015-0042-0

Abramowitz, J. S., & Bucholz, J. L. (2020). Pediatric obsessive-compulsive disorder. In E. A. Youngstrom, M. J. Prinstein, E. J. Mash, & R. A. Barkley (Eds.), *Assessment of disorders in childhood and adolescence* (5th ed., pp. 307–324). The Guilford Press.

Abrams, Z. (2022). Diagnosing and treating bipolar spectrum disorders. *Monitor on Psychology, 53*(1), 36–41. https://www.apa.org/monitor/2022/01/cc-bipolar-spectrum

Accurso, E. C., & Waller, G. (2021). A brief session-by-session measure of eating disorder psychopathology for children and adolescents: Development and psychometric properties of the Eating Disorder-15 for Youth (ED-15-Y). *International Journal of Eating Disorders, 54*(4), 569–577. https://doi.org/10.1002/eat.23449

Achenbach, T. M. (1999). The Child Behavior Checklist and related instruments. In M. E. Maruish (Ed.), *The use of psychological testing for treatment planning and outcomes assessment* (pp. 429–466). Lawrence Erlbaum Associates Publishers.

Achenbach, T. M., McConaughy, S. H., & Howell, C. T. (1987). Child/adolescent behavioral and emotional problems: Implications of cross-informant correlations for situational specificity. *Psychological Bulletin, 101*(2), 213–232. https://doi.org/10.1037/0033-2909.101.2.213

Achenbach, T. M., & Rescorla, L. A. (2004). The Achenbach System of Empirically Based Assessment (ASEBA) for ages 1.5 to 18 years. In M. E. Maruish (Ed.), *The use of psychological testing for treatment planning and outcomes assessment: Vol. 2. Instruments for children and adolescents* (3rd ed., pp. 179–213). Routledge.

Adams, G. B. (2011). *Students with OCD: A handbook for school personnel.* Pherson Creek Press.

Aguirre, L. (2021). Navigating the diagnostic challenges of bipolar disorder in youth. *Journal of the American Academy of Physician Assistants, 34*(8), 21–27. https://doi.org/10.1097/01.JAA.0000758200.80004.87

Aiken, C. B., Weisler, R. H., & Sachs, G. S. (2015). The Bipolarity Index: A clinician-rated measure of diagnostic confidence. *Journal of Affective Disorders, 177*, 59–64. https://doi.org/10.1016/j.jad.2015.02.004

Akiskal, H. S. (2004). Demystifying borderline personality: Critique of the concept and unorthodox reflections on its natural kinship with the bipolar spectrum. *Acta Psychiatrica Scandinavica, 110*(6), 401–407. https://doi.org/10.1111/j.1600-0447.2004.00461.x

Alexander, L. M., Salum, G. A., Swanson, J. M., & Milham, M. P. (2020). Measuring strengths and weaknesses in dimensional psychiatry. *The Journal of Child Psychology and Psychiatry, 61*(1), 40–50. https://doi.org/10.1111/jcpp.13104

Algorta, G. P., Youngstrom, E. A., Phelps, J., Jenkins, M. M., Youngstrom, J. K., & Findling, R. L. (2013). An inexpensive family index of risk for mood issues improves identification of pediatric bipolar disorder. *Psychological Assessment, 25*(1), 12–22. https://doi.org/10.1037/a0029225

Allain, N., Leven, C., Falissard, B., Allain, J.-S., Batail, J.-M., Polard, E., Montastruc, F., Drapier, D., & Naudet, F. (2017). Manic switches induced by antidepressants: An umbrella review comparing randomized controlled trials and observational studies. *Acta Psychiatrica Scandinavica, 135*(2), 106–116. https://doi.org/10.1111/acps.12672

Alston, J. F. (2007). The complex issue of attachment disorders. *The Psychiatric Times, 24*(12). https://www.psychiatrictimes.com/view/complex-issue-attachment-disorders

Althoff, R. R., Verhulst, F. C., Rettew, D. C., Hudziak, J. J., & van der Ende, J. (2010). Adult outcomes of childhood dysregulation: A 14-year follow-up study. *Journal of the American Academy of Child & Adolescent Psychiatry, 49*(11), 1105–1116.e1. https://doi.org/10.1097/00004583-201011000-00004

Álvarez, M. J., Roura, P., Osés, A., Foguet, Q., Solà, J., & Arrufat, F. X. (2011). Prevalence and clinical impact of childhood trauma in patients with severe mental disorders. *Journal of Nervous and Mental Disease, 199*(3), 156–161. https://doi.org/10.1097/NMD.0b013e31820c751c

Amemiya, J., Mortenson, E., & Wang, M.-T. (2020). Minor infractions are not minor: School infractions for minor misconduct may increase adolescents' defiant behavior and contribute to racial disparities in school discipline. *American Psychologist, 75*(1), 23–36. https://doi.org/10.1037/amp0000475

American Academy of Child & Adolescent Psychiatry. (2010, June). *Principles of care for treatment of children and adolescents with mental illnesses in residential treatment centers*. https://www.aacap.org/App_Themes/AACAP/docs/clinical_practice_center/principles_of_care_for_children_in_residential_treatment_centers.pdf

American Academy of Pediatrics. (n.d.). *The Brief Impairment Scale (BIS)*. HEARD Alliance. https://www.heardalliance.org/wp-content/uploads/2011/04/Brief-Impairment-Scale-English.pdf

American Psychiatric Association. (1994). *Diagnostic and statistical manual of mental disorders* (4th ed.).

American Psychiatric Association. (2013). *Diagnostic and statistical manual of mental disorders* (5th ed.). https://doi.org/10.1176/appi.books.9780890425596

American Psychiatric Association. (2022). *Diagnostic and statistical manual of mental disorders* (5th ed., text rev.). https://doi.org/10.1176/appi.books.9780890425787

American Psychological Association. (n.d.-a). Base rate. In *APA dictionary of psychology*. Retrieved November 5, 2020, from https://dictionary.apa.org/base-rate

American Psychological Association. (n.d.-b). Motivational interviewing. In *APA dictionary of psychology*. Retrieved March 3, 2024, from https://dictionary.apa.org/motivational-interviewing

American Psychological Association. (2003). Guidelines on multicultural education, training, research, practice, and organizational change for psychologists. *American Psychologist, 58*(5), 377–402. https://doi.org/10.1037/0003-066X.58.5.377

Americans With Disabilities Act of 1990, 42 U.S.C. § 12101 *et seq.* (1990). https://www.ada.gov/pubs/adastatute08.htm

Andrés, M. L., del-Valle, M. V., Richaud de Minzi, M. C., Introzzi, I., Canet-Juric, L., & Navarro-Guzmán, J. I. (2021). Distress tolerance and executive functions: A systematic review. *Psychology & Neuroscience, 14*(3), 280–297. https://doi.org/10.1037/pne0000259

Androutsos, C. H. (2012). Schizophrenia in children and adolescents: Relevance and differentiation from adult schizophrenia. *Psychiatriki, 23*(Suppl. 1), 82–93.

APA Presidential Task Force on Evidence-Based Practice. (2006). Evidence-based practice in psychology. *American Psychologist, 61*(4), 271–285. https://doi.org/10.1037/0003-066X.61.4.271

Arango, C., Fraguas, D., & Parellada, M. (2014). Differential neurodevelopmental trajectories patients with early-onset bipolar and schizophrenia disorders. *Schizophrenia Bulletin, 40*(Suppl. 2), S138–S146. https://doi.org/10.1093/schbul/sbt198

Archer, R. P., Handel, R. W., Ben-Porath, Y. S., & Tellegen, A. (2016). *Minnesota Multiphasic Personality Inventory–Adolescent-Restructured Form (MMPI-A-RF): Manual for administration, scoring, interpretation, and technical manual*. University of Minnesota Press.

Armstrong, J. (2011, March 9–13). *Trauma is more than PTSD: Preview of APA's trauma clinical assessment guidelines* [Paper presentation]. Annual Meeting of the Society for Personality Assessment, Boston, MA, United States.

Armstrong, J., Carlson, E. B., & Putnam, F. (n.d.). *Adolescent Dissociative Experience Scale-II*. [Measurement instrument]. Retrieved from https://www.emdrworks.org/Downloads/a-des.pdf

Armstrong, J. G., Putnam, F. W., Carlson, E. B., Libero, D. Z., & Smith, S. R. (1997). Development and validation of a measure of adolescent dissociation: The Adolescent Dissociative Experiences Scale. *Journal of Nervous and Mental Disease, 185*(8), 491–497. https://doi.org/10.1097/00005053-199708000-00003

Arnett, J. J. (2000). Emerging adulthood. A theory of development from the late teens through the twenties. *American Psychologist, 55*(5), 469–480. https://doi.org/10.1037/0003-066X.55.5.469

Axelson, D., Birmaher, B. J., Brent, D., Wassick, S., Hoover, C., Bridge, J., & Ryan, N. (2003). A preliminary study of the Kiddie Schedule for Affective Disorders and Schizophrenia for School-Age Children Mania Rating Scale for children and adolescents. *Journal of Child and Adolescent Psychopharmacology, 13*(4), 463–470. https://doi.org/10.1089/104454603322724850

Baca, L., & Smith, S. R. (2018). Evidence-based practice in diversity-sensitive personality assessment. In S. R. Smith & R. Krishnamurthy (Eds.), *Diversity-sensitive personality assessment* (pp. 3–24). Routledge. https://doi.org/10.4324/9780203551578-1

Baio, J., Wiggins, L., Christensen, D. L., Maenner, M. J., Daniels, J., Warren, Z., Kurzius-Spencer, M., Zahorodny, W., Robinson Rosenberg, C., White, T., Durkin, M. S., Imm, P., Nikolaou, L., Yeargin-Allsopp, M., Lee, L. C., Harrington, R., Lopez, M., Fitzgerald, R. T., Hewitt, A., . . . Dowling, N. F. (2018). Prevalence of autism spectrum disorder among children aged 8 years—Autism and Developmental Disabilities Monitoring Network, 11 Sites, United States, 2014. *MMWR Surveillance Summaries, 67*(SS-6), 1–23. https://doi.org/10.15585/mmwr.ss6706a1

Banks, C., & Priebe, S. (2020). Scales for assessing the therapeutic milieu in psychiatric inpatient settings: A systematic review. *General Hospital Psychiatry, 66*, 44–50. https://doi.org/10.1016/j.genhosppsych.2020.06.014

Bardone-Cone, A. M., & von Ranson, K. M. (2020). Eating and feeding disorders. In E. A. Youngstrom, M. J. Prinstein, E. J. Mash, & R. A. Barkley (Eds.), *Assessment of disorders in childhood and adolescence* (5th ed., pp. 584–618). The Guilford Press.

Barkley, R. A. (2012). *The Barkley Functional Impairment Scale-Children and Adolescents (BFIS-CA)*. The Guilford Press.

Barkley, R. A. (2016). Measuring impairment with the Barkley Functional Impairment Scale. In S. Goldstein & J. A. Naglieri (Eds.), *Assessing impairment: From theory to practice* (2nd ed., pp. 257–273). Springer. https://doi.org/10.1007/978-1-4899-7996-4_13

Barkley, R. A., & Benton, C. M. (2013). *Your defiant child: 8 steps to better behavior* (2nd ed.). The Guilford Press.

Basting, E. J., Naser, S., & Goncy, E. A. (2022). Assessing the factor structure and measurement invariance of the BASC-3 Behavioral and Emotional Screening

System Student Form across race/ethnicity and gender. *Assessment for Effective Intervention*, *48*(1), 43–51. https://doi.org/10.1177/15345084221095440

Bayes, A., Parker, G., & Fletcher, K. (2014). Clinical differentiation of bipolar II disorder from borderline personality disorder. *Current Opinion in Psychiatry*, *27*(1), 14–20. https://doi.org/10.1097/YCO.0000000000000021

Bebbington, P. E., Bhugra, D., Brugha, T., Singleton, N., Farrell, M., Jenkins, R., Lewis, G., & Meltzer, H. (2004). Psychosis, victimisation and childhood disadvantage: Evidence from the second British National Survey of Psychiatric Morbidity. *The British Journal of Psychiatry*, *185*(3), 220–226. https://doi.org/10.1192/bjp.185.3.220

Beck, J. S., Beck, A. T., Jolly, J. B., & Steer, R. A. (2005). *Beck Youth Inventories™: Manual* (2nd ed.). Pearson.

Bell, A., Palace, K., Allen, M., & Nelson, R. (2016). Using martial arts to address social and behavioral functioning in children and adolescents with autism spectrum disorder. *Therapeutic Recreation Journal*, *50*(2), 176–180. https://doi.org/10.18666/TRJ-2016-V50-I2-7287

Bellak, L., & Bellak, S. (1949). *Children's Apperception Test*. Consulting Psychologists Press.

Ben-Eliyahu, A. (2018, October 25). What is emotional regulation and how can mentors help? *The Chronical of Evidence-Based Mentoring*. https://www.evidencebasedmentoring.org/guest-research-corner-how-mentors-can-help-young-people-regulate-their-emotions/

Berboth, S., & Morawetz, C. (2021). Amygdala-prefrontal connectivity during emotion regulation: A meta-analysis of psychophysiological interactions. *Neuropsychologia*, *153*, Article 107767. https://doi.org/10.1016/j.neuropsychologia.2021.107767

Berg, E. A. (1948). A simple objective technique for measuring flexibility in thinking. *The Journal of General Psychology*, *39*(1), 15–22. https://doi.org/10.1080/00221309.1948.9918159

Bernstein, D. P., Fink, L., Handelsman, L., Foote, J., Lovejoy, M., Wenzel, K., Sapareto, E., & Ruggiero, J. (1994). Initial reliability and validity of a new retrospective measure of child abuse and neglect. *The American Journal of Psychiatry*, *151*(8), 1132–1136. https://doi.org/10.1176/ajp.151.8.1132

Bhowmik, D., Aparasu, R. R., Rajan, S. S., Sherer, J. T., Ochoa-Perez, M., & Chen, H. (2014). Risk of manic switch associated with antidepressant therapy in pediatric bipolar depression. *Journal of Child and Adolescent Psychopharmacology*, *24*(10), 551–561. https://doi.org/10.1089/cap.2014.0028

Biederman, J., Faraone, S., Milberger, S., Guite, J., Mick, E., Chen, L., Mennin, D., Marrs, A., Ouellette, C., Moore, P., Spencer, T., Norman, D., Wilens, T., Kraus, I., & Perrin, J. (1996). A prospective 4-year follow-up study of attention-deficit hyperactivity and related disorders. *Archives of General Psychiatry*, *53*(5), 437–446. https://doi.org/10.1001/archpsyc.1996.01830050073012

Biederman, J., Faraone, S. V., Chu, M. P., & Wozniak, J. (1999). Further evidence of a bidirectional overlap between juvenile mania and conduct disorder in children. *Journal of the American Academy of Child & Adolescent Psychiatry, 38*(4), 468–476. https://doi.org/10.1097/00004583-199904000-00021

Biederman, J., Fitzgerald, M., Woodworth, K. Y., Yule, A., Noyes, E., Biederman, I., Faraone, S. V., Wilens, T., & Wozniak, J. (2018). Does the course of manic symptoms in pediatric bipolar disorder impact the course of conduct disorder? Findings from four prospective datasets. *Journal of Affective Disorders, 238*, 244–249. https://doi.org/10.1016/j.jad.2018.05.020

Bird, H. R., Canino, G. J., Davies, M., Ramírez, R., Chávez, L., Duarte, C., & Shen, S. (2005). The Brief Impairment Scale (BIS): A multidimensional scale of functional impairment for children and adolescents. *Journal of the American Academy of Child & Adolescent Psychiatry, 44*(7), 699–707. https://doi.org/10.1097/01.chi.0000163281.41383.94

Birmaher, B., Brent, D. A., Chiappetta, L., Bridge, J., Monga, S., & Baugher, M. (1999). Psychometric properties of the Screen for Child Anxiety Related Emotional Disorders (SCARED): A replication study. *Journal of the American Academy of Child & Adolescent Psychiatry, 38*(10), 1230–1236. https://doi.org/10.1097/00004583-199910000-00011

Black, R. S., Curran, D., & Dyer, K. F. (2013). The impact of shame on the therapeutic alliance and intimate relationships. *Journal of Clinical Psychology, 69*(6), 646–654. https://doi.org/10.1002/jclp.21959

Blair, C. (2017). Educating executive function. *WIREs Cognitive Science, 8*(1–2), Article e1403. https://doi.org/10.1002/wcs.1403

Bland, A. R., Roiser, J. P., Mehta, M. A., Schei, T., Boland, H., Campbell-Meiklejohn, D. K., Emsley, R. A., Munafo, M. R., Penton-Voak, I. S., Seara-Cardoso, A., Viding, E., Voon, V., Sahakian, B. J., Robbins, T. W., & Elliott, R. (2016). EMOTICOM: A neuropsychological test battery to evaluate emotion, motivation, impulsivity, and social cognition. *Frontiers in Behavioral Neuroscience, 10*, Article 25. https://doi.org/10.3389/fnbeh.2016.00025

Bornstein, R. F. (1998). Implicit and self-attributed dependency needs in dependent and histrionic personality disorders. *Journal of Personality Assessment, 71*(1), 1–14. https://doi.org/10.1207/s15327752jpa7101_1

Bornstein, R. F. (2007). Toward a process-based framework for classifying personality tests: Comment on Meyer and Kurtz (2006). *Journal of Personality Assessment, 89*(2), 202–207. https://doi.org/10.1080/00223890701518776

Borsboom, D. (2006). When does measurement invariance matter? *Medical Care, 44*(11, Suppl. 3), S176–S181. https://doi.org/10.1097/01.mlr.0000245143.08679.cc

Boudjerida, A., Labelle, R., Bergeron, L., Berthiaume, C., Guilé, J. M., & Breton, J. J. (2022). Development and initial validation of the Disruptive Mood Dysregulation Disorder Questionnaire among adolescents from clinic settings. *Frontiers in Psychiatry, 13*, Article 617991. https://doi.org/10.3389/fpsyt.2022.617991

Bowen, M. (1993). *Family therapy in clinical practice*. Jason Aronson.

Bowlby, J. (1969). *Attachment and loss: Vol. 1. Attachment*. Basic Books.

Brabender, V. M. (2023). The value of multi-method psychological assessment. In J. H. Kleiger & I. B. Weiner (Eds.), *Psychological assessment of bipolar spectrum disorders* (pp. 19–34). American Psychological Association. https://doi.org/10.1037/0000356-002

Brabender, V. M., & Fallon, A. E. (Eds.). (2013). *Working with adoptive parents: Research, theory, and therapeutic interventions*. John Wiley & Sons. https://doi.org/10.1002/9781394260492

Brabender, V. M., & Mihura, J. L. (Eds.). (2016). *Handbook of gender and sexuality in psychological assessment*. Routledge.

Braconnier, M. L., & Siper, P. M. (2021). Neuropsychological assessment in autism spectrum disorder. *Current Psychiatry Reports*, *23*(10), Article 63. https://doi.org/10.1007/s11920-021-01277-1

Bram, A. D. (2010). The relevance of the Rorschach and patient–examiner relationship in treatment planning and outcome assessment. *Journal of Personality Assessment*, *92*(2), 91–115. https://doi.org/10.1080/00223890903508112

Bram, A. D. (2012). Meet an assessment professional. In R. J. Cohen, M. E. Swerdlik, & E. D. Sturman (Eds.), *Psychological testing and assessment: An introduction to tests and measurement* (8th ed., pp. 469–470). McGraw-Hill.

Bram, A. D. (2013). Psychological testing and treatment implications: We can say more. *Journal of Personality Assessment*, *95*(4), 319–331. https://doi.org/10.1080/00223891.2012.736907

Bram, A. D. (2015). To resume a stalled psychotherapy? Psychological testing to understand an impasse and reevaluate treatment options. *Journal of Personality Assessment*, *97*(3), 241–249. https://doi.org/10.1080/00223891.2014.997824

Bram, A. D. (2017). Reviving and refining psychodynamic interpretation of the Wechsler intelligence tests: The Verbal Comprehension subtests. *Journal of Personality Assessment*, *99*(3), 324–333. https://doi.org/10.1080/00223891.2016.1236342

Bram, A. D. (2018a, March 14–18). Testing the limits in personality assessment administration: Considerations and illustrations. In J. Yalof (Chair), *The assessment framework: Testing the limits in administration and interpretation* [Symposium]. Society for Personality Assessment Annual Convention, Washington, DC, United States.

Bram, A. D. (2018b). Understanding a therapeutic impasse: Use of R-PAS in a multimethod assessment of alliance dynamics and underlying developmental disruption. In J. L. Mihura & G. J. Meyer (Eds.), *Using the Rorschach Performance Assessment System® (R-PAS®)* (pp. 119–137). The Guilford Press.

Bram, A. D. (2021). Psychoanalytic assessment in private practice. In J. Yalof & A. D. Bram (Eds.), *Psychoanalytic assessment applications in different settings* (pp. 6–27). Routledge.

Bram, A. D., & Peebles, M. J. (2014). *Psychological testing that matters: Creating a road map for effective treatment*. American Psychological Association. https://doi.org/10.1037/14340-000

Bram, A. D., Viglione, D. J., Lee-Parritz, O., Gottschalk, K. A., Yalof, J. A., Kleiger, J. H., Dyette, K., & Khadivi, A. (2023). Rorschach assessment of ego involvement in affect regulation: Interrater reliability of form dominance in shading and achromatic color responses. *Psychoanalytic Psychology, 40*(4), 328–337. https://doi.org/10.1037/pap0000458

Bram, A. D., & Yalof, J. (2018). Two contemporary Rorschach systems: Views of two experienced Rorschachers on the CS and R-PAS. *SIS Journal of Projective Psychology & Mental Health, 25*(1), 35–43.

Brand, B. L., Armstrong, J. G., & Loewenstein, R. J. (2006). Psychological assessment of patients with dissociative identity disorder. *Psychiatric Clinics of North America, 29*(1), 145–168. https://doi.org/10.1016/j.psc.2005.10.014

Brazelton, T. B., & Cramer, B. G. (1991). *The earliest relationship: Parents, infants, and the drama of early attachment*. Da Capo Press.

Breton, É., Juster, R.-P., & Booij, L. (2023). Gender and sex in eating disorders: A narrative review of the current state of knowledge, research gaps, and recommendations. *Brain and Behavior, 13*(4), Article e2871. https://doi.org/10.1002/brb3.2871

Brobbey, G. (2018). Punishing the vulnerable: Exploring suspension rates for students with learning disabilities. *Intervention in School and Clinic, 53*(4), 216–219. https://doi.org/10.1177/1053451217712953

Brodey, B. B., McMullin, D., Kaminer, Y., Winters, K. C., Mosshart, E., Rosen, C. S., & Brodey, I. S. (2008). Psychometric characteristics of the Teen Addiction Severity Index–Two (T-ASI-2). *Substance Abuse, 29*(2), 19–32. https://doi.org/10.1080/08897070802092942

Brooks, S. J., & Kutcher, S. (2004). The Kutcher Generalized Social Anxiety Disorder Scale for Adolescents: Assessment of its evaluative properties over the course of a 16-week pediatric psychopharmacotherapy trial. *Journal of Child and Adolescent Psychopharmacology, 14*(2), 273–286. https://doi.org/10.1089/1044546041649002

Brustenghi, F., Mezzetti, F. A. F., Di Sarno, C., Giulietti, C., Moretti, P., & Tortorella, A. (2019). Eating disorders: The role of childhood trauma and the emotion dysregulation. *Psychiatria Danubina, 31*(Suppl. 3), 509–511.

Bryant-Waugh, R. J., Cooper, P. J., Taylor, C. L., & Lask, B. D. (1996). The use of the eating disorder examination with children: A pilot study. *International Journal of Eating Disorders, 19*(4), 391–397. https://doi.org/10.1002/(SICI)1098-108X(199605)19:4<391::AID-EAT6>3.0.CO;2-G

Buehler, C., & Welsh, D. P. (2009). A process model of adolescents' triangulation into parents' marital conflict: The role of emotional reactivity. *Journal of Family Psychology, 23*(2), 167–180. https://doi.org/10.1037/a0014976

Burke, N. L., Tanofsky-Kraff, M., Crosby, R., Mehari, R. D., Marwitz, S. E., Broadney, M. M., Shomaker, L. B., Kelly, N. R., Schvey, N. A., Cassidy, O., Yanovski, S. Z., & Yanovski, J. A. (2017). Measurement invariance of the Eating Disorder Examination in Black and White children and adolescents. *International Journal of Eating Disorders, 50*(7), 758–768. https://doi.org/10.1002/eat.22713

Burns, R. C., & Kaufman, S. (1970). *Kinetic Family Drawings (KFD): An introduction to understanding children through kinetic drawings*. Brunner/Mazel.

Butcher, J. N., Dahlstrom, W. G., Graham, J. R., Tellegen, A., & Kaemmer, B. (1989). *Minnesota Multiphasic Personality Inventory-2 (MMPI-2): Manual for administration and scoring*. University of Minnesota Press.

Butcher, J. N., Williams, C., Graham, J. R., Archer, R. P., Tellegen, A., Ben-Porath, Y. S., & Kaemmer, B. (1992). *Minnesota Multiphasic Personality Inventory–Adolescent*. University of Minnesota Press.

Byrne, B. M., & Watkins, D. (2003). The issue of measurement invariance revisited. *Journal of Cross-Cultural Psychology, 34*(2), 155–175. https://doi.org/10.1177/0022022102250225

Canino, G. J., Fisher, P. W., Alegria, M., & Bird, H. (2013). Assessing child impairment in functioning in different contexts: Implications for use of services and the classification of psychiatric disorders. *Open Journal of Medical Psychology, 2*(1), 29–34. https://doi.org/10.4236/ojmp.2013.21006

Carlson, G. A., & Youngstrom, E. A. (2003). Clinical implications of pervasive manic symptoms in children. *Biological Psychiatry, 53*(11), 1050–1058. https://doi.org/10.1016/S0006-3223(03)00068-4

Carpenter, R. W., & Trull, T. J. (2013). Components of emotion dysregulation in borderline personality disorder: A review. *Current Psychiatry Reports, 15*(1), Article 335. https://doi.org/10.1007/s11920-012-0335-2

Carpenter-Song, E. (2009). Caught in the psychiatric net: Meanings and experiences of ADHD, pediatric bipolar disorder and mental health treatment among a diverse group of families in the United States. *Culture, Medicine, and Psychiatry, 33*(1), 61–85. https://doi.org/10.1007/s11013-008-9120-4

Carter, J. C., Stewart, D. A., & Fairburn, C. G. (2001). Eating disorder examination questionnaire: Norms for young adolescent girls. *Behaviour Research and Therapy, 39*(5), 625–632. https://doi.org/10.1016/S0005-7967(00)00033-4

Castro-Blanco, D., & Karver, M. S. (Eds.). (2010). *Elusive alliance: Treatment engagement strategies with high-risk adolescents*. American Psychological Association. https://doi.org/10.1037/12139-000

Centers for Disease Control and Prevention. (2006). Mental health in the United States: Parental report of diagnosed autism in children aged 4–17 years—United States, 2003–2004. *Morbidity and Mortality Weekly Report, 55*(17), 481–486.

Cepeda, C., & Gotanco, L. (2017). *Psychiatric interview of children and adolescents*. American Psychiatric Association Publishing.

Chahin, S. S., Apple, R. W., Kuo, K. H., & Dickson, C. A. (2020). Autism spectrum disorder: Psychological and functional assessment, and behavioral treatment approaches. *Translational Pediatrics, 9*(Suppl. 1), S66–S75. https://doi.org/10.21037/tp.2019.11.06

Chansky, T. E. (2001). *Freeing your child from obsessive-compulsive disorder: A powerful, practical program for parents of children and adolescents*. Crown Publishers.

Cheung, R. Y. M., & Park, I. J. K. (2010). Anger suppression, interdependent self-construal, and depression among Asian American and European American college students. *Cultural Diversity & Ethnic Minority Psychology, 16*(4), 517–525. https://doi.org/10.1037/a0020655

Chiappetta, L., Stark, S., Mahmoud, K. F., Bahnsen, K. R., & Mitchell, A. M. (2018). Motivational interviewing to increase outpatient attendance for adolescent psychiatric patients. *Journal of Psychosocial Nursing and Mental Health Services, 56*(6), 31–35. https://doi.org/10.3928/02793695-20180212-04

Child and Adolescent Trauma Screen 2 (CATS-2): Self Report (7–17) Years. (n.d.). Oklahoma TF-CBT. https://oklahomatfcbt.org/wp-content/uploads/2023/04/CATS-2-Selfreport-English-DSM-scoring-only.pdf

Children's Yale-Brown Obsessive Compulsive Scale (CY-BOCS). (n.d.). Massachusetts Child Psychiatry Access Program. https://www.mcpap.com/pdf/CYBOCS.pdf

Cimbora, D. M., & Krishnamurthy, R. (2018). Asking difficult questions: Client definitions. In S. R. Smith & R. Krishnamurthy (Eds.), *Diversity-sensitive personality assessment* (pp. 27–42). Routledge. https://doi.org/10.4324/9780203551578-2

Cipani, E. (2017). *Functional behavioral assessment, diagnosis, and treatment: A complete system for education and mental health settings* (3rd ed.). Springer Publishing. https://doi.org/10.1891/9780826170330

Cogan, C. M., Paquet, C. B., Lee, J. Y., Miller, K. E., Crowley, M. D., & Davis, J. L. (2021). Differentiating the symptoms of posttraumatic stress disorder and bipolar disorders in adults: Utilizing a trauma-informed assessment approach. *Clinical Psychology & Psychotherapy, 28*(1), 251–260. https://doi.org/10.1002/cpp.2504

Cohen, J. A., Mannarino, A. P., Kliethermes, M., & Murray, L. A. (2012). Trauma-focused CBT for youth with complex trauma. *Child Abuse & Neglect, 36*(6), 528–541. https://doi.org/10.1016/j.chiabu.2012.03.007

Columbia University, Mailman School of Public Health. (n.d.). *Differential item functioning*. https://www.publichealth.columbia.edu/research/population-health-methods/differential-item-functioning

Comsa, M., Anderson, K. N., Sharma, A., Yadav, V. C., & Watson, S. (2022). The relationship between sleep and depression and bipolar disorder in children and young people. *BJPsych Open, 8*(1), Article e27. https://doi.org/10.1192/bjo.2021.1076

Conners, C. K. (2008). *Conners* (3rd ed.). Multi-Health Systems.

Conners, C. K. (2014a). *Conners Continuous Auditory Test of Attention*. Multi-Health Systems.

Conners, C. K. (2014b). *Conners Continuous Performance Test* (3rd ed.). Multi-Health Systems.

Conners, C. K. (2015). *Conners Kiddie Continuous Performance Test* (2nd ed.). Multi-Health Systems.

Constantino, G., Dana, R. H., & Malgady, R. G. (2007). *TEMAS (Tell-Me-A-Story) assessment in multicultural societies*. Routledge.

Constantino, J. N., & Gruber, C. P. (2012). *Social Responsiveness Scale* (2nd ed.). Western Psychological Services.

Cooper, M., & Norcross, J. C. (2016). A brief, multidimensional measure of clients' therapy preferences: The Cooper-Norcross Inventory of Preferences (C-NIP). *International Journal of Clinical and Health Psychology, 16*(1), 87–98. https://doi.org/10.1016/j.ijchp.2015.08.003

Cooper, S. H., Perry, J. C., & Arnow, D. (1988). An empirical approach to the study of defense mechanisms: I. Reliability and preliminary validity of the Rorschach Defense scales. *Journal of Personality Assessment, 52*(2), 187–203. https://doi.org/10.1207/s15327752jpa5202_1

Copeland, W. E., Brotman, M. A., & Costello, E. J. (2015). Normative irritability in youth: Developmental findings from the Great Smoky Mountains Study. *Journal of the American Academy of Child & Adolescent Psychiatry, 54*(8), 635–642. https://doi.org/10.1016/j.jaac.2015.05.008

Craba, A., Mazza, M., Marano, G., Rinaldi, L., Sani, G., & Janiri, L. (2021). Which comes first? New insights on comorbidity between eating disorders and bipolar disorders. *Emerging Trends in Drugs. Addictions, and Health*. Advance online publication. https://doi.org/10.1016/j.etdah.2021.100023

Cradock O'Leary, J., Nakamura, N., & Finn, S. E. (2020). The Thurston Cradock Test of Shame as a crucial "empathy magnifier": A therapeutic assessment of a teenager and her parents. *Rorschachiana, 41*(2), 144–161. https://doi.org/10.1027/1192-5604/a000128

Cramer, P. (1991). *The development of defense mechanisms: Theory, research, and assessment*. Springer-Verlag. https://doi.org/10.1007/978-1-4613-9025-1

Croskerry, P. (2003). The importance of cognitive errors in diagnosis and strategies to minimize them. *Academic Medicine, 78*(8), 775–780. https://doi.org/10.1097/00001888-200308000-00003

Crouch, W. (1998). The therapeutic milieu and treatment of emotionally disturbed children: Clinical application. *Clinical Child Psychology and Psychiatry, 3*(1), 115–129. https://doi.org/10.1177/1359104598031011

Cultural and Mental Health Disparities. (n.d.). *Understanding the impact of racism: UConn Racial/Ethnic Stress & Trauma Scale (UnRESTS)*. https://www.mentalhealthdisparities.org/unrests.php

D'Amico, E. J., Parast, L., Meredith, L. S., Ewing, B. A., Shadel, W. G., & Stein, B. D. (2016). Screening in primary care: What is the best way to identify at-risk youth for substance use? *Pediatrics, 138*(6), Article e20161717. https://doi.org/10.1542/peds.2016-1717

Dana, R. H. (2005). *Multicultural assessment: Principles, applications, and examples*. Routledge. https://doi.org/10.4324/9781410612540

Dawson, P., & Guare, R. (2018). *Executive skills in children and adolescents: A practical guide to assessment and intervention* (3rd ed.). The Guilford Press.

Dean, S., Britt, E., Bell, E., Stanley, J., & Collings, S. (2016). Motivational interviewing to enhance adolescent mental health treatment engagement: A randomized clinical trial. *Psychological Medicine, 46*(9), 1961–1969. https://doi.org/10.1017/S0033291716000568

Deighton, J., Croudace, T., Fonagy, P., Brown, J., Patalay, P., & Wolpert, M. (2014). Measuring mental health and wellbeing outcomes for children and adolescents to inform practice and policy: A review of child self-report measures. *Child and Adolescent Psychiatry and Mental Health*, *8*(1), Article 14. https://doi.org/10.1186/1753-2000-8-14

DelBello, M. P., Adler, C. M., Amicone, J., Mills, N. P., Shear, P. K., Warner, J., & Strakowski, S. M. (2004). Parametric neurocognitive task design: A pilot study of sustained attention in adolescents with bipolar disorder. *Journal of Affective Disorders*, *82*(Suppl. 1), S79–S88. https://doi.org/10.1016/j.jad.2004.05.014

DelBello, M. P., Lopez-Larson, M. P., Soutullo, C. A., & Strakowski, S. M. (2001). Effects of race on psychiatric diagnosis of hospitalized adolescents: A retrospective chart review. *Journal of Child and Adolescent Psychopharmacology*, *11*(1), 95–103. https://doi.org/10.1089/104454601750143528

DelCarmen-Wiggins, R., & Carter, A. S. (Eds.). (2019). *The Oxford handbook of infant, toddler, and preschool mental health assessment* (2nd ed.). Oxford University Press.

De Leersnyder, J., Boiger, M., & Mesquita, B. (2013). Cultural regulation of emotion: Individual, relational, and structural sources. *Frontiers in Psychology*, *4*, Article 55. https://doi.org/10.3389/fpsyg.2013.00055

DeMille, S., Tucker, A. R., Gass, M., Javorski, S., Vankanegan, C., Talbot, B., & Karoff, M. (2018). The effectiveness of outdoor behavioral healthcare with struggling adolescents: A comparison group study a contribution for the special issue: Social innovation in child and youth services. *Children and Youth Services Review*, *88*, 241–248. https://doi.org/10.1016/j.childyouth.2018.03.015

De Nadai, A. S., Karver, M. S., Murphy, T. K., Cavitt, M. A., Alvaro, J. L., Bengtson, M., Stock, S., Rakhshani, A. C., & Storch, E. A. (2017). Common factors in pediatric psychiatry: A review of essential and adjunctive mechanisms of treatment outcome. *Journal of Child and Adolescent Psychopharmacology*, *27*(1), 10–18. https://doi.org/10.1089/cap.2015.0263

Diamond, A. (2013). Executive functions. *Annual Review of Psychology*, *64*(1), 135–168. https://doi.org/10.1146/annurev-psych-113011-143750

Dimitrov, D. M. (2010). Testing for factorial invariance in the context of construct validation. *Measurement and Evaluation in Counseling and Development*, *43*(2), 121–149. https://doi.org/10.1177/0748175610373459

Duffy, A., Carlson, G., Dubicka, B., & Hillegers, M. H. J. (2020). Pre-pubertal bipolar disorder: Origins and current status of the controversy. *International Journal of Bipolar Disorders*, *8*(1), Article 18. https://doi.org/10.1186/s40345-020-00185-2

Duffy, A., Grof, P., Robertson, C., & Alda, M. (2000). The implications of genetics studies of major mood disorders for clinical practice. *The Journal of Clinical Psychiatry*, *61*(9), 630–637. https://doi.org/10.4088/JCP.v61n0906

DuPaul, G. J., Power, T. J., Anastopoulos, A. D., & Reid, R. (2016). *ADHD Rating Scale-5 for children and adolescents: Checklists, norms, and clinical interpretation*. The Guilford Press.

Durlak, J. A., Mahoney, J. L., & Boyle, A. E. (2022). What we know, and what we need to find out about universal, school-based social and emotional learning programs for children and adolescents: A review of meta-analyses and directions for future research. *Psychological Bulletin, 148*(11–12), 765–782. https://doi.org/10.1037/bul0000383

East-Richard, C. R., Mercier, A. R., Nadeau, D., & Cellard, C. (2020). Transdiagnostic neurocognitive deficits in psychiatry: A review of meta-analyses. *Canadian Psychology, 61*(3), 190–214. https://doi.org/10.1037/cap0000196

Eating Disorders in Youth–Questionnaire: English version. (n.d.). University of Leipzig Publication Server. https://ul.qucosa.de/api/qucosa%3A14486/attachment/ATT-0/

Eating Questionnaire–A (EDE-A). (n.d.). Child Outcomes Research Consortium. https://www.corc.uk.net/media/1272/ede-a-adolescentquestionnaire.pdf

Edyburn, K. L., Dowdy, E., DiStefano, C., Bertone, A., & Greer, F. (2020). Measurement invariance of the English and Spanish BASC-3 behavioral and emotional screening system parent preschool forms. *Early Childhood Research Quarterly, 51*, 307–316. https://doi.org/10.1016/j.ecresq.2019.12.002

Eklund, K., Rossen, E., Koriakin, T., Chafouleas, S. M., & Resnick, C. (2018). A systematic review of trauma screening measures for children and adolescents. *School Psychology Quarterly, 33*(1), 30–43. https://doi.org/10.1037/spq0000244

Elkins, R. M., Pincus, D. B., & Comer, J. S. (2014). A psychometric evaluation of the Panic Disorder Severity Scale for Children and Adolescents. *Psychological Assessment, 26*(2), 609–618. https://doi.org/10.1037/a0035283

Ellis, E. E., Yilanli, M., & Saadabadi, A. (2022). *Reactive attachment disorder*. StatPearls Publishing. https://www.ncbi.nlm.nih.gov/books/NBK537155/

Eskander, N., Emamy, M., Saad-Omer, S. M., Khan, F., & Jahan, N. (2020). The impact of impulsivity and emotional dysregulation on comorbid bipolar disorder and borderline personality disorder. *Cureus, 12*(8), Article e9581. https://doi.org/10.7759/cureus.9581

Evans, S. C., Karlovich, A. R., Khurana, S., Edelman, A., Buza, B., Riddle, W., & López Sosa, D. (2024). Evidence base update on the assessment of irritability, anger, and aggression in youth. *Journal of Clinical Child & Adolescent Psychology*. Advance online publication. https://doi.org/10.1080/15374416.2023.2292041

Exner, J. E. (2003). *The Rorschach: A Comprehensive System: Vol. 1. Basic foundations and principles of interpretation* (4th ed.). Wiley.

Exner, J. E., Andronikof, A., & Fontan, P. (2022). *The Rorschach: A Comprehensive System—Revised administration and coding manual*. Rorschach Workshops.

Extended Strengths and Weaknesses Assessment of Normal Behavior (E-SWAN). (n.d.). Child Mind Institute, UFRGS [Universidade Federal do Rio Grande do Sul], & UCI [University of California, Irvine]. http://www.eswan.org/dmdd/

Fairburn, C. G., & Cooper, Z. (1993). The Eating Disorder Examination. In C. G. Fairburn & G. T. Wilson (Eds.), *Binge eating: Nature, assessment, and treatment* (Vol. 12, pp. 317–360). The Guilford Press.

The Family Index of Risk for Mood (FIRM). (n.d.). Qualtrics. https://unc.az1.qualtrics.com/jfe/form/SV_25i6gZJ4cmV4K9L

Farmer, J. (n.d.). *What every parent should know about PBIS and IEP support in special education*. IEP Mommy. https://iepmommy.com/what-every-parent-should-know-about-pbis-and-iep-support-in-special-education/

Feinstein, A. R. (1970). The pre-therapeutic classification of co-morbidity in chronic disease. *Journal of Chronic Diseases*, *23*(7), 455–468. https://doi.org/10.1016/0021-9681(70)90054-8

Fela-Thomas, A. L., Olotu, O. S., & Esan, O. (2018). Risk of manic switch with antidepressants use in patients with bipolar disorder in a Nigerian neuro-psychiatric hospital. *The South African Journal of Psychiatry*, *24*, Article 1215. https://doi.org/10.4102/sajpsychiatry.v24i0.1215

Feriante, J., Shayani, A., Lauer, E., Pressman, A., & Rubin, E. (2022). Sibling support program: A novel peer support intervention for parents, caregivers and siblings of youth experiencing mental illness. *Healthcare*, *10*(5), Article 908. https://doi.org/10.3390/healthcare100509086

Finn, S. E., Fischer, C. T., & Handler, L. (Eds.). (2012). *Collaborative/therapeutic assessment: A casebook and guide*. John Wiley & Sons.

Flannery, K. A., & Wisner-Carlson, R. (2020). Autism and education. *Child and Adolescent Psychiatric Clinics of North America*, *29*(2), 319–343. https://doi.org/10.1016/j.chc.2019.12.005

Fleischer, N., Crane, M. E., & Kendall, P. C. (2020). Anxiety disorders. In E. A. Youngstrom, M. J. Prinstein, E. J. Mash, & R. A. Barkley (Eds.), *Assessment of disorders in childhood and adolescence* (5th ed., pp. 269–306). The Guilford Press.

Flückiger, C., Del Re, A. C., Wampold, B. E., & Horvath, A. O. (2018). The alliance in adult psychotherapy: A meta-analytic synthesis. *Psychotherapy*, *55*(4), 316–340. https://doi.org/10.1037/pst0000172

Fonagy, P., Gergely, G., Jurist, E. L., & Target, M. (2002). *Affect regulation, mentalization, and the development of the self*. Other Press.

Fontanella, C. A. (2008). The influence of clinical, treatment, and healthcare system characteristics on psychiatric readmission of adolescents. *American Journal of Orthopsychiatry*, *78*(2), 187–198. https://doi.org/10.1037/a0012557

Ford, B. Q., & Mauss, I. B. (2015). Culture and emotion regulation. *Current Opinion in Psychology*, *3*, 1–5. https://doi.org/10.1016/j.copsyc.2014.12.004

Ford, J. D., & Cloitre, M. (2009). Best practices in psychotherapy for children and adolescents. In C. A. Courtois & J. A. Ford (Eds.), *Treating complex traumatic stress disorders: An evidence-based guide* (pp. 59–81). The Guilford Press.

Fowke, A., Ross, S., & Ashcroft, K. (2012). Childhood maltreatment and internalized shame in adults with a diagnosis of bipolar disorder. *Clinical Psychology & Psychotherapy*, *19*(5), 450–457. https://doi.org/10.1002/cpp.752

Franklin, M. E., Freeman, J. B., & March, J. S. (2019). *Treating OCD in children and adolescents: A cognitive-behavioral approach*. The Guilford Press.

Frazier, T. W., Chetcuti, L., Al-Shaban, F. A., Haslam, N., Ghazal, I., Klingemier, E. W., Aldosari, M., Whitehouse, A. J. O., Youngstrom, E. A., Hardan, A. Y.,

& Uljarević, M. (2023). Categorical versus dimensional structure of autism spectrum disorder: A multi-method investigation. *JCPP Advances*, *3*(2), Article e12142. https://doi.org/10.1002/jcv2.12142

Frazier, T. W., Whitehouse, A. J. O., Leekam, S. R., Carrington, S. J., Alvares, G. A., Evans, D. W., Hardan, A. Y., & Uljarević, M. (2023). Reliability of the commonly used and newly-developed autism measures. *Journal of Autism and Developmental Disorders*. Advance online publication. https://doi.org/10.1007/s10803-023-05967-y

Freud, S. (1953a). The interpretation of dreams. In *The standard edition of the complete psychological works of Sigmund Freud* (Vol. 4–5; J. Strachey, Ed. & Trans.; pp. 1–751). Hogarth Press. (Original work published 1900)

Freud, S. (1953b). Introductory lectures on psycho-analysis. In *The standard edition of the complete psychological works of Sigmund Freud* (Vol. 16; J. Strachey, Ed. & Trans.; pp. 1–267). Hogarth Press. (Original work published 1917)

Frías, Á., Baltasar, I., & Birmaher, B. (2016). Comorbidity between bipolar disorder and borderline personality disorder: Prevalence, explanatory theories, and clinical impact. *Journal of Affective Disorders*, *202*, 210–219. https://doi.org/10.1016/j.jad.2016.05.048

Frías, Á., Palma, C., & Farriols, N. (2015). Comorbidity in pediatric bipolar disorder: Prevalence, clinical impact, etiology and treatment. *Journal of Affective Disorders*, *174*, 378–389. https://doi.org/10.1016/j.jad.2014.12.008

Fristad, M. A., & MacPherson, H. A. (2014). Evidence-based psychosocial treatments for child and adolescent bipolar spectrum disorders. *Journal of Clinical Child & Adolescent Psychology*, *43*(3), 339–355. https://doi.org/10.1080/15374416.2013.822309

Fristad, M. A., Verducci, J. S., Walters, K., & Young, M. E. (2009). Impact of multifamily psychoeducational psychotherapy in treating children aged 8 to 12 years with mood disorders. *Archives of General Psychiatry*, *66*(9), 1013–1021. https://doi.org/10.1001/archgenpsychiatry.2009.112

Fulford, D., Eisner, L. R., & Johnson, S. L. (2015). Differentiating risk for mania and borderline personality disorder: The nature of goal regulation and impulsivity. *Psychiatry Research*, *227*(2–3), 347–352. https://doi.org/10.1016/j.psychres.2015.02.001

Funder, D. (2020, January 31). MIsgivings: Some thoughts about "measurement invariance." *Funderstorms*. https://funderstorms.wordpress.com/2020/01/31/misgivings-some-thoughts-about-measurement-invariance/

Fung, A. L. C., & Lee, T. K. H. (2018). Effectiveness of Chinese martial arts and philosophy to reduce reactive and proactive aggression in schoolchildren. *Journal of Developmental and Behavioral Pediatrics*, *39*(5), 404–414. https://doi.org/10.1097/DBP.0000000000000565

Gabbard, G. O. (1995). Countertransference: The emerging common ground. *The International Journal of Psycho-Analysis*, *76*(3), 475–485.

Gadow, K. D., & Sprafkin, J. (2013). *Child & Adolescent Symptom Inventory-5 (ages 5 to 18 years)*. Checkmate Plus. https://www.checkmateplus.com/casi-5

Garno, J. L., Goldberg, J. F., Ramirez, P. M., & Ritzler, B. A. (2005). Impact of childhood abuse on the clinical course of bipolar disorder. *The British Journal of Psychiatry, 186*(2), 121–125. https://doi.org/10.1192/bjp.186.2.121

Geller, B., Warner, K., Williams, M., & Zimerman, B. (1998). Prepubertal and young adolescent bipolarity versus ADHD: Assessment and validity using the WASH-U-KSADS, CBCL and TRF. *Journal of Affective Disorders, 51*(2), 93–100. https://doi.org/10.1016/S0165-0327(98)00176-1

Gender Minority Stress and Resilience Measure for Adolescents (GMSR-A). (n.d.). National Institutes of Health Manuscript Submission. https://www.ncbi.nlm.nih.gov/pmc/articles/PMC7678225/bin/NIHMS1044230-supplement-Supplemental_Material.pdf

Gergov, V., Marttunen, M., Lindberg, N., Lipsanen, J., & Lahti, J. (2021). Therapeutic alliance: A comparison study between adolescent patients and their therapists. *International Journal of Environmental Research and Public Health, 18*(21), Article 11238. https://doi.org/10.3390/ijerph182111238

Gill, D., Warburton, W., Simes, D., & Sweller, N. (2018). Group therapy for emotional dysregulation: Treatment for adolescents and their parents. *Child and Adolescent Social Work Journal, 35*(2), 169–180. https://doi.org/10.1007/s10560-017-0510-8

Gioia, G. A., Isquith, P. K., Guy, S. C., & Kenworthy, L. (2015). *Brief Rating Inventory of Executive Function* (2nd ed.). PAR.

Goldstein, S., & Naglieri, J. A. (2010). *Autism Spectrum Rating Scales (ASRS)*. Multi-Health Systems.

Goldstein, S., & Naglieri, J. A. (2016a). Measuring impairment with the Rating Scale of Impairment. In S. Goldstein & J. A. Naglieri (Eds.), *Assessing impairment: From theory to practice* (2nd ed., pp. 247–255). Springer. https://doi.org/10.1007/978-1-4899-7996-4_12

Goldstein, S., & Naglieri, J. A. (2016b). *Rating Scale of Impairment (RSI)*. Multi-Health Systems.

Goldstein, T. R., Fersch-Podrat, R. K., Rivera, M., Axelson, D. A., Merranko, J., Yu, H., Brent, D. A., & Birmaher, B. (2015). Dialectical behavior therapy for adolescents with bipolar disorder: Results from a pilot randomized trial. *Journal of Child and Adolescent Psychopharmacology, 25*(2), 140–149. https://doi.org/10.1089/cap.2013.0145

González-Prendes, A. A. (2013). Culture-sensitive regulation of anger. In E. Fernandez (Ed.), *Treatments for anger in specific populations: Theory, application, and outcome* (pp. 236–254). Oxford University Press. https://doi.org/10.1093/med:psych/9780199914661.003.0013

Gorske, T. T., & Smith, S. R. (2009). *Collaborative therapeutic neuropsychological assessment*. Springer. https://doi.org/10.1007/978-0-387-75426-0

Gottesman, I. I., Laursen, T. M., Bertelsen, A., & Mortensen, P. B. (2010). Severe mental disorders in offspring with 2 psychiatrically ill parents. *Archives of General Psychiatry, 67*(3), 252–257. https://doi.org/10.1001/archgenpsychiatry.2010.1

Gracious, B. L., Youngstrom, E. A., Findling, R. L., & Calabrese, J. R. (2002). Discriminative validity of a parent version of the Young Mania Rating Scale. *Journal of the American Academy of Child & Adolescent Psychiatry, 41*(11), 1350–1359. https://doi.org/10.1097/00004583-200211000-00017

Greene, R., & Winkler, J. (2019). Collaborative & proactive solutions (CPS): A review of research findings in families, schools, and treatment facilities. *Clinical Child and Family Psychology Review, 22*(4), 549–561. https://doi.org/10.1007/s10567-019-00295-z

Greene, R. W. (2016). *Lost & found: Helping behaviorally challenging students (and, while you're at it, all the others)*. Jossey-Bass.

Greene, R. W. (2021). *The explosive child: A new approach for understanding and parenting easily frustrated, chronically inflexible children* (6th ed.). Harper Paperbacks.

Greene, R. W., & Ablon, J. S. (2005). *Treating explosive kids: The collaborative problem-solving approach.* The Guilford Press.

Greene, R. W., & Haynes, S. (2021). An alternative to exclusionary discipline. *Childhood Education, 97*(5), 72–76. https://doi.org/10.1080/00094056.2021.1982300

Greenwald, R., & Rubin, A. (1999). Assessment of posttraumatic symptoms in children: Development and preliminary validation of parent and child scales. *Research on Social Work Practice, 9*(1), 61–75. https://doi.org/10.1177/104973159900900105

Gross, J. J. (1998). The emerging field of emotion regulation: An integrative review. *Review of General Psychology, 2*(3), 271–299. https://doi.org/10.1037/1089-2680.2.3.271

Groth-Marnat, G., & Wright, A. J. (2016). *Handbook of psychological assessment* (6th ed.). John Wiley & Sons. https://doi.org/10.1002/9781394258918

Groves, S., Backer, H. S., van den Bosch, W., & Miller, A. (2012). Dialectical behaviour therapy with adolescents. *Child and Adolescent Mental Health, 17*(2), 65–75. https://doi.org/10.1111/j.1475-3588.2011.00611.x

Guilé, J. M., Boissel, L., Alaux-Cantin, S., & Garny de La Rivière, S. (2018). Borderline personality disorder in adolescents: Prevalence, diagnosis, and treatment strategies. *Adolescent Health, Medicine and Therapeutics, 9*, 199–210. https://doi.org/10.2147/AHMT.S156565

Gullone, E. (n.d.). *Psychological measures for downloading.* https://eleonoragullone.wordpress.com/2018/09/20/psychological-measures-for-downloading/#more-484

Gullone, E., Hughes, E. K., King, N. J., & Tonge, B. (2010). The normative development of emotion regulation strategy use in children and adolescents: A 2-year follow-up study. *The Journal of Child Psychology and Psychiatry, 51*(5), 567–574. https://doi.org/10.1111/j.1469-7610.2009.02183.x

Gullone, E., & Taffe, J. (2012). The Emotion Regulation Questionnaire for Children and Adolescents (ERQ-CA): A psychometric evaluation. *Psychological Assessment, 24*(2), 409–417. https://doi.org/10.1037/a0025777

Haeyen, S. (2018). *Art therapy and emotion regulation problems: Theory and workbook*. Palgrave Macmillan. https://doi.org/10.1007/978-3-319-96773-8

Hall, H., & Nielsen, E. (2020, May 26). *How do children spend their time? Time use and skill development in the PSID, FEDS Notes*. Board of Governors of the Federal Reserve System. https://doi.org/10.17016/2380-7172.2577

Haller, S. P., Kircanski, K., Stringaris, A., Clayton, M., Bui, H., Agorsor, C., Cardenas, S. I., Towbin, K. E., Pine, D. S., Leibenluft, E., & Brotman, M. A. (2020). The Clinician Affective Reactivity Index: Validity and reliability of a clinician-rated assessment of irritability. *Behavior Therapy, 51*(2), 283–293. https://doi.org/10.1016/j.beth.2019.10.005

Hamrin, V., & Iennaco, J. D. (2017). Evaluation of motivational interviewing to improve psychotropic medication adherence in adolescents. *Journal of Child and Adolescent Psychopharmacology, 27*(2), 148–159. https://doi.org/10.1089/cap.2015.0187

Harkness, A. R., & McNulty, J. L. (1994). The Personality Psychopathology Five (PSY-5): Issues from the pages of a diagnostic manual instead of a dictionary. In S. Strack & M. Lorr (Eds.), *Differentiating normal and abnormal personality* (pp. 291–315). Springer Publishing Company.

Harlacher, J. E., & Rodriguez, D. J. (2017). *Schoolwide positive behavioral interventions and supports*. Marzano Resources.

Hartford HealthCare. (n.d.). *DIAMOND and DIAMOND-KID interviews, articles, training course and rater certification*. Hartford Hospital. https://giving.hartfordhospital.org/diamond/

Hasler, G., Drevets, W. C., Gould, T. D., Gottesman, I. I., & Manji, H. K. (2006). Toward constructing an endophenotype strategy for bipolar disorders. *Biological Psychiatry, 60*(2), 93–105. https://doi.org/10.1016/j.biopsych.2005.11.006

Hays, P. A. (2008). *Addressing cultural complexities in practice: Assessment, diagnosis, and therapy* (2nd ed.). American Psychological Association. https://doi.org/10.1037/11650-000

He, Y., Gewirtz, A. H., Lee, S., & August, G. (2018). Do parent preferences for child conduct problem interventions impact parenting outcomes? A pilot study in community children's mental health settings. *Journal of Marital and Family Therapy, 44*(4), 716–729. https://doi.org/10.1111/jmft.12310

Heckwolf, J. I., Bergland, C., & Mouratidis, M. (2014). Coordinating principles of art therapy and DBT. *The Arts in Psychotherapy, 41*(4), 329–335. https://doi.org/10.1016/j.aip.2014.03.006

Helping Give Away Psychological Science. (n.d.). *Child Mania Rating Scale (CMRS)—Parent Version*. Qualtrics. https://unc.az1.qualtrics.com/jfe/form/SV_2huLjI4IrsPKjyZ

Helzer, J. E., van den Brink, W., & Guth, S. E. (2006). Should there be both categorical and dimensional criteria for the substance use disorders in *DSM-V*? *Addiction, 101*(s1), 17–22. https://doi.org/10.1111/j.1360-0443.2006.01587.x

Henin, A., Mick, E., Biederman, J., Fried, R., Hirshfeld-Becker, D. R., Micco, J. A., Miller, K. G., Rycyna, C. C., & Wozniak, J. (2009). Is psychopharmacologic treatment associated with neuropsychological deficits in bipolar youth? *The Journal of Clinical Psychiatry*, *70*(8), 1178–1185. https://doi.org/10.4088/JCP.08m04696

Henry, C., Mitropoulou, V., New, A. S., Koenigsberg, H. W., Silverman, J., & Siever, L. J. (2001). Affective instability and impulsivity in borderline personality and bipolar II disorders: Similarities and differences. *Journal of Psychiatric Research*, *35*(6), 307–312. https://doi.org/10.1016/S0022-3956(01)00038-3

Herbell, K., & Banks, A. J. (2020). “Fighting tooth and nail”: Barriers to accessing adolescent mental health treatment from mothers’ perspectives. *Administration and Policy in Mental Health and Mental Health Services Research*, *47*(6), 935–945. https://doi.org/10.1007/s10488-020-01026-1

Herpertz-Dahlmann, B. (2021). Intensive treatments in adolescent anorexia nervosa. *Nutrients*, *13*(4), Article 1265. https://doi.org/10.3390/nu13041265

Herrera, C., & Karcher, M. J. (2014). School-based mentoring. In D. L. DuBois & M. J. Karcher (Eds.), *Handbook of youth mentoring* (2nd ed., pp. 203–220). SAGE Publications. https://doi.org/10.4135/9781412996907.n14

Hidalgo, M. A., Petras, H., Chen, D., & Chodzen, G. (2019). The Gender Minority Stress and Resilience Measure: Psychometric validity of an adolescent extension. *Clinical Practice in Pediatric Psychology*, *7*(3), 278–290. https://doi.org/10.1037/cpp0000297

Hilbert, A., & van Dyck, Z. (2016). Eating Disorders in Youth–Questionnaire. English version. University of Leipzig. http://nbn-resolving.de/urn:nbn:de:bsz:15-qucosa-197246

Hillegers, M. H., Reichart, C. G., Wals, M., Verhulst, F. C., Ormel, J., & Nolen, W. A. (2005). Five-year prospective outcome of psychopathology in the adolescent offspring of bipolar parents. *Bipolar Disorders*, *7*(4), 344–350. https://doi.org/10.1111/j.1399-5618.2005.00215.x

Hirschfeld, R. M., Williams, J. B., Spitzer, R. L., Calabrese, J. R., Flynn, L., Keck, P. E., Jr., Lewis, L., McElroy, S. L., Post, R. M., Rapport, D. J., Russell, J. M., Sachs, G. S., & Zajecka, J. (2000). Development and validation of a screening instrument for bipolar spectrum disorder: The Mood Disorder Questionnaire. *The American Journal of Psychiatry*, *157*(11), 1873–1875. https://doi.org/10.1176/appi.ajp.157.11.1873

Hlastala, S. A., Kotler, J. S., McClellan, J. M., & McCauley, E. A. (2010). Interpersonal and social rhythm therapy for adolescents with bipolar disorder: Treatment development and results from an open trial. *Depression and Anxiety*, *27*(5), 457–464. https://doi.org/10.1002/da.20668

Hoag, M. J., Massey, K. E., & Roberts, S. D. (2014). Dissecting the wilderness therapy client: Examining clinical trends, findings, and patterns. *Journal of Experiential Education*, *37*(4), 382–396. https://doi.org/10.1177/1053825914540837

Hoffman, L., Rice, T. R., & Prout, T. A. (2016). *Manual of regulation-focused psychotherapy for children (RFP-C) with externalizing behaviors: A psychodynamic approach*. Routledge.

Holt, R. R. (Ed.). (1968). *Diagnostic psychological testing* (rev. ed.). International Universities Press.

Hopwood, C. J. (2022). (Ed.). *The evolution of personality assessment in the 21st century: Understanding the people who understand people*. Routledge.

Hopwood, C. J., & Bornstein, R. F. (Eds.). (2014). *Multimethod clinical assessment*. The Guilford Press.

Horn, K., Roessner, V., & Holtmann, M. (2011). Neurocognitive performance in children and adolescents with bipolar disorder: A review. *European Child & Adolescent Psychiatry, 20*(9), 433–450. https://doi.org/10.1007/s00787-011-0209-x

Hou, J., Song, B., Chen, A. C. N., Sun, C., Zhou, J., Zhu, H., & Beauchaine, T. P. (2017). Review on neural correlates of emotion regulation and music: Implications for emotion dysregulation. *Frontiers in Psychology, 8*, Article 501. https://doi.org/10.3389/fpsyg.2017.00501

Hunsley, J., & Meyer, G. J. (2003). The incremental validity of psychological testing and assessment: Conceptual, methodological, and statistical issues. *Psychological Assessment, 15*(4), 446–455. https://doi.org/10.1037/1040-3590.15.4.446

IDEA: Individuals with Disabilities Education Act. (n.d.). U.S. Department of Education. https://sites.ed.gov/idea/

Independent Educational Consultants Association. (n.d.). *Therapeutic needs*. https://www.iecaonline.com/quick-links/parents-students/therapeutic-needs/

Individuals With Disabilities Education Act, Pub. L. 101–476, 104 Stat. 1142 (1990).

International Rorschach Institute. (n.d.). *CHESSSS 2* [Computer software]. https://www.rorschach-institute.org/purchase_chessss2.html#:~:text=Experience%20CHESSSS%202:%20Bridging%20Tradition%20and%20Modernity.,advancement%20in%20the%20field%20of%20Rorschach%20assessment

International Society for Traumatic Stress Studies. (n.d.). *Child/adolescent trauma instruments*. https://istss.org/clinical-resources/child-trauma-assessments

Janjhua, Y., Chaudhary, R., Sharma, N., & Kumar, K. (2020). A study on effect of yoga on emotional regulation, self-esteem, and feelings of adolescents. *Journal of Family Medicine and Primary Care, 9*(7), 3381–3386. https://doi.org/10.4103/jfmpc.jfmpc_153_20

Janson, P., & Vavra, A. (2017). The procrustean bed: The danger in the proliferation of protocols [Letter to the editor]. *The Journal of Emergency Medicine, 52*(2), e53–e54. https://doi.org/10.1016/j.jemermed.2016.01.036

Jenkins, M. M., & Youngstrom, E. A. (2016). A randomized controlled trial of cognitive debiasing improves assessment and treatment selection for pediatric bipolar disorder. *Journal of Consulting and Clinical Psychology, 84*(4), 323–333. https://doi.org/10.1037/ccp0000070

Jensen, P. S., Hinshaw, S. P., Kraemer, H. C., Lenora, N., Newcorn, J. H., Abikoff, H. B., March, J. S., Arnold, L. E., Cantwell, D. P., Conners, C. K., Elliott, G. R., Greenhill, L. L., Hechtman, L., Hoza, B., Pelham, W. E., Severe, J. B., Swanson, J. M., Wells, K. C., Wigal, T., & Vitiello, B. (2001). ADHD comorbidity findings from the MTA study: Comparing comorbid subgroups. *Journal of the American Academy of Child & Adolescent Psychiatry, 40*(2), 147–158. https://doi.org/10.1097/00004583-200102000-00009

Johnston, M. H., Holzman, P. S., Solovay, M. R., Shenton, M. E., Gasperetti, C., Coleman, M., Kestnbaum, E., & Carpenter, J. T. (1986). Scoring manual for the Thought Disorder Index. *Schizophrenia Bulletin, 12*(3), 483–496. https://doi.org/10.1093/schbul/12.3.483

Jones, K. D. (2012). Dimensional and cross-cutting assessment in the *DSM-5*. *Journal of Counseling & Development, 90*(4), 481–487. https://doi.org/10.1002/j.1556-6676.2012.00059.x

Joseph, M. F., Frazier, T. W., Youngstrom, E. A., & Soares, J. C. (2008). A quantitative and qualitative review of neurocognitive performance in pediatric bipolar disorder. *Journal of Child and Adolescent Psychopharmacology, 18*(6), 595–605. https://doi.org/10.1089/cap.2008.064

Joseph, M. F., Youngstrom, E. A., & Soares, J. C. (2009). Antidepressant-coincident mania in children and adolescents treated with selective serotonin reuptake inhibitors. *Future Neurology, 4*(1), 87–102. https://doi.org/10.2217/14796708.4.1.87

Joshi, G., Biederman, J., Petty, C., Goldin, R. L., Furtak, S. L., & Wozniak, J. (2013). Examining the comorbidity of bipolar disorder and autism spectrum disorders: A large controlled analysis of phenotypic and familial correlates in a referred population of youth with bipolar I disorder with and without autism spectrum disorders. *The Journal of Clinical Psychiatry, 74*(6), 578–586. https://doi.org/10.4088/JCP.12m07392

Joshi, G., & Wilens, T. (2009). Comorbidity in pediatric bipolar disorder. *Child and Adolescent Psychiatric Clinics of North America, 18*(2), 291–319, vii–viii. https://doi.org/10.1016/j.chc.2008.12.005

Jurist, E. L. (2005). Mentalized affectivity. *Psychoanalytic Psychology, 22*(3), 426–444. https://doi.org/10.1037/0736-9735.22.3.426

Kafali, H. Y., Bildik, T., Bora, E., Yuncu, Z., & Erermis, H. S. (2019). Distinguishing prodromal stage of bipolar disorder and early onset schizophrenia spectrum disorders during adolescence. *Psychiatry Research, 275*, 315–325. https://doi.org/10.1016/j.psychres.2019.03.051

Kahneman, D., & Tversky, A. (1972). Subjective probability: A judgment of representativeness. *Cognitive Psychology, 3*(3), 430–454. https://doi.org/10.1016/0010-0285(72)90016-3

Kalb, L. G., Singh, V., Hong, J. S., Holingue, C., Ludwig, N. N., Pfeiffer, D., Reetzke, R., Gross, A. L., & Landa, R. (2022). Analysis of race and sex bias in the Autism Diagnostic Observation Schedule (ADOS-2). *JAMA Network Open, 5*(4), Article e229498. https://doi.org/10.1001/jamanetworkopen.2022.9498

Kambanis, P. E., Kuhnle, M. C., Wons, O. B., Jo, J. H., Keshishian, A. C., Hauser, K., Becker, K. R., Franko, D. L., Misra, M., Micali, N., Lawson, E. A., Eddy, K. T., & Thomas, J. J. (2020). Prevalence and correlates of psychiatric comorbidities in children and adolescents with full and subthreshold avoidant/restrictive food intake disorder. *International Journal of Eating Disorders, 53*(2), 256–265. https://doi.org/10.1002/eat.23191

Kaminer, Y., Bukstein, O., & Tarter, R. E. (1991). The Teen-Addiction Severity Index: Rationale and reliability. *The International Journal of the Addictions, 26*(2), 219–226. https://doi.org/10.3109/10826089109053184

Karalunas, S. L., Gustafsson, H. C., Fair, D., Musser, E. D., & Nigg, J. T. (2019). Do we need an irritable subtype of ADHD? Replication and extension of a promising temperament profile approach to ADHD subtyping. *Psychological Assessment, 31*(2), 236–247. https://doi.org/10.1037/pas0000664

Karcher, N. R., Barch, D. M., Avenevoli, S., Savill, M., Huber, R. S., Simon, T. J., Leckliter, I. N., Sher, K. J., & Loewy, R. L. (2018). Assessment of the Prodromal Questionnaire–Brief Child Version for measurement of self-reported psychoticlike experiences in childhood. *JAMA Psychiatry, 75*(8), 853–861. https://doi.org/10.1001/jamapsychiatry.2018.1334

Karver, M. S., De Nadai, A. S., Monahan, M., & Shirk, S. R. (2018). Meta-analysis of the prospective relation between alliance and outcome in child and adolescent psychotherapy. *Psychotherapy, 55*(4), 341–355. https://doi.org/10.1037/pst0000176

Karver, M. S., De Nadai, A. S., Monahan, M., & Shirk, S. R. (2019). Alliance in child and adolescent psychotherapy. In J. C. Norcross & M. J. Lambert (Eds.), *Psychotherapy relationships that work: Vol. 1. Evidence-based therapist contributions* (3rd ed., pp. 79–116). Oxford University Press. https://doi.org/10.1093/med-psych/9780190843953.003.0003

Kaufman, J., Birmaher, B., Axelson, D., Perepletchikova, F., Brent, D., & Ryan, N. (2016). *K-SADS-PL DSM-5*. Advanced Center for Intervention and Services Research (ACISR) for Early Onset Mood and Anxiety Disorders, Western Psychiatric Institute and Clinic. https://www.pediatricbipolar.pitt.edu/sites/default/files/assets/AH/AK/KSADS_DSM_5_SCREEN_Final.pdf

Kazdin, A. E. (2009). *Parenting your defiant child: The Kazdin method for managing difficult behavior.* Piatkus.

Kelly, S. M., Gryczynski, J., Mitchell, S. G., Kirk, A., O'Grady, K. E., & Schwartz, R. P. (2014). Validity of brief screening instrument for adolescent tobacco, alcohol, and drug use. *Pediatrics, 133*(5), 819–826. https://doi.org/10.1542/peds.2013-2346

Kernberg, O. (1965). Notes on countertransference. *Journal of the American Psychoanalytic Association, 13*(1), 38–56. https://doi.org/10.1177/000306516501300102

Kernberg, O. F., & Yeomans, F. E. (2013). Borderline personality disorder, bipolar disorder, depression, attention deficit/hyperactivity disorder, and narcissistic personality disorder: Practical differential diagnosis. *Bulletin of the Menninger Clinic, 77*(1), 1–22. https://doi.org/10.1521/bumc.2013.77.1.1

Khadivi, A. (2023). Clinical interview methods for assessing bipolar spectrum disorders. In J. H. Kleiger & I. B. Weiner (Eds.), *Psychological assessment of bipolar spectrum disorders* (pp. 37–45). American Psychological Association. https://doi.org/10.1037/0000356-003

Kim, P., Evans, G. W., Angstadt, M., Ho, S. S., Sripada, C. S., Swain, J. E., Liberzon, I., & Phan, K. L. (2013). Effects of childhood poverty and chronic stress on emotion regulatory brain function in adulthood. *PNAS, 110*(46), 18442–18447. https://doi.org/10.1073/pnas.1308240110

Kleiger, J. H. (1997). Rorschach shading responses: From a printer's error to an integrated psychoanalytic paradigm. *Journal of Personality Assessment, 69*(2), 342–364. https://doi.org/10.1207/s15327752jpa6902_7

Kleiger, J. H. (1999). *Disordered thinking and the Rorschach: Theory, research, and differential diagnosis*. The Analytic Press.

Kleiger, J. H. (2016). Sex, gender identity, and the assessment of psychosis. In V. M. Brabender & J. L. Mihura (Eds.), *Handbook of gender and sexuality in psychological assessment* (pp. 233–255). Routledge.

Kleiger, J. H. (2017). *Rorschach assessment of psychotic phenomena: Clinical, conceptual, and empirical developments*. Routledge. https://doi.org/10.4324/9781315271385

Kleiger, J. H. (2023). Rating scales and screening assessment of bipolar spectrum disorders. In J. H. Kleiger & I. B. Weiner (Eds.), *Psychological assessment of bipolar spectrum disorders* (pp. 107–122). American Psychological Association. https://doi.org/10.1037/0000356-000

Kleiger, J. H., & Khadivi, A. (2015). *Assessing psychosis: A clinician's guide*. Routledge. https://doi.org/10.4324/9781315882006

Kleiger, J. H., & Weiner, I. B. (Eds.). (2023). *Psychological assessment of bipolar spectrum disorders*. American Psychological Association. https://doi.org/10.1037/0000356-000

Klein, D. N., Dougherty, L. R., Kessel, E. M., Silver, J., & Carlson, G. A. (2021). A transdiagnostic perspective on youth irritability. *Current Directions in Psychological Science, 30*(5), 437–443. https://doi.org/10.1177/09637214211035101

Knight, J. R., Harris, S. K., Sherritt, L., Van Hook, S., Lawrence, N., Brooks, T., Carey, P., Kossack, R., & Kulig, J. (2007). Adolescents' preference for substance abuse screening in primary care practice. *Substance Abuse, 28*(4), 107–117. https://doi.org/10.1300/J465v28n04_03

Knight, J. R., Sherritt, L., Shrier, L. A., Harris, S. K., & Chang, G. (2002). Validity of the CRAFFT substance abuse screening test among adolescent clinic patients. *Archives of Pediatrics & Adolescent Medicine, 156*(6), 607–614. https://doi.org/10.1001/archpedi.156.6.607

Kochman, F. J., Hantouche, E. G., Ferrari, P., Lancrenon, S., Bayart, D., & Akiskal, H. S. (2005). Cyclothymic temperament as a prospective predictor of bipolarity and suicidality in children and adolescents with major depressive disorder.

Journal of Affective Disorders, 85(1–2), 181–189. https://doi.org/10.1016/j.jad.2003.09.009

Kothgassner, O. D., Goreis, A., Robinson, K., Huscsava, M. M., Schmahl, C., & Plener, P. L. (2021). Efficacy of dialectical behavior therapy for adolescent self-harm and suicidal ideation: A systematic review and meta-analysis. *Psychological Medicine, 51*(7), 1057–1067. https://doi.org/10.1017/S0033291721001355

Kowatch, R. A., Fristad, M., Birmaher, B., Wagner, K. D., Findling, R. L., Hellander, M., & the Child Psychiatric Workgroup on Bipolar Disorder. (2005). Treatment guidelines for children and adolescents with bipolar disorder. *Journal of the American Academy of Child & Adolescent Psychiatry, 44*(3), 213–235. https://doi.org/10.1097/00004583-200503000-00006

Krupnick, J. L., Sotsky, S. M., Simmens, S., Moyer, J., Elkin, I., Watkins, J., & Pilkonis, P. A. (1996). The role of the therapeutic alliance in psychotherapy and pharmacotherapy outcome: Findings in the National Institute of Mental Health Treatment of Depression Collaborative Research Program. *Journal of Consulting and Clinical Psychology, 64*(3), 532–539. https://doi.org/10.1037/0022-006X.64.3.532

KSADS-COMP. (n.d.). *About KSADS-COMP.* https://www.ksadslogin.net/ksads-comp/AboutKC.aspx?ID=clinuse&val=mhc

Kuypers, L. (2011). *The Zones of Regulation™: A curriculum designed to foster self-regulation and emotional control.* Think Social Publishing.

LaForce, C. (2021). *Mindful monsters: Development of a DBT-Informed art therapy method for traumatized children in an acute inpatient residential program* [Master's thesis, Lesley University]. Lesley Digital Commons. https://digitalcommons.lesley.edu/expressive_theses/413

Lång, U., Mittal, V. A., Schiffman, J., & Therman, S. (2021). Measurement invariance of psychotic-like symptoms as measured with the Prodromal Questionnaire, Brief Version (PQ-B) in adolescent and adult population samples. *Frontiers in Psychiatry, 11*, Article 593355. https://doi.org/10.3389/fpsyt.2020.593355

Langer, D. A., Kritikos, T. K., Asarnow, J. R., & Tompson, M. C. (2021). Parent and youth preferences in the treatment of youth depression. *Child Psychiatry and Human Development, 52*(2), 236–247. https://doi.org/10.1007/s10578-020-01006-4

Larivière, M., Couture, R., Ritchie, S. D., Cote, D., Oddson, B., & Wright, J. (2012). Behavioural assessment of wilderness therapy participants: Exploring the consistency of observational data. *Journal of Experiential Education, 35*(1), 290–302. https://doi.org/10.1177/105382591203500106

Lauth, B., Levy, S. R., Júlíusdóttir, G., Ferrari, P., & Pétursson, H. (2008). Implementing the semi-structured interview Kiddie-SADS-PL into an in-patient adolescent clinical setting: Impact on frequency of diagnoses. *Child and Adolescent Psychiatry and Mental Health, 2*(1), Article 14. https://doi.org/10.1186/1753-2000-2-14

Laviano, J., & Swanson, J. (2017). *Your special education rights: What your school district isn't telling you.* Skyhorse.

LeBeau, R., Bögels, S., Möller, E., & Craske, M. (2015). Integrating dimensional assessment and categorical diagnosis in *DSM-5*: The benefits and challenges of the paradigm shift for the anxiety disorders. *Psychopathology Review*, *2*(1), 83–99. https://doi.org/10.5127/pr.036414

Lee, H.-A., Lee, H.-J., Moon, J.-H., Lee, T., Kim, M.-G., In, H., Cho, C.-H., & Kim, L. (2017). Comparison of wearable activity tracker with actigraphy for sleep evaluation and circadian rest-activity rhythm measurement in healthy young adults. *Psychiatry Investigation*, *14*(2), 179–185. https://doi.org/10.4306/pi.2017.14.2.179

Leffler, J. M., Riebel, J., & Hughes, H. M. (2015). A review of child and adolescent diagnostic interviews for clinical practitioners. *Assessment*, *22*(6), 690–703. https://doi.org/10.1177/1073191114561253

Lehmann, P. S., Azimi, A. M., Fortney, K., & Alaniz, K. (2022). Racial and ethnic disparities in school discipline: The interactive effects of gender and parental educational attainment. *Crime & Delinquency*, *68*(10), 1631–1669. https://doi.org/10.1177/00111287211029879

Leichtman, M. (1996). *The Rorschach: A developmental perspective*. The Analytic Press.

Leopold, K., Bauer, M., Bechdolf, A., Correll, C. U., Holtmann, M., Juckel, G., Lambert, M., Meyer, T. D., Pfeiffer, S., Kittel-Schneider, S., Reif, A., Stamm, T. J., Rottmann-Wolf, M., Mathiebe, J., Kellmann, E. L., Ritter, P., Krüger-Özgürdal, S., Karow, A., Sondergeld, L. M., . . . Pfennig, A. (2020). Efficacy of cognitive-behavioral group therapy in patients at risk for serious mental illness presenting with subthreshold bipolar symptoms: Results from a prespecified interim analysis of a multicenter, randomized, controlled study. *Bipolar Disorders*, *22*(5), 517–529. https://doi.org/10.1111/bdi.12894

Lerner, P. M. (1990). Rorschach assessment of primitive defenses: A review. *Journal of Personality Assessment*, *54*(1–2), 30–46.

Levy, D. L., Smith, M., Robinson, D., Jody, D., Lerner, G., Alvir, J., Geisler, S. H., Szymanski, S. R., Gonzalez, A., Mayerhoff, D. I., Lieberman, J. A., & Mendell, N. R. (1993). Methylphenidate increases thought disorder in recent onset schizophrenics, but not in normal controls. *Biological Psychiatry*, *34*(8), 507–514. https://doi.org/10.1016/0006-3223(93)90192-G

Levy, S., Weiss, R., Sherritt, L., Ziemnik, R., Spalding, A., Van Hook, S., & Shrier, L. A. (2014). An electronic screen for triaging adolescent substance use by risk levels. *JAMA Pediatrics*, *168*(9), 822–828. https://doi.org/10.1001/jamapediatrics.2014.774

Lewin, A. B., McGuire, J. F., Murphy, T. K., & Storch, E. A. (2014). The importance of considering parent's preferences when planning treatment for their children—The case of childhood obsessive-compulsive disorder. *The Journal of Child Psychology and Psychiatry*, *55*(12), 1314–1316. https://doi.org/10.1111/jcpp.12344

Lewis, C. C., Boyd, M., Puspitasari, A., Navarro, E., Howard, J., Kassab, H., Hoffman, M., Scott, K., Lyon, A., Douglas, S., Simon, G., & Kroenke, K. (2019).

Implementing measurement-based care in behavioral health: A review. *JAMA Psychiatry, 76*(3), 324–335. https://doi.org/10.1001/jamapsychiatry.2018.3329

Life Problems Inventory (LPI). (n.d.). Squarespace. https://static1.squarespace.com/static/54d67392e4b08579c6a861e7/t/5c94cb3ef4e1fc7eec3de221/1553255231328/LPI+Scale.doc

Lindfors, K. U. M., Therman, S., Lindgren, M., Kekkonen, V., & Tolmunen, T. (2022). Factor structure, measurement invariance, and abbreviated versions of the Adolescent Dissociative Experiences Scale (A-DES). *Journal of Trauma & Dissociation, 23*(4), 464–479. https://doi.org/10.1080/15299732.2022.2064575

Linehan, M. M. (2014). *DBT skills training manual* (2nd ed.). The Guilford Press.

Lippold, M. A., Greenberg, M. T., & Collins, L. M. (2014). Youths' substance use and changes in parental knowledge-related behaviors during middle school: A person-oriented approach. *Journal of Youth and Adolescence, 43*(5), 729–744. https://doi.org/10.1007/s10964-013-0010-x

Lochman, J. E., Powell, N. P., Boxmeyer, C. L., & Jimenez-Camargo, L. (2011). Cognitive-behavioral therapy for externalizing disorders in children and adolescents. *Child and Adolescent Psychiatric Clinics of North America, 20*(2), 305–318. https://doi.org/10.1016/j.chc.2011.01.005

Loewy, R., & Cannon, T. D. (2010). *The Prodromal Questionnaire, Brief Version (PQ-B)*. University of California.

Loewy, R. L., Pearson, R., Vinogradov, S., Bearden, C. E., & Cannon, T. D. (2011). Psychosis risk screening with the Prodromal Questionnaire–Brief Version (PQ-B). *Schizophrenia Research, 129*(1), 42–46. https://doi.org/10.1016/j.schres.2011.03.029

Lohse, A., Lemelle, I., Pillet, P., Duquesne, A., Ballot, C., Tran, T. A., Sparsa, L., Goumy, L., Reumaux, H., Rossi, L., Solau-Gervais, E., Arbault, A., Alleyrat, C., Guillemin, F., & Devauchelle-Pensec, V. (2021). Therapeutic alliance is associated to treatment adherence in children with juvenile idiopathic arthritis. *Joint Bone Spine, 88*(4), Article 105151. https://doi.org/10.1016/j.jbspin.2021.105151

López, S. R. (2002). Teaching culturally informed psychological assessment: Conceptual issues and demonstrations. *Journal of Personality Assessment, 79*(2), 226–234. https://doi.org/10.1207/S15327752JPA7902_06

Lord, C., Rutter, M., DiLavore, P. C., Risi, S., Gotham, K., & Bishop, S. (2012). *Autism Diagnostic Observation Schedule* (2nd ed.). Western Psychological Services.

Lozada, F. T., Riley, T. N., Catherine, E., & Brown, D. W. (2022). Black emotions matter: Understanding the impact of racial oppression on Black youth's emotional development: Dismantling systems of racism and oppression during adolescence. *Journal of Research on Adolescence, 32*(1), 13–33. https://doi.org/10.1111/jora.12699

Lydecker, J. A., & Grilo, C. M. (2017). Does your child's weight influence how you judge yourself as a parent? A cross-sectional study to define and examine parental overvaluation of weight/shape. *Preventive Medicine, 105*, 265–270. https://doi.org/10.1016/j.ypmed.2017.10.009

Lyons, M. D., & McQuillin, S. D. (2019). Risks and rewards of school-based mentoring relationships: A reanalysis of the student mentoring program evaluation. *School Psychology, 34*(1), 76–85. https://doi.org/10.1037/spq0000265

Mahler, M. S., Pine, F., & Bergman, A. (1975). *The psychological birth of the human infant: Symbiosis and individuation*. Basic Books.

Malik, H. B., & Norman, J. B. (2023). Best practices and methodological strategies for addressing generalizability in neuropsychological assessment. *Journal of Pediatric Neuropsychology, 9*(2), 47–63. https://doi.org/10.1007/s40817-023-00145-5

Mandell, D. S., Ittenbach, R. F., Levy, S. E., & Pinto-Martin, J. A. (2007). Disparities in diagnoses received prior to a diagnosis of autism spectrum disorder. *Journal of Autism and Developmental Disorders, 37*(9), 1795–1802. https://doi.org/10.1007/s10803-006-0314-8

Mandell, D. S., Listerud, J., Levy, S. E., & Pinto-Martin, J. A. (2002). Race differences in the age at diagnosis among Medicaid-eligible children with autism. *Journal of the American Academy of Child & Adolescent Psychiatry, 41*(12), 1447–1453. https://doi.org/10.1097/00004583-200212000-00016

Manning, J. (2015). Aggressive suicide. *International Journal of Law, Crime and Justice, 43*(3), 326–341. https://doi.org/10.1016/j.ijlcj.2015.05.002

Mapi Research Trust. (2010). *Mini-International Neuropsychiatric Interview for Children and Adolescents (MINI-KID)*. ePROVIDE. https://eprovide.mapi-trust.org/instruments/mini-international-neuropsychiatric-interview-for-children-and-adolescents#coas_member_access_content

Marangoni, C., De Chiara, L., & Faedda, G. L. (2015). Bipolar disorder and ADHD: Comorbidity and diagnostic distinctions. *Current Psychiatry Reports, 17*(8), Article 67. https://doi.org/10.1007/s11920-015-0604-y

March, J. S. (2012). *Multidimensional Anxiety Scale for Children* (2nd ed.). Multi-Health Systems. https://doi.org/10.1037/t05050-000

March, J. S., & Mulle, K. (1998). *OCD in children and adolescents: A cognitive-behavioral treatment guide*. The Guilford Press.

March, J. S., Parker, J. D., Sullivan, K., Stallings, P., & Conners, C. K. (1997). The Multidimensional Anxiety Scale for Children (MASC): Factor structure, reliability, and validity. *Journal of the American Academy of Child & Adolescent Psychiatry, 36*(4), 554–565. https://doi.org/10.1097/00004583-199704000-00019

Marchand, W. R., Clark, S. C., Wirth, L., & Simon, C. (2005). Validity of the Parent Young Mania Rating Scale in a community mental health setting. *Psychiatry, 2*(3), 31–35.

Marcus, E. R. (2017). *Psychosis and near psychosis: Ego function, symbolic structure, and treatment*. Routledge. https://doi.org/10.4324/9781315675855

Margari, L., Buttiglione, M., Craig, F., Cristella, A., de Giambattista, C., Matera, E., Operto, F., & Simone, M. (2013). Neuropsychopathological comorbidities in learning disorders. *BMC Neurology, 13*(1), Article 198. https://doi.org/10.1186/1471-2377-13-198

Martin, J. A., Tarantino, D. M., & Levy, K. N. (2023). Investigating gender-based differential item functioning on the McLean Screening Instrument for Borderline Personality Disorder (MSI-BPD): An item response theory analysis. *Psychological Assessment, 35*(5), 462–468. https://doi.org/10.1037/pas0001229

Masi, G., Milone, A., Brovedani, P., Pisano, S., & Muratori, P. (2018). Psychiatric evaluation of youths with disruptive behavior disorders and psychopathic traits: A critical review of assessment measures. *Neuroscience and Biobehavioral Reviews, 91*, 21–33. https://doi.org/10.1016/j.neubiorev.2016.09.023

Masia-Warner, C., Storch, E. A., Pincus, D. B., Klein, R. G., Heimberg, R. G., & Liebowitz, M. R. (2003). The Liebowitz Social Anxiety Scale for Children and Adolescents: An initial psychometric investigation. *Journal of the American Academy of Child & Adolescent Psychiatry, 42*(9), 1076–1084. https://doi.org/10.1097/01.CHI.0000070249.24125.89

Massachusetts Sibling Support Network. (n.d.). *Explore sibling services*. https://www.masiblingsupport.org/sibling-services

Mavranezouli, I., Megnin-Viggars, O., Daly, C., Dias, S., Stockton, S., Meiser-Stedman, R., Trickey, D., & Pilling, S. (2020). Research review: Psychological and psychosocial treatments for children and young people with post-traumatic stress disorder: A network meta-analysis. *The Journal of Child Psychology and Psychiatry, 61*(1), 18–29. https://doi.org/10.1111/jcpp.13094

Mazefsky, C. A., Conner, C. M., Breitenfeldt, K., Leezenbaum, N., Chen, Q., Bylsma, L. M., & Pilkonis, P. (2021). Evidence base update for questionnaires of emotion regulation and reactivity for children and adolescents. *Journal of Clinical Child & Adolescent Psychology, 50*(6), 683–707. https://doi.org/10.1080/15374416.2021.1955372

Mazefsky, C. A., Yu, L., & Pilkonis, P. A. (2021). Psychometric properties of the emotion dysregulation inventory in a nationally representative sample of youth. *Journal of Clinical Child & Adolescent Psychology, 50*(5), 596–608. https://doi.org/10.1080/15374416.2019.1703710

Mazefsky, C. A., Yu, L., White, S. W., Siegel, M., & Pilkonis, P. A. (2018). The emotion dysregulation inventory: Psychometric properties and item response theory calibration in an autism spectrum disorder sample. *Autism Research, 11*(6), 928–941. https://doi.org/10.1002/aur.1947

McCarney, S. B., & House, S. N. (2019). *Attention Deficit Disorder Evaluation Scale* (5th ed.). Hawthorne Educational Services.

McClain, M. B., Harris, B., Schwartz, S. E., & Golson, M. E. (2020). Evaluation of the Autism Spectrum Rating Scales in a diverse, nonclinical sample. *Journal of Psychoeducational Assessment, 38*(6), 740–752. https://doi.org/10.1177/0734282919880051

McClain, M. B., Harris, B., Schwartz, S. E., & Golson, M. E. (2021). Differential item and test functioning of the Autism Spectrum Rating Scales: A follow-up evaluation in a diverse, nonclinical sample. *Journal of Psychoeducational Assessment, 39*(2), 247–257. https://doi.org/10.1177/0734282920945529

McClellan, J., Kowatch, R., Findling, R. L., & the Work Group on Quality Issues. (2007). Practice parameter for the assessment and treatment of children and adolescents with bipolar disorder. *Journal of the American Academy of Child & Adolescent Psychiatry, 46*(1), 107–125. https://doi.org/10.1097/01.chi.0000242240.69678.c4

McDonnell, M. A. (2010). *Race, gender, and age effects on the assessment of bipolar disorder in youth* [Unpublished doctoral dissertation]. Northeastern University, School of Nursing. https://repository.library.northeastern.edu/files/neu:1718

McElroy, S. L., Kotwal, R., Keck, P. E., Jr., & Akiskal, H. S. (2005). Comorbidity of bipolar and eating disorders: Distinct or related disorders with shared dysregulations? *Journal of Affective Disorders, 86*(2–3), 107–127. https://doi.org/10.1016/j.jad.2004.11.008

McGoldrick, M., Gerson, R., & Petry, S. (2020). *Genograms: Assessment and treatment* (4th ed.). W. W. Norton & Company.

McGuffin, P., Rijsdijk, F., Andrew, M., Sham, P., Katz, R., & Cardno, A. (2003). The heritability of bipolar affective disorder and the genetic relationship to unipolar depression. *Archives of General Psychiatry, 60*(5), 497–502. https://doi.org/10.1001/archpsyc.60.5.497

McIntosh, K., Girvan, E. J., Fairbanks Falcon, S., McDaniel, S. C., Smolkowski, K., Bastable, E., Santiago-Rosario, M. R., Izzard, S., Austin, S. C., Nese, R. N. T., & Baldy, T. S. (2021). Equity-focused PBIS approach reduces racial inequities in school discipline: A randomized controlled trial. *School Psychology, 36*(6), 433–444. https://doi.org/10.1037/spq0000466

McMahon, K., Berger, M., Khalsa, K. K., Harden, E., & Khalsa, S. B. S. (2021). A non-randomized trial of kundalini yoga for emotion regulation within an after-school program for adolescents. *Journal of Child and Family Studies, 30*(3), 711–722. https://doi.org/10.1007/s10826-021-01911-9

Mennin, D. S., Holaway, R. M., Fresco, D. M., Moore, M. T., & Heimberg, R. G. (2007). Delineating components of emotion and its dysregulation in anxiety and mood psychopathology. *Behavior Therapy, 38*(3), 284–302. https://doi.org/10.1016/j.beth.2006.09.001

Menschner, C., & Maul, A. (2016, April). *Key ingredients for successful trauma-informed care* (Issue brief). Substance Abuse and Mental Health Services Administration. https://www.samhsa.gov/sites/default/files/programs_campaigns/childrens_mental_health/atc-whitepaper-040616.pdf

Merriam-Webster. (n.d.). Procrustean bed. In *Merriam-Webster.com dictionary*. Retrieved May 23, 2024, from https://www.merriam-webster.com/dictionary/procrustean%20bed

Meyer, G. J. (2002). Exploring possible ethnic differences and bias in the Rorschach Comprehensive System. *Journal of Personality Assessment, 78*(1), 104–129. https://doi.org/10.1207/S15327752JPA7801_07

Meyer, G. J., Erdberg, P., & Shaffer, T. W. (2007). Toward international normative reference data for the comprehensive system. *Journal of Personality Assessment, 89*(Suppl. 1), S201–S216. https://doi.org/10.1080/00223890701629342

Meyer, G. J., Giromini, L., Viglione, D. J., Reese, J. B., & Mihura, J. L. (2015). The association of gender, ethnicity, age, and education with Rorschach scores. *Assessment, 22*(1), 46–64. https://doi.org/10.1177/1073191114544358

Meyer, G. J., & Kurtz, J. E. (2006). Advancing personality assessment terminology: Time to retire "objective" and "projective" as personality test descriptors. *Journal of Personality Assessment, 87*(3), 223–225. https://doi.org/10.1207/s15327752jpa8703_01

Meyer, G. J., Viglione, D. J., Mihura, J. L., Erard, R. F., & Edberg, P. (2011). *Rorschach Performance Assessment System: Administration, coding, interpretation, and technical manual.* Rorschach Performance Assessment System.

Midgley, N., & Kennedy, E. (2011). Psychodynamic psychotherapy for children and adolescents: A critical review of the evidence base. *Journal of Child Psychotherapy, 37*(3), 232–260. https://doi.org/10.1080/0075417X.2011.614738

Miguez, M., Weber, B., Debbané, M., Balanzin, D., Gex-Fabry, M., Raiola, F., Barbe, R. P., Vital Bennour, M., Ansermet, F., Eliez, S., & Aubry, J. M. (2013). Screening for bipolar disorder in adolescents with the Mood Disorder Questionnaire–Adolescent version (MDQ-A) and the Child Bipolar Questionnaire (CBQ). *Early Intervention in Psychiatry, 7*(3), 270–277. https://doi.org/10.1111/j.1751-7893.2012.00388.x

Mihura, J. L., & Brabender, V. M. (2016). Sex, gender, and sexuality in psychological assessment: Where do we go from here? In V. M. Brabender & J. L. Mihura (Eds.), *Handbook of gender and sexuality in psychological assessment* (pp. 655–678). Routledge.

Mihura, J. L., Meyer, G. J., Dumitrascu, N., & Bombel, G. (2013). The validity of individual Rorschach variables: Systematic reviews and meta-analyses of the comprehensive system. *Psychological Bulletin, 139*(3), 548–605. https://doi.org/10.1037/a0029406

Miller, C. (n.d.). *Is it ADHD or bipolar disorder?* Child Mind Institute. https://childmind.org/article/is-it-adhd-or-bipolar-disorder/

Miller, D. C., & Maricle, D. E. (2019). *Essentials of school neuropsychological assessment* (3rd ed.). Wiley.

Millon, T., Tringone, R., Grossman, S., & Millon, C. (2020). *Millon® Adolescent Clinical Inventory-II (MACI®-II)*. Pearson.

Millon, T., Tringone, R., Millon, C., & Grossman, S. (2005). *Millon® Pre-Adolescent Clinical Inventory (M-PACI®)*. Pearson.

Minuchin, S., Reiter, M. D., & Borda, C. (2021). *The craft of family therapy: Challenging certainties* (2nd ed.). Routledge. https://doi.org/10.4324/9781003110996

Mneimne, M., Fleeson, W., Arnold, E. M., & Furr, R. M. (2018). Differentiating the everyday emotion dynamics of borderline personality disorder from major depressive disorder and bipolar disorder. *Personality Disorders: Theory, Research, and Treatment, 9*(2), 192–196. https://doi.org/10.1037/per0000255

Monette, S., Cyr, C., Terradas, M. M., Couture, S., Minnis, H., & Lehmann, S. (2022). Development and validation of a measure of attachment disorders based on *DSM-5* criteria: The Early TRAuma-Related Disorders Questionnaire (ETRADQ). *Assessment, 29*(3), 556–571. https://doi.org/10.1177/1073191120981763

Montemagni, C., Bellino, S., Bracale, N., Bozzatello, P., & Rocca, P. (2020). Models predicting psychosis in patients with high clinical risk: A systematic review. *Frontiers in Psychiatry, 11*, Article 223. https://doi.org/10.3389/fpsyt.2020.00223

Mood Center. (n.d.). *General Behavior Inventory: Parent Version (P-GBI) Short Form—H/B (Revised Version, 2008)*. https://moodcenter.org/wp-content/uploads/2015/08/PGBI-Clinical-Version-.pdf

Moran, L. V., Ongur, D., Hsu, J., Castro, V. M., Perlis, R. H., & Schneeweiss, S. (2019). Psychosis with methylphenidate or amphetamine in patients with ADHD. *The New England Journal of Medicine, 380*(12), 1128–1138. https://doi.org/10.1056/NEJMoa1813751

Moreno, R., Buckelew, S. M., Accurso, E. C., & Raymond-Flesch, M. (2023). Disparities in access to eating disorders treatment for publicly-insured youth and youth of color: A retrospective cohort study. *Journal of Eating Disorders, 11*(1), Article 10. https://doi.org/10.1186/s40337-022-00730-7

Morey, L. C. (2007). *Personality Assessment Inventory–Adolescent (PAI-A) professional manual*. Psychological Assessment Resources.

Morey, L. C., & Meyer, J. K. (2014). Conceptualizing youth borderline personality disorder within a PAI framework. In C. Sharp & J. L. Tackett (Eds.), *Handbook of borderline personality disorder in children and adolescents* (pp. 49–64). Springer Science+Business Media. https://doi.org/10.1007/978-1-4939-0591-1_5

Morrison, J., & Flegel, K. (2016). *Interviewing children and adolescents: Skills and strategies for effective* DSM-5® *diagnosis* (2nd ed.). The Guilford Press.

Mortensen, P. B., Pedersen, M. G., & Pedersen, C. B. (2010). Psychiatric family history and schizophrenia risk in Denmark: Which mental disorders are relevant? *Psychological Medicine, 40*(2), 201–210. https://doi.org/10.1017/S0033291709990419

Multi-Health Systems. (n.d.). *MASC 2™: Multidimensional Anxiety Scale for Children 2nd Edition™*. https://storefront.mhs.com/collections/masc-2

Mürner-Lavanchy, I., Kaess, M., & Koenig, J. (2023). Diagnostic instruments for the assessment of disruptive mood dysregulation disorder: A systematic review of the literature. *European Child & Adolescent Psychiatry, 32*(1), 17–39. https://doi.org/10.1007/s00787-021-01840-4

Murray, H. (1943). *Thematic Apperception Test manual*. Harvard University Press.

Myers, D. V. (1978). Toward an objective evaluation procedure of the Kinetic Family Drawings (KFD). *Journal of Personality Assessment, 42*(4), 358–365. https://doi.org/10.1207/s15327752jpa4204_5

Myers, M. (2021). *When reactive attachment disorder looks like something else and the medication consequences*. https://www.radadvocates.org/post/when-reactive-attachment-disorder-looks-like-something-else-and-the-medication-consequences

Naar, S., & Suarez, M. (2021). *Motivational interviewing with adolescents and young adults* (2nd ed.). The Guilford Press.

National Center for Learning Disabilities. (n.d.). *Learning disabilities checklist*. Pediatric Neurologists of Palm Beach. https://pedineurologists.com/learning-disabilities-checklist.pdf

National Council for Mental Wellbeing. (2022). *How to manage trauma*. https://www.thenationalcouncil.org/wp-content/uploads/2022/08/Trauma-infographic.pdf

National Disability Rights Network. (n.d.). *NDRN member agencies*. https://www.ndrn.org/about/ndrn-member-agencies/

National Eating Disorders Association. (n.d.). *Avoidant restrictive food intake disorder (ARFID)*. https://www.nationaleatingdisorders.org/avoidant-restrictive-food-intake-disorder-arfid/

National Institute on Drug Abuse. (n.d.). *Screening tools for adolescent substance use*. https://nida.nih.gov/nidamed-medical-health-professionals/screening-tools-resources/screening-tools-adolescent-substance-use

National Institute of Mental Health. (n.d.). *What is prevalence?* https://www.nimh.nih.gov/health/statistics/what-is-prevalence

Newhall, P. W. (2011). *Language-based learning disabilities*. Landmark School Outreach Program.

Norcross, J. C., & Wampold, B. E. (2011). Evidence-based therapy relationships: Research conclusions and clinical practices. *Psychotherapy*, *48*(1), 98–102. https://doi.org/10.1037/a0022161

Novin, S., & Rieffe, C. (2015). Validation of the Brief Shame and Guilt Questionnaire for Children. *Personality and Individual Differences*, *85*, 56–59. https://doi.org/10.1016/j.paid.2015.04.028

Núñez, D., Villacura-Herrera, C., Celedón, K., Ulloa, J. L., Ramos, N., Spencer, R., & Fresno, A. (2022). Identifying self-report measures of emotion regulation and evaluating their psychometric properties: A protocol for a systematic review. *BMJ Open*, *12*(5), Article e056193. https://doi.org/10.1136/bmjopen-2021-056193

Nusslock, R., & Frank, E. (2011). Subthreshold bipolarity: Diagnostic issues and challenges. *Bipolar Disorders*, *13*(7–8), 587–603. https://doi.org/10.1111/j.1399-5618.2011.00957.x

Ogden, T. H. (1977). *Projective identification & psycho-therapeutic technique*. Rowman & Littlefield Publishers.

O'Keefe, M., Mennen, F., & Lane, C. J. (2006). An examination of the factor structure for the youth self report on a multiethnic population. *Research on Social Work Practice*, *16*(3), 315–325. https://doi.org/10.1177/1049731505285340

Olgiati, P., & Serretti, A. (2022). Post-traumatic stress disorder and childhood emotional abuse are markers of subthreshold bipolarity and worse treatment outcome in major depressive disorder. *International Clinical Psychopharmacology, 37*(1), 1–8. https://doi.org/10.1097/YIC.0000000000000380

Olivares, J., Sánchez-García, R., & López-Pina, J. A. (2009). The Liebowitz Social Anxiety Scale for Children and Adolescents. *Psicothema, 21*(3), 486–491.

Otto, M. W., Perlman, C. A., Wernicke, R., Reese, H. E., Bauer, M. S., & Pollack, M. H. (2004). Posttraumatic stress disorder in patients with bipolar disorder: A review of prevalence, correlates, and treatment strategies. *Bipolar Disorders, 6*(6), 470–479. https://doi.org/10.1111/j.1399-5618.2004.00151.x

Owen, J., & Hilsenroth, M. J. (2014). Treatment adherence: The importance of therapist flexibility in relation to therapy outcomes. *Journal of Counseling Psychology, 61*(2), 280–288. https://doi.org/10.1037/a0035753

Pagel, T., Baldessarini, R. J., Franklin, J., & Baethge, C. (2013). Characteristics of patients diagnosed with schizoaffective disorder compared with schizophrenia and bipolar disorder. *Bipolar Disorders, 15*(3), 229–239. https://doi.org/10.1111/bdi.12057

Palmer, B. A., Pahwa, M., Geske, J. R., Kung, S., Nassan, M., Schak, K. M., Alarcon, R. D., Frye, M. A., & Singh, B. (2021). Self-report screening instruments differentiate bipolar disorder and borderline personality disorder. *Brain and Behavior, 11*(7), Article e02201. https://doi.org/10.1002/brb3.2201

Palmer, N. A., & Greytak, E. A. (2017). LGBTQ student victimization and its relationship to school discipline and justice system involvement. *Criminal Justice Review, 42*(2), 163–187. https://doi.org/10.1177/0734016817704698

Pan, P. M., Salum, G., & Bressan, R. A. (2019). Debate: Dimensions of mania in youth: Possibly bipolar, probably risk indicators, certainly impairing. *Child and Adolescent Mental Health, 24*(1), 103–105. https://doi.org/10.1111/camh.12310

Papachristou, E., Ormel, J., Oldehinkel, A. J., Kyriakopoulos, M., Reinares, M., Reichenberg, A., & Frangou, S. (2013). Child Behavior Checklist–Mania Scale (CBCL-MS): Development and evaluation of a population-based screening scale for bipolar disorder. *PLOS ONE, 8*(8), Article e69459. https://doi.org/10.1371/journal.pone.0069459

Papolos, D. (2006). *CBQ and JJ: Frequently asked questions*. Juvenile Bipolar Research Foundation. https://www.jbrf.org/cbq-and-j-j-frequently-asked-questions/

Parry, P. I., & Levin, E. C. (2012). Pediatric bipolar disorder in an era of "mindless psychiatry." *Journal of Trauma & Dissociation, 13*(1), 51–68. https://doi.org/10.1080/15299732.2011.597826

Passarotti, A. M., Trivedi, N., Dominguez-Colman, L., Patel, M., & Langenecker, S. A. (2016). Differences in real world executive function between children with pediatric bipolar disorder and children with ADHD. *Journal of the Canadian Academy of Child and Adolescent Psychiatry, 25*(3), 185–195.

Paterniti, S., & Bisserbe, J.-C. (2018). Factors associated with false positives in MDQ screening for bipolar disorder: Insight into the construct validity of the scale. *Journal of Affective Disorders*, *238*, 79–86. https://doi.org/10.1016/j.jad.2018.05.058

Paulhus, D. L. (1991). Measurement and control of response bias. In J. P. Robinson, P. R. Shaver, & L. S. Wrightsman (Eds.), *Measures of personality and social psychological attitudes* (pp. 17–59). Academic Press. https://doi.org/10.1016/B978-0-12-590241-0.50006-X

Pavuluri, M. N., Henry, D. B., Devineni, B., Carbray, J. A., & Birmaher, B. (2006). Child Mania Rating Scale: Development, reliability, and validity. *Journal of the American Academy of Child & Adolescent Psychiatry*, *45*(5), 550–560. https://doi.org/10.1097/01.chi.0000205700.40700.50

Pavuluri, M. N., O'Connor, M. M., Harral, E. M., Moss, M., & Sweeney, J. A. (2006). Impact of neurocognitive function on academic difficulties in pediatric bipolar disorder: A clinical translation. *Biological Psychiatry*, *60*(9), 951–956. https://doi.org/10.1016/j.biopsych.2006.03.027

Payakachat, N., Tilford, J. M., Kovacs, E., & Kuhlthau, K. (2012). Autism spectrum disorders: A review of measures for clinical, health services and cost-effectiveness applications. *Expert Review of Pharmacoeconomics & Outcomes Research*, *12*(4), 485–503. https://doi.org/10.1586/erp.12.29

Peebles, M. J. (2012). *Beginnings: The art and science of planning psychotherapy* (2nd ed.). Routledge.

Peebles-Kleiger, M. J. (2002). Elaboration of some sequence analysis strategies: Examples and guidelines for level of confidence. *Journal of Personality Assessment*, *79*(1), 19–38. https://doi.org/10.1207/S15327752JPA7901_02

Perry, B. D., & Szalavitz, M. (2006). *The boy who was raised as a dog*. Basic Books.

Perry, B. D., & Winfrey, O. (2021). *What happened to you? Conversations on trauma, resilience, and healing*. Flatiron Books.

Perugia, G., Hantouche, E., & Vannucchia, G. (2017). Diagnosis and treatment of cyclothymia: The "primacy" of temperament. *Current Neuropharmacology*, *15*(3), 372–379. https://doi.org/10.2174/1570159X14666160616120157

Peterson, B. S. (2019). Editorial: Common factors in the art of healing. *The Journal of Child Psychology and Psychiatry*, *60*(9), 927–929. https://doi.org/10.1111/jcpp.13108

Piehler, T. F., Lee, S. K., Stockness, A., & Winters, K. C. (2020). The correspondence of parent-reported measures of adolescent alcohol and cannabis use with adolescent-reported measures: A systematic review. *Substance Abuse*, *41*(4), 437–450. https://doi.org/10.1080/08897077.2019.1692123

Pisano, S., Senese, V. P., Bravaccio, C., Santangelo, P., Milone, A., Masi, G., & Catone, G. (2020). Cyclothymic-hypersensitive temperament in youths: Refining the structure, the way of assessment and the clinical significance in the youth population. *Journal of Affective Disorders*, *271*, 272–278. https://doi.org/10.1016/j.jad.2020.03.155

Pollastri, A. R., & Wang, L. (2019). Research and evaluation of CPS outcomes. In A. R. Pollastri, J. S. Ablon, & M. J. B. Hone (Eds.), *Collaborative problem-solving: An evidence-based approach to implementation and practice* (pp. 149–177). Springer Nature. https://doi.org/10.1007/978-3-030-12630-8_8

Putnam, F. W., Helmers, K., & Trickett, P. K. (1993). Development, reliability, and validity of a child dissociation scale. *Child Abuse & Neglect, 17*(6), 731–741. https://doi.org/10.1016/S0145-2134(08)80004-X

Putnick, D. L., & Bornstein, M. H. (2016). Measurement invariance conventions and reporting: The state of the art and future directions for psychological research. *Developmental Review, 41*, 71–90. https://doi.org/10.1016/j.dr.2016.06.004

Pylypow, J., Quinn, D., Duncan, D., & Balbuena, L. (2020). A measure of emotional regulation and irritability in children and adolescents: The Clinical Evaluation of Emotional Regulation–9. *Journal of Attention Disorders, 24*(14), 2002–2011. https://doi.org/10.1177/1087054717737162

Quello, S. B., Brady, K. T., & Sonne, S. C. (2005). Mood disorders and substance use disorder: A complex comorbidity. *Science & Practice Perspectives, 3*(1), 13–21. https://www.ncbi.nlm.nih.gov/pmc/articles/PMC2851027/

Rapaport, D., Gill, M. M., & Schafer, R. (1968). *Diagnostic psychological testing* (rev. ed.). International Universities Press.

Rathus, J. H., Wagner, D., & Miller, A. L. (2015). Psychometric evaluation of the life inventory, a measure of borderline personality features in adolescents. *Journal of Psychology & Psychotherapy, 5*(4), Article 1000198. https://doi.org/10.4172/2161-0487.1000198

Raver, C. C., Roy, A. L., Pressler, E., Ursache, A. M., & Charles McCoy, D. (2016). Poverty-related adversity and emotion regulation predict internalizing behavior problems among low-income children ages 8–11. *Behavioral Sciences, 7*(1), Article 2. https://doi.org/10.3390/bs7010002

REAACT Research Program. (n.d.). *About our program.* University of Pittsburgh. https://www.reaact.pitt.edu/

Reddy, L. A., Weissman, A. S., & Hale, J. B. (Eds.). (2013). *Neuropsychological assessments and Interventions for youth: An evidence-based approach to emotional and behavioral disorders*. American Psychological Association. https://doi.org/10.1037/14091-000

Reinstein, D. K., & Burau, D. E. (2014). *Integrating neuropsychological and psychological evaluations: Assessing and helping the whole child.* Routledge. https://doi.org/10.4324/9781315885889

Relationship Problems Questionnaire. (n.d.). University of Glasgow. https://www.gla.ac.uk/media/Media_475581_smxx.pdf

Rettew, D. C., Lynch, A. D., Achenbach, T. M., Dumenci, L., & Ivanova, M. Y. (2009). Meta-analyses of agreement between diagnoses made from clinical evaluations and standardized diagnostic interviews. *International Journal of Methods in Psychiatric Research, 18*(3), 169–184. https://doi.org/10.1002/mpr.289

Reynolds, C. R., & Kamphaus, R. W. (2015). *Behavior Assessment System for Children* (3rd ed.). Pearson.

Rice, T. R., Prout, T., Cohen, J., Russo, M., Clements, T., Kufferath-Lin, T., Joaquin, M., Kui, T., Kim, S., Zaidi, A., & Hoffman, L. (2021). Psychodynamic psychotherapy for children as a trauma-informed intervention. *Psychodynamic Psychiatry, 49*(1), 73–85. https://doi.org/10.1521/pdps.2021.49.1.73

Riley, T. N., DeLaney, E., Brown, D., Lozada, F. T., Williams, C. D., The Spit for Science Working Group, & Dick, D. M. (2021). The associations between African American emerging adults' racial discrimination and civic engagement via emotion regulation. *Cultural Diversity & Ethnic Minority Psychology, 27*(2), 169–175. https://doi.org/10.1037/cdp0000335

Roberts, G. E., & Gruber, C. (2005). *Roberts-2*. Western Psychological Service.

Rojas, E. B., & Tuber, S. (1991). The Animal Preference Test and its relationship to behavioral problems in young children. *Journal of Personality Assessment, 57*(1), 141–148. https://doi.org/10.1207/s15327752jpa5701_16

Rosenfeld, G. W. (2008). *Beyond evidence-based psychotherapy: Fostering the eight sources of change in child and adolescent treatment*. Routledge. https://doi.org/10.4324/9780203889428

Roussouw, T., Wiwe, M., & Vrouva, I. (2021). *Mentalization-based treatment for adolescents: A practical treatment guide*. Routledge.

Sabol, T. J., Kessler, C. L., Rogers, L. O., Petitclerc, A., Silver, J., Briggs-Gowan, M., & Wakschlag, L. S. (2022). A window into racial and socioeconomic status disparities in preschool disciplinary action using developmental methodology. *Annals of the New York Academy of Sciences, 1508*(1), 123–136. https://doi.org/10.1111/nyas.14687

Sachser, C., Berliner, L., Risch, E., Rosner, R., Birkeland, M. S., Eilers, R., Hafstad, G. S., Pfeiffer, E., Plener, P. L., & Jensen, T. K. (2022). The Child and Adolescent Trauma Screen 2 (CATS-2)—Validation of an instrument to measure *DSM-5* and ICD-11 PTSD and complex PTSD in children and adolescents. *European Journal of Psychotraumatology, 13*(2), Article 2105580. https://doi.org/10.1080/20008066.2022.2105580

Safran, J. D., Muran, J. C., & Eubanks-Carter, C. (2011). Repairing alliance ruptures. *Psychotherapy, 48*(1), 80–87. https://doi.org/10.1037/a0022140

Salagre, E., Grande, I., Vieta, E., Mezquida, G., Cuesta, M. J., Moreno, C., Bioque, M., Lobo, A., González-Pinto, A., Moreno, D. M., Corripio, I., Verdolini, N., Castro-Fornieles, J., Mané, A., Pinzon-Espinosa, J., Bonnin, C., Bernardo, M., & PEPs Group. (2020). Predictors of bipolar disorder versus schizophrenia diagnosis in a multicenter first psychotic episode cohort: Baseline characterization and a 12-month follow-up analysis. *The Journal of Clinical Psychiatry, 81*(6), 19m12996. https://doi.org/10.4088/JCP.19m12996

Salamon, S., Santelmann, H., Franklin, J., & Baethge, C. (2018). Test–retest reliability of the diagnosis of schizoaffective disorder in childhood and adolescence—A systematic review and meta-analysis. *Journal of Affective Disorders, 230*, 28–33. https://doi.org/10.1016/j.jad.2017.12.070

Salem, T., Walters, K. A., Verducci, J. S., & Fristad, M. A. (2021). Psychoeducational and skill-building interventions for emotion dysregulation. *Child and Adolescent Psychiatric Clinics of North America, 30*(3), 611–622. https://doi.org/10.1016/j.chc.2021.04.010

Sanches, M. (2019). The limits between bipolar disorder and borderline personality disorder: A review of the evidence. *Diseases, 7*(3), Article 49. https://doi.org/10.3390/diseases7030049

Sandstrom, A., Perroud, N., Alda, M., Uher, R., & Pavlova, B. (2021). Prevalence of attention-deficit/hyperactivity disorder in people with mood disorders: A systematic review and meta-analysis. *Acta Psychiatrica Scandinavica, 143*(5), 380–391. https://doi.org/10.1111/acps.13283

Scahill, L., Riddle, M. A., McSwiggin-Hardin, M., Ort, S. I., King, R. A., Goodman, W. K., Cicchetti, D., & Leckman, J. F. (1997). Children's Yale-Brown Obsessive Compulsive Scale: Reliability and validity. *Journal of the American Academy of Child & Adolescent Psychiatry, 36*(6), 844–852. https://doi.org/10.1097/00004583-199706000-00023

Schafer, R. (1954). *Psychoanalytic interpretation of Rorschach testing*. Grune & Stratton.

Schore, A. N. (1994). *Affect regulation and the origin of the self: The neurobiology of emotional development*. Lawrence Erlbaum Associates.

Screen for Child Anxiety Related Disorders (SCARED): Child Version. (n.d.). American Academy of Child & Adolescent Psychiatry. https://www.aacap.org/App_Themes/AACAP/docs/member_resources/toolbox_for_clinical_practice_and_outcomes/symptoms/ScaredChild.pdf

Section 504 of the Rehabilitation Act of 1973, as amended, 29 U.S.C. § 794 (2008).

Sedky, K., Bennett, D. S., & Carvalho, K. S. (2014). Attention deficit hyperactivity disorder and sleep disordered breathing in pediatric populations: A meta-analysis. *Sleep Medicine Reviews, 18*(4), 349–356. https://doi.org/10.1016/j.smrv.2013.12.003

Sellbom, M., & Jarrett, M. A. (2014). Conceptualizing youth borderline personality disorder within a PAI framework. In C. Sharp & J. L. Tackett (Eds.), *Handbook of borderline personality disorder in children and adolescents* (pp. 65–79). Springer Science+Business Media. https://doi.org/10.1007/978-1-4939-0591-1_6

Sharma, A., & McClellan, J. M. (2020). Early-onset schizophrenia. In E. A. Youngstrom, M. J. Prinstein, E. J. Mash, & R. A. Barkley (Eds.), *Assessment of disorders in childhood and adolescence* (5th ed., pp. 569–583). The Guilford Press.

Shectman, F. (1997). *Advanced inference making* [Seminar]. Menninger Clinic Postdoctoral Program in Clinical Psychology, Topeka, KS, United States.

Shectman, F., & Harty, M. K. (1986). Treatment implications of object relationships as they unfold during the diagnostic interaction. In M. Kissen (Ed.), *Assessing object relations phenomena* (pp. 279–303). International Universities Press.

Shectman, F., & Smith, W. H. (Eds.). (1982). *Diagnostic understanding and treatment planning: The elusive connection*. John Wiley & Sons.

Shedler, J. (2018). Where is the evidence for "evidence-based" therapy? *Psychiatric Clinics of North America, 41*(2), 319–329. https://doi.org/10.1016/j.psc.2018.02.001

Sheehan, D. V. (2016). Mini International Neuropsychiatric Interview for Children and Adolescents (MINI-KID) (English Version 7.0.2 for *DSM-5*). D. V. Sheehan and Mapi Research Trust.

Simonds, L. M., John, M., Fife-Schaw, C., Willis, S., Taylor, H., Hand, H., Rahim, M., Winstanley, H., & Winton, H. (2016). Development and validation of the Adolescent Shame-Proneness Scale. *Psychological Assessment, 28*(5), 549–562. https://doi.org/10.1037/pas0000206

Singh, M. K. (Ed.). (2019). *Clinical handbook for the diagnosis and treatment of pediatric mood disorders*. American Psychiatric Publishing.

Singh, T., & Rajput, M. (2006). Misdiagnosis of bipolar disorder. *Psychiatry, 3*(10), 57–63.

Skinner, H. A. (1982). The drug abuse screening test. *Addictive Behaviors, 7*(4), 363–371. https://doi.org/10.1016/0306-4603(82)90005-3

Skokauskas, N., & Frodl, T. (2015). Overlap between autism spectrum disorder and bipolar affective disorder. *Psychopathology, 48*(4), 209–216. https://doi.org/10.1159/000435787

Slesnick, N., Erdem, G., Bartle-Haring, S., & Brigham, G. S. (2013). Intervention with substance-abusing runaway adolescents and their families: Results of a randomized clinical trial. *Journal of Consulting and Clinical Psychology, 81*(4), 600–614. https://doi.org/10.1037/a0033463

Sloan, E., Hall, K., Moulding, R., Bryce, S., Mildred, H., & Staiger, P. K. (2017). Emotion regulation as a transdiagnostic treatment construct across anxiety, depression, substance, eating and borderline personality disorders: A systematic review. *Clinical Psychology Review, 57*, 141–163. https://doi.org/10.1016/j.cpr.2017.09.002

Slobodin, O., & Masalha, R. (2020). Challenges in ADHD care for ethnic minority children: A review of the current literature. *Transcultural Psychiatry, 57*(3), 468–483. https://doi.org/10.1177/1363461520902885

Smith, B. L. (2021). Cross-cultural considerations in the assessment of disordered thought and perception. In I. B. Weiner & J. H. Kleiger (Eds.), *Psychological assessment of disordered thinking and perception* (pp. 287–302). American Psychological Association. https://doi.org/10.1037/0000245-017

Smith, S. R., & Krishnamurthy, R. (Eds.). (2018a). *Diversity-sensitive personality assessment*. Routledge. https://doi.org/10.4324/9780203551578

Smith, S. R., & Krishnamurthy, R. (2018b). Evidence-based practice in diversity-sensitive personality assessment. In S. R. Smith & R. Krishnamurthy (Eds.), *Diversity-sensitive personality assessment* (pp. 363–372). Routledge. https://doi.org/10.4324/9780203551578-20

Society of Clinical Psychology. (n.d.). *Psychological treatments*. https://div12.org/treatments/

Soto, E. F., Irwin, L. N., Chan, E. S. M., Spiegel, J. A., & Kofler, M. J. (2021). Executive functions and writing skills in children with and without ADHD. *Neuropsychology, 35*(8), 792–808. https://doi.org/10.1037/neu0000769

Sparta, S. N., & Koocher, G. P. (Eds.). (2006). *Forensic mental health assessment of children and adolescents*. Oxford University Press. https://doi.org/10.1093/med:psych/9780195145847.001.0001

Spruyt, K., & Gozal, D. (2011). Pediatric sleep questionnaires as diagnostic or epidemiological tools: A review of currently available instruments. *Sleep Medicine Reviews, 15*(1), 19–32. https://doi.org/10.1016/j.smrv.2010.07.005

Stein, M. B., & Slavin-Mulford, J. (2018). *The Social Cognition and Object Relations Scale–Global Rating Method (SCORS-G)*. Routledge.

Stern, D. N. (2004). The motherhood constellation: Therapeutic approaches to early relational problems. In A. J. Sameroff, S. C. McDonough, & K. L. Rosenblum (Eds.), *Treating parent–infant relationship problems: Strategies for intervention* (pp. 29–42). The Guilford Press.

Stevanovic, D., Jafari, P., Knez, R., Franic, T., Atilola, O., Davidovic, N., Bagheri, Z., & Lakic, A. (2017). Can we really use available scales for child and adolescent psychopathology across cultures? A systematic review of cross-cultural measurement invariance data. *Transcultural Psychiatry, 54*(1), 125–152. https://doi.org/10.1177/1363461516689215

Stokes, J., Pogge, D., Wecksell, B., & Zaccario, M. (2011). Parent–child discrepancies in report of psychopathology: The contributions of response bias and parenting stress. *Journal of Personality Assessment, 93*(5), 527–536. https://doi.org/10.1080/00223891.2011.594131

Stokes, J. M., Sapoff, M., Pogge, D. L., Zaccario, M., & Barbot, B. (2019). A dimensional understanding of borderline personality features in adolescence: The relationship between the MMPI-A PSY-5 scales and PAI-A borderline features. *Personality and Individual Differences, 140*(1), 27–32. https://doi.org/10.1016/j.paid.2018.04.025

Strauss, E., Sherman, E. M. S., & Spreen, O. (2006). *A compendium of neuropsychological tests: Administration, norms, and commentary* (3rd ed.). Oxford University Press.

Strayhorn, J. M., & Strayhorn, J. C. (2009). Martial arts as a mental health intervention for children? Evidence from the ECLS-K. *Child and Adolescent Psychiatry and Mental Health, 3*, Article 32. https://doi.org/10.1186/1753-2000-3-32

Stricker, G. (2006). Assimilative psychodynamic psychotherapy integration. In G. Stricker & J. Gold (Eds.), *A casebook of psychotherapy integration* (pp. 55–63). American Psychological Association. https://doi.org/10.1037/11436-005

Stricker, G., & Trierweiler, S. J. (1995). The local clinical scientist: A bridge between science and practice. *American Psychologist, 50*(12), 995–1002. https://doi.org/10.1037/0003-066X.50.12.995

Stringaris, A., Goodman, R., Ferdinando, S., Razdan, V., Muhrer, E., Leibenluft, E., & Brotman, M. A. (2012). The Affective Reactivity Index: A concise irritability scale for clinical and research settings. *The Journal of Child Psychology and Psychiatry, 53*(11), 1109–1117. https://doi.org/10.1111/j.1469-7610.2012.02561.x

Suarez, M., & Martinez-Kaig, V. (2022). Using motivational interviewing to enhance neuropsychological practice for adults with depression and neurocognitive difficulties. In S. M. McClintock & J. Choi (Eds.), *Neuropsychology of depression* (pp. 249–261). The Guilford Press.

Substance Abuse and Mental Health Services Administration. (n.d.). *Evidence-based practices resource center*. https://www.samhsa.gov/resource-search/ebp

Sullivan, A. L. (2013). School-based autism identification: Prevalence, racial disparities, and systemic correlates. *School Psychology Review, 42*(3), 298–316. https://doi.org/10.1080/02796015.2013.12087475

Swift, J. K., Callahan, J. L., Cooper, M., & Parkin, S. R. (2018). The impact of accommodating client preference in psychotherapy: A meta-analysis. *Journal of Clinical Psychology, 74*(11), 1924–1937. https://doi.org/10.1002/jclp.22680

Tapert, S. F., Schweinsburg, A. D., & Brown, S. A. (2008). The influence of marijuana use on neurocognitive functioning in adolescents. *Current Drug Abuse Reviews, 1*(1), 99–111. https://doi.org/10.2174/1874473710801010099

Tay, L., Meade, A. W., & Cao, M. (2015). An overview and practical guide to IRT measurement equivalence analysis. *Organizational Research Methods, 18*(1), 3–46. https://doi.org/10.1177/1094428114553062

Tennessee State Government. (n.d.). *Parent Version of the Young Mania Rating Scale (P-YMRS)*. https://www.tn.gov/content/dam/tn/mentalhealth/documents/Pages_from_CY_BPGs_483-488.pdf

Testa, R. J., Habarth, J., Peta, J., Balsam, K., & Bockting, W. (2015). Development of the Gender Minority Stress and Resilience Measure. *Psychology of Sexual Orientation and Gender Diversity, 2*(1), 65–77. https://doi.org/10.1037/sgd0000081

Tharinger, D. J., Rudin, D. I., Frackowiak, M., & Finn, S. E. (2022). *Therapeutic assessment with children: Enhancing parental empathy through psychological assessment*. Routledge. https://doi.org/10.4324/9781003000174

Thurston, N. S., & Cradock O'Leary, J. (2009). *The Thurston-Cradock Test of Shame (TCTS)*. Western Psychological Services.

Timbrook, R. E., & Graham, J. R. (1994). Ethnic differences on the MMPI-2? *Psychological Assessment, 6*(3), 212–217. https://doi.org/10.1037/1040-3590.6.3.212

Tolin, D. F., Sain, K. S., Davis, E., Gilliam, C., Hannan, S. E., Springer, K. S., Stubbing, J., George, J. R., Jean, A., Goldblum, R., Katz, B. W., Everhardt, K., Darrow, S., Ohr, E. E., Young, M. E., & Serchuk, M. D. (2023). The DIAMOND-KID: Psychometric properties of a structured diagnostic interview for *DSM-5* anxiety, mood, and obsessive-compulsive and related disorders in children and adolescents. *Assessment, 30*(8), 2351–2363. https://doi.org/10.1177/10731911221143994

Torio, C. M., Encinosa, W., Berdahl, T., McCormick, M. C., & Simpson, L. A. (2015). Annual report on health care for children and youth in the United States: National estimates of cost, utilization and expenditures for children with mental health conditions. *Academic Pediatrics, 15*(1), 19–35. https://doi.org/10.1016/j.acap.2014.07.007

Trauma Institute & Child Trauma Institute. (n.d.). *Assessment instruments*. https://www.ticti.org/resources/assessment-instruments/

Trompeter, N., Bussey, K., Forbes, M. K., Hay, P., Goldstein, M., Thornton, C., Basten, C., Heruc, G., Roberts, M., Byrne, S., Griffiths, S., Lonergan, A., & Mitchison, D. (2022). Emotion dysregulation and eating disorder symptoms: Examining distinct associations and interactions in adolescents. *Research on Child and Adolescent Psychopathology, 50*(5), 683–694. https://doi.org/10.1007/s10802-022-00898-1

Tronick, E. (2007). *The neurobehavioral and social-emotional development of infants and children*. W. W. Norton & Company.

Tsai, J. (2022). *Culture and emotion*. Noba. https://nobaproject.com/modules/culture-and-emotion

Tsuchiya, K. J., Byrne, M., & Mortensen, P. B. (2003). Risk factors in relation to an emergence of bipolar disorder: A systematic review. *Bipolar Disorders, 5*(4), 231–242. https://doi.org/10.1034/j.1399-5618.2003.00038.x

Tuber, S. (2022). Review of *Hermann Rorschach's Psychodiagnostics: Newly translated and annotated 100th anniversary edition* [Review of the book *Hermann Rorschach's Psychodiagnostics: Newly translated and annotated 100th anniversary edition*, by P. J. Keddy, R. Signer, P. Erdberg, & A. Schnedier-Stocking, Eds.]. *Psychoanalytic Psychology, 39*(4), 344–346. https://doi.org/10.1037/pap0000414

Tufnell, G. (2005). Eye movement desensitization and reprocessing in the treatment of pre-adolescent children with post-traumatic symptoms. *Clinical Child Psychology and Psychiatry, 10*(4), 587–600. https://doi.org/10.1177/1359104505056320

Tyrer, P. (2017). Comorbidity, consanguinity, and co-occurrence. *BJPsych Advances, 23*(3), 167–168. https://doi.org/10.1192/apt.bp.116.016444

University of California, San Francisco. (2010, November 3). *Prodromal Questionnaire, Brief Version (PQ-B)* [Letter followed by copy of the PQ-B]. Semel Institute for Neuroscience and Human Behavior. https://www.semel.ucla.edu/sites/default/files/pdf/High%20Risk%20Psychosis%20Screener.pdf

UPMC Western Psychiatric Hospital, Child & Adolescent Bipolar Spectrum Services. (n.d.-a). *Lab gallery*. University of Pittsburgh. https://www.pediatricbipolar.pitt.edu/resources/instruments

UPMC Western Psychiatric Hospital, Child & Adolescent Bipolar Spectrum Services. (n.d.-b). *Modified K-SADS Mania Rating Scale*. University of Pittsburgh. https://www.pediatricbipolar.pitt.edu/sites/default/files/assets/AH/AK/Mania%20Rating%20Scale_RiskCalculator%20(modified-no%20boxes).pdf

U.S. Department of Health and Human Services. (2010). *Infant/toddler development, screening, and assessment*. National Infant & Toddler Child Care Initiative. https://childcareta.acf.hhs.gov/sites/default/files/infant-toddler_development_screening_and_assessment.pdf

Vacher, C., Goujon, A., Romo, L., & Purper-Ouakil, D. (2020). Efficacy of psychosocial interventions for children with ADHD and emotion dysregulation: A systematic review. *Psychiatry Research, 291*, Article 113151. https://doi.org/10.1016/j.psychres.2020.113151

van Benthem, P., Spijkerman, R., Blanken, P., Kleinjan, M., Vermeiren, R. R. J. M., & Hendriks, V. M. (2020). A dual perspective on first-session therapeutic alliance: Strong predictor of youth mental health and addiction treatment outcome. *European Child & Adolescent Psychiatry, 29*(11), 1593–1601. https://doi.org/10.1007/s00787-020-01503-w

van Bergen, A. H., Verkooijen, S., Vreeker, A., Abramovic, L., Hillegers, M. H., Spijker, A. T., Hoencamp, E., Regeer, E. J., Knapen, S. E., Riemersma-van der Lek, R. F., Schoevers, R., Stevens, A. W., Schulte, P. F. J., Vonk, R., Hoekstra, R., van Beveren, N. J., Kupka, R. W., Sommer, I. E. C., Ophoff, R. A., . . . Boks, M. P. M. (2019). The characteristics of psychotic features in bipolar disorder. *Psychological Medicine, 49*(12), 2036–2048. https://doi.org/10.1017/S0033291718002854

Van Meter, A. R., & Youngstrom, E. A. (2012). Cyclothymic disorder in youth: Why is it overlooked, what do we know and where is the field headed? *Neuropsychiatry, 2*(6), 509–519. https://doi.org/10.2217/npy.12.64

Vervoort, E., De Schipper, J. C., Bosmans, G., & Verschueren, K. (2013). Screening symptoms of reactive attachment disorder: Evidence for measurement invariance and convergent validity. *International Journal of Methods in Psychiatric Research, 22*(3), 256–265. https://doi.org/10.1002/mpr.1395

Viapiana, V. F., Rodrigues, A. C. R. B. G., Peters, R., Tramontina, S., Passos, I. C., & Fonseca, R. P. (2022). Pediatric bipolar disorder: Executive, linguistic, mnemonic, and cognitive efficiency mapping. *Applied Neuropsychology: Child, 11*(3), 350–363. https://doi.org/10.1080/21622965.2020.1848568

Viglione, D. J. (2010). *Rorschach coding solutions: A reference guide for the Comprehensive System* (2nd ed.).

Viglione, D. J., & Senecal, S. (2014, March 13–17). *Research and development of a scale to measure unusual beliefs and experiences among children and adolescents* [Paper presentation]. Annual Meeting of the Society for Personality Assessment, Arlington, VA, United States.

Wachtel, P. L. (1997). *Psychoanalysis, behavior therapy, and the relational world*. American Psychological Association. https://doi.org/10.1037/10383-000

Wachtel, P. L. (2010). Beyond "ESTs": Problematic assumptions in the pursuit of evidence-based practice. *Psychoanalytic Psychology, 27*(3), 251–272. https://doi.org/10.1037/a0020532

Wagner, K. D., Hirschfeld, R. M., Emslie, G. J., Findling, R. L., Gracious, B. L., & Reed, M. L. (2006). Validation of the Mood Disorder Questionnaire for bipolar disorders in adolescents. *The Journal of Clinical Psychiatry*, *67*(5), 827–830. https://doi.org/10.4088/JCP.v67n0518

Walker, T. M., Frick, P. J., & McMahon, R. J. (2020). Conduct and oppositional disorders. In E. A. Youngstrom, M. J. Prinstein, E. J. Mash, & R. A. Barkley (Eds.), *Assessment of disorders in childhood and adolescence* (5th ed., pp. 132–156). The Guilford Press.

Wang, C., Liu, J. L., Havewala, M., Zhu, Q., Do, K. A., & Shao, X. (2021). Parent–Child Connect: A culturally responsive parent training for Asian American parents at school. *Psychology in the Schools*, *58*(8), 1624–1641. https://doi.org/10.1002/pits.22520

Waxmonsky, J. G., Waschbusch, D. A., Belin, P., Li, T., Babocsai, L., Humphery, H., Pariseau, M. E., Babinski, D. E., Hoffman, M. T., Haak, J. L., Mazzant, J. R., Fabiano, G. A., Pettit, J. W., Fallahazad, N., & Pelham, W. E. (2016). A randomized clinical trial of an integrative group therapy for children with severe mood dysregulation. *Journal of the American Academy of Child & Adolescent Psychiatry*, *55*(3), 196–207. https://doi.org/10.1016/j.jaac.2015.12.011

Wechsler, D. (2003). *Wechsler Intelligence Scale for Children–Fourth Edition (WISC-IV)*. The Psychological Corporation.

Wechsler, D. (2008). *Wechsler Adult Intelligence Scale–Fourth Edition (WAIS-IV)*. The Psychological Corporation.

Wechsler, D. (2011). *Wechsler Abbreviated Scale of Intelligence–Second Edition (WASI-II)*. Pearson.

Wechsler, D. (2014). *Wechsler Intelligence Scale for Children–Fifth Edition (WISC-V)*. Pearson.

Weiner, I. B. (1998). *Principles of Rorschach interpretation*. Lawrence Erlbaum Associates.

Weiner, I. B. (2000). Making Rorschach interpretation as good as it can be. *Journal of Personality Assessment*, *74*(2), 164–174. https://doi.org/10.1207/S15327752JPA7402_2

Weiner, I. B., & Greene, R. L. (2006). *Handbook of personality assessment*. John Wiley & Sons.

Weiner, I. B., & Greene, R. L. (2017). *Handbook of personality assessment* (2nd ed.). Wiley.

Werry, J. S., McClellan, J. M., & Chard, L. (1991). Childhood and adolescent schizophrenic, bipolar, and schizoaffective disorders: A clinical and outcome study. *Journal of the American Academy of Child & Adolescent Psychiatry*, *30*(3), 457–465. https://doi.org/10.1097/00004583-199105000-00017

West, A. E., Weinstein, S. M., Peters, A. T., Katz, A. C., Henry, D. B., Cruz, R. A., & Pavuluri, M. N. (2014). Child- and family-focused cognitive-behavioral therapy for pediatric bipolar disorder: A randomized clinical trial. *Journal of the American Academy of Child & Adolescent Psychiatry, 53*(11), 1168–1178. https://doi.org/10.1016/j.jaac.2014.08.013

West, M. L., & Sharif, S. (2023). Cannabis and psychosis. *Child and Adolescent Psychiatric Clinics of North America, 32*(1), 69–83. https://doi.org/10.1016/j.chc.2022.07.004

Westen, D., Lohr, N., Silk, K. R., Gold, L., & Kerber, K. (1990). Object relations and social cognition in borderlines, major depressives, and normals: A Thematic Apperception Test analysis. *Psychological Assessment, 2*(4), 355–364. https://doi.org/10.1037/1040-3590.2.4.355

Westen, D., & Morrison, K. (2001). A multidimensional meta-analysis of treatments for depression, panic, and generalized anxiety disorder: An empirical examination of the status of empirically supported therapies. *Journal of Consulting and Clinical Psychology, 69*(6), 875–899. https://doi.org/10.1037/0022-006X.69.6.875

Westen, D., Novotny, C. M., & Thompson-Brenner, H. (2004). The empirical status of empirically supported psychotherapies: Assumptions, findings, and reporting in controlled clinical trials. *Psychological Bulletin, 130*(4), 631–663. https://doi.org/10.1037/0033-2909.130.4.631

Whitehead, M. L. (2016). Hidden in plain sight: Gender and sexuality in the clinical assessment interview. In V. M. Brabender & J. L. Mihura (Eds.), *Handbook of gender and sexuality in psychological assessment* (pp. 81–107). Routledge.

Williams, M. T., Metzger, I., Leins, C., & DeLapp, C. (2018). Assessing racial trauma within a *DSM–5* framework: The UConn Racial/Ethnic Stress and Trauma Survey. *Practice Innovations, 3*(4), 242–260. https://doi.org/10.1037/pri0000076

Wilson, S. N. (2010). *Comparative validity of the MMPI-A scales scores in African American and Caucasian male juvenile delinquents* [Doctoral dissertation, Old Dominion University]. ODU Digital Commons. https://digitalcommons.odu.edu/cgi/viewcontent.cgi?article=1327&context=psychology_etds

Winner, M. G. (2006). *Think social*. Think Social Publishing.

Winnicott, D. W. (1958). *Collected papers: Through paediatrics to psycho-analysis*. Basic Books.

Winnicott, D. W. (1965). *The maturational processes and the facilitating environment: Studies in the theory of emotional development*. International Universities Press.

Winters, K. C. (1992). Development of an adolescent alcohol and other drug abuse screening scale: Personal Experience Screening Questionnaire. *Addictive Behaviors, 17*(5), 479–490. https://doi.org/10.1016/0306-4603(92)90008-J

Winters, K. C., Anderson, N., Bengston, P., Stinchfield, R. D., & Latimer, W. W. (2000). Development of a parent questionnaire for use in assessing adolescent drug abuse. *Journal of Psychoactive Drugs, 32*(1), 3–13. https://doi.org/10.1080/02791072.2000.10400207

Winters, K. C., & Henly, G. A. (1989). *Personal Experience Inventory Test and manual*. Western Psychological Services.

Winters, K. C., & Kaminer, Y. (2008). Screening and assessing adolescent substance use disorders in clinical populations. *Journal of the American Academy of Child & Adolescent Psychiatry, 47*(7), 740–744. https://doi.org/10.1097/CHI.0b013e31817395cf

World Health Organization. (2019). *International statistical classification of diseases and related health problems* (11th ed.). https://icd.who.int/

Wozniak, J., Biederman, J., Kiely, K., Ablon, J. S., Faraone, S. V., Mundy, E., & Mennin, D. (1995). Mania-like symptoms suggestive of childhood-onset bipolar disorder in clinically referred children. *Journal of the American Academy of Child & Adolescent Psychiatry, 34*(7), 867–876. https://doi.org/10.1097/00004583-199507000-00010

Wright, A. J. (2022). *The Cambridge handbook of clinical assessment and diagnosis* [Review of the book *The Cambridge handbook of clinical assessment and diagnosis*, edited by M. Sellbom and J. A. Suhr]. *Journal of Personality Assessment, 104*(6), 857–859. https://doi.org/10.1080/00223891.2021.1991360

Wright, P. W. P., & Wright, P. D. (2002). *From emotions to advocacy: The special education survival guide*. Harbor House Law Press.

Wright, P. W. P., & Wright, P. D. (2006). *From emotions to advocacy: The special education survival guide* (2nd ed.). Harbor House Law Press.

Wright, P. W. P., & Wright, P. D. (2007). *Wrightslaw: Special education law* (2nd ed.). Harbor House Law Press.

Yalof, J. A., & Bram, A. D. (Eds.). (2021). *Psychoanalytic assessment applications for different settings*. Routledge.

Yapıcı Eser, H., Taşkıran, A. S., Ertınmaz, B., Mutluer, T., Kılıç, Ö., Özcan Morey, A., Necef, I., Yalçınay İnan, M., & Öngür, D. (2020). Anxiety disorders comorbidity in pediatric bipolar disorder: A meta-analysis and meta-regression study. *Acta Psychiatrica Scandinavica, 141*(4), 327–339. https://doi.org/10.1111/acps.13146

Yim, E. P. (2022). Effects of Asian cultural values on parenting style and young children's perceived competence: A cross-sectional study. *Frontiers in Psychology, 13*, Article 905093. https://doi.org/10.3389/fpsyg.2022.905093

Youngstrom, E., Meyers, O., Demeter, C., Youngstrom, J., Morello, L., Piiparinen, R., Feeny, N., Calabrese, J. R., & Findling, R. L. (2005). Comparing diagnostic checklists for pediatric bipolar disorder in academic and community mental health settings. *Bipolar Disorders, 7*(6), 507–517. https://doi.org/10.1111/j.1399-5618.2005.00269.x

Youngstrom, E. A., Birmaher, B., & Findling, R. L. (2008). Pediatric bipolar disorder: Validity, phenomenology, and recommendations for diagnosis. *Bipolar Disorders, 10*(1p2), 194–214. https://doi.org/10.1111/j.1399-5618.2007.00563.x

Youngstrom, E. A., Choukas-Bradley, S., Calhoun, C. D., & Jensen-Doss, A. (2015). Clinical guide to the evidence-based assessment approach to diagnosis and treatment. *Cognitive and Behavioral Practice, 22*(1), 20–35. https://doi.org/10.1016/j.cbpra.2013.12.005

Youngstrom, E. A., Findling, R. L., Calabrese, J. R., Gracious, B. L., Demeter, C., Bedoya, D. D., & Price, M. (2004). Comparing the diagnostic accuracy of six potential screening instruments for bipolar disorder in youths aged 5 to 17 years. *Journal of the American Academy of Child & Adolescent Psychiatry, 43*(7), 847–858. https://doi.org/10.1097/01.chi.0000125091.35109.1e

Youngstrom, E. A., Findling, R. L., Danielson, C. K., & Calabrese, J. R. (2001). Discriminative validity of parent report of hypomanic and depressive symptoms on the General Behavior Inventory. *Psychological Assessment, 13*(2), 267–276. https://doi.org/10.1037/1040-3590.13.2.267

Youngstrom, E. A., Frazier, T. W., Demeter, C., Calabrese, J. R., & Findling, R. L. (2008). Developing a 10-item mania scale from the Parent General Behavior Inventory for children and adolescents. *The Journal of Clinical Psychiatry, 69*(5), 831–839. https://doi.org/10.4088/JCP.v69n0517

Youngstrom, E. A., Freeman, A. J., & Jenkins, M. M. (2009). The assessment of children and adolescents with bipolar disorder. *Child and Adolescent Psychiatric Clinics of North America, 18*(2), 353–390, viii–ix. https://doi.org/10.1016/j.chc.2008.12.002

Youngstrom, E. A., Genzlinger, J. E., Egerton, G. A., & Van Meter, A. R. (2015). Multivariate meta-analysis of the discriminative validity of caregiver, youth, and teacher rating scales for pediatric bipolar disorder: Mother knows best about mania. *Archives of Scientific Psychology, 3*(1), 112–137. https://doi.org/10.1037/arc0000024

Youngstrom, E. A., Jenkins, M. M., Jensen-Doss, A., & Youngstrom, J. K. (2012). Evidence-based assessment strategies for pediatric bipolar disorder. *The Israel Journal of Psychiatry and Related Sciences, 49*(1), 15–27.

Youngstrom, E. A., Morton, E. E., & Murray, G. (2020). Bipolar spectrum disorders. In E. A. Youngstrom, M. J. Prinstein, E. J. Mash, & R. A. Barkley (Eds.), *Assessment of disorders in childhood and adolescence* (5th ed., pp. 192–244). The Guilford Press.

Youngstrom, E. A., Prinstein, M. J., Mash, E. J., & Barkley, R. A. (Eds.). (2020). *Assessment of disorders in childhood and adolescence* (5th ed.). The Guilford Press.

Yulaf, Y., Gümştaş, F., Gökçe, S., & Yazgan, Y. (2018). Executive functions profile in children and adolescents with or without ADHD: By using performance-based measures and homework and work habits questionnaire. *Psychiatry and Clinical Psychopharmacology, 28*(Suppl. 1), 283–286.

Zajac, K., Randall, J., & Swenson, C. C. (2015). Multisystemic therapy for externalizing youth. *Child and Adolescent Psychiatric Clinics of North America, 24*(3), 601–616. https://doi.org/10.1016/j.chc.2015.02.007

Zanarini, M. C., Vujanovic, A. A., Parachini, E. A., Boulanger, J. L., Frankenburg, F. R., & Hennen, J. (2003). A screening measure for BPD: The McLean Screening Instrument for Borderline Personality Disorder (MSI-BPD). *Journal of Personality Disorders, 17*(6), 568–573. https://doi.org/10.1521/pedi.17.6.568.25355

Zeanah, C. H., Jr. (Ed.). (2009). *Handbook of infant mental health* (3rd ed.). The Guilford Press.

Zimmerman, M., Balling, C., Chelminski, I., & Dalrymple, K. (2021). Patients with borderline personality disorder and bipolar disorder: A descriptive and comparative study. *Psychological Medicine, 51*(9), 1479–1490. https://doi.org/10.1017/S0033291720000215

Zimmerman, M., & Morgan, T. A. (2013). The relationship between borderline personality disorder and bipolar disorder. *Dialogues in Clinical Neuroscience, 15*(2), 155–169. https://doi.org/10.31887/DCNS.2013.15.2/mzimmerman

Zurhellen, W., Lessin, H. R., Chan, E., Allan, C. C., Wolraich, W., Sprecher, E., & Evans, S. W. (2019). *Caring for children with ADHD: A practical resource toolkit for clinicians* (3rd ed.). American Academy of Pediatrics.

Index

C

D

S

T

U

V

W

Y

Z

About the Author

Anthony D. Bram, PhD, ABAP, FABP, is a psychologist and psychoanalyst in private practice in Lexington, Massachusetts, where he conducts psychological assessment, psychodynamic and cognitive behavior therapy, and psychoanalysis with children and adults. He is a part-time lecturer in psychology in the Department of Psychiatry at Cambridge Health Alliance/Harvard Medical School and is on the faculty of the Boston Psychoanalytic Society & Institute (BPSI), where he also serves as vice chair of the Child and Adolescent Psychoanalysis Training Program.

Dr. Bram received his doctorate from the University of Kansas and is a graduate of the 2-year Postdoctoral Training Program at the Menninger Clinic in Topeka, Kansas, where he was subsequently a staff psychologist. Dr. Bram completed adult psychoanalytic training at the Greater Kansas City Psychoanalytic Institute and child analytic training at BPSI. He is a board-certified diplomate in Assessment Psychology and in Child/Adolescent Psychoanalysis. He has received a fellowship from the American Psychoanalytic Association, the Martin Mayman Award (two times) from the Society for Personality Assessment, the Scientific Writing Award from the Menninger Clinic, the Biennial Award for Research in Psychological Assessment from Psychodiagnostics, Inc., and the Johanna Tabin Book Prize from Division 39, the Society for Psychoanalysis and Psychoanalytic Psychology, of the American Psychological Association (APA).

Dr. Bram's first book, *Psychological Testing That Matters: Creating a Road Map for Effective Treatment*, coauthored with Mary Jo Peebles, was published by APA Books in 2014. He also coedited with Jed Yalof the book *Psychoanalytic Assessment Applications for Different Settings*, which was published in 2021.